## DATE DUE

The First Chinese Democracy

LINDA CHAO

RAMON H. MYERS

# The First Chinese Democracy

*Political Life in the Republic of China
on Taiwan*

THE JOHNS HOPKINS UNIVERSITY PRESS

*Baltimore and London*

© 1998 The Johns Hopkins University Press
All rights reserved. Published 1998
Printed in the United States of America on acid-free paper
07 06 05 04 03 02 01 00 99 98   5 4 3 2 1

All photographs are reproduced courtesy of the Government
Information Office, Republic of China and by Yang Yongzhi of
*China Times Weekly*.

The Johns Hopkins University Press
2715 North Charles Street
Baltimore, Maryland 21218–4319
The Johns Hopkins Press Ltd., London

Library of Congress Cataloging-in-Publication Data will be found
at the end of this book.
A catalog record for this book is available from the British Library.

ISBN 0-8018-5650-7

This book is dedicated to those leaders, activists, and voters whose commitment, sacrifice, and belief in democracy made it possible for the people of Taiwan to perfect the first democracy in the history of Chinese civilization.

# CONTENTS

# ILLUSTRATIONS

Only recently have Western and Chinese scholars begun to explore Taiwan's unusual twentieth-century history, from a colony of imperial Japan (1895–1945) to the island state of the Republic of China on Taiwan (ROC) today. In the 1980s the government of the People's Republic of China (PRC) even established some dozen research institutes to examine the ROC's past and present, and in 1992 National Beijing University's Department of History organized a team to study the ROC's recent political development.

China's autocratic polity had no tradition of the democratic ideology and institutions that slowly evolved in the Western societies of Europe and North America. After imperial China clashed with Western states and Japan in the nineteenth century, a dim awareness of democracy became evident among certain Chinese elites and intellectuals. How did that awareness translate to allow a small Chinese society like Taiwan to make a peaceful but rapid transition toward democracy in the second half of the twentieth century while maintaining its national security and achieving modernization?

To anwer that question, we began studying Chinese political life on Taiwan in the fall of 1989 during the December 2 local and national elections. We continued to monitor later political changes, and in 1991 the Hoover Institution supported our research. Soon after, we were assisted by funding from the Luce Foundation and the ROC's Government Information Office, which enabled us to interview more than fifty leading politicians who had been involved in the important political events of recent decades. These and other historical materials form the basis of this book.

Our study, a narrative of key events, also analyzes those distinctive historical patterns in which the main protagonists competed for political power in the name of Chinese democracy. This remarkable story tells how a part of China has experienced a democratic transition.

Our greatest intellectual debt is to our colleague Thomas A. Metzger, whose writings, ideas, and encouragement have not only inspired our efforts but helped to give them an analytic-conceptual form. In particular, we are grateful for his sharing with us an unpublished essay discussing political repression and political culture after the December 10, 1979, Kaohsiung incident. We particularly thank James A. Robinson for his encouragement and comments on early drafts and Virginia Sheng of the ROC's Government Information Office for carefully reading the last draft.

We are also indebted to the staff of the East Asian Collection at the Hoover Institution for helping us obtain relevant documents. Other libraries also greatly aided our research: the National Central Library of the ROC, the Taiwan Provincial Library, the Kuomintang Archives, and the National Archives of the ROC. A number of individuals kindly read our preliminary draft and offered useful criticisms and suggestions. In this regard we are especially grateful to Cheng Tun-jen, John F. Copper, Thomas A. Metzger, Liao Ta-chi, Kuo Tai-chün, Lucian W. Pye, Steven Goldstein, and several unknown critics in Taiwan and the United States. Finally, we want to thank our spouses for their encouragement and patience, which allowed us to spend many hours away from home to complete this study. We thank the reference department of the *Zhongyang ribao* (Central daily news) for assistance. We are grateful for the photographs provided by the Government Information Office of the ROC and Mr. Yang Yongzhi of the *Shibao zhoukan* (China times weekly). In romanizing Chinese names and terms we have generally used the pinying system except for standard name spelling listed in ROC Government Information Office, *The Republic of China Yearbook* for relevant years and the Zhungguo minren zhuanji zhongxin (Biographical Center for Famous Chinese Persons), *Who's Who of the Republic of China* (Taipei: Yatai guoji chuban shiye you xian gongsi, 1982), in English and Chinese. When a person's name appeared in both sources we selected the version we believed to be the preferred, official spelling. All special terms and places in mainland China are in pinyin, but for romanizing place-names in Taiwan we have used the preferred form commonly used in Taiwan sources. Readers interested in obtaining a detailed bibliography of Chinese, Western, and Japanese sources about Taiwan's political development can obtain a computer disk of such materials from the authors.

The First Chinese Democracy

# CHAPTER ONE

# Posing the Problem

*The Democratization of a Chinese Society*

When Alexis de Tocqueville observed in 1840 that "the nations of our time cannot prevent the conditions of men from becoming equal," he might have been foretelling what Samuel P. Huntington recently described as the world's three waves of democratizing nations. According to Huntington, the first wave occurred between 1826 and 1926, with some reversal in the next two decades; then there was a single short wave from 1943 to 1962 with a short reversal during 1958–75; and finally there was a third wave after 1974 in which thirty-odd countries adopted democracy, giving people what Tocqueville called the "unlimited power of the majority."[1]

One of those thirty-odd countries was the Republic of China on Taiwan, on the semitropical island of Taiwan, the size of the American state of Maryland, situated some one hundred miles east of the Chinese mainland.[2] Taiwan, a frontier area of the Chinese mainland, was ruled by the Qing monarchy from 1683 to 1885, when Peking upgraded the island to a province of the Qing empire. But when Japan defeated China in a short war (1894–95), the Qing court ceded Taiwan to Japan with the signing of the Treaty of Shimonoseki on April 17, 1895. Taiwan was a Japanese colony, then, until October 25, 1945, when it reverted to China, coming under the administrative control of the Nationalist government of the Republic of China (ROC), which had claimed sovereignty over mainland China since 1911. The civil war then raging on the mainland ended in 1949; remnants of the ROC regime, including members of that government's ruling party, the Kuomintang (KMT), and civilian refugees, fled to Taiwan for a last-ditch stand.

How these refugees and the Chinese people living on Taiwan survived the Chinese civil war and built a democracy is the theme of this book. The story began in Taipei on May 19, 1949, when Chen Cheng, who had been sworn in as the Nationalist governor of Taiwan, ordered that martial law take effect the next day at zero hour on the grounds that communist troops were moving into Fujian province, thus threatening Taiwan.[3] The provincial government and the Garrison Command then sealed off Taiwan from the mainland, searched every ship entering its harbors, and monitored everyone entering and leaving the island. Martial law outlined the security measures for protecting the island and mandated that public assembly, political criticism, and any action endangering public order were seditious, to be adjudicated by military court and punished by long prison terms or death. Until July 15, 1987, when martial law was lifted, political power was concentrated within a single political party, the KMT, which controlled Taiwan's political life. Lifting martial law marked an important political watershed, in effect initiating the transition to democracy and making the ROC part of Huntington's third wave. To compare Taiwan under martial law with Taiwan under democracy, let us look at four examples.

## Political Dissent

In late 1977 Hsu Hsin-liang was elected magistrate of Taoyuan county but was accused by the government of participating in an unlawful street demonstration.[4] In late December 1979, Hsu departed for the United States, where he helped establish the Taiwan Revolutionary Party, an organization dedicated to overthrowing the ROC government. He wrote articles advocating urban guerrilla warfare in Taiwan for the September and October 1982 issues of *Meilidao* (Beautiful Formosa), a prominent Taiwan independence journal published in the United States. Introducing the translation of a Cuban urban guerrilla terrorist manual, he wrote,

"Urban guerrilla" warfare will be a most important strategy and tactic in the Taiwan reconstruction revolutionary movement, because Taiwan has been an "urbanized" area; the urban guerrilla will become the vanguard of the revolution. Therefore, we would like to translate and introduce this essay, "The Mini-Manual of the Urban Guerrilla," to serve as a reference for those Taiwan countrymen, both at home and abroad, who are dedicating themselves to the revolution.[5]

In 1986, Hsu established the Taiwan Democratic Party in San Francisco. After the Democratic Progressive Party (DPP) was formed (in violation of martial law) in Taiwan on September 28, 1986, Hsu offered to make his party the overseas branch of the DPP.

On November 29, 1986, Hsu Hsin-liang left New York for Tokyo with a scheduled stop for refueling in Taipei.[6] Thus on December 1 some two thousand people congregated at Taiwan's International Airport to meet him; when military and airport police attempted to disperse the crowd, fighting broke out. Three policemen were injured, stones were thrown, and the police used water hoses and tear gas on the crowds. On December 3, Hsu Hsin-liang flew from Tokyo to Manila, intending to fly to Taiwan, but the authorities in Manila refused him, saying he lacked a valid visa. On December 3, the Philippine government placed Hsu on a Japanese airplane, returning him to Tokyo.

When martial law was lifted, Hsu returned to Taiwan and the government dropped all charges of sedition against him. He joined the DPP, whose members had registered as a legal political party in 1989, and became a member of the central committee. At the banquet opening of the National Affairs Conference (Guoshi huiyi) on June 27, 1990, television cameras caught Hsu and President Lee Teng-hui smiling and talking; later, Hsu and Premier Hau Pei-tsun smiled and toasted each other.[7] In November 1991 the DPP elected Hsu Hsin-liang chairman, succeeding party veteran Huang Hsin-chieh. For the next two years Hsu boasted that the DPP would become the ruling party. The DPP, however, suffered a bitter defeat in the December 21, 1991, election,though it fared much better in the December 1992 election for the Legislative Yuan and again in December 1994 when its candidate, Chen Shui-bian, was elected mayor of Taipei. But when the DPP won only six county magistrate seats in the November 27, 1993, local election, Hsu, as he had promised, resigned because his party had failed to expand its control over local government.

Hsu Hsin-liang is emblematic of a significant pattern in Taiwanese political life: under martial law, dissidents charged with sedition fled the country and engaged in revolutionary activities; after martial law was lifted, they returned to Taiwan to live as free citizens, some acquiring high positions in the main opposition party, the DPP, and competing in national elections.

## Constitutional Law

Between August and December 1947 the ROC government held national elections throughout the China mainland and Taiwan to select national representatives of the National Assembly, the Legislative Yuan, and the Control Yuan. The National Assembly, with nearly four thousand national representatives, elected the nation's president and vice president for a six-year term; the Legislative Yuan recommended and passed laws and approved the national budget; the Control Yuan had the power to impeach, censure, and audit. In 1948 the National Assembly adopted the Temporary Provisions, which deactivated the constitution and conferred power on the Office of the President. When China divided that same year, national elections for these three organs could not be held. How could the defeated ROC government survive in Taiwan if it could not elect its own national representatives? To justify the ROC's claim to represent all the people of China, including the mainland, in 1953 the ROC's Executive Yuan requested that the Judicial Yuan rule on whether those ROC representatives elected in 1947 on the mainland could hold office without a new election. On January 29, 1954, Justice Wang Zonghui of the Council of Grand Justices ruled as follows:

Our country has gone through enormous changes, and elections cannot be held according to the law. If we allow the Legislative and Control Yuans to fall into disarray, the principle of our five-power system of government will be violated. Therefore, until the second-term delegates are elected, the first-term elected delegates of the National Assembly can continue to serve and enjoy their rights.[8]

The national representatives elected from the mainland and Taiwan in 1947 thus retained their power until elections in late 1991 and 1992 replaced them.

For more than forty years, then, KMT mainlanders ran Taiwan, appointing the ROC's president and vice president, controlling the legislative machinery, and monitoring the activities of government officials. Although in 1969 the government allowed supplementary elections to replace those representatives who had died or resigned, the power brokers ensured that KMT rule was never threatened. In those elections, which were held concurrently with triennial local elections, non-KMT politicians ran and even won some seats. Although they never seriously challenged KMT rule until 1986, they campaigned to remove the First National Assembly and elect a new National Assembly to reform the constitution.

A signal change in the constitution came when the Council of Grand Justices ruled on June 21, 1990, that by December 31, 1991, all those elected in 1947 to the First National Assembly, Legislative Yuan, and Control Yuan must resign. In April 1991 the First National Assembly abolished the Temporary Provisions, thus revitalizing the constitution, and added articles whereby a Second National Assembly would be elected on December 21, 1991. In May 1992 the Second National Assembly further amended the constitution to expand elections for national representatives. After a skillful campaign, opposition politicians for the first time won enough seats in the December 1992 election for the second Legislative Yuan to initiate coalition politics with the KMT. In August 1994 the Second National Assembly again amended the constitution to empower the people to elect a president, a vice president, and the Third National Assembly on March 23, 1996. On that day the Chinese people on Taiwan had truly completed the process to democracy.

The 1947 constitution established the rule of law both before and after martial law was lifted. The ruling elites tried to preserve the 1947 constitution to promote the unification of a democratic China. The opposition elites used it to demand national elections, establish opposition parties, and create a *real* democracy, not a pseudodemocracy. Under martial law a deactivated constitution enabled the ruling party to hold forth the promise of democracy and emboldened the opposition to press for fulfillment. After the lifting of martial law a reactivated constitution allowed for reform, national elections, and the establishment of a true democracy.

## Free Speech

Under martial law the Garrison Command and other national security organs controlled all information circulated in society, including the media. Guo Yidong (nom de plume, Bo Yang),[9] a journalist, was arrested on March 4, 1968, for drawing a newspaper cartoon lampooning Chiang Kai-shek. At his trial the authorities charged that Bo Yang had "used a girlfriend to find out from a Nationalist military officer how many bicycles there were in his regiment and that he attempted to persuade a friend to remain behind in Communist China rather than flee to Taiwan."[10] Bo Yang claimed that the military court that sentenced him to eighteen years in prison never informed him of the law he had violated or of his crime.[11] Bo Yang was pardoned and left prison on April 1, 1977, after serving more than nine years of his sentence.

In 1986 Bo Yang published a book titled *The Ugly Chinese People*, a satire depicting the failings of the Chinese people on both sides of the Taiwan Strait. The mainland authorities immediately banned the book, but the ROC government allowed it to circulate freely. On January 1, 1988, the government removed restrictions on the press, ending censorship of the written word in Taiwan. In the summer of 1992 Bo Yang declared that the ROC was the freest society that had ever existed in Chinese history.[12]

## Political Party Competition

In the late 1960s new politicians began opposing the KMT by competing in the triennial local and national elections, publishing journals, and criticizing government policies and officials. Their activities coalesced on November 24, 1978, when a group led by Huang Hsin-chieh formed the Nonparty Organization to Promote Elections throughout the Province (Chuansheng dangwai zhuxuan),[13] whose stated purpose was to elect non-KMT politicians. On September 8, 1979, those same politicians began publishing the magazine *Meilidao*, which became a platform for winning voter support in local elections.

On December 10, 1979, some of these opposition politicians spoke at a human rights rally in Kaohsiung. Violence broke out between rally participants and local police; arrests followed, with more than a dozen opposition politicians tried in military court and given long prison terms. But anti-KMT political activity did not cease. On March 11, 1984, another group of anti-KMT politicians established the Public Policy Association (Gong zhenghui) to discuss public policy and promote democracy. The KMT and the government reminded its leaders not to form a political party because it was prohibited by martial law.

In March 1986 KMT chairman Chiang Ching-kuo decided to reform the polity but did not mention lifting martial law. He instructed the KMT to plan for political reforms, including political parties competing in elections. Opposition leaders met on September 19, 1986, and organized a new political party; sixteen individuals signed the new party's charter. They dared not go public until nine days later, on September 28, 1986, when, at the Grand Hotel in Taipei, they declared the illegal formation of the Democratic Progressive Party (DPP). Although they had defied martial law, Chiang Ching-kuo did not arrest them, and in 1989 both the DPP and the KMT registered as political parties. The KMT leadership's tolerance and the opposition elite's courage marked a new stage in Taiwan's democratic transition. Political party competition, outlawed under martial law, now became a way of life in Taiwan.

These four examples illuminate the dramatic changes in political life before and after martial law. The power that had been concentrated in a single leader and his ruling party during thirty-eight years of martial law was quickly transferred to the people. In March 1996, only nine years after martial law was lifted, national elections were held for Taiwan's leaders and national representatives. Unlike the prolonged bloody struggles between the people and the autocrats of imperial Russia, France, England, and other countries, Taiwan's democratization had occurred rapidly and peacefully.[14]

## Posing the Problem

Why has Taiwan, but no other part of China, experienced democratization? After World War II a large, prosperous middle class emerged in Hong Kong and Macao because of enlightened colonial rule, but democracy never took place because the colonial rulers prohibited it and the Chinese elites never organized to demand it. In Hong Kong, political pluralism briefly emerged after December 1984, when the PRC and England's leaders signed the Sino-British Declaration allowing the PRC to reestablish sovereignty over Hong Kong on July 1, 1997. In 1987 limited elections for a Legislative Council began and others followed until the last election in September 1995. In early 1997 Beijing's leaders declared that all elected Legislative Council members would be replaced after July 1, 1997, when Hong Kong reverted to a special administrative region under Chinese sovereignty. Hong Kong was to have "decolonization without democracy." [15] The future of Hong Kong's embryonic democracy is problematic, and democracy has yet to evolve in Macao which too reverts to China in 1999. As for Singapore, a single party has always stifled political opposition, and to date there exists no embryonic democracy championed by an opposition group and tolerated by the authorities.

As for the Chinese mainland, the Celestial Kingdom had always been ruled by powerful autocrats, whether unified, divided, or under foreign rule. Its rulers were toppled (usually on the pretext of losing the mandate of heaven or being morally undeserving) by coup, rebellion, or foreign invasion, with power soon concentrated in new autocrats and their advisers and officials. Personal power, not the rule of law or the will of the people, determined how China was governed. Ruler after ruler drafted legal codes but never established the rule of law, nor was there any political theory developed to justify a polity organized by checks and balances with leaders and representatives elected by the people. The Legalists, a group of philosophers, tried to make law the basis for guiding rulers and citizens, but the political culture, the society, and the economy resisted. Confucian elites forever debated how to organize the political center under sage-kings who could link cosmic forces, the political center, and society into one perfectly moral, sacred order.

By the early twentieth century, some Chinese had begun to champion the rule of law and the transfer of power to the people, but they had little success. The Communist Party, which unified China in 1949, paid lip service to these goals but replicated the patterns of the past and continued to amass and project power. Taiwan's democratization, as this book argues, seems unique when compared with other Chinese societies in the twentieth century. To sharpen the comparison, let us compare how the ruling elites on the two sides of the Taiwan Strait used power after 1949. We adopted a typology developed by Thomas A. Metzger and based on Edward A. Shils's concept of the "political center," defined as the "legally most powerful roles and collectivities in a society, along with their subordinates and centripetal elites." [16] We use this typology to personify the structural relationships between the political center and the rest of society.

One such relationship uses relatively free elections and free public media to subordinate the center to the demands of the rest of society. There are hypothetical democratic societies in which power has been transferred to the people and some form of "civil society" exists. David Held describes three modern models of democracy as John S. Mill's "developmental democracy," Joseph A. Schumpeter's "competitive elitist democracy," and R. A. Dahl, C. E. Lindblom, and others' "pluralistic democracy."[17] These three models of democracy can be subsumed under a particular type of political center we refer to as the *subordinated political center,* which rapidly evolved after martial law was lifted.

Another relationship between the political center and society is one in which the center possesses enormous power because of its autocratic core, made up of a ruling party, government structure, and the ruling party's auxiliary organs and its domination of ideology.[18] This center dominates through what Amitai Etzioni's typology delineates as normative, remunerative, and coercive sanctions. This center has the power to mobilize the population and the skills to maintain leadership stability by recruitment and replacement; it successfully avoids conflicts in the international arena while enhancing its global status. We call this type the *uninhibited political center* because society passively complies with the center's ideology, policies, and sanctions.

The final relationship between the political center and society is one in which the "center does not control many of society's resources, and it gives much leeway to other loci of decision making, such as 'self-propelled adults' using their own judgement rather than following state commands to decide where to reside, how to pursue education, what intellectual and moral choices to make, and what political causes to support."[19] We call this type the *inhibited political center,* which can apply to various types of authoritarian regimes that have existed in the twentieth century.

In the 1950s Taiwan's ruling elite established an inhibited center that four decades later became a subordinated center, or democracy. Mainland China's ruling elite opted instead for an uninhibited center that only since the 1980s has evolved into an inhibited center. Thus Taiwan's transition can be understood only by analyzing why Taiwan's ruling elite's decided to establish a relationship between the political center and the society that we will refer to as *limited democracy,*[20] by which we mean the inhibited center is committed to promoting full democracy but without a timetable. This political center also set limits for the permissible behavior of a political opposition, but under limited democracy a political opposition formed to challenge the inhibited political center to establish a real democracy. What were the major characteristics of Taiwan's inhibited center that made possible limited democracy and the emergence of a political opposition? What kind of political development made possible Taiwan's transition to a subordinated center, or democracy? To answer these questions, we offer the following.

## The First Chinese Democracy

After fifty years of Japanese colonial rule, on October 25, 1945, national government officials, troops, and KMT officials took over Taiwan and established the Taiwan provincial government as part of China. By late 1949, however, the communist-led military had taken over the mainland, and in that interim period nearly two million people had chosen to migrate to Taiwan. Some of these migrants were Taiwanese returning to their homeland to join their three million island brethren, but most were political and military refugees along with their families. The migrants' military and police power, combined with that of the Taiwan provincial government, made it possible to relocate the old central government in Taiwan as the Republic of China. In June 1950 the United States government entered the Korean War and dispatched the Seventh Fleet to patrol the Taiwan Strait and prevent a communist invasion. American military and economic aid to Taiwan soon followed.

The ROC confronted not only a powerful communist enemy across the Taiwan Strait but a hostile Taiwanese people who spoke a dialect very different from the national language of Mandarin and who had been profoundly Japanized. To make matters worse for the new mainlander regime, the new authorities had harshly suppressed an indigenous uprising on February 28, 1947. Many Taiwanese had fled overseas and begun plotting to overthrow the ROC and establish a Republic of Taiwan independent of mainland China. Thus establishing martial law gave the ROC the power not only to deal with communist subversion but also to suppress any indigenous political movement that appeared to threaten the government. The first task for these mainlander refugees was to rebuild the shattered KMT.

Between late 1949 and late 1952, the ROC's powerful leaders, led by Chiang Kai-shek and his son Chiang Ching-kuo, rebuilt the shattered KMT into a new party dedicated to transforming Taiwan into a model society based on Sun Yat-sen's Three Principles of the People. Chapter 2 describes how this new

CHART 1
*The Inhibited Political Center*

1. *Leading political principles:* A Chinese society based on Sun Yat-sen's Three Principles of the People. The ruling KMT was committed to full democracy, but only after lifting martial law.
2. *Major objectives:* The center formulates policy, enacts laws, and produces budgets; it promotes modernization, maintains domestic order, and preserves national security for the purpose of eventually unifying with the mainland under a democratic constitution.
3. *Key agents:* KMT, First National Assembly, Office of the President, Executive Yuan and central government, and other *yuan.*
4. *The structure of political power.*

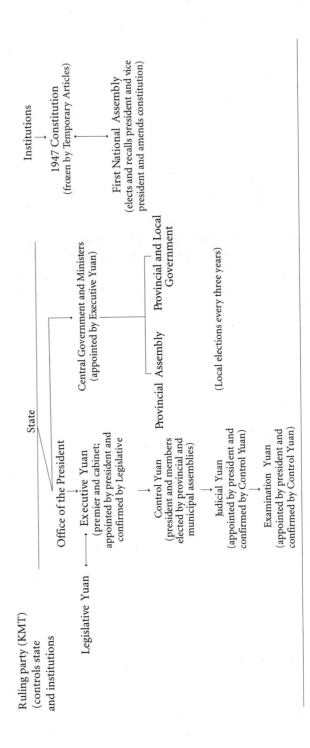

Ruling party (KMT)
(controls state
and institutions

State                          Institutions

1947 Constitution
(frozen by Temporary Articles)

First National Assembly
(elects and recalls president and vice
president and amends constitution)

Office of the President

Central Government and Ministers
(appointed by Executive Yuan)

Provincial and Local
Government

Provincial Assembly

(Local elections every three years)

Legislative Yuan

Executive Yuan
(premier and cabinet;
appointed by president and
confirmed by Legislative

Control Yuan
(president and members
elected by provincial and
municipal assemblies)

Judicial Yuan
(appointed by president and
confirmed by Control Yuan)

Examination Yuan
(appointed by president and
confirmed by Control Yuan)

party was rebuilt and deeply embedded in the national, provincial, and local governments. From the outset, the KMT leadership decided to use the 1947 constitution as its guideline for political rule. That constitution postulated a democratic republic whose citizens enjoyed civil liberties and elected local leaders but whose central government leaders were indirectly elected by an assembly of nationally elected representatives. China's civil war, however, had prevented the implementation of this constitution. On April 18, 1949, the First National Assembly, elected on the mainland, "deactivated" the constitution by adding articles called the "Temporary Provisions," which the government adopted on May 10, 1949. Those new articles allowed the powers normally vested in the constitution to be transferred to the president, who also was the KMT chairman, thus melding the party and the state. Single-party, authoritarian rule had become the order of the day, with the promise of establishing democracy tomorrow.

Confronted by enemies from within and without, the new KMT created a polity we will characterize as an inhibited political center (chart 1). To legitimize this center, the regime used the "deactivated" 1947 constitution and its governance structure, which was now dominated by single-party control. The KMT leaders adhered to the political principles, derived from Sun Yat-sen's doctrine, that called for vesting power in the people *(minzhu)*, but only after lifting martial law. The regime would use the laws and security forces created under martial law to repress any political opposition that seemed to threaten public order and undermine regime legitimacy. Therefore the regime did not tolerate any political opposition party, but it was willing to promote a limited democracy with the promise of eventually establishing full democracy when favorable conditions allowed.

Meanwhile, to legitimize its powers the inhibited center used the governance structure that had been created on the mainland when the 1947 constitution had been approved by the First National Assembly. That assembly elected the president and vice president to a six-year term and amended the constitution. Along with the Office of the President and five *yuan*, there were the Taiwan provincial and local governments. Coordinating and controlling this structure was the KMT, whose chairman also served as president (chart 1).

In the inhibited political center, the KMT and the Office of the President determined policy, conceived laws, and drafted budgets. Five principal agencies called *yuan* administered the government: the Executive Yuan (premier and cabinet) actually ran the government, the Legislative Yuan governed through a parliament, the Judicial Yuan rendered judicial decisions, the Control Yuan provided government oversight, and the Examination Yuan selected and promoted officials. Because the ROC leaders hoped to recover the mainland, they insisted on maintaining a Taiwan provincial government complete with governor, assembly, and local government.

The expressed goals of this polity were to build a powerful, wealthy modern economy and prepare to recover the mainland. By the late 1950s, however, that dream had faded as the mainland regime robustly demonstrated its ability to survive. The ROC regime continued to advocate the Sinicizing of a populace that had been isolated from Chinese culture for a half century, to attempt to educate a middle class while avoiding the inequalities of wealth distribution, to grant business enterprises the right to contract and use the marketplace, and to nurture a limited democracy. Most important but least understood was the nurturing of limited democracy by the KMT-dominated political center.

As chapters 3 and 4 will show, limited democracy constituted the first evolutionary phase of Taiwan's polity toward democratization (see chart 2). Although local and provincial elections were first held in spring 1946, it was not until 1950 that the KMT's inhibited political center allowed for local elections of village, township, city, and district leaders and assemblies, as well as a provincial assembly election, to be routinely held. The KMT permitted discussion and debate of Western liberalism but banned Marxism and socialist thought. This ruling party also insisted upon strict adherence to the 1947 constitution with the intent of reactivating it to establish full democracy when conditions permitted. Finally, it allowed regime critics to hold public meetings and critically evaluate the regime as long as the authorities judged such behavior did not threaten party-state rule. Limited democracy received further encouragement when the regime passed a law in 1969 permitting a small quota of national representatives to be elected every three years. These characteristics of limited democracy constituted an embryonic political market process in which an incipient opposition began to challenge the KMT to accelerate the pace of democratization.

Limited democracy coexisted with extreme repression. The inhibited political center still possessed enormous power and repeatedly used it whenever the authorities believed the opposition had overstepped the proper bounds. Fearful of communist subversion as well as an incipient Taiwanese nationalist movement both at home and abroad dedicated to replacing the KMT regime with one of its own, the KMT party and state machine ruthlessly crushed any dissent and activity regarded as threatening national security.

The KMT, therefore, tried to perform a difficult balancing act: maintaining its authority and power while trying to nurture a democracy that would elicit popular support at home and respect and support from the international community, particularly the United States. As chapters 3 and 4 will demonstrate, this difficult balancing act proved successful. Taiwan's people gradually learned to play by the rules of democracy. A political opposition gradually emerged and skillfully expanded its political influence, and the ruling party gradually learned how to tolerate and live with a political opposition. The evolutionary phase of limited democracy was crucial for Taiwan's democratic breakthrough and consolidation because it provided enough time for the people and elites to "learn democracy by practicing it" and for their political cultural values to become conducive to the practice of democracy.

The KMT's limited democracy under martial law was rarely praised, but Taiwan's economic development and social transformation became widely recognized and acknowledged. The record reveals that the party-state encouraged resources to move to high-value activities and maintain high economic growth rates. Although an economic slowdown began in the 1980s, households and enterprises adjusted to new patterns of demand, and the economy continued to prosper while experiencing great structural change. Individuals could express their ideas as long as these were not perceived to threaten the inhibited center's legitimacy. Therefore, Taiwan's dynamic economic market process and the evolution of its ideological market process, in which Sunist ideology, Confucian humanism, Western liberalism, and the ideology of ordinary Taiwanese people competed for acceptance and predominance, helped to promote the development of a civil society having new organizational forms that critically evaluated the performance of the government, always urging it to do better, and established an atmosphere of ruling elite tolerance toward an emerging political opposition. Thus the KMT-dominated inhibited political center became even more inhibited by complex market processes and the rise of civil society, which encouraged an embryonic democratic process.

Compare the stark differences between the ROC's inhibited political center and society and that of Communist China's uninhibited political center. In mainland China the Maoist-Marxist ideology was the only means whereby one could obtain knowledge and interpret phenomena; no other ideas were allowed to compete. The Communist Party—through its organizations and agencies—regulated, monitored, and controlled every aspect of society. Private associations were eliminated or marginalized. The party and state apparatus controlled the economy through state-owned enterprises, collectives, and communes, leaving no scope for the market process. A combination of workplace control mechanisms separated rural and urban society and made it difficult for a civil society to evolve. In 1957 communist leaders mobilized massive campaigns to terrorize backsliding, hostile intellectuals; in 1958 they

CHART 2

*The Five Phases of ROC Democratization*

| Evolutionary phase | Period | Key characteristics |
|---|---|---|
| 1. Limited democracy | May 19, 1949–March 1986 | Martial law, a mixture of repression and liberalization. |
| 2. KMT chairman Chiang Ching-kuo expands democracy and lifts martial law | March 1986 | Chiang Ching-kuo instructs KMT to study political reform |
| | September 1986 | DPP illegally establishes a political party, but Chiang Ching-kuo takes no action |
| | June 1987 | Legislative Yuan passes new security law to replace martial law |
| | July 15, 1987 | Martial law lifted |
| 3. KMT chairman Lee Teng-hui initiates a political pact between the ruling and opposition parties and launches constitutional reform | 1987–89 | Liberalization of press and laws allowing political parties |
| | December 2, 1989 | First election after martial law (peaceful) |
| | March 1990 | First severe political crisis in KMT and the First National Assembly over whether to reelect Lee Teng-hui |
| | June–July 1990 | President Lee Teng-hui convenes National Affairs Conference |
| | April 22, 1991 | President Lee abolishes Temporary Provisions, and First National Assembly amends constitution to permit election of Second National Assembly |
| | December 21, 1991 | Second National Assembly is elected |
| 4. Constitutional reform and election of national representatives | March 1992 | President Lee persuades KMT to delay amending constitution for indirect elections of president and vice president |
| | May 27, 1992 | Second National Assembly approves electing new national representatives |
| | December 19, 1992 | Voters elect 161 members to Second Legislative Yuan |
| 5. Stage two of constitutional reform and elections for national representatives and leaders | July 29, 1994 | Second National Assembly adds ten articles to constitution, which include direct election of president and vice president |
| | December 3, 1994 | Taiwan governor and mayors of Taipei and Kaohsiung elected |
| | December 2, 1995 | Voters elect 164 members to Third Legislative Yuan |
| | March 23, 1996 | President and vice president (four-year terms) and Third National Assembly elected |

established rural communes. Beginning in 1966 and ending only with Mao's death on September 9, 1976, the Great Proletarian Cultural Revolution rooted out enemies of the Communist Party. Even the elected National People's Congress, controlled and manipulated by the Communist Party, rubber-stamped all party decisions. The limited democracy that evolved in Taiwan was never practiced, nor did the Communist Party promise even a bona fide socialist democracy; it continued to revise its constitution while never affirming its political rules. Private enterprise, free markets, and ideas competing with Maoist-Marxist thought did not begin to exist until the 1980s and 1990s. In a structural sense, then, the political paths of these two Chinese societies rapidly diverged after 1949, when their political centers formed, although developments now taking place suggest that the two societies might gradually be converging.

In Taiwan, the relationship between the inhibited political center and society underwent a profound transformation after the first phase of limited democracy (see chart 2). Chapters 5 and 6 describe phase two, the democratic breakthrough, in which the KMT leadership replaced martial law with new laws and promised political reform. At the same time, an opposition party illegally formed. Enlightened and astute political leadership made possible these two developments. Our focus therefore shifts to the critical role played by Chiang Ching-kuo, who resolved the new crises that began to overwhelm the KMT in the early and mid-1980s and initiated a democratic breakthrough. The opposition leaders, displaying courage and political skill, also organized their new party without resorting to bloodshed. These leadership successes depended on political brokers' skillfully mediating compromise and agreements between the opposition political elites so that reform advanced to expand the political market process.

In phase three (chart 2), some momentous events, described in chapters 7 through 9, took place that threatened to reverse the democratic transition or create anarchy. The death of Chiang Ching-kuo in January 1988 brought great uncertainty to political life. In 1989 the shrill voice of Taiwanese nationalism challenged the political center's ruling party. In that same year the KMT experienced its first election setback, and public demonstrations intensified. In 1990 the KMT split as Chiang's successor, the Taiwanese Lee Teng-hui, fought a severe power struggle with mainlander party leaders. The First National Assembly began losing its legitimacy in the eyes of the elites and the public. The new opposition party, the DPP, threatened to go to the streets to mobilize public support for speeding up democracy. These crises were resolved only in 1990, by the innovative leadership of President Lee Teng-hui, along with that of the DPP's moderate leadership wing, in establishing a "political pact" between the parties to respect the nation's political institutions and play by the rules of democracy. This pact made possible the crucial election for the Second National Assembly on December 21, 1991, which brought into power a new generation of elites to reform the constitution and expand the democratic process.

Phases four and five (chart 2) are covered in chapters 10 through 12, which describe the complex events surrounding constitutional reform and the national elections that began taking place from December 19, 1992, when the people elected the Second Legislative Yuan, until March 23, 1996, the first time in Chinese history the people elected a president, a vice president, and the Third National Assembly. The elections during this period empowered the people to choose their legislators (two elections held for the Legislative Yuan, in December 1992 and 1995 respectively), the governor of Taiwan province, and the mayors of Taipei and Kaohsiung cities. Constitutional reform continued, but the bulk of that reform, already completed, now guaranteed regular elections for Taiwan's leaders and representatives at the national, provincial, and local levels of government.

Intense disagreements between elites and the political parties marked these reforms and elections, yet the protagonists agreed to disagree, and their disagreements were peacefully resolved. The competing elites continued to respect the ROC's political institutions, those rules that had evolved in the initial phase of limited democracy, which now served as the political guidelines for their parties to participate in political life.

In all political parties there were intense debates, and party factionalism eventually eliminated the many small parties that had formed in 1989, even transforming the KMT from a large, bureaucratic party into a smaller party streamlined to campaign and win votes. A minor political realignment took place in August 1994, when a small group of KMT members left their party to form the New Party. Further realignment occurred in the summer of 1996, when some members of the DPP, along with independents, formed the National Building Party, a pro-Taiwanese independent party. Taiwan's open, free society now allows for vigorous, critical discourse about that island nation's problems and future prospects. Civil liberties are fully guaranteed. Political parties vigorously compete. Although the KMT has lost power, it has yet to be replaced by another political party.

By the spring of 1996 the old inhibited center had been transformed into a subordinated center, or democracy, characterized by competing political parties, routine elections, unrestrained media, laws that protected individual lib-

CHART 3
## The Subordinated Political Center

### Functional Elements

1. Routine national elections prescribed by a constitution for national leaders and representatives—president; vice president; Taiwan provincial governor; mayors of Taipei, Kaohsiung, and all cities; Legislative Yuan and the National Assembly; as well as for all local elected officials and the Taiwan provincial and municipal assemblies—by a registered voting electorate living in Taiwan and offshore islands.

2. Political parties select their candidates for national and local elections and compete according to prescribed law. Opposition parties have achieved sufficient strength in parliament and some municipal-provincial assemblies to engage in coalition politics.

3. Human rights and liberties protected under the law to ensure freedom of speech, movement, and political activity.

4. Public media, except electronic media, have the freedom to publish information and critically evaluate political life according to prescribed law.

5. Fundamental political rules as embodied in the revised 1947 constitution serve as the basis for democracy.

### The Structure of Power

| | Means of subordinating political center to civil society (political market process) | Replacement of authority in political center and checks and balances on the center |
| --- | --- | --- |
| Civil society | | |
| Political parties | Competing for votes | Ruling party is elected by number of votes won in national and local elections |
| | | Legislative Yuan elected every three years and checks and balances Executive Yuan and Office of President |
| Private associations | Exerting pressure on Legislative Yuan and government agencies | Taiwan provincial governor elected and works with elected Taiwan Provincial Assembly and other elected local officials and councils, who check and balance national government |
| Public media | Monitoring, describing, and evaluating | National Assembly elected by voters every four years |
| Business enterprises | Financial gifts to political parties and candidates | President and vice president elected every four years |
| Voters | Voting in local and national elections for Legislative Yuan, president and vice president, Taiwan provincial governor, mayorships, district chiefs, councils, and assemblies | Government officials and leaders respond to demands by private associations, monitoring and evaluating by media, and preferences of voters |

erties and rights, and a civil society whose members affirmed democracy even though they differed over how that democracy should develop. The nation now elected all its national representatives and leaders according to prescribed constitutional amendments drafted and approved by the First and Second National Assemblies. Chart 3 presents the salient features of contemporary Taiwan, in which society—or the will of the people—subordinates the political center to its demands, thus fulfilling the criteria for democracy developed by most experts. In essence, the ROC's citizens freely and by law formulate their preferences; they signify those preferences to their fellow citizens and the government; and their preferences are weighed reasonably equally in the conduct of government.[21] The concluding chapter summarizes our narrative's findings according to four patterns of political development, showing how this Chinese society was transformed from an inhibited political center into a subordinated political center.

That this Chinese polity, which had been governed by an inhibited political center, transformed itself into a democracy is remarkable. Our narrative, which examines the major events and personalities that signified the momentous transformation of this Chinese polity, is a history of a half century of Taiwan's political life. To understand the complexities of that political life, in the following chapters we describe the interaction between the ideas and actions of leading personalities—leaders and elites; examine what people valued or preferred, or both, as well as their claims and perceptions; and specify the key events that produced relevant political decisions, agreements, reforms, and so forth.[22] This mix we call political life reflects the reality of history.

# Political Life under Martial Law

# CHAPTER TWO

# Building a New Party

Between 1941 and early 1945 the Republic of China government prepared for the takeover of Taiwan. When Japan surrendered on August 15, 1945, ROC troops and civil affairs officers began streaming into Taiwan to set up a new administration to make Taiwan a province of China. In September and October the Taiwanese warmly welcomed their mainland brethren, but disillusionment quickly set in as they began to realize that new foreign rulers had merely replaced old ones.

The new governor, Chen Yi, preferred to govern from his office rather than mingling with the people. He refused to speak in Taiwanese and Japanese, though he spoke those languages easily, instead insisting that the people use Mandarin. His administration did not auction off the Japanese wealth that the Taiwanese had labored to produce. His officials rejected the market economy approach to reviving the economy and imposed a system of monopoly bureaus to control the economy, thereby making shortages worse. Stocks of grain and coal were shipped to the mainland instead of being used to stabilize prices in Taiwan. About 36,000 Taiwanese officials formerly employed in the Japanese colonial bureaucracy lost their jobs.[1] The new administration refused to appoint any qualified Taiwanese to top-level positions. Taiwan's unemployment and inflation immediately worsened. The high expectations of those ruled under fifty years of Japanese colonialism quickly soured and became grievances.

Chen Yi believed in Sunist doctrine and decided to hold islandwide elections on April 15, 1946, an event the people greatly welcomed. These elections went off peacefully and produced a threefold increase in Taiwanese representation in the provincial and city assemblies and local government offices compared with the Japanese colonial period. The media also could publish what they wanted. This leap into democracy softened the mounting grievances, but only momentarily. By January 1947 not only had economic conditions deteriorated, but popular resentment had increased because of administration corruption and many grievances.

On the evening of February 27, 1947, officials of the Taipei City Monopoly Bureau arrested a forty-year-old widow for selling contraband cigarettes on Taiping Street in Taipei. The next day a huge public demonstration took place in front of the governor's office in Taipei and soon became violent. News of the event quickly spread throughout the island, and public demonstrations began occurring in all the large cities. The Nationalist government had now lost control over the island. Governor Chen had declared martial law on February 28, but in the next few days the people formed Resolution Committees in all major cities to replace all mainland officials and govern those cities. Negotiations between the Taipei Resolution Committee and Chen Yi began immediately but never achieved any satisfactory agreement. Meanwhile, Chen Yi appealed to Chiang Kai-shek for troops, which arrived on March 9, fanned out over the island, and in a series of massacres that horrified the populace, quickly restored Nationalist control.

Some estimates of the killings ranged from ten thousand to over twenty thousand; others indicated fewer. Whatever the true number, the February 28, 1947, uprising became the reference point for Taiwanese hatred of the mainlander-dominated provincial administration. Meanwhile, thousands fled to China, Japan, and North America. Their intentions were to continue the political struggle to overthrow the Nationalist regime. On May 15 Wei Taoming replaced Chen Yi. For the next two years the provincial government struggled to revive the economy but without any major success except to begin land reform in early 1949. Hyperinflation was now in full swing, and unemployment increased. These were the conditions on Taiwan that awaited the defeated KMT in 1949.

The KMT's defeat on the mainland was total, with provinces collapsing like dominoes. The United States secretary of state, Dean Acheson, told President Harry Truman that "the Nationalist armies did not have to be defeated; they disintegrated."[2] The president of the ROC and KMT chairman Chiang Kai-shek agreed. Writing in his journal on January 22, 1949, Chiang reflected: "The biggest reason for our defeat was that we had never established a new, solid organization type of system. The old one had long deteriorated and collapsed. In the current, crucial phase between the old and the new, we have lost the basic means to build and save a country. This is why we have been defeated."[3] But the KMT had seen better days.

KMT members trace their party's origin to the Revive China Society (Xing-zhonghui), set up by Sun Yat-sen in Hawaii in 1894. The society then merged with two other groups in Japan in 1905 to become the Chinese United League (Tongmenghui), with Sun as one of the principal leaders. After spearheading the revolution that toppled the Qing monarchy in 1911, the Chinese United League was reorganized in April 1912 by Song Jiaoren into the Chinese Nationalist Party (Kuomintang), which President Yuan Shikai soon outlawed. In July 1914, Sun reorganized the Kuomintang, whose members pledged loyalty to him. Then in Shanghai on October 10, 1919, Sun announced the reorganization of the Chinese Revolutionary Party as the Chinese Kuomintang. In the next few years Sun's party adopted the Bolshevik party's organizational structure and V. I. Lenin's principle of "democratic centralism" in 1924.[4] Sun and his followers believed this revitalized party could defeat the warlords and build an unequaled democratic polity and modern economy. Although Sun died in 1925, his followers, assisted by Soviet aid, defeated the major warlords and reconciled with the minor ones to expand KMT power over the country. But Sun's followers failed to capitalize on that early success, and after 1943 the KMT began losing its popular support and by 1949 had collapsed.

## Chiang Kai-shek Resolves to Fight On

On May 7, 1949, while still on the mainland, the government's paramount leader, Chiang Kai-shek, vowed that "in spite of the layers of darkness around me, I will maintain hope and remain committed and loyal to Sun Yat-sen." He was "determined to struggle without ever giving up" (*CTTC*, vol. 7, pt. 2, p. 296).[5] Believing that only he could regroup his countrypeople to "escape from the Iron Curtain and achieve a happy and peaceful life," Chiang flew to Makung city in the Pescadores and then to Kaohsiung, arriving on Taiwanese soil for the first time on May 25 (p. 288). Nationalist troops were still retreating to the southwest and southeast provinces. In subsequent weeks Chiang suffered acute pain from stomach ulcers brought on by stress and mental depression. To ease his many ills, Chiang constantly reminded himself to review "past mistakes and errors in order to expunge all of the harmful effects of our previous defeat." Realizing that Taiwan might become the last line of defense, Chiang began planning how to rebuild the KMT with the "correct social conditions and to determine the party's political direction"(pp. 367–68).

By early June he was in Taipei. On June 26, 1949, at a memorial service for Sun Yat-sen, Chiang explained why the KMT had been defeated and how its defeat could serve as the launching pad for a new party.[6] On July 14, 1949, he flew to Canton to meet with surviving KMT Central Standing Committee (CSC) members. At their first meeting, on July 18, Chiang revealed his plan for party reform,[7] and the CSC agreed to review it. Chiang then flew to Chongqing in Sichuan Province to rally party, military, and government officials, but the Nationalist forces in that region were too disorganized to continue a war of resistance against the Communists. Taiwan was now Chiang's last hope, and he returned to Taipei, never to set foot on the mainland again.

From September 1949 until mid-1950 an atmosphere of doom hung over the island. The KMT members who had fled the mainland were divided about their fate: should they try to negotiate a truce with the Communists or organize a last-ditch stand and prepare to die? The United States had abandoned the KMT, and only a few shipments of military weapons were in the pipeline for Taiwan. Every day brought news of communist military successes and an impending assault on Taiwan. Determined to fight to the bitter end, Chiang continued to organize Taiwan's defense while training new party cadres.

On October 16, 1949, Chiang founded a party cadres' school called the Academy for the Study of Carrying out Revolution (Geming shijian yanjiuyuan) in a cluster of large hills just north of Taipei called the Yangming Mountains. Over the next thirty months his academy graduated more than three thousand elite cadres in four- to six-week training cycles. Chiang told the first graduating class that "the reason that I founded this Academy was to make it possible for everyone to review our past mistakes and to have a solid understanding of our past defeats. Only then can we study how to defeat our enemies and win a great victory" (*CTCC*, vol. 7, pt. 2, p. 393).

Chiang explained the academy's name of "revolution" as "transforming one's mind." He urged the graduates to undergo an "inner" change by purging themselves of "selfishness, corruption, and bureaucratism" (p. 395). Chiang insisted that "if [party leaders] do not eliminate their psychological problems, the future is without hope" (p. 396). As for "putting into practice," Chiang explained that "party cadres in the past had never carried out their work in any practical way, because they had been vain, had worked superficially at their tasks and had never been truthful in their everyday actions" (p. 399). Finally, Chiang explained that "study" meant the following: "For all of you here today, this will be your last chance to repay your party and country. You must be determined to rid yourselves of the past and only be aware of the present in order to learn how to become revolutionaries, acquire the proper spirit and knowledge to carry out the Three Principles of the People, and rebuild our country" (p. 400). Like some charismatic religious leader, Chiang urged his top leaders to purify their thinking and lay down their lives for the revolutionary task of putting into practice Sun's Three Principles of the People (Sanmin zhuyi).

On October 31, 1949, Chiang turned sixty-three years old. On that day he wrote in his journal that "the past year has been the most tragic, darkest year of my life" (p. 410). Some months before, his party's headquarters had evacuated from Nanking and relocated in Taipei. In January 1950 only fifty thousand KMT members of a party that once comprised more than four million had managed to reach the island.[8] Most now struggled to support their families. Some early arrivals helped local government officials reduce tenant rents to a flat 37.5 percent of the harvest.

About four hundred cadres met that same month in Taipei to discuss party reform. Roughly half of them finally agreed on a draft proposal, which was sent to party headquarters, Chiang Kai-shek, and other CSC members. By April 1950 the party had recruited only a thousand new Taiwanese members,[9] and economic conditions were fast deteriorating. With the party in shambles, public morale declining, and a communist military attack expected by late summer, all seemed lost.

## Selecting the Party's Leadership Core

The outbreak of the Korean War on June 25, 1950, gave the KMT a new life. As United States warships sped to the Taiwan Straits to defend Taiwan and its offshore islands, Chiang Kai-shek realized that a communist invasion was impossible. On July 12, 1950, he informed 214 KMT and Control Yuan members in the Taipei Pinkuan (guest house) that he intended to immediately rebuild the KMT.[10] On July 26 he announced a new leadership team called the Central Reform Committee (Gaizao weiyuanhui) (CRC) to be in charge of rebuilding the party (see table 1) and be assisted by an advisory committee of twenty-five members.[11]

With the average age of CRC members only forty-seven, this youthful leadership was highly educated—many had advanced degrees from Japan, the United States, and Europe—and they shared a modern, cosmopolitan outlook. They also held important party-government positions and after 1952 contin-

TABLE 1

*Leadership Profile of the Reform Committee, July 26, 1950*

| Name | Age | Highest education attained | Former profession and official position | Official position in 1952 | Higher positions held since 1952 |
|---|---|---|---|---|---|
| Chen Cheng | 54 | Graduate, Baoding Military Academy (eighth class) | Chief of staff, chief commander in the army, governor of Taiwan | Premier | Vice president |
| Chang Chi-yun | 50 | B.A., National Normal University, Nanjing, Jiangsu | Professor, member of National Assembly, member, Central Standing Committee (KMT) | Head, Central Propaganda Department (KMT) | President of Chinese Cultural University, Minister of Education |
| Chang Tao-fan | 52 | B.A., Art Department, University of London | Professor, vice minister of social affairs, vice minister of communication, interior, and education | Member, Central Standing Committee (KMT) | Chairman, Legislative Yuan |
| Ku Cheng-kang | 48 | B.A., University of Berlin; honorary Ph.D., Dong Guk University, Korea | Minister of social affairs, minister of the interior | Minister of social affairs | National policy adviser to the president; president, ROC chapter, Asian-Pacific Anti-Communist League |
| Cheng Yen-fen | 48 | B.A., National Guangdong University; member secretariat, UN | Secretary general, Guangdong provisional government; secretary-general, Central Executive Committee, KMT; director, Department of Overseas Affairs, KMT; legislator | Secretary-general, Central Executive Committee (KMT); member, Central Standing Committee | Senior adviser to the president; minister of justice |
| Chen Hsueh-ping | 49 | B.A., National Beijing University; M.A., Columbia University | Professor; acting minister of education | Head, Taiwan province education department | National policy adviser to the president |

| Name | Age | Highest education attained | Former profession and official position | Official position in 1952 | Higher positions held since 1952 |
|---|---|---|---|---|---|
| Hu Chien-chung | 48 | B.A., Fudan University, Shanghai | Professor; director and chief editor, (*Zhongyang ribao*) | Legislator; member, central committee, KMT | President, *Zhongyang ribao* |
| Yuan Shou-chien | 47 | B.A., Whampoa Military Academy (first class) | Secretary-general of San Min Chu I Youth Corps; member, Central Standing Committee | Vice minister of national defense | National policy adviser to the president; minister of communication |
| Tsui Shu-chin | 45 | B.A., Nankai University; Ph.D., Harvard University | Professor at many universities | Legislator | Chairman, Planning and Examination Department of KMT central party headquarters |
| Ku Feng-hsiang | 44 | B.A., Beijing Chaoyang University Law School | Professor | Comissioner, Control Yuan | Secretary-general, KMT |
| Tseng Hsu-pai | 56 | B.A., St. John's University, Shanghai; honorary Ph.D., Chinese Cultural University | Director, International Department; vice minister of information, Graduate School of Journalism, National Cheng-chih University | Vice president, China Broadcasting | National policy adviser to the president; chairman of the board, Central China News Agency |
| Chiang Ching-kuo | 41 | Studied at Sun Yat-sen University, Moscow | Director, Section for Youth, Military, and Politics, KMT; commissioner, central committee | Director, Political Department, Department of Defense | President, ROC; premier, ROC |
| Hsiao Tzu-cheng | 44 | B.A., Central Political University; M.A., Columbia University | Professor; vice president, *Zhongyang ribao* | Chief, Section 6, KMT Reconstruction Committee | President, *Zhongyang ribao*; president, *Zhonghua ribao* |

TABLE 1 (continued)

| Name | Age | Highest education attained | Former profession and official position | Official position in 1952 | Higher positions held since 1952 |
|------|-----|---------------------------|----------------------------------------|---------------------------|----------------------------------|
| Shen Chang-huan | 38 | B.A., Hwanghua University; M.A., University of Michigan; honorary LL.D., Yonsei University, Seoul | Director, Protocol Department, Ministry of Foreign Affairs; director, Government Information Office; adviser, Executive Yuan | Government spokesman; vice minister, Central Propaganda Committee | Ambassador to Thailand; ambassador to Spain; minister of foreign affairs; senior adviser to the president; |
| Kuo Cheng | 43 | B.A., China University, Beijing | Member, KMT Central Standing Committee | Vice director, KMT Party, Shansi | |
| Lien Chen-tung | 41 | B.A., Keio University, Tokyo | Delegate to National Assembly | Secretary, Taiwan provincial delegation to National Assembly | Vice premier; senior adviser to the president |

SOURCE: Information in the first five columns is based on data from the excellent study by Xu Fuming, *Zhongguo guomindang di gaizao*, pp. 59–62. Some of the information in the last column was provided by the staff of *Zhongyang ribao* (Central daily news), Taipei.

ued to serve in high party and government posts. More important, they were unswervingly loyal and devoted to Chiang and shared his Sunist vision. The advisory committee had similar characteristics.[12]

## The Reform Committee Begins Work

On August 5, 1950, at ten in the morning, Chiang Kai-shek, along with the advisory committee to the CRC, other politicians, and several government-party workers assembled at KMT headquarters, just off Chungshan South Road near Taipei's South Gate. After Chiang briefly addressed the group, the sixteen CRC members stood up and took the following oath:

I swear with the utmost sincerity to carry out the will of Sun Yat-sen and to obey the Leader of our country; to strive to create a perfect, moral society without selfishness; to use all my wisdom and to strive with utmost loyalty to unite all loyal comrades in the party; to propagate a revolutionary spirit and to carry out and complete all our party reform tasks; and to strive to put into practice the Three Principles of the People. If I violate this oath or oppose it in any way, I willingly submit to severe punishment according to our party rules. With this oath, I so swear. (Ibid., p. 63)

Chiang then spoke:

The responsible comrades of the party should recognize our determination to reform the party, to propagate a revolutionary spirit, to carry out the duty of party political reform, and to reform the nation. We must begin to do all these things right now. This is the duty of the Central Reform Committee. At the same time, it is the expectation of all party members. (P. 63)

At eleven o'clock Chiang and the CRC met behind closed doors and reached the following decisions: to inform the old central committee members of the group's activities and ask them to perform new duties; to establish procedures for rotating the chairmanship; to appoint a secretary-general and a vice secretary-general; and finally, to appoint a chair for a new committee responsible for party reform (p. 64).

Next day, at the same time, the CRC reconvened to establish the organization that would carry out party reform. At the top was the paramount leader, Chiang Kai-shek; next was the sixteen-person CRC, assisted by a twenty-five-person advisory group and a secretary-general and deputy appointed from its ranks. This structure now took charge of thirteen new agencies: a secretariat, seven committees to study and carry out specific reform tasks, and five committees for training party cadres, recording party reforms, managing party financial affairs, editing party history, and making plans (pp. 65–66). The CRC concluded with plans to publish a statement on the political situation facing the new party, to define the basic characteristics of the new party and to establish rules for recruiting members and assigning party tasks (p. 67). The committee then adjourned.

## Party Reconstruction Reaches the Grass Roots

By August 31, 1950, the CRC was organizing the new party throughout Taiwan. Now calling itself a revolutionary-democratic political party that intended "to use revolutionary means to build democracy" (p. 68), the CRC requested that all former KMT members reregister in the new party and then assigned them to area headquarters units *(qu)* that covered the entire island. In every unit there was to be a locally selected and approved reform committee modeled on the Taipei CRC and charged with the task of building the new party in that area (p. 71). The process of party building at the grass roots worked as follows.

On October 2, 1950, the CRC sent Ni Wen-ya, along with eleven others, to instruct the Taiwan Provincial Reform Committee on how to establish reform committees in area headquarters for the district *(xian)*, city *(shi)*, township *(zhen)*, or hamlet *(xiang)*. Ni and his team then met with these area reform committee members, who had just reregistered, and instructed them in how to establish party work teams *(xiaozu)* (pp. 72–74). The work teams would recruit new members, discuss party tasks, conduct socioeconomic, cultural, and political surveys, and make recommendations to the area headquarters reform committee. Throughout the final months of 1950 the new reform committees in each area steadily organized their area teams.

The Nantou district in southern Taiwan, where 276 former KMT members had reregistered, illustrates how the party was reconstituted.[13] After their reregistration had been approved by party central, in mid-March the new members elected their provisional reform committee, which then toured Nantou, visiting with party members and local elite. On March 28, 1951, this committee elected a preparatory reform committee, which then took the same oath sworn to by the CRC when it formed in Taipei. On April 1, this area reform committee began assigning all registered party members to new party teams and asking each team to elect a leader and recruit new members. These new teams then became linked to a designated party unit headquarters *(qu)* and its relevant party section group. By April 10, Nantou district had thirteen such headquarters, seventy-two party section groups, and 298 work teams. In addition, there were five headquarters assigned to the Nantou district government and four more to the district's education system. Nantou's party teams were already recruiting new members; by mid-April Nantou's party membership had reached 1,713, more than six times the original number, and team leaders or cadres were attending the rotational training seminars.

To recruit work team members, two standing members had to vouch for the candidate's character and background, which the team leader submitted to headquarters for approval or rejection. The work team meetings, held at least once a month, typically began with the team leader reading Sun Yat-sen's will and reporting on the team's current activities; other reports, an open discussion, a review of new business, and final adjournment followed. Team leaders encouraged all members to participate but dissuaded those prone to monopolize the discussion.[14] The party tried to promote a familylike atmosphere of self-help and unity based on warm personal relations and close attachments.[15]

Every month, Taipei party headquarters asked the work teams throughout the island to provide information, submit suggestions, or carry out assigned work related to public security, economy, society, polity, and education.[16] In this way the party used the work teams to monitor society, carry out party policy, and evaluate policy outcomes. Party teams were expected to recruit young, educated, patriotic members, train them, and encourage them to participate vigorously in party work and life.[17]

Team members paid a monthly fee to the party, a dependable source of party revenue in those early years, but the party already had staked out claims to real estate and other physical assets that later contributed substantially to its income. Team members continued their lives as officials, teachers, professionals, workers, farmers, or businesspeople yet secretly met each month in small meetings to receive their assigned work. In this way these KMT members, believing they were part of an elite group, volunteered on behalf of Taiwan's society to participate in an anticommunism crusade. The party work teams embodied not only the goals and missions of the new KMT but, for the first time in KMT history, an organizational structure tightly connected the party's leaders to its members.[18]

## A New Party Takes Form

In early 1950, party statistics revealed that only 63,263 former party members had reregistered, but by the fall 16,780 more party veterans did so. The new work teams continued recruiting, and by fall 1952 the party's total membership increased to 270,000.[19] The population of Taiwan province in fall 1952 stood at 8,000,000, so that the ratio of party workers to population was a meager 0.034, a small party indeed.

Despite having only some 270,000 members, party leaders described their organization as a "revolutionary-democratic party representing the nation's people and all their interests; the party makes the interests of the people their interests, and it does not represent any particular class." According to party statistics for early 1951, farmers and workers made up 38 percent of the membership, with academics, writers, and the like making up the remainder.[20] Forty-nine percent of the members were under thirty years of age, and Taiwanese membership was steadily increasing.

By late 1952, however, the party's social profile had changed somewhat. Although still male dominated and young (48 percent were under forty years of age), only a third came from the farming and laboring classes. A tenth were businesspeople, with the rest being young intellectuals, students, and such. Some two-fifths had an elementary, high-school, or college-university education. This party now had a broad social base but tilted toward the youth and intelligentsia, with Taiwanese now making up slightly more than half the membership, or about 56 percent.

By late 1952 there were some thirty thousand work teams throughout Taiwan, with thirteen thousand party-trained cadres making up the party's elite core. Of the 270,000 registered members at that time, more than 14,000 lived in Taipei city and worked in the provincial government. Nearly 3,000 party members, organized into 295 work teams, served in the central government (see table 2). These work teams had been established by those reform committees designated by the CRC, so that they operated in each of the new headquarters units connected to the Office of the President, the five *yuan,* and the ministries belonging to the Executive Yuan. The work teams in government and society functioned as the party base whereby party members were integrated.[21]

These work teams were integrated into the party through four component structures: one structure interfaced with the nation's industry and mining, maritime activities, and public transportation; another embraced all levels of provincial and local government; a third took responsibility for the Legislative and Control Yuans and other central government organs; a final structure linked party loyalists living abroad (chart 4). These four party structures directed the political activities of the state and local governments, monitored the labor and professional associations, women's groups, and so forth, and linked up with the overseas Chinese to win their financial and political support. Top party cadres and government leaders, being one and the same, tried to guide the polity and economy and coordinate the public and private sectors of economic and social life. The work teams in the provincial government and occupational structures also reported to their party unit headquarters

TABLE 2

*Distribution of Party Workers in the Central Government, August 1952*

| Party unit headquarters | No. of sections | Work teams | Party members | Administrative unit |
|---|---|---|---|---|
| First | 10 | 45 | 414 | Central Reform Committees |
| Second | 8 | 45 | 380 | Office of the President |
| Third | 14 | 110 | 1,095 | Executive Yuan |
| Fourth | 2 | 13 | 139 | Legislative Yuan |
| Fifth | 3 | 11 | 68 | Judicial Yuan |
| Sixth | 3 | 13 | 112 | Examination Yuan |
| Seventh | 3 | 13 | 146 | Control Yuan |
| Eighth | 2 | 10 | 96 | Practical Revolutionary Study Academy |
| Ninth | 6 | 35 | 261 | Central administrative organs |
| TOTAL | 51 | 295 | 2,971 | |

SOURCE: See Xu Fuming, *Zhongguo guomindang di gaizo,* p. 89.

CHART 4
*The Organizational Structure of the KMT (1952)*

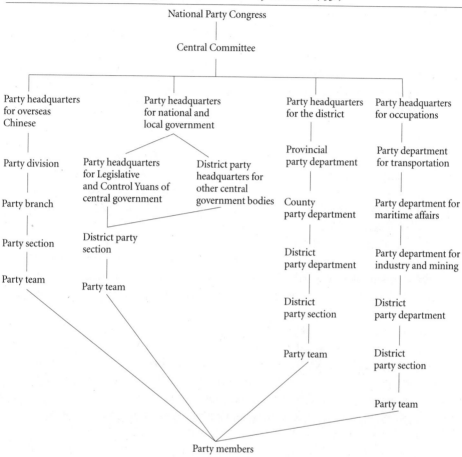

(qudangbu), whereas central government work teams participated in special party units *(tuan)* located in each ministry and throughout the ROC's five-power governmental structure (table 2). What kind of spirit and organizing principles characterized this new party?

## The New Party as Political Sect

Those Chinese who fled the mainland and joined the new KMT between 1950 and 1952 shared many haunting experiences, including the humiliation of defeat. The collapse of the once-powerful ROC central government had been a great shock to them, and a way of life suddenly disappeared. Expecting to die for having fled to Taiwan, they waited stoically or in terror for the communist invasion. The arrival of the United States Seventh Fleet meant a sudden reprieve from a death sentence, and most believed they had been given a new life.[22] They now looked toward this new party as the vehicle of their salvation and, like a sect, the party gave their lives new meaning. The party's leader, Chiang Kai-shek, inspired them to follow his lead, believe in his message, and identify with his vision.

### The Sect's Sage

Chiang Kai-shek was born October 13, 1887, in Qikou, a small town of Ningpo prefecture in Zhejiang. Raised by his mother, he decided early on a military career, studying first at a military school in Baoding, Hebei province, and later at the Shimbu Gakkô in Tokyo. He became a follower of Sun Yatsen's revolutionary movement to overthrow the Qing monarchy; with the help of the Shanghai revolutionary Chen Qimei, he met Sun, who decided to make use of his military expertise. Thus in March 1918 Sun summoned Chiang to Canton, where he soon became one of Sun's most trusted military officials. After Sun's death in 1925, Chiang rapidly ascended in the KMT, becoming the country's most powerful leader and commander of the Nationalist military forces. He achieved world fame in the early 1940s as the leader of one of the three major Allied powers cooperating with the United States to defeat Japan. After Japan's defeat, Chiang's fortunes plummeted; by 1949 communist military forces had defeated his government and military forces.

For many who had fled to Taiwan, Chiang's reputation was legendary. He had known Sun Yat-sen and had interacted with every major figure in twentieth-century Chinese history as well as with many world leaders. Chiang had not sought refuge abroad but instead chose to make a last stand on Taiwan with his few loyal troops, government officials, and party members, marking him as their natural leader in Taiwan. But could he organize any meaningful, lasting resistance to the Communists who controlled the China mainland in 1950? After all, Chiang had been largely responsible for the loss of the mainland to the Communists, and was that not because of failed leadership? One of Chiang's closest advisers, Chen Li-fu, judged Chiang to be skillful at political maneuvering, especially at using checks and balances to maintain his power, but that tactic had produced mixed results. According to Chen, "This method of his created distrust, fear, and suspicion; therefore, unity among his subordinates was always in doubt. In spite of this failing, Chiang's firm, strong anticommunist beliefs, however, made him the natural leader of our national revolution."[23] Moreover, Chiang had been overwhelmed by historical events and the awesome problems facing China. His aloof style made it difficult for the public to rally behind him. In his party, opposition to his efforts had been intense and widespread. Yet he soldiered on as the odds mounted against him after 1937. Increasingly isolated, he surrounded himself with advisers of questionable ability. From 1945 onward, Chiang began to miscalculate and opt for wrong strategies that caused the KMT's defeat.[24] So why did so many think that Chiang could lead them once again?

First, Chiang courageously shouldered most of the blame for his nation's defeat and asked only that everyone learn from that tragedy. On April 27, 1949, while still on the mainland, Chiang made a radio broadcast to the Chinese people in which he confessed that "I ought to bear the main responsibility for our defeat on the mainland" (*CTCC*, vol. 7, pt. 2, p. 288). Whenever Chiang addressed KMT members, he urged them to understand their defeat, purify themselves of indecision, fear, and guilt, and resolve in their hearts to learn from that bitter experience and never be defeated again.

Second, Chiang offered his followers a heroic vision. Understanding their anger, humiliation, and confusion over their defeat, Chiang emphasized that the Communists threatened China's five-thousand-year-old civilization and that only the KMT stood between them and the destruction of China's culture and heritage. Chiang appealed to everyone to join him in a great crusade to defeat this evil.

This grand mission could be achieved only by building a new party capable of waging "a people's war to oppose totalitarianism" (p. 369). To fight the Communists this new party had to use different methods, because they were like no other enemy the Chinese people had ever faced.

The political and military actions of the Communists are entirely based on their methods of "struggle" in society. To be anti-communist is to wage a people's democratic war, but the success or failure of such action will not be determined by military force and politics alone but by social and cultural methods. The Communists' social struggle today is to destroy our entire society. Their cultural work is to destroy our historical culture. Their activities are counter to our social and cultural traditions. Therefore, our party reform will review our party's organization, determine our party's social foundations, and plan our party's cultural work. We want to make the party's organization a product of our society's foundations. All party members will work on behalf of the people and be organized for the party's tasks. We must do this in order to carry out the Principle of People's Livelihood and to solve the social and economic problems that now exist as well as to carry out our mission of reforming society. (Pp. 370–71)

To lead the crusade against communist totalitarianism, the new KMT must mobilize by using moral power. Having been defeated by the Communists, Chiang believed that he alone understood the KMT's failings and that he could overcome the party's setbacks by building a new political organization. Chiang thus cast himself as possessing special knowledge and having a new doctrine for saving China.

## The Sect's Historical Mission

Whenever Chiang spoke to his party colleagues and officials, he reminded them of the KMT's unique, heroic history, which dated back to the Revive China Society (Xingzhonghui), established by Sun Yat-sen in 1894, and the United League, also founded by Sun Yat-sen in Tokyo in 1905.

Chiang argued that their party had struggled heroically to remove the foreigners from China, unite the country, modernize the military and the economy, and resist Japanese aggression. But in the past half century, the party had suffered more defeats than victories. Chiang referred to those defeats as testing the party's resolve, bringing it new crises but always leaving it more weakened. Such defeats included Yüan Shikai's illegitimate seizure of political power in 1913; Sun Yat-sen's departure from the office of president in 1918; Chen Qiongming's rebellion in Guangdong province in 1922; Sun's military defeat in Jiangxi in 1924; Wang Jingwei's collaboration with the Communists in 1927; the May Third Incident in 1928; the Japanese invasion and takeover of Manchuria in 1931; the Japanese invasion of China in 1937; and finally, the loss of the mainland to the Communists in 1949 (CTCC, vol. 7, pt. 2, pp. 360–65). According to Chiang, "After each defeat, our party's organization became more disconnected; the will of our party members further weakened, and party opportunists even betrayed the party in order to seek wealth and personal gain" (p. 366).

Other KMT members also acknowledged their party's sixty-odd years of victories followed by defeats. Like Chiang, they stressed that the 1949 defeat threatened the very survival of Chinese civilization.[25] How to save Chinese civilization after its half century of severe struggles and defeats became a common party refrain. Rather than remain mired in defeatism, Chiang urged his followers to take pride in their party's struggles and learn from them.

To dramatize the party's saga of heroism in the midst of defeat, the Taipei CRC published numerous accounts of party revolutionaries who had given their lives to the party, stressing the high moral character, nobility, and heroism of these martyrs.[26] If party members followed their example and developed that same heroic spirit, the KMT would never perish.

Chiang also called on party members to cultivate a spirit of self-sacrifice. Addressing the CRC at a Sun Yat-sen memorial on January 8, 1951, he applauded the "new spirit in the party, which gives me great confidence,"[27] but he emphasized that more had to be done to nurture that spirit:

With regard to "spirit," the psychology of our colleagues has not been completely reformed. Our party still has factions. I want the highest level of party cadres to adopt a spirit of complete self-sacrifice. Previously, after new members had been recruited, we had no way to continually train them. This is one of the main reasons why our party was defeated. This time, our reform will aggressively focus on establishing the deep foundations of our party base, and that is what our reform must accomplish.[28]

Chiang urged his new party to adopt a revolutionary spirit without selfishness, and he appealed to everyone in Taiwan to participate in the great war against Chinese communism and Soviet aggression. This great battle already was being fought by the nations of the free world, led by the United States, against the Soviet Union and its satellite communist regimes, including the one on the Chinese mainland. The ROC's role in this epic struggle was to transform Taiwan into an anticommunist bastion capable of recovering the mainland. Therefore Taiwan's new party must take the lead by building a perfect moral society without selfishness *(dagong wusi)* and making Sun Yat-sen's Three Principles of the People the centerpiece of reform.[29] Sunist doctrine was to be transplanted to Taiwan by giving all new party cadres and members a blueprint for reform that would also be used in civics courses at the elementary, high school, college, and university levels. Every citizen must be exposed to Sun's doctrine and encouraged to apply its principles, because it was the only way for the Chinese on Taiwan to defeat communism. To take the lead in this crusade, all party workers must soldier in the front line of society to save Chinese civilization by building a new moral order on Taiwan second to none in the world. The new party must eradicate the communist plague on the mainland and be ready to return to the mainland should the opportunity arise.

Throughout his political career, Chiang Kai-shek had used Confucian rhetoric and values to appeal to the nation to reform its ways, as in the New Life Movement that he launched in early 1934 but that sputtered out for lack of popular support. In Taiwan his followers, numbering only a few, took seriously his moral message of living virtuous lives by practicing benevolence, sincerity, tolerance, and mutual respect. Taiwan's new moral society should also distribute wealth equally so that it might resemble that ideal Confucian moral order *(datong)* of humaneness, benevolence, and virtue that the sages of the past had envisioned for China. Each KMT member must strive to build such a society. Taking their cue from Chiang, some KMT members proposed that everyone adopt a "politics of reverence" *(renzheng)* to nurture charity and self-help throughout society.[30]

Still other party members encouraged "nurturing a sense of worth or spirit," relating that to a strong desire to contribute to society and help others.[31] Feelings of pessimism and despair must be jettisoned. Trying to "get by" was not an appropriate attitude. Party members should take advantage of every opportunity, rely on the collective efforts of all party members, and propagate this spirit in all walks of life. If party members failed in these tasks and the party could not accomplish its glorious mission, then they would be labeled "criminals" for the rest of eternity. Falling short of these goals implied a profound moral failure of self. Each party member's moral salvation therefore became identified with making Taiwan into a new moral force to save Chinese civilization. As one party member put it: "I joined the party to save our country and our people."[32]

### The Sect's New Elite Core

For Chiang Kai-shek to build this new political organization based on Sun's creed and his vision, the party's new spirit, and each member's profound awareness of the party's heroic past, he needed an elite core of like-minded leaders dedicated to ensuring the integrity of the organization. This elite core must possess the proper values, persevere in the party's mission, and be immune from interest groups and external pressures.[33]

Chiang's first step in building this elite core, as mentioned earlier, was to open the Academy for the Study of Carrying out Revolution in October 1949 in the Yangming Mountains. From its first eight graduating classes, he selected his sixteen-person CRC, the CRC's advisory committee, and other key leaders. Everyone agreed that poor cadre training had contributed to the party's defeat and that in the future "the quality of cadres would influence the party's revolutionary mission, the security of the country, and the fortunes and disasters of the people."[34]

From the beginning, then, Chiang carefully selected and trained the cadres to serve the party's leader, carry out the party's mission, and lead party members. Three criteria determined their selection: to be committed anticommunists and eager to participate in the party's crusade to destroy communism;

to have practical leadership skills and the qualities of selflessness, discipline, hard work, and courage in the face of adversity; and finally, to have made a signal contribution to Taiwanese political and economic life.[35]

Chiang and the CRC opted for a three-tier cadre-training system.[36] The top-tier cadres attended the academy in the Yangming Mountains. Chiang managed the academy, visiting with each graduating class member and addressing each class several times. By personally examining every cadre's background and progress, he identified those people suitable for promotion. Student life in the academy was spartan, and the training was intense. Weekly discussion sessions brought everyone together, and at least once a term each student presented his or her personal history and told why the party had become a special vocation. By late 1952, eighteen classes had graduated 3,075 cadres who immediately took up posts in the party and central government.

Middle-level party cadres in each county received their training by rotating through a two-month training series. The first group began its training on May 9, 1951. By late 1952, 8,605 cadres had been trained. Groups of five to seven heard lectures on party history, theory, international affairs, and the like and participated in seminars. On completing their courses, they served in middle-echelon party units.

The lowest level of cadre training, established in 1951–52, involved three-week winter and summer camp seminars that trained those between ages fifteen and thirty. Young people from schools, technical colleges, and universities were invited to lectures on party history, theory, and international affairs, with heavy doses of Sunist doctrine and the writings of Chiang Kai-shek. Guest lecturers spoke about party affairs and rebuilding the party. In a two-year period 1,124 young people received such training.

By the end of 1952 some thirteen thousand people—only 0.05 percent of the party membership—had been trained in these three tiers. Party members elected them; the party trained them. This elite cadre received better organizational training than had been offered on the mainland, as witness one party member's recollection of the mainland party in 1934:

We always aimed at getting positions at the top of the party. We never considered the foundations and our work at that level. At that time, in my area's party central headquarters there were over one thousand workers, but at the base no one worked. Our party had a big head and small feet. The party could not project any power. As we continued to develop like that, we constantly shook.[37]

In addition to training an elite cadres core, however, the new party also needed a different institutional foundation.

*Organization*

For an organization to have integrity and fulfill its mission, its social structure must embody the purposes of the organization.[38] Thus the organization's personnel must be organized so that they convey the purpose of the organization and adhere to its rules. As already mentioned, the work team of eight to fifteen persons was to interact with society, make reports to party headquarters, perform assigned tasks, and carry out the party's mission.

On October 13, 1950, the CRC drew up nineteen articles stipulating how the small teams should be established. Article 16 required that each party member belong to a team and that the team structure be secret, thus enabling the party to keep its operations secret.[39] This penchant for secrecy was dictated by tradition. The KMT's antecedent organizations, which had been formed in secret by Sun Yat-sen, resembled the secret societies of mainland China, whose members swore an oath to the leader and maintained absolute silence about their activities and members.[40] The KMT also insisted on secrecy to protect its power, avoid public scrutiny and criticism, and prevent its enemies from understanding its operations. One party member put it this way:

The party's power and strength lay in its organization. The organization belonged to the members. Only the members knew the source of power. If the organization was made public, our power was revealed; that might constrain the organization. The party could never allow the enemy to know about its power.[41]

With the KMT's penchant for secrecy, oaths, and rituals, its reliance on an inner elite core, its adherence to a powerful moral vision, its loyalty to a sage-like leader, and its belief in a heroic history, it resembled a political sect of zealots led by a self-anointed patriarch.

Virtually all its members shared the deep humiliation of their party's defeat and agonized over why they had devoted so much of their adult lives to a failed party. After arriving in Taiwan, there was no place to hide from the Communists except to "jump into the sea," as many cadres reminded their comrades. But as the new party formed, they swore to uphold its aims and fulfill its founder's will: to plant deep in Chinese hearts the spirit and meaning of the Three Principles of the People. Their secret meetings and rituals epitomized their commitment to a cause even higher than family or personal ambition.

## A Leninist Party?

Was this new KMT Leninist? Many have claimed[42] that the new party was Bolshevik-like because it pursued a revolutionary agenda, practiced "democratic centralism," permeated society, penetrated the state, and controlled the military and security forces.[43] Although the KMT was organized like the Bolshevik party, its goals, leadership conduct, and party behavior were not the same. The Leninist label denotes a party organized like V. I. Lenin's, which seized power in 1917 in Russia to create the first socialist state and society. Before that time, the political parties in Western Europe had been described as either confessional or national, the former "seeking to adapt the needs of life here below," the latter promoting new nationalist policies.[44] The Bolshevik, or Leninist, party in Russia, however, signaled a "party of a new type," as noted by Bertram D. Wolfe,[45] and had three specific features.

First, this party believed in the myth and power of Marxist ideology. The Bolsheviks claimed that history evolved according to strict laws, and they embraced a common vision: to build a futuristic, communist society for that final stage in human history in which mankind would "pass completely beyond the narrow horizon of bourgeois rights, and for society to inscribe on its banners: From each according to his ability; to each according to his needs!"[46] The Bolsheviks fervently embraced this ideology, just as Joseph Stalin and Mao Tse-tung did when they articulated their parties' mission. Closely related to this ideology was the communist leadership's belief that, because their party represented only the workers and peasants, it must destroy all class enemies and vigilantly prevent their resurgence. The KMT never adhered to laws of history, a vision of a communist society, or class warfare.

Second, a Leninist party required an authoritarian core controlled by a dominant leader who determined the party's strategy and policies. The self-disciplined party loyalists adhered to their party's rules and "line." The party's authoritarian core also exercised extraordinary power over its members, manifesting, as Ken Jowitt put it, a "charismatic impersonality" totally unlike the "procedural impersonal" style of Western political organizations.[47] The KMT was dominated by Chiang Kai-shek and later by his son, Chiang Ching-kuo, but neither adhered to a party line, nor did its elite core exercise the great power over its membership as was the case in a Leninist party.

Finally, personal inclusion within the Leninist party overrode individual considerations, with that party assuming heroic proportions and projecting its power to perform superhuman tasks. Any leader or member failing in his or her duties was judged as having betrayed the party and often was condemned to death, imprisonment, or exile. Families of these victims became social outcasts. By concentrating awesome power to itself, a Leninist party tried to regulate every aspect of its members' public and private lives. Therefore the Leninist party and state were one, as were party and society. Transforming society into collective organizations also gave the Leninist party even greater control over the individual. The KMT never tried to control its members that tightly, nor did it seek totalitarian control over society. The Leninist parties that came to power in Eastern Europe and North Korea after World War II (thanks to the Red Army) and in China, Vietnam, and Cuba (by revolutionary skill) had all of the characteristics above.

Political organizations, even of the Leninist type, evolve and change. According to Philip Selznick, they experience specific kinds of life cycles because certain problems inevitably plague the organization over time: standards decline for recruiting and promoting party personnel; building an institutional core conflicts with selective recruiting within the party; and formalizing procedures is difficult to uphold over long periods.[48] As time passes, an organization's leadership and personnel change, and it loses the singular traits that distinguished its early formation. The parties of Brezhnev and Gorbachev were not the parties of Lenin and Stalin. Nor was Deng Xiaoping's party the party of Mao. As a Leninist party decays, its special features disappear, and it becomes merely a "hard" authoritarian party as in China today.[49] Or it can collapse altogether, as was the case in the old Soviet Union.

## The New Party Flexes Its Muscles

The revitalized KMT of the early 1950s, like the mainland's Chinese Communist Party (CCP), wanted to build a new society.[50] But the two parties went about this very differently. Between 1950 and 1956 the CCP used a mixture of violence, coercion, terror, and incentives in an effort to replace the age-old private property, family-firm, market economy with a public property, centrally planned, collectivized state-owned and state-managed economy. In that same period, the CCP also replaced the pre-1949 multiparty system with a one-party dictatorship that concentrated enormous power in its leaders and functionaries. Finally, the CCP replaced the ideological market process of competing foreign and domestic ideas with a single-thought system based on Marxist-Leninist-Maoist ideas. By 1956 this Leninist party had established its totalitarian control over the Chinese mainland.

In Taiwan, by contrast, between 1950 and 1956 the KMT developed a reform package that its leaders described as "implementating the Three Principles of the People in Taiwan."[51] The KMT's reform package removed the barriers that had blocked individuals from enriching themselves, educating themselves, and elevating their social status and power, what Ralph Dahrendorf has called enhancing "life chances,"[52] to unleash Taiwan's human energy. It was this new energy that made possible the evolution of new economic, political, and ideological market processes that transformed Taiwan's society.

The reform package addressed the economy through five policies designed to increase resource productivity, expand markets and private enterprise, and raise living standards.[53] Beginning in April 1949, under the auspices of an evolving land reform program, property rights were redistributed to some 350,000 poor rural households (more than two million persons). In 1953 the government introduced indicative economic planning to allocate, through the market mechanism, resources to industries targeted for growth. In that same year the government increased spending for water conservancy and irrigation, electrical energy, and public transportation. From 1950 onward the government transferred many state industries to the private sector. In 1951–52 the government approved workers' industrial accident insurance and increased base wages in the state-owned enterprises of salt production, mining, and manufacturing.

Other elements of the reform package initiated political reform. In 1950 the government authorized elections for governing councils and leaders of villages, townships, cities, districts, and the province, thus establishing local self-governance.[54] Two final policies, aiming at societal change and stability, completed the reform package: the government (1) subsidized primary education and promoted a core curriculum for Mandarin-language instruction, including propagating Sun Yat-sen's thought while stressing the evils of communism; and (2) established a comprehensive public security system.[55] KMT officials and representatives initiated these reform laws in the Legislative Yuan and approved new government budgets in the Executive Yuan to implement the reform package. These policies became the means by which the government regulated and guided the private sector.

By 1960 the economy had become more productive. Local elections were routine, and KMT-supported candidates often lost. Student enrollments and public literacy, health, and welfare had improved. All these developments accelerated by the late 1960s, as Taiwan became a society of rapid acquisition of household wealth, increased social mobility, and improved education and technical training.

Taiwan's traditional, entrenched interest groups, made up of many local elite, tried to resist these reforms, but they were overwhelmed. The KMT mobilized broad public support for its reform package. Party work teams throughout the island held rallies, lectures, and demonstrations to explain the reforms to the Taiwanese. Teams visited villages that had undergone land reform to recruit members for the party.[56] In late 1952 teams in Taoyuan district held rallies at public schools to publicize the party's mission, a tactic that then spread to the rest of the island.[57] The Taichung party team held seminars and invited leading citizens to discuss Sunist doctrine and the KMT's grand mission.[58] Some teams organized drama and entertainment tours around the island to advertise a new Chinese society based on Sun's Three Principles of the People. These same teams stressed the evils of communism on the mainland and emphasized how the KMT's reforms were improving Taiwan's living standards. In Taitung district, touring groups visited miners, farmers, and city workers to inform them of the reform's benefits.[59]

Party work teams also tried to win public support for the KMT by targeting all kinds of social groups and initiating public campaigns to improve citizens' welfare. Some work teams visited the military camps to elevate troop morale.[60] Other teams cleaned up city dumps, gave lectures on how to improve public health, promoted public frugality campaigns, and helped to regulate city traffic.[61] They also helped to select popular candidates for local elections.[62]

By the end of the 1950s, a small party of zealots had been spearheading significant economic, political, and social change. At first the party's efforts proved feeble because the KMT was rebuilding; by late 1953 its work teams volunteered their activism in every district and township. They respected the worth of the Chinese family and its private associations and tried to improve the party's image in Taiwanese society. Most important, perhaps, the KMT reform policies gave new incentives for families and businesses to produce greater wealth and to replace the old elites in rural and urban communities. Finally, Taiwan's citizens were better educated and trained for a society that was rapidly becoming urban, industrialized, and linked to the world economy.

Many Taiwanese elite still detested this authoritarian party because of its ruthless suppression of the February 28, 1947, uprising.[63] The public's memory of that tragedy had cast a huge dark shadow over Taiwan's society, dividing its citizenry and elite into two great camps: those who embraced the new ruling party and willingly aligned with its power structure and those who resented the mainlander-dominated KMT government power structure and devoted their lives to challenging it to become a true democracy. The resentment of the latter toward the KMT deepened after the imposition of martial law and its domination of the polity. This social cleavage afflicted Taiwan society for many decades, and within this sorely wounded and divided society the new KMT tried to legitimate its rule and establish laws to discourage any political opposition.

# The "Inhibited" Political Center

On October 10, 1952, at 8:00 on a clear and sunny morning, KMT elected delegates, central government representatives, and top party leaders gathered in the Chungshanlou Auditorium in the Yangming Mountains for the Seventh KMT Congress. As the sixty-six-year-old Chiang Kai-shek strode toward the podium to the accompaniment of martial music, he presented a heroic figure, dressed in a military uniform and wearing his medals. Chiang asked the five-hundred-person audience for three minutes of silence to remember Sun Yat-sen, the revolutionary martyrs, and their fellow Chinese suffering on the mainland.

He then spoke, reminding them of their party's recent shameful defeat and exhorting them to erase that humiliation:

When we retreated to Taiwan, everyone realized that we had been humiliated by the Communists and the entire world held us in contempt. How shameful it was for our party to have to learn the bitter lessons of that defeat. Anyone having the ambition and possessing the virtue to be a revolutionary must feel enormous regret about that defeat. Everyone now wants to overcome that sense of shame, make up for our crimes and sins, and use that triumph to comfort our leader, Sun Yat-sen, and those martyrs who died and are in heaven.[1]

Chiang warned his listeners to study their enemy, the Communists, and adjust party policy to world trends. He then urged the party to adopt a plan for recovering the mainland and said how delighted he was that party reform had been completed. Buses finally took congress attendees to places where they could watch the gala parades commemorating the anniversary of the 1911 revolution. Although there was little that was new in Chiang's remarks or in the next ten days of the congress, their convening demonstrated the new party's unity, its revitalized spirit, and its mission.

Over the next twenty-odd years, this 270,000-member political sect grew to more than two million members who dominated the polity. This party not only controlled the "inhibited" political center but had the power to influence society.[2] Yet it never controlled the lives of individuals in any compelling way. Household members had the freedom to choose their careers, change residence, speak their minds, and build their social attachments. In political life the center merely insisted on society's adhering to four implicit rules delineating the boundary between acceptable and unacceptable political behavior. The rules reflected the center's willingness to tolerate a very limited political opposition as long as it did not try to change the distribution of political power and threaten the center's legitimacy. They were never formally publicized but can be deduced from the "inhibited" center's political activities and statements.

— Adjusting the 1947 constitution to the political realities of Taiwan to make it the basis for law, authority, and political legitimation
— Preserving single-party rule of the KMT through martial law but allowing two client parties to exist: the Young China Party (YCP) and the China Democratic Socialist Party (CDSP)
— Promoting "limited democracy" in Taiwan province by allowing for elections of local government assemblies and offices and eventually (1969) limited numbers of national representatives
— Permitting the competition of ideas while not tolerating Marxism, Leninism, socialist thought, or criticisms likely to delegitimize the political center

These implicit rules defined the structural relationship between society and the political center. Society could participate in a defined sphere of political life and discourse until the ruling party decided that conditions were appropriate for adopting democracy by revitalizing the 1947 constitution and allowing political parties to compete. As one KMT member put it in 1952:

If we consider the theory and experience of those countries having political parties, we can say that the current conditions in Taiwan at this time are not yet appropriate for having political parties compete. For political parties to compete, there must be a powerful party, and at the same time we need to have a powerful opposition party. Then the two political parties can monitor each other and compete against each other. Only in this way can there be political progress.[3]

For the ruling party's elites, then, democracy meant that the opposition party played by the rules, both parties shared similar goals, and political competition required that each monitor the other's behavior.

The ruling party could not tolerate any political opposition that prematurely tried to organize another party adhering to a political mission different from its own. Nor could it tolerate an opposition that tried to discredit the authorities either in the public media or through public demonstrations. But the ruling party's insistence on a timetable before democracy was permissible also worked to the KMT's disadvantage. The political opposition would repeatedly condemn the political center's lack of sincerity in promoting genuine democracy, a charge the ruling party found increasingly difficult to reject while appealing for support from the elites and public.

Vesting power in the Office of the President and relying on martial law naturally enabled the political center to project enormous power. Yet the center's power was increasingly constrained because of its stated commitment to fully enact Sun's Three Principles of the People, which called for building democracy and improving people's welfare. Moreover, the ruling party had repeatedly promised full democracy to impress on the Chinese people and the world that its polity was very different from that of the communist-ruled mainland. Its ability to deliver democracy was highly suspect at first because of the February 28, 1947, uprising and the suppression that had followed. Therefore, the new regime tried to establish implicit political rules that would allow for a mixture of suppressing the political behavior it disapproved while nurturing the limited democracy and free speech it could tolerate.

## Adjusting the 1947 Constitution

Ever since June 30, 1895, when Kang Youwei urged Emperor Guang Xu (1875–1908) to undertake political reform, Chinese reformers had advocated a constitution. Although opponents tried to block their efforts, China adopted a constitution in 1912. Constitutional government remained a sham, however, until 1930, when Chiang Kai-shek, urged on by KMT leaders Wang Jingwei, Yen Xisheng and Feng Yuxiang, considered establishing a constitutional government and terminating the KMT's dictatorial rule. Hu Hanmin, however, opposed the idea of a provisional constitutional government, arguing that the party had not yet established democratic local governance at the county *(xian)* level, as advocated by Sun Yat-sen.[4] Those differences of opinion escalated into serious political struggles within the party, culminating in Hu Hanmin's house arrest by Chiang on March 1, 1931.[5]

On May 5, 1935, the Nationalist government published its first draft constitution, based on Sun Yat-sen's concept of a five-power government. On December 2, 1935, after extensive revision, the party and government approved this draft and called for the people to elect a national assembly that would approve the constitution and initiate constitutional government. This election was to take place in the following year on Sun Yat-sen's birthday, November 12.[6] Japan's invasion of China, however, ended such ideas and delayed constitutional government.

After the war the KMT was strongly opposed by the Communists and other political parties. To resolve their differences and try to form a coalition government, all parties met at a political consultative affairs conference in January 1946,[7] during which the Communists refused to participate in elections for a national assembly. To demonstrate their commitment to constitutional government and legitimation of the regime even as the civil war intensified, the ROC government and the KMT went ahead with the elections. Believing that democratic elections and a Western-style constitution would strengthen party and ROC legitimacy, Chiang Kai-shek and other KMT leaders made every effort to hold national elections for a national assembly that would then ratify a new constitution and establish a constitutional government.

The members of the newly elected National Assembly convened on November 15, 1946, to approve the revised prewar constitution. That constitution, which became law on January 1, 1947, required appointing a new government with new laws of governance and holding another election for the First National Assembly.[8] Meanwhile, the Nationalist government suffered major defeats at the hands of the Communists in northeast and north China, and its troops retreated southward toward the Yangtze. How could constitutional rule be organized under such conditions? Wang Shizhe, a legal expert, proposed that the First National Assembly draw up new articles to the 1947 constitution, suspending the constitution but empowering the ROC's president to manage any crises threatening the ROC government until conditions improved to restore full constitutional authority.[9] The First National Assembly, elected between August and December 1947, met in Nanking on March 29, 1948, attended by some 2,800 delegates.

On April 18 the assembly adopted Wang's suggestion and passed a group of articles called the Temporary Provisions Effective during the Period of Communist Rebellion (Dongyuan kanluan shiqi lingshi) that became law on May 10. (The assembly adjourned on May 1, 1948.)

Those Temporary Provisions nullified Articles 39, 43, and 57, section 2, of the constitution and took away the Legislative Yuan's power to check the president and the Executive Yuan.[10] The president and the Executive Yuan now had unlimited power to authorize any policies deemed necessary to deal with threats to national security, natural disasters, and economic catastrophes and, with the approval of the assembly, the power to abolish the Temporary Provisions. These legal actions concentrated enormous power to the president; if the president was also the KMT chairman, that party then was able to control the polity and dominate society.

By early 1950 the Nationalist government had relocated to Taiwan and begun administering the five-power government as it had done in Nanking, but with salient differences (see chart 1). The party and the government now had to adjust the constitution to the political realities of Taiwan until the constitution could be fully restored. For example, the constitution required that a new national assembly be elected before May 20, 1954, but this could not be done because China was divided into two states: the PRC and the ROC.[11] Therefore the Judicial Yuan ruled on January 29, 1954, that the First National Assembly representatives and other elected central government representatives in Taiwan could serve indefinitely.[12]

Article 8 of the ROC's National Assembly Organization Law required that unless at least half the First National Assembly delegates were present to choose a chair, the assembly could not be convened. The elected members of the First National Assembly numbered 3,045, but a survey by the ROC's Ministry of the Interior in 1953 found that more than half these delegates lived outside the ROC, and thus the assembly could not be convened.[13] Therefore on December 17, 1953, the Executive Yuan asked the Legislative Yuan to amend the law so that only one-third of the delegates need convene to elect a chair and conduct assembly affairs.[14]

Finally, after amending various laws, on March 24, 1954, the first assembly elected Chiang Kai-shek to his second term as president and Chen Cheng as vice president.[15] The way was now clear for the assembly to elect future presidents and vice presidents and revise the Temporary Provisions when appropriate.[16]

Over the next fifteen years National Assembly members died, became too ill to participate, or retired, so that membership steadily declined, putting the organization in peril. Without a functioning national assembly, neither the KMT nor the government could uphold the constitution or remain legitimate. On March 16, 1966, two days before electing Chiang Kai-shek to a fourth term as president with Yen Chia-kan as vice president, the assembly added an additional article to the Temporary Provisions that mandated supplementary elections for the National Assembly, Legislative Yuan, and Control Yuan and gave the elected candidates the right to serve indefinitely.[17]

The first supplementary elections (along with local elections) took place on December 20, 1969. Voters elected fifteen KMT candidates to the National Assembly and eight KMT plus three nonparty candidates to the Legislative Yuan. One political commentator remarked that this election revealed "an intensity and excitement unique in recent years."[18] In the fifteen-day preelection campaigning, several opposition candidates severely criticized the KMT, but the government took no action. One such opposition candidate, who would later be the chairman of the DPP, Huang Hsin-chieh, chastised the ruling party, so enraging his listeners that they nearly attacked him. When Chang Pao-shu, the general secretary of the KMT's Central Committee, learned of the episode, he assigned police protection to Huang, fearing that any attack on him would be blamed on the KMT. Huang, under heavy police guard for the rest of the campaign, continued to criticize the ruling party.

On March 17, 1972, the National Assembly voted in new Temporary Provisions stipulating that the president could select members of the Legislative and Control Yuans from Chinese nationals residing overseas and that before standing for reelection, new delegates to the National Assembly must serve six years, delegates to the Legislative Yuan three years, and delegates to the Control Yuan six years.[19] These new provisions guaranteed an influx of central government representatives to offset those being lost through attrition and enabled the party and the government to claim that democratization continued. The KMT still controlled the National Assembly and the power structure upholding the constitution.

Those actions preserving the National Assembly's power did not go unnoticed. Critics of the KMT complained that the government granted special privileges to National Assembly members that were unfair and very costly. In 1971 Lai Zuyi pointed out that the government had purchased property in Shihlin, Neihu, and Pihu so National Assembly members could buy cheap land and build homes with interest-free loans.[20] Lai charged that in less than a decade that property, purchased for NT$240,000 (about US$6,000), had increased in value to NT$1.2 and 2 million [US$30,000 to $50,000].[21] Other critics charged that the government annually spent NT$1.1 billion (about US$27 million) of taxpayers' money to cover expenses for National Assembly members.[22]

By 1981, nearly 16 percent of the representatives were over eighty, with another 50 percent in their seventies. A critic complained that these "eternal representatives" (wannien yiyuan) had already served thirty-eight years, were too old, and lived overseas, which put them out of touch with political conditions in Taiwan.[23] In 1948, 2,841 National Assembly members had convened, but in November 1984 only 1,046 members (797 original members and another 249 chosen in supplementary elections) did so.[24] Some opposition elite also complained that in the "past thirty years, as our nation rapidly developed, the senior representatives have always constituted a special, privileged group, but they lack the ability to react and reflect the changes taking place around them."[25] The KMT and the government either tolerated these criticisms or closed down the journals and newspapers that printed them. Their attacks on the National Assembly intensified in the 1970s and early 1980s, but they never dared stage public demonstrations to denounce the assembly for fear of arrest and imprisonment.

By modifying laws, the KMT and the government adjusted the 1947 constitution to the peculiar conditions of Taiwan. In this way they preserved the 1947 constitution until that time when it could be "reactivated." The political center also endured mounting criticism of the National Assembly's legitimacy but persevered to support this political body until it could amend the constitution. Using legal maneuvers to preserve the constitution and the National Assembly was relatively easy, but countering the challenges of the people opposing single-party rule was far more difficult.

## Preserving the KMT's Power through Martial Law

Taiwan's proximity to the mainland and the many small craft navigating the Taiwan Straits made it possible to smuggle weapons, people, and contraband into the country even though the military and police intensively patrolled the seacoast. Because sealing Taiwan off from the mainland was crucial for national security, the ROC government created the Taiwan Garrison Command to enforce the May 19, 1949, emergency decree of martial law and ordered that it be assisted by the Security Bureau, the Bureau of Investigation, and other agencies. These agencies also monitored the flow of information in and out of the island along with any social and political activity they saw as threatening security and stability. The party and the government constantly worried about communist subversion as well as the dissidents who had fled Taiwan after the February 28, 1947, uprising or remained on the island.

Distinguishing between constructive criticism and criticism that might discredit the center's legitimacy was a constant challenge for the authorities. How could one differentiate between the critics who wanted to make government accountable to the people and those trying to undermine government authority? The authorities responded to this challenge by adhering to a large body of laws (some had been promulgated as early as November 29, 1934) and preferring to err on the side of repression rather than allow criticisms to be repeated too often.[26] Such repression was always justified by the argument that Taiwan was the last anticommunist Chinese society.

To enforce compliance with martial law, the Taiwan Garrison Command, Security Bureau, police, and military courts arrested, tried, and imprisoned or executed any individual they considered a threat to national security and public order. That meant arresting and imprisoning any individuals trying to organize an opposition party and closing journals and newspapers that printed information threatening public order or the regime's legitimacy.

There are no reliable data on the countless arrests, trials, imprisonments, and even executions between 1949 and July 15, 1987, when martial law was lifted. The following examples, only selective and incomplete, indicate that suppression was severe in the early 1950s and never relaxed thereafter. Yang Kuei, who lived in Taiwan, wrote a "peace declaration" that appeared in the April 6, 1949, Shanghai *Dagongbao* newspaper. The authorities promptly arrested him and imprisoned him for twelve years.[27] In May 1950 police arrested thirty-three persons in the town of Matou for threatening to overthrow the government. A military court sentenced three of them to death, nine to life imprisonment, and the rest to prison for periods of ten, twelve, and fifteen years.[28] In May 1951 the government arrested sixty-three individuals in Taichung; a military court charged these students, schoolteachers, and workers with planning to overthrow the government and sentenced seven to death, twelve to life imprisonment, and the rest to prison terms of ten, twelve, and fifteen years.[29] During the early 1950s the authorities arrested unknown numbers of students, intellectuals, and teachers on charges of sedition, giving rise to charges that in those years the regime perpetrated a reign of "white terror."[30] In 1960 the regime even arrested a prominent KMT member like Lei Chen for trying to establish a political party.

Lei Chen was born in 1897 in Zhejiang province; in 1917 he went to Japan to study.[31] In Tokyo, two KMT members, Dai Jitao and Zhang Ji, introduced Lei to the Nationalist Party, and he became a KMT member. Lei Chen graduated from the Faculty of Law of Kyoto Imperial University in 1926, and in 1926, at age thirty, he returned to China, where he was a professor at the National Central University from 1930 to 1932; during 1933–38 he served as the director of the General Affairs Department in the Ministry of Education. From 1939 to 1947 Lei Chen was assistant secretary-general of the People's Political Council in the ROC government and in 1947 became a minister without portfolio in the Executive Yuan and an adviser on national strategy to the Office of the President. In 1949 he fled with his family to Taiwan. Later that year, funding from the Ministry of Education enabled him to launch *Ziyou zhongguo* (Free China fortnightly), a magazine that for the next eleven years represented the voice of democratic liberalism in the party and government.

As the driving force behind the *Ziyou zhongguo*, Lei Chen persuaded the scholar-diplomat Hu Shih, who headed the prestigious Academia Sinica, and the philosopher-professor Yin Hai-kuang, who taught at National Taiwan University, to serve on the editorial board and contribute articles. *Ziyou zhongguo* published articles critical of the KMT, the First National Assembly, various branches of the five-power government, and the KMT's management of local elections.

Although Lei Chen only wanted to see the KMT become powerful and influential, his candor and bluntness earned him the enmity of many of the party's top leaders. In 1950 Lei Chen, along with many others, was invited to work on one of Chiang Kai-shek's committees to reorganize the KMT. Lei argued that the KMT should be separate from the military; when Chiang Kai-shek learned of this, he was furious. On April 16, 1951, Chiang spoke about the party's reform efforts and publicly rebuked Lei Chen and another KMT critic, Hong Lanyou, as being "no different from communist sympathizers and traitors."[32]

In March 1951, at a memorial service honoring the party's revolutionary martyrs, Chiang Ching-kuo asked Lei Chen if he intended to continue his campaign opposing the party's activities in the ROC military. Lei responded, "Yes! Why should the party have administrative units in the military when party people already are there?" Chiang angrily responded, "You are perpetuating the evils of the Communists. Your thinking is extremely reactionary. Because of people like you, our party was defeated. Even today, you still do not realize the great harm you cause the party."[33] (Lei later said that he felt sad about that exchange with Chiang Ching-kuo.) But after Lei Chen wrote an article criticizing the Security Bureau's deputy commander, General Peng Meng-chi, for saying that all students from the mainland were Communists, Peng ordered Lei Chen placed under surveillance for "insulting the government."[34] Only after Lei Chen appealed to powerful friends to intervene did this harassment end.

Lei Chen's advocacy of Western-style liberal democracy set him apart from other KMT elites. He believed that the KMT's defeat on the mainland originated in "single-party, authoritarian rule" (*yidang zhuanzheng*)[35] and that, if open discussion and criticism had been allowed in the party, leadership decisions would have been more successful. According to Lei Chen's view, a major reason for the KMT's defeat on the mainland was that it had not practiced democracy.

As for party unity, Lei Chen's views did not differ radically from those of other KMT politicians. He believed that "in order to propagate the power of the KMT and to eliminate completely factional struggles, we must start from a strong organization and have a clear liaison between the party and its members" (14:60). But after the Seventh Party Congress in October 1952, Lei Chen expressed the hope that there would be no secrecy in politics, only "a strong compliance with the law" (14:63), even though many in the KMT disagreed with him. Lei also advocated that "those KMT members who are public-spirited under heaven [tianxia weigong] have the great task of becoming magnanimous and tolerant" (14:66). Although many party leaders concurred with this view, they increasingly regarded him as a "misfit" whose views they must tolerate in order to demonstrate party unity.

When Lei Chen spoke in favor of a unified party making every effort to bring all patriotic Chinese into one great, "powerful anticommunist organization that will unite with similar people in Hong Kong and overseas," few disagreed (14:14). But when he said that he wanted the KMT to cultivate democracy in every dimension of Taiwan's political and economic life, many party members could not agree. His voice was only one of a few calling for the government to guarantee individual liberties, allow a free economy to develop, and create a political system of checks and balances in which political parties could compete as in America and England (14:14, 89).

The KMT never responded to Lei Chen's appeal. Aware of the KMT's intransigence, Lei Chen continued to criticize it for wanting to "rule the entire country" instead of cultivating democracy. He argued that the KMT had no business meddling in the military, in educational institutions, or in the economy (15:83). He lashed out at the National Assembly for adding the Temporary Provisions to the 1947 constitution, arguing that constitutional revisions should be undertaken by all the Chinese people and not simply by the assembly:

The Constitution is for all of the people of our nation, including the people of the mainland who have given us the great task of carrying out [those rules]. If we want to revise the Constitution, we must wait until we return to the mainland to obtain the opinions of all the people. (16:231)

Similarly, he took the Executive Yuan to task for flouting the authority of the Legislative Yuan and establishing the Defense Council and the Anticommunist Youth Corps without first obtaining the Legislative Yuan's consent (16:231).

One of Lei Chen's political goals now began to take form: the KMT must permit an opposition party to compete in all elections (16:108). In May 1960 he called for the following:

I hope that everyone who believes in democratic politics will gather to form an opposition party in order to break the monopoly hold of the KMT. The rationale for a new party is that it must gain political authority by competing in elections. Our constitution (Article 14) empowers individuals with the freedom to form a party. This new opposition party can be organized immediately, but it must be protected by the law. (16:71)

For a decade Lei Chen had criticized the ruling party's unwillingness to allow any opposition group to nominate candidates in local elections. But he now appealed for the KMT to be more responsive to the "people's will" and adhere to the following dictum: "Whatever the people like, you must like! Whatever the people hate, you must hate!" (16:74).

He and a few like-minded intellectuals became impatient with the KMT. Meeting in late spring and summer, they discussed how to organize a new party and even drafted a party charter. Then, on September 4, 1960, the Taiwan Garrison Command arrested Lei Chen, along with several of his junior editors, and confiscated the party's charter along with other documents. The last issue of *Ziyou zhongguo* appeared on September 1, 1960.

The authorities charged Lei Chen with sedition, including advocating the hopelessness of recovering the mainland; urging the United States to interfere in the internal affairs of the ROC; stirring up dissension between the military and the government; writing articles that helped the Chinese Communists to promote their "united front" tactics in Taiwan province; promoting ill will between the Taiwanese and mainlanders; and encouraging people to hate the government. A military court reviewed Lei Chen's case and on October 8, 1960, sentenced him to prison for ten years.

In July 1962 authorities arrested thirty military students for conspiring to establish an independent Taiwan republic.[36] In September of that same year, authorities arrested National Taiwan University professor Peng Ming-min and several students for distributing leaflets advocating one Taiwan and one China and arguing that recovering the China mainland was a fantasy. Although Peng later escaped to the United States after being let out on bail, his students Xie Congming and Wei Tingchao received, respectively, ten and eight years in prison. In July 1968 thirty-six persons were arrested for trying to organize a nationalist group called the National Taiwan Alliance; a military court ordered the leaders imprisoned for ten years. More such incidents occurred between 1970 and 1987, but the numbers are incomplete (see table 3).

By the end of the 1960s the regime's more angry opponents realized the

TABLE 3
*Political Arrests in the ROC, 1970–1987*

| | |
|---|---|
| February 13, 1970 | Students Yang Bichuan and Deng Lienhuang arrested for discussing Taiwan independence; imprisoned for 10 years |
| February 23, 1971 | Xie Congming, Wei Tingchao, and Li Ao arrested for sedition; imprisoned 15, 12, and 10 years, respectively |
| February 1973 | Chen Guying arrested and detained for several weeks |
| May 1, 1976 | Yan Mingzheng and Yang Jinghai arrested for illegal activities to topple the government; imprisoned for 12 years and life, respectively |
| October 19, 1976 | Huang Hua, assistant editor of *Taiwan Zhenglun,* arrested for trying to overthrow the government; imprisoned for 10 years |
| November 27, 1976 | Seven persons arrested and charged with collaborating with communist agents in Tokyo to facilitate a PRC takeover of Taiwan; imprisoned for terms ranging from 7 to 15 years |
| January 21, 1979 | Arrest of Rui Yan and Wu Taian on charges of collaborating with the PRC to organize a network in Taiwan |
| August 7, 1979 | Arrest of the publisher of *Chao Liu* magazine, Yang Yurong of the Ming-hui Publishing Company, and Chen Bowen, an editor, in Taichung |
| January 1980 | Arrest of Meilidao organizers (January 12, 65 individuals arrested; February 1, another 61 arrested; February 20, 8 more arrested) |
| March 11, 1980 | Meilidao personnel Yao Guojian and Qiu Shengxiong arrested and imprisoned 3 years and 30 months, respectively |
| April 18, 1980 | Meilidao organizers (see January 1980) sentenced and imprisoned |
| January 5, 1983 | Yang Huan arrested for Taiwanese independence activities |
| July 2–3, 1985 | Three persons arrested on charges of possessing and leaking military secrets |
| July 4, 1985 | Circulation of the United States book *The Soong Dynasty* suspended and Huang Tienfu, chief of *dangwai* magazine *Penglaidao,* arrested |
| April 15, 1987 | Qui Jingyuan, an overseas Chinese from Malaysia, arrested; imprisoned for 12 years on charges of sedition |

SOURCE: Ihara Kichinosuke, *Taiwan no seiji kaikaku nempō: oboegaku (1943–1987)* (A yearbook of Taiwan political reforms: Major events, 1943–1987), vol. 1 (Nara: Tezukayama University, Faculty of Culture, 1992).

futility of organizing public opposition to KMT rule. In the 1970s those individuals who might have risked public demonstrations now joined those political opponents who had long been participating in local elections and the marketplace of ideas (see below). As more and more opponents of the regime became active in local politics (see chapter 4) and won voter support, some of them became careless and went too far. One such example was the Kaohsiung incident.

From August 16, 1979, until December 10, 1979, the Meilidao Publishing Company printed a magazine called *Meilidao* (Beautiful Formosa) that contained articles critical of Taiwan's political authorities.[37] The regime allowed the magazines to circulate, and early issues were quickly sold out. In those months Meilidao organizers convened fourteen political gatherings, established eleven branches of their magazine, and increased magazine circulation to about 100,000 subscribers.[38] Their political meetings around the island attracted as many as a thousand people per meeting. These activities alarmed the authorities, who began monitoring the meetings. When Huang Hsin-chieh, one of the magazine's chief editors who had been elected to the Legislative Yuan in 1969, asked the Kaohsiung authorities for permission to hold a public meeting commemorating Human Rights Day on December 10, 1979, at Fulun Park across from Kaohsiung city's Dadong Department Store, they turned him down. From here on, accounts differ regarding the events that led up to a bloody clash between a huge crowd and military police at a large traffic circle near the Meilidao office.

This much, however, seems clear. In the late afternoon of December 9, 1979, police seized Yao Guojian and Qiu Shengxiong, who were driving a van carrying Meilidao publications, at the intersection of Gushan erlu and Luchuan Streets and took them to the Gushan police station for questioning. Hours later the police released the two men, who appeared to have been severely beaten.[39] Meilidao leaders charged the police with brutality and unlawfully confiscating published materials. The police claimed that the men had resisted the legal confiscation of a truck carrying published materials and that they had not been beaten.[40] News of the event spread, and the next day many individuals from other cities arrived in Kaohsiung. When the police learned of this, they immediately sealed off Fulun Park. In the late afternoon, however, crowds began assembling in front of the Meilidao office not far from the park. Huang Hsin-chieh arrived by train from Taipei at 6:30 P.M. General Chang Zhixiu, the southern garrison deputy commander, met Huang at the Kaohsiung railway station and apparently agreed that the rally could be held in front of the Meilidao office as long as there were no torches, sticks, or chemicals, and no march.[41] When Huang arrived at the Meilidao office, the crowd already exceeded several thousand people; during the next hour or so, they moved to a large traffic circle nearby.

Here again it becomes difficult to know exactly what took place. It appears that, beginning about seven o'clock, various Meilidao leaders, through microphones, spoke to the crowd, shouted political slogans, or sang songs. Some speakers urged the crowd to go home. Later (and it is the timing of what followed that was hotly disputed by five newspapers, government authorities, and Meilidao leaders), the police launched tear gas as unruly crowd members began attacking the military police (who were assembled nearby to maintain crowd control) with long wooden clubs. They also threw bricks, bottles, and other debris at the city police, who used their shields to protect themselves.

In the days that followed, the press reported as many as 183 injured, including 139 military police, 43 city police, and one private citizen.[42] General Wang Jingxi, head of the Taiwan Garrison Command, later stated that 500 people had started the violence.[43] The city police claimed to have arrested only two rioters on the spot, but human rights activists abroad claimed that the authorities rounded up 152 persons, released 50 on bail, released another 40 subject to recall, and imprisoned 62.[44]

The government eventually sent thirty-three prisoners to be tried in civilian courts, charged eight with sedition in military court, and released the rest. The eight charged with sedition were Huang Hsin-chieh; four of the five individuals managing *Meilidao* magazine (Shih Ming-teh, Yao Chia-wen, Chang Chun-hong, and Lin Yixiong; Hsu Hsin-liang was abroad); Zhen Zhu, the acting director of the Kaohsiung office; Lin Hongxuan, general secretary; and Lu Xiulian, deputy director of the magazine, a proponent of women's rights, and candidate in the aborted 1978 supplementary election for the National Assembly.[45]

The government charged those individuals with organizing to overthrow the government. Huang Hsin-chieh was also indicted for conspiring to obtain money from communist agents in Japan to import baby eels from the PRC; the income thus derived would support the group's plan to destabilize the ROC government. In prison, all eight confessed to the government charges, but they later recanted, stating that they had been deprived of sleep until they confessed.

The trial began in a military court outside Taipei on March 18, 1980. On April 18, the court found all eight defendants guilty. The court sentenced Shih Ming-Teh to life imprisonment; Huang Hsin-chieh received fourteen years, and the other six received twelve years each. The harshness of these sentences stunned many. (The government later reduced the sentences, then commuted them; by 1990 all had been freed.)

Were the charges fair? Was the trial just? Under the United States legal system, the outcome would likely have been very different. But Taiwan was under martial law, and its authorities were charged with crushing those groups perceived as disturbing the peace and with severely punishing the ringleaders. The Kaohsiung incident was the largest clash between the public and police since the February 28, 1947, uprising, and interviews with ROC citizens after the event revealed that most were unhappy that such violence had occurred and did not want it repeated.[46] The government tack was that the Meilidao activists had "underestimated the people, overevaluated themselves, and erroneously judged the government."[47] Moreover, these activists threatened to reverse Taiwan's social and economic progress and create the social turmoil that had befallen societies like the Republic of Korea.[48] The Kaohsiung incident, then, served notice to all opponents of the regime that if they tried to establish a political party, they did so at their peril. For the next six years, the political opposition was extremely cautious (see chapter 6).

Under martial law, regime repression was neither capricious nor aimed at bending every individual to the whims of the state. The authorities simply did not want to risk competing with political parties for resources or debating issues on which the KMT's position was firm: spending heavily (10 to 12 percent of gross domestic product) for defense; suppressing the Taiwanese independence movement; and guiding the national economy and society according to Sunist doctrine. Committed to its special vision of democracy but nervous about possible weak popular support if political parties were allowed to compete, the KMT preferred to regulate political life rather than experiment with political pluralism and risk losing control. Thus the regime continued to celebrate democracy as a goal for Chinese society: school texts expounded Western democratic virtues such as checks and balances; government and sponsored institutes of Sun Yat-sen studies extolled the democratic ideals of the KMT's founding father. But there was to be no competing political party.

## Limited Democracy

Local elections without opposition parties became a learning experience in which the people participated to select their leaders, council members, and representatives for local governance in the province, districts, townships, cities, villages, and urban wards. Early on the central government decided to hold local elections according to the following principles: elect national leaders indirectly but subprovincial leaders directly; allow persons twenty or older to register as candidates except for district magistrates, who had to be under sixty-one; allow any number of candidates to compete but allow no candidate to threaten or coerce other candidates; grant women as well as minorities such as the aborigines a fixed quota of elected seats in each election.[49] Local election laws also stipulated that candidates must not oppose or violate the constitution or the Temporary Provisions and must never engage in activities that would undermine the government's legitimacy.[50]

In the early summer of 1950, government officials held seminars for high-level provincial officials in which election experts outlined the new election law and explained the election procedures. These seminars were then held at the subdistrict level; eventually some forty thousand to fifty thousand officials learned the rudiments of how to establish the machinery for electing local leaders and people's representatives.[51] From July 2, 1950, until January 28, 1951, the government supervised the election of first-term district and city council members, dividing the island's twenty-one district and city areas into 155 election districts *(qu)* in which multiple candidates competed.[52] In January 1951 voters elected 831 new council members. Every two years thereafter, voters went to the polls and elected their district and city council members. In August 1950 the first elections were held for district and city magistrates and mayors; thereafter they were held every three years.[53] Similarly, the first elections for the Taiwan Provincial Council, village and township heads, urban wards and neighborhood leaders, and people's representatives were held in these same years (provincial assembly election was in 1959) and continued on a regular basis.

Although these elections appeared to be peaceful and orderly, *Ziyou zhongguo* complained of low voter turnout and voter apathy because too many single-candidate contests were dominated by KMT-nominated candidates.[54] If potential candidates learned that the KMT was supporting a single candidate, they decided not to run, even if they had a popular base. Some KMT leaders also engaged in dirty tricks. In the 1956 election for the Taoyuan district magistrate, it appeared that the KMT nominee would be decisively defeated. The day before the election, the popular opposition candidate received a government summons notifying him he must immediately begin serving his military conscription time.[55] Such incidents were not infrequent.

Party leaders soon learned that excessive intervention was counterproductive and produced a backlash of popular resentment. Moreover, the character of elections quickly changed as younger, more capable candidates representing different local interests began competing. After land reform was completed about 1957–58, the powerful rural power holders who had dominated the elections before 1955 began to decline in influence. After 1960 Taiwan's accelerated economic growth also brought new business and professional people into local elections.

A survey by political scientists at National Taiwan University compared the backgrounds of local leaders elected in 1950–51 with those elected in 1971.[56] In the early period, wealthy elite families supplied 60 percent of those elected; in 1971, only 10 percent. The middle elites supplied 32 percent in the early period compared with 65 percent in 1971, and finally, the less wealthy elites supplied only 10 percent in the early period compared with 25 percent in 1971. Similar changes took place in politicians' families' annual earned income over this same period: middle- and lower-income groups supplied 80 percent of the elected politicians in 1971 compared with only 28 percent in 1950–51. Meanwhile, the educational levels of candidates also improved over these same decades.

As Taiwan's economy prospered and its society became more differentiated, the pool of political candidates changed, producing election races between highly educated businesspeople and professionally oriented politicians who sought prestige and power. Some observers interpreted this as a common pattern of early political modernization: the political-cultural values of a national elite emphasizing harmony, unity, and order clashing with those of people who wanted cheaper, more abundant public goods, laws changed in favor of their interests, and the tax burden shifted from the local to the national level.[57]

Criticisms of the regime became commonplace, but candidates also criticized each other. The wealthier candidates tried to buy votes, and the KMT continued to try to manipulate the election results. In these multimember local elections, all sorts of factions and interest groups competed. When candidates realized they could not be elected without local factional support, whether in villages, towns, or large cities, they allied themselves with factions (paixi) connected by blood ties or lineages, ethnic groups like Hakka, Taiwanese speaking the Minan dialect, mainlanders sharing a common language and cultural beliefs, or those sharing the same business or professional interests, such as farmers' associations, business associations, and so forth.

Without an organized political opposition in the 1950s and 1960s, the KMT played factional candidates against one another to ensure that enough KMT politicians were elected to exercise party control over local budgets, laws, and other matters.[58] The KMT looked for the best-qualified people from the most powerful local factions to nominate as party candidates, hoping to co-opt local power groups into supporting the party's programs.[59] By the 1960s local elections had become routine, with better-educated political candidates and more voters turning out but still electing representatives of local factions.[60] Vote buying during this period never declined and probably even increased as candidates became wealthier.[61]

In these same years, the ruling KMT allowed politicians of all stripes to compete, but never as a legal, organized political party. The voting turnout was high, and the KMT easily dominated these elections, as table 4 indicates. The voting turnout was usually over 70 percent of the registered voters. The KMT typically won 80–90 percent of the district-city leadership race and three-quarters or more of the Taiwan provincial assembly seats (see table 4). The elected nonparty candidates then tried to organize coalitions with KMT

## TABLE 4
### Local Elections for County and City Leaders and the Taiwan Provincial Assembly, 1951–1981

| Year | 1951 (79%)[a] | 1954 (74%) | 1957 (78%) | 1960 (72%) | 1964 (69%) | 1968 (74%) | 1972 (70%) | 1977 (80%) | 1981 (71%) |
|---|---|---|---|---|---|---|---|---|---|
| *Xian Magistrates and City Mayors* | | | | | | | | | |
| Elected seats | 21 | 21 | 21 | 21 | 21 | 20 | 20 | 20 | 19 |
| No. of seats won by party | | | | | | | | | |
| KMT | 17 | 19 | 20 | 19 | 17 | 17 | 20 | 16 | 15 |
| YCP | 0 | 0 | 0 | 0 | 0 | 0 | 0 | 0 | 0 |
| CDSP | 0 | 0 | 0 | 0 | 0 | 0 | 0 | 0 | 0 |
| Other | 4 | 2 | 1 | 2 | 4 | 4 | 0 | 4 | 4 |
| *Taiwan Provincial Assembly* | | | | | | | | | |
| Elected seats | 55 | 57 | 66 | 73 | 74 | 71 | 73 | 77 | 77 |
| No. of seats won by party | | | | | | | | | |
| KMT | 43 | 48 | 53 | 58 | 61 | 61 | 58 | 56 | 59 |
| YCP | 1 | 0 | 1 | 1 | 1 | 1 | 0 | 0 | 1 |
| CDSP | 0 | 0 | 0 | 0 | 0 | 0 | 0 | 0 | 0 |
| Other | 11 | 9 | 12 | 14 | 12 | 9 | 15 | 21 | 18 |

SOURCE: The April 1946 provincial election chose forty-one representatives (two were women, and thirty-eight were Taiwanese), of whom twenty were KMT, four were YSP, seven were CDSP, and nine were other. For the years 1946 and 1951–1954 to elect the Taiwan Assembly, see Taiwan sheng yi hui (Secretariat of Taiwan Provincial Assembly), *Taiwan sheng yihui ziliao xuan zhu* (Materials on the Elections of the Taiwan Provincial Assembly) (Taichung: Taiwan sheng yi hui mishu ju, 1973), p. 69. Other data can be found in Wu Wen-cheng and Chen I-hsin, *Elections and Political Development in Taiwan* (Taipei: Government Information Office, 1989). We have omitted data for elections of the Taipei and Kaohsiung city assemblies.
[a]Figures in parentheses are voting rates.

members to influence the allocation of resources and the approval of local laws. The KMT never relaxed its efforts to control these elections. The party's election laws permitted anyone to register and campaign in elections as long as the candidates obeyed the law, which the non-KMT politicians did. But in the late 1960s and early 1970s some opposition politicians began to exercise their broad rights of free speech while carefully refraining from seditious discourse yet criticizing the prevailing political order.

Many of these opposition politicians were university educated or had successful business experience or both (see chapter 4). Some had joined the KMT in the 1960s but left in disillusion. They turned to editing and publishing intellectual magazines critical of the KMT and the ROC government. Not a few were arrested and had their magazines shut down on charges of sedition. They also registered and campaigned in the local elections and for national representatives' supplementary elections that were legalized in 1969. They shared the ideals of liberal democracy as articulated earlier by Lei Chen and others, referring to themselves as "politicians outside the KMT" (dangwai) (their KMT critics used this label to identify them at election time).[62]

The 1972 local elections marked the first time that dangwai candidates increased their seats in local assemblies and became national representatives. Then in 1977 a former KMT headquarters member Hsu Hsin-liang decided to run in the Taoyuan magistrate race. The KMT withheld its endorsement of Hsu because he had written a book titled The Sound of Wind and Rain that criticized the Taiwan Provincial Assembly and embarrassed the KMT.[63] Instead, the KMT endorsed KMT member Ou Xianyu. On voting day in the town of Chungli, rumors spread of election box tampering in a public school precinct, where a group of Hsu supporters gathered to protest. They became unruly, and a major altercation erupted that left one person dead, another wounded, and numerous automobiles overturned and burned, the worst violence since the February 28, 1947, uprising. But Hsu, who was extremely popular, won the election by 220,000-odd votes to 130,000 for his opponent. This incident embarrassed and shocked the KMT. For the first time in local elections, the KMT's share of the overall popular vote dropped to an all-time low of 64.2 percent (the high was 69.1 percent in 1972);[64] the opposition's share of elected seats in the Taiwan Provincial Assembly increased to 27 percent.

The government, meanwhile, had decided in 1969 to establish supplementary elections for national representatives. Several reasons prompted this action. First, both party and government leaders realized that the mainlander national representatives were disappearing from office and had to be replaced if the government expected to function and be legitimate. Second, most KMT leaders were committed to gradual democratization and believed their party was capable of retaining political power even as national elections expanded. Finally, KMT leaders expected to retain broad popular support because their polling of voters' sentiments revealed they merely wanted stability, progress, and tranquility.[65]

Campaigning for a very important supplementary national representative election, slated for December 23, 1978, began on December 8, with 896 political rallies scheduled. Some 126 candidates, including many *dangwai*, competed for thirty-eight seats in the Legislative Yuan; another 151 competed for fifty-six seats in the First National Assembly. Then, on December 15, President Jimmy Carter announced that the United States intended to abrogate formal relations with the ROC and initiate diplomatic ties with the PRC. On December 17 the Taiwan press announced that "the ROC president had ordered that all election activities by candidates immediately cease."[66] A number of candidates publicly announced that "we must be cool and remain united to save China." A patriotic frenzy swept the country. Faced with its most serious international crisis since the spring of 1950, the government promptly postponed the December 23 election until the international furor abated.

In early 1979 the government decided to combine the expanded national elections with local elections, scheduling them for December 23, 1980: seventy-six seats were open in the National Assembly, five times the number available in 1969 and roughly half as many as in 1973; ninety-seven for the Legislative Yuan, slightly less than double the number of seats in 1973 and 1975; and thirty-two for the Control Yuan, or sixteen times the number in 1969 and more than double the number elected in 1973.

These elections became the most important political contest since "limited democracy" had commenced in 1950.[67] The KMT candidates boasted of their party's successful economic policies and the island's booming prosperity. The *dangwai* criticized the ruling party and called for increasing national election seats, appointing more Taiwanese in government, allowing political parties to form, expanding freedoms of speech, assembly, and the press, abolishing the Temporary Provisions, and reviewing the sentences of political prisoners and releasing many of them. As the campaign heated up, many opposition politicians became vituperative, complaining of police harassment and lambasting the ruling party for its bribery, corruption, and special privileges. On election day there were no voting irregularities; voter turnout was lower than expected because of rain (little more than two-thirds of the registered voters). The KMT won sixty-one of the seventy-six National Assembly seats and seventy-nine of the ninety-seven seats in the Legislative Yuan (table 5). Although *dang-*

TABLE 5
Supplementary Elections for National Representatives, 1969–1983

| Year | 1969 (55%)[a] | 1972–73 (68%) | 1975 (75%) | 1980 (66%) | 1983 (63%) |
|---|---|---|---|---|---|
| | Legislative Yuan Supplementary Seats | | | | |
| Elected seats | 11 | 51 | 52 | 97 | 98 |
| No. of seats won by party | | | | | |
| KMT | 8 | 41 | 42 | 79 | 83 |
| YCP | 0 | 1 | 1 | 2 | 1 |
| CDSP | 0 | 0 | 0 | 0 | 1 |
| Others | 3 | 9 | 9 | 16 | 13 |
| | First National Assembly Supplementary Seats | | | | |
| Elected seats | 15 | 53 | 0 | 76 | 0 |
| No. of seats won by party | | | | | |
| KMT | 15 | 43 | 0 | 61 | 0 |
| YCP | 0 | 0 | 0 | 0 | 0 |
| CDSP | 0 | 0 | 0 | 1 | 0 |
| Other | 0 | 10 | 0 | 14 | 0 |

SOURCE: Wu Wen-cheng and Chen I-hsin, *Elections and Political Development in Taiwan.*
[a] Figures in parentheses are voting rates.

*wai* candidates won only 19 percent of the additional National Assembly seats and 17 percent of the additional Legislative Yuan seats, they could claim that some of their winners had received the most popular votes. Thus both sides claimed victory. In the supplementary elections held between 1969 and 1983, opposition candidates won slightly less than one-fifth of the expanded national representative seats for the Legislative Yuan and First National Assembly (see table 5).

## An Ideological Marketplace Evolves

The marketplace of ideas represents the free discourse among elite and intellectuals who describe, explain, interpret, evaluate, and recommend. According to Thomas A. Metzger, after 1950 five major political modes of discourse competed:[68]

— An official doctrine based on Sun's doctrine of the Three Principles of the People
— A petty bourgeois outlook represented by the businessman Gu Ying (Min Hongkuei) criticizing Sunist doctrine, praising the free market, and supporting Buddhist-Confucian morality
— Modern Confucian humanism represented by such writers as Tang Zhunyi, Mou Zongsan, and others who extol the quintessential aspects of Chinese culture
— Chinese liberalism as elaborated by the famous scholars and intellectu-

als Hu Shih, Yin Hai-kuan, Lei Chen, and, more recently, Yang Guo-shu and others

— Writers and activists like Peng Ming-min who supported the Taiwan independence movement and the endeavor to create a new Republic of Taiwan that will represent the will of the people

Metzger notes that these major strands of Chinese thinking interacted to mute the Confucian utopian ideas for governing a polity that were based on sacred moral values and beliefs and promote an acceptance of instrumental rationality and a tolerance of political opposition.

The two modes of political discourse identified by Metzger—Chinese liberalism and the Taiwan independence movement—criticized the ROC polity and evaluated it as always falling short of an ideal system based on theories of Western liberalism and a Chinese moral-intellectual elite being the only group qualified to rule the polity *(xianren zhengfu).*[69] In the new intellectual magazines of the 1960s, 1970s, and 1980s those strands of thinking produced a biting rhetoric severely critical of the KMT and the government.

After 1970, in particular, these two modes of political discourse frequently challenged the regime to differentiate between a genuine, constructive criticism that could be tolerated and seditious statements that undermined authority and legitimacy and harmed public order. The authorities struggled to define the fine line between those kinds of statements but erred on the side of stricture to guarantee social tranquility and political stability. To that end, in the 1970s and 1980s the authorities closed down many journals and arrested their publishers and editors, a form of regime repression that steadily increased during those years.[70] The examples that follow show why the regime opted for suppression while still allowing for the critical evaluation of the political center just mentioned.

The periodical *Taiwan zhenglun* (Taiwan political review) caused a sensation because of its audacious criticism of the KMT and the government. By year's end, the authorities had closed it and arrested and imprisoned several editors. One of that journal's most outspoken writers was Huang Hua, who had already served eight years of a commuted ten-year sentence at Green Island, one of the regime's infamous penal institutions. (Huang commented after he was freed in 1975 that he was amazed at Taiwan's material progress during the years of his incarceration.) Yet Huang continued to criticize Taiwan's political system, informing his readers that "the fact that we still dream to recover the mainland is really unrealistic."[71] Huang believed in individual freedom and the right to express one's opinions, move about, and hold different religious beliefs; to form a political party to compete with and replace the ruling party through peaceful elections; and to elect a congress of representatives reflecting the people's will. Based on these standards, he criticized the First National Assembly as being unfit to represent Taiwan's people. He called for political reforms that would create a polity based on human rights and demanded the release of those political prisoners who were staunch anticommunists and willing to cooperate with the government.

To explain why he never joined the KMT, Huang said that people's having to believe in one way of thinking was "inhuman" and that, because he was a liberal, he had no need of the KMT.[72] Huang then challenged the authorities to accept his standards of freedom:

As long as I believed I must give myself to society, I was prepared for all kinds of hardship, even to suffer accusations of which I was innocent, and even to go to jail. Our government should not be undemocratic; it should not be unreasonable; and it should not be so foolish as not to allow me to say what I want to say and do what I want to do.[73]

Huang said that many had advised him to join the KMT if he wanted to play any role in political life. But he rejected that advice.

To be afraid of politics and the KMT is a widespread pathology of our society. Conditions now are worse than ten years ago. Many businesspeople, students, working people, and government officials do not understand the KMT's ideology and do not like that party, but they still have joined that party. Why? Because they fear the KMT. Why do they fear the KMT? Because that party made trouble for them: increased their taxes; caused them to lose their jobs; refused to promote them; and could arrest, imprison, and execute them. It is unreasonable, however, to be so afraid. The KMT is only a political party representing the people. According to the constitution, the KMT, Youth Party, and Chinese Democratic Socialist Party are all the same. The people do not fear the latter two parties, so why do they fear the KMT?[74]

Although Huang expressed no fear of the KMT and was often contemptuous of it, he recognized that the KMT, the state, and the military acted as a unified force, held great power, and could arrest people and sentence them to prison for an undetermined period. The First National Assembly, noted Huang, was merely an instrument of that power structure, and although the KMT had committed terrible blunders—losing the mainland, withdrawing from the United Nations, and so forth—it never feared being ejected from office or being violently overthrown because the people of Taiwan were cowed by it. Arguing that the people of Taiwan were ashamed of living under a political system dominated by mainlanders, Huang continued to insult and ridicule the KMT and the government. By so infuriating the authorities,

Huang went too far. They decided by the year's end to close the *Taiwan zheng-lun,* arrested Huang Hua and others, and returned Huang to prison.[75]

Numerous other magazines also appeared in these same years, whose titles translate as names like the *China Tide, This Generation,* the *Eighties,* the *Forward,* and *Beautiful Formosa (Meilidao);* they experienced the same fate. In an early issue of *Meilidao* seven of its editors attacked government censorship by arguing that martial law should apply only to the communist menace and that civil society should be allowed to publish freely.[76] An article by former KMT member and legislator Fei Hsi-ping described his interpellation of Premier Sun Yun-suan in the Legislative Yuan. Fei had asked the premier if "the ruling party could be tolerant enough to accept political parties of different ideologies." Replied the premier, "In this special period of history we are now experiencing, any political parties having an ideology different from that of the Three Principles of the People cannot be allowed, because they do not share our national strategy and mission."[77]

These new magazines scolded the regime for not performing according to the normative standards of political democracy. But the ruling elites were not impressed. They complained that their critics created a mainlander versus Taiwanese mentality and encouraged social divisiveness; discredited the KMT and the government as greedy, corrupt, inept, and ignorant in its handling of international problems and domestic affairs; and projected the opposition as being the "fearless champions of the popular will, always identifying with the masses."[78] A point finally was reached at which the authorities suppressed these voices of dissent. But the regime was now in an uphill struggle.

As more small and medium-sized businesses prospered, they provided the funds for the intellectuals and activists to publish their magazines. These publishers improved their magazines' formats, introduced high-quality photographs, and published essays and stories lampooning public officials, thereby gaining readerships of 100,000 or more. The authorities responded as in the past by suspending magazines and newspapers and arresting those publishers and writers they believed were inflaming public passions. And so a pattern began to take form: the publishers conceiving of imaginative ways to criticize the government while amusing their readers; the authorities selectively closing the magazines they regarded as most offensive and arresting their editors. This ideological marketplace exhibited an excitement and tension not seen in the 1950s and early 1960s. Meanwhile, the regime managed to maintain public order and calm, unlike those in the Philippines and South Korea, where public demonstrations and student strikes increased.

One of the regime's most effective ways to control the opposition and prevent social disturbances was to control the universities. Take the example of the country's premier state-financed university, National Taiwan University. Under Japanese rule, it was called Taipei Imperial University and was the island's top university for training lawyers, physicians, engineers, and educators. After Taiwan reverted to Nationalist rule, the Ministry of Education changed the name to National Taiwan University. This government-controlled university attracted renowned academics to teach and conduct research, and potential college students dreamed of walking through its exalted corridors and studying in its classrooms. Early in the 1950s the government established the Disciplinary Office *(Xundaochu)* in all Taiwan's universities to monitor and control information and student activities.[79] That office vetted all student newspapers, fliers, and posters; scrutinized student and faculty speeches; and required prior knowledge and permission for any public assembly on the campus. Anyone violating the rules of this office was first warned, then reprimanded, and finally expelled. Chinese students and faculty lacked any means to circumvent these controls.

Another way the regime defused student activities that might otherwise have become politicized and led to public demonstrations challenging the regime was for the Ministry of Education to permit military training activities on all university campuses, thus co-opting many students. The ministry also encouraged student dances and other social events to divert attention from controversial issues like human rights.[80] By encouraging students to form networks of nonpolitical interests, the regime channeled students' idealism to developing a career, forming a healthy, middle-class family, and participating in civic groups to contribute to society. Finally, the inhibited political center was able to win the support of a large majority of new urban middle strata who had benefited from Taiwan's rapid modernization.

## A New Society Takes Form

Between 1950 and 1986 Taiwan's economy and society changed dramatically. Taiwan's per capita gross domestic product, only about US$100 in 1950, reached nearly US$4,000 in 1986, with people saving 38 percent of their income. Because of this great increase in income, households that had spent half or more of their earnings for food, drink, and tobacco in 1950 spent little more than one-third for the same items in 1986, while spending more for education, travel, health care, and recreation. Manufacturing and services had become the main generators of employment and income. Whereas more than half of the people lived in villages in the 1950s, by the early 1980s society had

TABLE 6
*Taiwan Independence Movement Politicans Who Returned to Taiwan (1965–1974)*

| Date | Politician |
| --- | --- |
| May 14, 1965 | Liao Wenyi, former president of the provisional government in Tokyo (ROC government returned his assets) |
| April 12, 1966 | Zheng Wanfu |
| January 1968 | Xu Xilin, member of the Taiwan Youth Independent Alliance, expelled by the Japanese government to Taiwan |
| March 27, 1968 | Liu Wenxiang, member of the Taiwan Youth Independent Alliance, expelled by the Japanese governmnet to Taiwan |
| February 22, 1972 | Gu Kuanmin, former executive head of the Taiwan Independence Movement |
| April 2, 1972 | Qiu Yonghan, former secretary-general of the Taiwan Independence Party |
| April 6, 1972 | Wang Wuchao, former member of the Taiwan Democratic Freedom Party in Japan |
| September 10, 1972 | Fu Jinchuan, former member of the Taiwan Independence Movement in Japan |
| April 28, 1973 | Huang Yongzun, former member of the Taiwan Independence Movement in Japan |
| June 23, 1973 | Gao Qiyong, former member of the Taiwan Independence Movement in Japan |
| October 7, 1974 | Six former members who left the Taiwan Independence Movement in Japan |

SOURCE: See Ihara Kichinosuke, *Taiwan no seiji kaikaku nempô oboe gaka (1943–1987)* (Taiwan political reform yearbook memoir [1943–1987]) (Nara, Japan: Tezukayama University, Department of Liberal Arts, 1992). See relevant dates.

become so urbanized that nearly 90 percent lived in cities and a middle class predominated. These great changes owed much to the vibrant economic marketplace encouraged by the party and the government. By allowing households to make economic decisions, acquire and transfer private property, and take advantage of the market, the ruling party unleashed powerful economic forces that the government sustained for many decades through its policies of sound money management, avoiding government budget deficits, and maintaining exchange rate stability. This prospering market economy fueled a new social development observed by Hung-mao Tien and others: an emerging civil society having publishing houses, numerous civic groups, and a highly educated group of professionals who were not afraid to critically appraise the political center's performance. This emerging economic market process and civil society interacted with the evolving ideological market process to vitalize Taiwan's "limited democracy" in the 1970s and early 1980s. Although critics of Taiwan's polity consistently judged its performance as woefully deficient in terms of Western democracy and human rights standards, overall progress was not ignored by members of the overseas Taiwan independence movement in Japan. From the mid-1960s to the mid-1970s, many of those dissidents, some of the regime's severest critics who had long advocated overthrowing the ROC government, began returning to Taiwan (see table 6). Some were lured by the promise of having their assets returned, and others were simply homesick, but Taiwan's social and economic progress was also a compelling reason to come in "out of the cold."

In these same years when the regime allowed "limited democracy" to flourish, it single-mindedly pursued its mission without any interference from an organized opposition. Those who repeatedly disregarded the regime's implicit rules paid the price by risking arrest, imprisonment, and even death. The inhibited political center insisted on adhering to martial law and its mission of making Taiwan an anticommunist bastion. As the political center became accustomed to governing a prosperous economy and an increasingly differentiated society in the early 1980s, it also became more tolerant of political opposition as long as it played by the rules. That opposition also learned to play by the implicit rules already described above, but it never relented from trying to change those rules in order to establish a legitimate political party that could compete in national elections—in other words, to transcend "limited democracy" and achieve full democracy.

# CHAPTER FOUR

# Legitimating a Political Opposition

From earliest times, China's elites had judged those in authority by high moral standards and relentlessly criticized them even when they performed well. Those in power either ignored such criticism or lost patience with their critics and cruelly repressed them. Relatives, friends, and sympathizers of the victimized responded by demanding justice; thus a vicious cycle of critical opposition, repression, revenge, and again critical opposition characterized Chinese autocratic rule over the centuries. Critical opposition of the political center was never legitimized in any legal-cultural way.

In Taiwan there was little reason to expect that the Chinese elite would behave differently. Why *should* a ruling party tolerate political opposition, especially after fifty years of Japanese colonial rule? Similarly, could the political opposition ever moderate its behavior to win the grudging respect of those in power? Who were the members of the political opposition that emerged in the 1970s and 1980s and willingly dedicated their lives to challenging political authority in Taiwan?

## The Political Opposition

Even before martial law, the ROC government had suppressed public demonstrations and banned published statements critical of KMT rule. In the 1950s a few courageous mainland KMT members had used Western political theory to criticize KMT rule in their journal *Ziyou zhongguo* (Free China), but in 1960 the regime banned this journal. During the 1960s a few Taiwanese elite like Peng Ming-min, Gao Yuxu, and Wu Sanlian had dared to publicly challenge the KMT, and they too were silenced. Then in the middle and late 1970s a small group began opposing the KMT in local elections and publicly criticizing the ruling party. Most of these politicians, who called themselves "outside the party" or "non-KMT politicians" *(dangwai)*,[1] were born in Taiwan of parents who strongly identified with the island's three-hundred-year-old culture and language and were one or more generations removed from the mainland.

By the 1970s most people basked in Taiwan's new prosperity, and the habits of the cities penetrated into the countryside. A new generation of local elite served as provincial and city council members or district magistrates, and they enjoyed unusual social and political prestige. One of Taiwan's oldest critics of the KMT, Yu Dengfa, explained why more people had begun to speak out more openly about Taiwan's political life:

The reason we were able to put in place a democratic government was because we have increasingly made secure our nation's foundations. In these past thirty years, the government has promoted compulsory public education, and, as a consequence, countless *dangwai* politicians have responded and continuously trained themselves in endless battles.[2]

Although Yu frequently praised the ROC government's reforms and successes, he was no friend of the KMT. Born in Tainan city in 1903, Yu graduated from Tainan's Professional Business School, part of the Japanese education system. He passed the law exams and, under Japanese rule, served on Tainan's local council. After Taiwan's retrocession to Nationalist rule, he became a ward chief. In 1947 he was elected to the ROC's National Assembly. In 1948 Yu went to Nanjing to attend the first meeting of the assembly, where he witnessed people protesting the elections and learned that the KMT had bribed voters to elect its nominees. Becoming disillusioned with the KMT, he decided never to become a party member. During the 1950s and 1960s he won the first, second, and fourth triennial elections for magistrate of Kaohsiung district, but when he lost the next election, he asserted that the KMT had cheated him.

Yu evaluated the KMT as follows: "Although the KMT organization is not bad, the majority of party workers were bad. . . . When the KMT say their elections are fair, open, and just, they lie" (*Dangwai di shengyin*, p. 32). Yu also complained that the KMT mobilized military personnel, young people, the police, and ward chiefs to get out the vote: "How is that fair? The KMT says all *dangwai* are bandits *[tufei]* and only the KMT candidates are loyal and behave like gentlemen" (p. 32). Citing the preponderance of KMT members in the national and provincial governments, Yu said, "That is not right." He resented the top-heavy KMT power structure and lamented, "I wish more *dangwai* would compete so that democracy could improve" (p. 37). Although contemptuous of the KMT's unfair lock on power and angry about its injustices and bending the rules to win elections, Yu did not support the Taiwan independence movement.

I feel that regarding the Taiwan independence issue, whether in a new or old form, it is not possible. We are all Chinese, and it is only right that China is unified. If someone advocates Taiwan independence, I believe they cannot obtain the endorsement of the international community and they will merely disgrace themselves. (P. 37)

This aging champion of opposition to the KMT fervently believed in democracy and clung to the idea of Taiwan's eventually being unified with the mainland.

The opposition magazine *Taiwan zhenglun* (Taiwan Political Review), which appeared in 1975, celebrated Taiwan democracy in the spirit of the 1950s *Ziyou zhongguo*. Thus a new generation of young opposition politicians began discussing democratization in earnest, focusing on how to improve Taiwan's polity. Within a year the authorities banned the magazine and accused its editors of seditious behavior and being Communists.

One of those editors, Huang Hsin-chieh, who had been educated in Taiwan's Japanese education system, graduating from Taipei's Administration Technical College in 1951, had actually joined the KMT. He left the party because he "felt that the KMT basically depended on personal relations. One could not get anywhere in that party without personal ties" (p. 94). Believing that he could never achieve a high position in the KMT without mainlander contacts, he began helping Gao Yuxu and other opposition politicians in their local election campaigns. In those campaigns he observed how the KMT had intimidated local businessmen who supported the opposition candidates, thus violating the Three Principles of the People that the KMT insisted Taiwan's schoolchildren should learn in their primary school texts. If martial law could be lifted and an opposition party formed, then a real democratic system could be established; Huang then argued the following proposition: "We must strive to abolish martial law, establish a judicial system, have fair laws, and allow the formation of a strong, idealistic opposition party" (p. 100). Huang, now an opposition activist, helped establish the magazine *Meilidao,* which sparked the opposition that organized the December 1979 Kaohsiung political rally. But when that rally ended in violence, key *dangwai* leaders, including Huang, were arrested and imprisoned.

Not all opposition politicians were so outspoken or active. Some cherished the same goals but chose to work more cautiously by complying with the four implicit rules the KMT enforced during the martial law era. Such an opposition politician was Kang Ning-hsiang, a Taiwanese. Kang was born into a poor family in Taipei, and his mother died while he was still a child. As a primary and secondary school student, he sold cloth in the streets to help support his family. In the mid-1970s he was elected to the Legislative Yuan. Kang believed that the KMT's long rule without competition prevented it from improving the people's welfare. For that reason, that party had become "an obstacle blocking Taiwan's political and social progress." Kang recognized that many supported the KMT, but to him it had become a huge machine in which individuals could not express themselves or have any influence. He believed that another political party was necessary to check and balance the KMT and force it to perform better. Kang opined, "I could be outside the party and adopt a critical, evaluative role to serve the people." He realized that Taiwan had dramatically changed in the previous two decades, meaning that those who were "outside the KMT and were *dangwai* politicians no longer suffered as in the past, because the political environment had much improved." Kang also admitted that "KMT efforts were positive and had brought about these improvements" (p. 107).

As for *dangwai* politicians, Kang noted that they were a disorganized, disparate group with greatly differing attitudes (p. 108). If the political opposition was to become a major force, each person had to set personal ambitions aside, desist from playing the role of the hero, and encourage the others. Kang pointed out that 1977 was a watershed year for *dangwai* politicians because more people than ever before had voted them into political office. He attributed their victory to the continued improvement of Taiwan's democracy.

Other moderate opposition politicians like Su Nan-cheng, although they willingly played by the political rules, were dedicated to creating an opposition party to check the KMT and make it accountable and more democratic. Su was also born into a poor family in Tainan city. He sold bean curd after school to help his mother, who rose early to make almond tea and sell it in the streets because her husband was ill and unemployed much of the time (p. 157). In high school Su read Sun's Three Principles of the People and was so deeply moved that he joined the KMT (p. 160). After serving in the military, he ran for Tainan City Council but failed because he lacked political experience. In 1968, however, he won the highest number of votes to enter the Tainan City Council and reluctantly agreed to run for council head. While visiting Taichung city to seek financial help for his campaign, he learned that much of that city's entertainment services industry gave generous bribes to local politicians (p. 163). Rather than accept such funding, he returned to Tainan and lost his bid for council head. Vowing to fight corruption, he blew the whistle on the bribing activities of local construction companies and the police force (p. 165). Su's achievements did not go unnoticed by KMT local cadres, who, fearing his power and popularity, tried to discredit him to their superiors, calling him a communist agent and a supporter of Taiwan independence. Su then decided to leave the KMT and compete against it: "I declared that I was not a nonparty or nonfaction person. I also was not one of the *dangwai*. I was a free agent" (p. 167). Su noted that even "within the KMT there also are free agents. In the current political situation, transferring political power to another party is impossible. Therefore, I respect this kind of political structure" (p. 167). Respectful but critical of the KMT, Su continued his battle as a political independent and opposition leader.

One of the most popular opposition candidates was Hsu Hsin-liang, who in 1973 received the most votes to become Taoyuan district's representative in the Taiwan Provincial Assembly and in 1977 was elected as Taoyuan district's magistrate. Hsu's family first lived in Tansui, then moved to Hsinchu and finally to the Chungli countryside, where Hsu attended Chungli Middle School and Hsinchu City High School. He became interested in politics and entered National Zhengzhi University to study political science. As a freshman and a great admirer of the KMT's history and achievements, he joined the party. He later grew critical, saying:

The KMT has contributed to Taiwan's development in the past twenty years. Yet it has done a lot of things we do not like, although that does not mean that everything it did was wrong. As for the party's membership, the party has gathered enormous power to itself in the hands of diverse individuals. Many cannot say they reflect the old guard but only that they have a lot of power. Even so, the party has progressed, and 80 percent of the members represent new blood. They grew up in Taiwan's new society. These KMT members are trying to modernize the party through their struggles. But the party needs to be pressured more to force it to modernize. (P. 168)

According to Hsu, outside pressure was needed to force major changes within the KMT. He pointed out two of the KMT's difficulties. "There were some, a minority possessing absolute power, who represented the old society and culture. Second, the KMT carries a heavy historical burden. Because of that, the old leadership hangs on to its political power" (p. 187).

Some opposition leaders came from educated families who admired Japan and its people. Chang Chun-hong, who grew up in such surroundings, joined the KMT as a young man. But when he tried to win his party's nomination for the Taipei city council, he was passed over. Angrily resigning, he returned to his hometown in Nantou district, where he was elected as a representative to the Taiwan provincial council. Although Chang admitted that the "KMT is the only true party that contributed to the Chinese Revolution" (pp. 244–45), there were no checks and balances of its power. "It allowed no competition, yet it held great power and destroyed any outside force before it could ever get started" (p. 245). Chang accused the KMT of using only yes-men who pleased the party leaders, adding to the inflexibility and deterioration of the party. The KMT had only itself to blame for driving talented people into the opposition, because they had been outraged over the way the KMT used ruthless and unfair tactics against them (p. 246). Chang admitted, however, that the opposition was divided and did not understand how to initiate a political process for checking and balancing the KMT.

The political opposition still managed to attract those with legal skills to its ranks. Yao Chia-wen grew up in the countryside of Changhua district. His parents were illiterate, and his father sold cloth. Yao attended the Changhua Business School, and at twenty-five years of age he passed the exam to enter the Faculty of Law of National Taiwan University. He graduated at age thirty-one, and in 1972 he went to the United States, specializing in legal assistance to the poor. He returned to Taiwan and set up law offices in Taipei, Taichung, and Tainan. Believing that the local KMT members "did not have any political ideals and solely worried about how to elect their party's nominees and whether the party could control them once elected" (p. 276), Yao charged that the KMT performed poorly because there were no checks and balances on the party. Taiwan's political progress, therefore, depended on more democracy, not less. "For Taiwan to really improve and stand tall in the world, we absolutely need political reform. We need some force to check and balance KMT power to create an equivalent competitive power and, when necessary, to replace it" (p. 277). According to Yao, the KMT could not be depended on to improve Taiwan's democracy; an opposition was necessary to build a new political system.

These educated, dynamic, courageous political opposition leaders were the beneficiaries of a society that had educated them and given them new opportunities. Their ranks included an older generation that had been educated and had become adults under Japanese colonial rule and a younger generation who had received only a Japanese elementary education and then were educated within a Chinese educational system. The older generation regarded the KMT as corrupt and lacking any moral legitimacy to govern. The younger generation believed in democracy in which an opposition party could compete with the ruling party to make it perform better or even replace it.

Some of these young, ambitious, and idealistic elite had joined the KMT, only to reject it because it did not live up to their political expectations or use their talents. Others, morally outraged or disillusioned by the KMT's behavior, never joined. They shared a political ideology, based on their admiration of Western democracy, in which political parties competed, monitored and critiqued each other, and tried to win popular support in elections. Disillusioned by the KMT's monopoly of political power, they used their ingenuity and skills to criticize the political center and try to win local elections. And when some were elected as national representatives, they even challenged cabinet ministers in interpellations conducted in the Legislative Yuan. Finally, they reached out to "liberal" KMT professionals and intellectuals to support their mission, and in those interactions the two groups exerted a moderating influence on each other.

### Criticizing the "Inhibited" Political Center

The coalescing of opposition politicians into a political movement during the 1970s was associated with their wide-ranging criticisms of the KMT-dominated polity, or what we have called the "inhibited" political center. These politicians were interested neither in legitimating that center nor in supporting it. They wanted to transform it into a "subordinated" political center, or democracy, because they had come to believe that democracy represented the ideal polity.

From the mid-1970s until the mid-1980s, their periodicals described and evaluated every aspect of Taiwan's polity. Informative, humorous, and bitingly critical of party-state leaders and their organizations and policies, the opposition's periodicals could be found in newsstands and stores throughout the island. As word of their contents rapidly spread among the avidly reading public, the number of readers multiplied.

The opposition's main tactic was to illustrate how the government's repeated promises to promote democracy had not been realized in practice. By showing the persistent gap between the promise and the reality of democracy, the opposition could criticize the regime's insincerity about building democracy. If the ruling party was insincere, it lacked morality and was unworthy to govern. By gradually delegitimizing the ruling party in the eyes of citizens, the opposition hoped to persuade more voters to elect their candidates and support their efforts to accelerate democratization.

With each passing year, then, the opposition asked how long martial law was supposed to continue.[3] Criticizing martial law was done by ridicule and by showing how Taiwan's "limited democracy" lagged far behind the democracy of the advanced countries. In spring 1986 a critic described Taiwan's martial law as being like a raincoat that "does not have any moral attributes, but if you still wear that raincoat, even if it never rains, for over thirty years, you have a problem."[4] The critic continued, "Martial law is not supposed to be used to deal with every type of possible crisis and then become a permanent institution. If martial law is perpetually used, you are trying to change the constitutional system. In the case of Taiwan, by 1986, martial law had been in effect for thirty-seven years, which is the longest period that any country in the world has imposed martial law. In democratic nations, martial law is only a temporary provision."[5]

Government officials rebutted such criticisms by arguing that martial law must remain in place as long as the communist-dominated polity on the mainland existed. That polity threatened Taiwan, and therefore only martial law could protect the island's people from communist subversion.

Under martial law, laws had proliferated, and according to the opposition, Taiwan had become an overregulated society: "Taiwan had far too many laws that were impractical, out of date, and worthless," complained one critic.[6] Too many laws made for "too many police, tax collectors, and officials who gambled, consorted with prostitutes, and broke the laws they were supposed to enforce." Readers of these periodicals knew only too well about local corruption, and opposition critics could escape police censorship by appealing to the authorities to clean up corruption and simplify laws.[7]

Martial law also gave the Garrison Command enormous power to censor the public media and to regulate society. Opposition periodicals reminded their readers that the

KMT's censorship policy was everywhere in society and for no explicable reason the KMT prohibited every kind of behavior: it forbade any revision of the constitution before recovering the mainland; it forbade any new party from forming; it forbade the registration of any new newspaper; it forbade strikes, demonstrations, and criticisms of national policy; it forbade the election of a provincial governor and the mayors of Taipei and Kaohsiung cities; it forbade the reading of works published by mainland China authors; it forbade the expression of views by political rallies; it forbade students to have long hair and to help politicians in elections. Most of these kinds of activities do not violate the constitution. They are merely the subjective views held by those in power and run counter to society's contemporary trends and the natural inclinations of our people.[8]

The opposition also complained that the government's severe censorship violated the constitution. Under Article 11, section 1 of martial law, the government could prohibit lectures, speeches, newspapers, periodicals, and public gatherings it disapproved or feared. But the opposition insisted that such social discourse did not pose any threat to the island's security, whereas denying people their rights to have such discourse certainly violated the constitution. By painting this dark picture of a society "without freedom of speech and the people so fearful of their government,"[9] the opposition concluded that the people could never have the right to form a political party. "Without an opposition party, how was it possible for the people to change the legislative process?" Why did the KMT jealously protect its power and rigidly regulate society by "closing it off and making it a 'bound foot'?"[10] Readers were asked to ponder such questions.

According to the opposition's critique, building democracy required that people have their freedoms of speech and assembly and the right to form an opposition party to monitor the ruling party, make officials more accountable to the people, and ensure that the people's will could be realized. By the early 1980s, the opposition had intensified its criticisms of the KMT, always emphasizing that the "KMT repeatedly talked about democracy but never explained why the political opposition could not have a political party, merely saying that until the appropriate conditions were ripe there should not be an opposition party."[11] The KMT rebutted this criticism by saying that "democracy requires having a powerful opponent, and the Communist Party on the mainland was the KMT's opponent." This war of words raged through the early 1980s and included negative evaluations of the center's foreign policy, its mainland China policy, and various organs of the government.

The opposition was not afraid to label the government's foreign policy as "money diplomacy" and wasting taxpayers' money.[12] They cited the government's lavish spending to buy the friendship of United States leaders and congressmen and to provide economic aid to small African and Latin American countries. They singled out the Ministry of Foreign Affairs as never conducting serious research and not calling on experts for advice. They charged that the Ministry of Foreign Affairs had the "most bureaucratic atmosphere of all the cabinet ministries."[13] Foreign Minister Shen Chang-huan was a classic example of official incompetence: he had spent many years in the ministry but never traveled. "His English was good, his temper moderate, and his relationships with other politicians satisfactory, but he talked too much nonsense; many criticized him as always wearing a smile. While cultured and always controlled, he was like a twice-cooked oil stick: you cannot chew it, cannot swallow it, and cannot cut it; you only can put it back. This kind of a minister was just like the KMT."[14]

The government's mainland policy also came under criticism for always fluctuating and being applied in unfair ways.[15] If a mainland Chinese visited his hometown, he was not punished, but when a Taiwanese went to the mainland, he would be accused of espionage and punished. Similarly, when trade flows through Hong Kong to the mainland doubled in value between 1979 and 1981, many large companies illegally shipped products and the government never took any action. Yet the government still charged certain businessmen with violating the law and punished them.[16]

Nor did the opposition spare the Legislative Yuan, the First National Assembly, and the constitution its criticisms. One critic who observed the seventy-first session of the Legislative Yuan in 1985 described its activities as a "huge political festival" that always celebrated the KMT's achievements. He noted that KMT legislators were poorly informed, rarely prepared, and "disconnected from reality." He sarcastically recounted how legislator Wang Mengyun interpellated the minister of education: "Should not all Chinese women in Taiwan be required to wear a bra?"[17] He also recalled how another legislator expressed his dissatisfaction with the practice of contraception by informing the legislative body that "if a man simply behaved like a gentleman, then even when a girl sat on your lap you would never be sexually aroused (zuohuai buluan)."[18] These anecdotes lampooned KMT legislators as frauds and incompetents unworthy of representing the people.

As early as 1978 opposition politicians like Wu Feng-shan, who later owned a famous newspaper, Zuli wanbao (Independent evening post), lambasted mainlander national representatives as being out of touch with reality. He pointed out that in 1978 "Taiwan still had 1,300 national assembly members, over 400 legislators, and another 70 in the Control Yuan. Having so many mainlanders control the government was like a small person wearing an oversized suit. It is ridiculous, stupid, and does not accord with reality."[19] Wu continued that "times have now changed, and there must be a changing of the guard." Still other critics charged that the mainlander majority rule disgraced Taiwan's democracy and disrespected its people.

Opposition politicians had carefully studied the constitution, and they wanted it reactivated to compel the government to permit political party competition. Kang Ning-hsiang, director of Bashi niandai (Eighties monthly), declared that the "greatest expectation shared by all dangwai of the ruling party was for it to carry out a true democratic political process."[20] He argued that the ruling party should not use "all kinds of excuses and procedures to restrict constitutional law and deprive the people of their rights under the constitution."[21]

*Trying to Win Elections*

Undismayed that their criticisms of the government had not persuaded it to permit the formation of an opposition party, *dangwai* politicians began entering the triennial local and supplementary quota elections for local and national representatives. Before 1970, only a few outspoken government critics, mainly in southern Taiwan, had dared to compete in local elections. But in the 1970s more regime opponents saw a great opportunity to achieve national political fame if they could win some elections, because there were now more resources to compete against the candidates supported by the powerful ruling party. The election of 1977 signaled a small breakthrough for the *dangwai* when voters elected Hsu Hsin-liang as Taoyuan county magistrate and a small group of *dangwai* to the Taiwan provincial assembly.[22] Then in 1980 voters even elected some *dangwai* politicians like Kang Ning-hsiang and Mrs. Xu Rongshu to the Legislative Yuan and others to the National Assembly.

*Dangwai* critics now argued that they "only wanted to use the voting system to demonstrate the power of the opposition."[23] After all, they claimed, in 1981 there were 389 ruling party legislators who did not have any responsibility toward the voters because they had not been elected. If the *dangwai* could win a few elections and behave in a responsible way, they hoped to convince the KMT leadership that the "politics of checks and balances" did not threaten the ruling party but might promote Taiwan's democratization. They also argued that checks and balances were possible only if four political conditions were created: "First, there must be a two party polity; second, there must be an independent judiciary; third, there should be an environment of fair criticism; and finally, there should be a strong legislature."[24] Although none of these conditions existed in the early 1980s, the *dangwai* politicians regarded winning elections as a means to begin to create those conditions.

Opposition election candidates carefully studied the election system and paid attention to the procedures that regulated elections and the management of local and national representative bodies. They developed special techniques to attract voters to their cause. In the 1980s elections, for example, *dangwai* leaders encouraged the wives of those politicians who had been arrested and imprisoned because of their involvement with the Meilidao incident of December 1979 in Kaohsiung to become election candidates. These women appealed to voters by calling for greater democracy and displaying their courage and loyalty to their imprisoned husbands by demanding their early release. So successful were these women that voters overwhelmingly elected Mrs. Zhou

Qingyu and Mrs. Xu Rongshu to give them the highest number of ballots cast for any of the competing candidates.[25]

At first the *dangwai* were severely disadvantaged in these election campaigns because the KMT had abundant resources to support their candidates' campaigning methods. The *dangwai* learned to approach the small and medium business enterprises and ask for financial contributions; they appealed to contributors to provide gifts in secret; and they held preelection banquets to ask potential voters to donate funds for the *dangwai* candidates; finally, they distributed handbills and fliers that described their platform and directly appealed for voters' support.[26]

*Dangwai* candidates campaigned on the theme that "society, particularly the intellectuals and various elites, holds high expectations of the *dangwai* and hopes they can offer an ideal blueprint that is legally and ideologically different from the KMT that not only can solve Taiwan's political problems but offers solutions for resolving the ills of society and the economy."[27] By projecting their candidates as more intelligent and morally superior, the *dangwai* tried to differentiate them from those of the ruling party. But to demonstrate the superiority of their candidates over those of the ruling party, the *dangwai* opposition had to find young, dynamic, attractive candidates who could attract voters' support, a difficult challenge that often defied their lofty intentions.

After studying the election trends of previous years, *dangwai* intellectuals concluded that the voting participation rate had been declining since the 1950s but began to rise after 1977, a trend they welcomed.[28] They also learned that voters had become more prosperous, a majority now lived in cities and regarded themselves as middle class, and they had access to more diverse information.[29] Males voted more often than females, and a higher proportion of mainlanders than Taiwanese tended to vote. They also recognized that as people became more urban and educated, they tended to vote less but usually voted more often for the KMT. More women tended to vote KMT, whereas more males voted for the *dangwai*. The older voters, especially those over forty, supported the KMT, whereas younger voters sympathized with the *dangwai*.

Voters who inclined toward reform, liked "checks and balances," and favored specific personalities tended to vote for *dangwai* candidates. Those voters desiring stability, economic growth, and security preferred the KMT. Survey after survey seemed to show that voters worried more about "bread and butter" issues: narrowing the gap between rich and poor; constructing more available, cheaper housing; improving personal security and preserving social stability; and promoting more social services and welfare. Based on such information, *dangwai* candidates tried to pitch their campaign rhetoric to emphasize "checks and balances," ending censorship, lifting martial law, and granting more self-governance for local people. For the younger voters more likely to view politics with passion and moral fervor, the *dangwai* message struck a responsive chord. But how well did *dangwai* candidates do in certain elections? The election results in Kaohsiung city and Pingtung county reveal that voters sometimes preferred *dangwai* over KMT candidates, but special circumstances seemed to have produced this new trend.

Kaohsiung city, situated almost at the southern tip of the island, had become the largest harbor and transshipment city in Taiwan under Japanese rule. A large business class coexisted with sociopolitical factions that competed for political patronage and prestige. It was in this more open, cosmopolitan city that some unusual politicians chose to challenge the KMT and win enough voter support to be elected to important political positions.

Take the example of Guo Guoqi, born in 1900 in Pingtung city, who graduated from the Faculty of Law of Meiji University in Japan.[30] In 1927, after marrying a Japanese woman, Guo returned to Kaohsiung and joined the Taiwan People's Party, which campaigned for greater Taiwanese self-rule. The Japanese arrested and imprisoned him in 1942 on the charge of receiving funds from the Nationalist government to organize local resistance against Japan. After he was freed in 1945, Kaohsiung voters elected him to the Kaohsiung city assembly in April 1946, in which he often critized the Nationalist regime. After the February 28, 1947, uprising Nationalist troops arrested him and imprisoned him for four months. Emerging from prison angry and furious at the Nationalist government, he devoted the rest of his life to criticizing the KMT. Guo was a fiery speaker, unafraid to speak his mind, and in touch with that stratum of Kaohsiung citizens who were unhappy with the KMT regime.

By 1968 Guo had been elected to a fourth term in the Taiwan provincial assembly. In 1969 he was easily elected to the Legislative Yuan. His slogan, which had great appeal among Kaohsiung voters, was "Let me die honorably on the platform of the Legislative Yuan" (*Ciwo guangrung zhanshi yitan*).[31] He was famous for his outspoken political demands: "Taiwan's vice president should be a Taiwanese"; "the provincial governor should be a Taiwanese"; "the deputy directors in the ministries should be Taiwanese."[32] He advocated the lifting of martial law, the popular election of national representatives and the president, the establishing of an independent judiciary, the competition of political parties, and the separation of political parties from the state. Guo

Guoqi represented that generation of Japanized Taiwanese elite who had learned about Western democracy through their Japanese education and believed that after Taiwan was retroceded to the Republic of China full democracy would be established throughout the island.

Another opposition politician, Su Qiuchen, was born in Kaohsiung in 1935.[33] Su graduated from the Faculty of Law of National Taiwan University. As a young man he had read Lei Chen's articles and knew the Kaohsiung opposition politician Yu Dengfa. He had participated in the Meilidao incident, was arrested, and was released on February 13, 1980. He decided to run for the Legislative Yuan in December 1980 by using such slogans as "I would rather be in prison if I cannot be elected" and "Our hometown needs our protection, and our people need our care." Kaohsiung's voters enthusiastically elected Su to the Legislative Yuan. During the next three years Su acquired the reputation of asking the most questions during interpellations of government officials and speaking on the floor whenever an opportunity permitted. He claimed his style would be a model for future legislators. Su represents that young generation of Taiwan elite who received their education under National government rule and had learned about democracy from KMT liberals and well-known opposition politicians.

Under Japanese colonial rule, Pingtung city and its environs had been famous for anti-Japanese activities. After retrocession, the KMT local cadres used local factions to establish their influence and control. The KMT nominated a local leader named Qiu Lianhui to run in the local elections, but Qiu proved too independent, and the KMT refused to nominate him in later elections.[34] When the *dangwai* emerged in the 1977 elections, Qiu had left the KMT and independently campaigned for the provincial assembly. He received enough votes to win and became an outspoken critic of the KMT in the provincial assembly. He was arrested after the Meilidao incident and then released. In December 1980 the citizens of Pingtung district elected him as their magistrate to become the first *dangwai* magistrate of Pingtung since retrocession.[35] Qiu represented those young opposition politicians who carved out a niche in local politics by their abilities to satisfy voters and appeal to their anti-KMT sentiments.

Another *dangwai* politician, Su Tseng-chang, was born in Pingtung city July 28, 1947, and he too graduated from the Faculty of Law of National Taiwan University.[36] He worked as a legal assistant to Kang Ning-hsiang and then served as Yao Chia-wen's defense attorney after the authorities arrested Yao for his activist role in the Meilidao incident. In 1981 Su entered the Pingtung district election for the Taiwan Provincial Assembly. A witty and magnetic speaker, Su attracted thousands of spectators to his campaign rallies. The critical barbs he unleashed at the KMT won him the admiration and respect of Pingtung voters, and in 1981 they solidly elected him to the Taiwan Provincial Assembly. Other famous young opposition politicians from the south during these same years were Qiu Maonan, Li Jingxiung, Pan Lifu, and Huang Zhengxiung.[37] They knew the old opposition politicians and admired their courage. They also had been influenced by the writings on democracy of Lei Chen and other KMT liberals. As part of an expanding network of elites who campaigned in elections to criticize the KMT for its failure to accelerate democratization, they successfully appealed to voters to elect them to promote democracy.

### Serving as National Representatives

Once elected as national representatives, how did these opposition politicians behave? There were too few of them in the Legislative Yuan to propose laws or block the actions of KMT legislators, but they distinguished themselves in the interpellations of the prime minister and cabinet, which the law allowed. In 1980 there were enough *dangwai* legislators to take advantage of the interpellation. By raising questions while criticizing the government's failure to promote democracy, the *dangwai* hoped to discredit the government in the eyes of voters.

For example, on March 24, 1981, about 170 legislators, along with Premier Sun Yun-Suan and his cabinet officials, had taken their seats in the Legislative Yuan's chambers. After chairman Ni Wen-ya called the ninth session to order, the opposition legislator named Fei Hsi-ping stood up to present an interpellation signed by ten *dangwai* legislators.[38]

Fei discussed seven key issues: lifting martial law, permitting political parties to compete, expanding personal freedom, allowing freedom of speech, establishing an independent judiciary, separating the party and state, and accelerating democracy. For more than five years the *dangwai* had repeated this same message to the ruling party and government. Now the debate was being conducted inside the Legislative Yuan for the public to evaluate. Fei directed his remarks to the government's leading official, the premier. "I do not really understand why it is still necessary to have martial law, which has now become a normal political practice. It deprives our citizens of all their rights under the constitution. Martial law should be a temporary measure."[39] Fei complained that "martial law prohibits public assembly and the right to organize political parties, thereby depriving the people of their basic rights and exercising their constitutional rights." Premier Sun offered the government's standard position: "We cannot lift martial law because we fear the communist threat, and we must preserve the national security of our country." These words from different sides of the chambers had been repeated many times in public, but for the first time political opposition members calmly presented their arguments to the government in a procedural and dignified manner.

The *dangwai* legislators carefully assembled evidence to make their interpellations persuasive and credible, and they continued to hammer away at the government's violations of the constitution and its laws. When *dangwai* legislator Huang Tienfu interpellated Premier Sun, he described how the Garrison Command had closed down a legal periodical even before the first issue was published.[40] According to Huang, the owner of *Zhonggulou* (Political monitors magazine) had registered with the Government Information Office and received permission to publish the first issue in September 1980. But several months before the scheduled time, Garrison Command personnel had investigated the magazine's staff and banned publication. Huang said the Garrison Command had justified its actions because "some articles about the Meilidao incident might threaten the peace and disturb the public's sense of morality." Huang complained that the government had violated its citizens' freedom of speech and that such behavior was intolerable in a democracy.

Huang then charged the government with violating its election laws. He recounted how government officials had separately interviewed the victims of the Meilidao incident and taped their comments without their knowledge or permission.[41] To make matters worse, government officials had instructed KMT-nominated candidates to use these tapes during political rallies in the December 1980 elections to attack the *dangwai* candidates. By citing government "dirty tricks" and showing how officials violated the election laws, the *dangwai* tried to portray the government as immoral. Although government officials denied Huang's charges, these interpellations enabled the opposition to argue that the ruling party and government only talked about building democracy and used democracy as a slogan.

*Dangwai* legislators also argued that a polity dominated by a single party could never become a democracy. Female legislator Xu Rongshu said as much in her interpellation of the premier on March 17, 1982: "In Taiwan there has been unlimited party power, overexpanded military power, and overused money power. These phenomena are due to a single large party system and the delay in establishing our constitutional political system. These conditions have consequently weakened the morale of our people."[42] Xu went on to say, "It is worrisome that the KMT cannot separate the party from the government. In all of the elections held in Taiwan, whether for city councils or mayors, party and government resources always have been merged to help the KMT to win elections."[43] Kang Ning-hsiang had made a study of the widespread bribery in elections and reported his findings in an interpellation. He claimed that KMT candidates were able to bus voters to tourist sites, supply box lunches, and entertain them with lotteries and banquets as well as distributing small presents. According to Kang, "the KMT did this all over the island. How can the KMT claim that it conducts fair elections? In a local election the KMT will even offer a government position to an opposition candidate as a bribe not to run."[44] In still other interpellations, *dangwai* legislators complained that Taiwan's universities only used educators who were KMT members, so that party membership became the criterion for university employment.[45]

In order to capitalize on their success in the 1980 election, Kang Ning-hsiang conceived the idea of the *dangwai*'s joining with liberal critics in the KMT and liberal academics to advocate greater democracy. He did this through a peculiar Chinese institution called the *discussion forum (zuotanhui)*.

*Mobilizing Other Elites*

On February 18, 1981, Kang Ning-hsiang invited twenty-three *dangwai* and liberals, including KMT scholars like Hu Fu, Chang Chung-tung, Yang Guoshu, and Tao Pai-chuan, KMT members like Shen Chun-shan and Kuan Chung, as well as *dangwai* supporters like Wu Feng-shan and Sima Wenwu to a one-day conference sponsored by Kang's magazine, *Bashi niandai,* at the Pacific International Club in Taipei. Kang's magazine published the proceedings in March 1981.[46] This gathering was the first time that famous elites of different political backgrounds had assembled to discuss and evaluate the progress of democracy in Taiwan during the 1980s, a decade many elite now regarded as likely to be a turning point in the island's political development.

Kang told the participants that he and others were eager to understand how the KMT intended to deal with the political opposition in the next few years, because KMT behavior would determine the future of the *dangwai* opposition movement. Participants agreed to consider the role of political parties in theory and history and the use of political power by the opposition and ruling parties in emerging democratic societies. This agenda made it possible for various participants to evaluate the KMT's policies and performance to determine whether that ruling party had satisfied popular expectations.

Wu Feng-shan reported that if one scored the KMT's political performance so far, it did not deserve a perfect score of 100 but more likely deserved a "barely passing" score of 60. But Wu then criticized both the *dangwai* and the KMT. He noted that the *dangwai* had assumed the heavy burden of critically evaluating the KMT's efforts to promote democracy, but they would be advised to be more constructive and gracious in their appraisal of the KMT's performance in building democracy. As for the KMT, it "has not understood the rapid changes of the past thirty years and how successfully the people have become educated in Taiwan." For that reason, "since the 1970s the KMT has reacted to these broad developments in an insensitive and unproductive way, and it never built any relationships with the opposition."[47] Because of Taiwan's complex developments and progress, "everyone now has a different opinion, but the ruling party still emphasizes a single form of national political policy, and it fails to realize that Taiwan is now a pluralistic society and must be dealt with accordingly."

Liberal scholars like Yang Guoshu told the audience that "there is no single political group that can satisfy a pluralistic society unless it too has become pluralistic."[48] Therefore, how should the ruling party treat the opposition's use of power? Yang advised that "the KMT should avoid taking any extreme view to oppose everything the opposition suggests or proposes." "The KMT, for example, should not refuse to have a dialogue with the opposition movement." Yang urged that the "KMT should allow the opposition to publish its views. The ruling party should treat the opposition as it treats any group of responsible citizens. It should not adopt a double standard to deal with the opposition. Finally, the KMT should become more flexible and generous by inviting opposition politicians to serve in the government. This would help the government."[49]

But Yang also counseled the opposition movement:

After listening to the opposition politicians express their political views, they often commit a strategic mistake by always denying what the KMT has done well. You must at least affirm and praise the KMT's good deeds and then criticize. For example, you can affirm that under the ROC constitutional system the KMT is trying to carry out democratization. Second, we are anticommunist because the other side adheres to totalitarian control, and for that reason we too oppose them. We do not oppose them because we are striving for our own power. But we have a democratic polity to uphold, and we should make use of that polity to oppose communist totalitarianism. Third, we must affirm China's unification. We must draw the line with regard to Taiwan's independence. Fourth, the opposition should also affirm the contributions the government has made rather than claim that everything is done by the people. Fifth, you must affirm the ruling party's achievements. Unless the opposition uses these means to affirm the ruling party and the government, then you cannot argue for checks and balances. The KMT would accept this line of argument, and many more people would believe that you too are fair.[50]

Yang advised the *dangwai* to be patient and adopt the spirit of carrying a heavy cross. Meanwhile, their members should strive to improve their behavior. He urged the *dangwai* to have more tolerance and respect for the ruling party, and he applauded their efforts to perform even better in local elections. Chang Chung-tung and Tao Pai-chuan also declared that democracy had come far in Taiwan. Chang recounted how "one year ago, Hu Fu, Yang Guo-shu, and I went to a *dangwai* meeting, but we could not enter and participate because of so many obstructions. Then, one year later, there was no problem, and we have had a wonderful conference. Our society has learned tolerance and now understands how to respect a legal gathering."[51] On this note the conference ended. In the next few years contacts between liberal academics, KMT members, and *dangwai* members continued, even though the ruling party adhered to its principle of having no informal or formal meetings with the *dangwai*. Meanwhile, Taiwan's "limited democracy" was being judged more tolerantly and favorably by different groups in society.

## Four "Advertisements" of Political Beliefs and Sentiments

How did different sociopolitical strata view and evaluate the political changes in Taiwan during the late 1970s and early 1980s? Political culture and ideology continually evolve out of interactions between shared orientations, personalities, and episodes in concrete history reality, a point recently stressed by the American sociologist Robert Bellah.[52] These orientations are expressed through rhetoric expressed by various individuals who represent different sociopolitical strata. This rhetoric is actually a form of "advertising," or an expression of personal political viewpoints or evaluations that involves both a claim and a perception of political reality and behavior. The assertion of such claims and perceptions, or what we will call "advertising," is continual, ever-changing, and connected with and reflective of the different subcultures and social strata of any society, as John Dunn has tried to eludicate.[53] In the case of the ROC, there was the *official theory* of the ruling elite and their supporters—namely, KMT doctrine based on the writings of Sun Yat-sen and his followers, best embodied in Sun's Three Principles of the People. Second, there was the advertising by the opposition and liberal critics of the ruling elite, as well as the more educated in society, or academics, called *intellectual theory*.

Much of this theory related to Western liberalism, often mixed with Confucianist-humanist terms. Then there was a third form of advertising expressed by the less educated strata of society that reflected not only common sense but the values and beliefs of the ordinary people, which is called *amateur theory*. Finally, there gradually developed a fourth form of advertising as reflected by *modern mass media theory*, which represented a mix of the three forms above.

In describing these four forms of advertising as articulating the elites' and ordinary people's political thoughts, beliefs, and feelings, we note a gradual acceptance and tolerance by the ruling elites of a political opposition and its activities. At the same time, we note that the opposition politicians also became more tolerant of the ruling elite and were willing to play by their rules if there was a level playing field and the rules were fairly umpired by the ruling elite. It was this gradual adjustment of political cultural values and a new political behavior that made possible an ethos of accepting democracy during the mid-1980s.

### The Official View of the Political Opposition

The KMT and its supporters adhered to the belief that only by implanting the doctrine of Sun Yat-sen, the "father of our nation" *(guofu)*, in Taiwan could they "save the nation and save the world" *(jiuguo jiushi)*. Only a strong, prosperous, democratic Taiwan could help suffering compatriots on the mainland and through "firm, strong struggle bring security and peace to the world."[54] Their thinking was as follows.

The Taiwan people must engage in a "revolution" to achieve those goals. That revolution depended on acquiring a system of moral-scientific knowledge that would serve as the basis for action. Having that knowledge enabled one to find a deep sense of conviction, which in turn generated action. Sun had discovered this doctrine by extracting the "finer essence" *(jinghua)* from the Eastern and Western doctrines, including both ancient morality and science as well as his insight.

Sun's doctrine was an architectonic system derived from the highest principles in the material realm and the spirit of compassion, which united both heaven and earth. Chiang Kai-shek extended Sun's doctrine to include the concept of the "political ideal." According to Chiang, in that political ideal "the wise and the capable will be elected to office and mutual faith, and neighborly relations will be cultivated ... there would be no need for conspiracies and underhanded dealings, nor for robberies, thefts, civil commotions, and usurpations." In the Sunist polity "there would be everlasting peace, and everyone would be guided by the principle that everything under heaven is for the public good" *(tianxia weigong)*.[55]

Chiang and his party tried to translate Sun's exalted moral vision into national action, impressing on every citizen that such a "project will alarm the heavens and move the earth" *(jingtian dongdi)*. All KMT members and citizens must study this doctrine, act on it, and transmit it. How did they feel about undertaking this grand mission? As one follower expressed it in late spring of 1979: "As I have undertaken this sort of work emphasizing both understanding and action, it has constituted a process of moral effort pervading my thought, work, life, intellect, and spirit. . . . I only wish that every Chinese could take on his back this Cross of the Three Principles of the People." [56] Said President Chiang Ching-kuo, "This is a heavy and a great responsibility which can be fulfilled only with the greatest spirit and the determination to endure humiliation and shoulder heavy burdens." [57]

KMT leaders frequently berated themselves and their followers for failing to fulfill their grave responsibilities and resolutely continuing to struggle against setbacks. As Chiang Ching-kuo said, "Whatever the circumstances one confronts, it is only the power we have within ourselves that is real and true power." [58] With this official view, the KMT leaders also took pains to inform the people, cultivate their understanding of the ruling party's goals, and avoid coercion and force. For example, the govenment instructed security and police personnel not to precipitate public violence and to exercise restraint when dealing with public demonstrations and disturbances. The KMT had learned an important lesson from the February 28, 1947, uprising: overreacting when controlling street violence risked losing the legitimacy to govern. Therefore when the Chungli city riot erupted on November 19, 1977, a voting day, the police, acting with great restraint, kept physical injuries on both sides to a minimum; at the December 8, 1979, rally in Kaohsiung city, the police controlled crowd violence, and only police were injured. The regime feared alienating the citizenry and wanted to uphold the rule of law.

When their opponents broke the law, however, the ruling elite conveyed their moral outrage using a rich vocabulary of vituperation. Violent dissidents were hoodlums *(baotu)*, criminal elements *(bufa fenzi)*, and power-hungry elements *(yexin fenzi)* who "cannot distinguish right from wrong" and "the loyal from the treasonous" *(buming shifei, bubian zhungjian)* and who "lack any sense of law or morality" *(wufa wutian)*. Such persons "cause trouble" *(zishi)* by "acting with blatant disrespect for authority" *(xiaozhang bahu)*, "distorting the true facts" *(waiqu shishi)*, trying to "inflame the masses," and threatening the peace and security of Taiwan at times of crisis. Such "criminals" lack all popular support and instead arouse the "hatred" and the "anger" of the people; only sincere persons can move with history's "tide" of moral power. Selective repression, which frequently occurred under martial law, was synonymous with proper moral action in the eyes of the ruling elite.

From 1960 until the mid-1970s the KMT leadership adhered to its informal rules regulating an incipient democracy and ideological marketplace while exuding confidence that the party was laying the foundations for a new society based on the Three Principles of the People. By the late 1970s, however, political opponents were publishing journals calling for a speeding up of democracy and blaming the KMT for Taiwan's lack of political progress. Trying to monitor and determine when these writings became seditious proved difficult and frustrating for the authorities. Finally, on April 7, 1977, a frustrated Chiang Ching-kuo instructed his security personnel that "from now on we must pay special attention to those who have special intentions. If someone writes a ten-page article, he is using nine and a half pages to conceal his crime in the other half-page." But the November 1977 elections shocked and angered Chiang Ching-kuo. The riot in Chungli city over alleged ballot tampering and the unprecedented display of voter support for *dangwai* politicians throughout the island worried him. On July 6, 1978, he issued these instructions: "Do not spend time on paper and meetings. Be determined to go out among the people and control them so that we can take aim at our enemies and defeat them."[59] Chiang believed that the Taiwan nationalist enemies in the ranks of the political opposition must be removed to avoid any crises on the home front. In 1980, after the government arrested, sentenced, and imprisoned the *dangwai* hard-core activist leaders, the opposition abandoned the tactic of the public rally. In that same year the *dangwai* politician Kang Ning-hsiang escorted a group of wives of imprisoned dissidents on an islandwide tour, and some of them even campaigned for the December 1 elections. Their very presence elicited a great outpouring of sympathy. In the next few years the *dangwai* published magazines and pressed for a public policy association that could facilitate islandwide discussions of politics. Although Chiang Ching-kuo and other KMT leaders saw a budding political party in the making, Chiang was becoming more confident that the KMT could have a dialogue with these politicians and even establish new rules to broaden democracy. By 1983 Chiang did not perceive these politicians as enemies; a West German journalist quoted him as saying, "The political opponents in our society serve to generate progress."[60] He was becoming conciliatory toward the *dangwai*. In early 1986, Chiang Ching-kuo finally agreed to KMT representatives' meeting with representatives of the opposition.

*The Intellectual View of Political Opposition*

Embedded in the thinking of the elite who wrote about and practiced politics, whether supporting the KMT or the opposition, were some crucial assumptions about knowledge and its implications for understanding and taking action.[61] According to one Chinese viewpoint, morality is a matter of knowledge and reason just as much as science is. Morality, then, is a matter of "clearly distinguishing between right and wrong" *(mingbian shifei)* and "seeking what is right by following the facts" *(shishi jiushi).*

Thus if I have successfully distinguished between right and wrong and you disagree with me, my view supersedes yours because it is based on a standard that exists independent of our wishes and inherently demands respect from both of us. The Chinese do not accept the relativism that Harold Bloom alludes to in American society. The Chinese concept of moral knowledge, at odds with the Western tradition of philosophical skepticism, has never been questioned in modern China. Therefore the Chinese belief in moral knowledge tends to define political conflict as a Manichaean struggle between good and evil.

This idea of objectively knowing right and wrong was intertwined with a vision of being heroically dedicated to this standard and fighting those opposed to it. The hero perceived himself as dealing with opponents who had failed to follow absolute moral standards and who inflicted "humiliating setbacks" *(cuozhe)* on the moral hero. One had to struggle *(fendou)* to oppose these bad people, endure "setbacks," and rededicate oneself to the absolute standards all men should respect. Connected with the morally dedicated ego, absolute moral standards, and the struggle against evil enemies was the theme of unifying the morally dedicated ego with "the people," who in turn were associated with the existence of a powerful historical "tide" supporting the ego's struggle against its enemies. This basic vision of oneness with the people and with cosmic-historical processes involved a complex, tradition-rooted set of ideas widely shared among the Chinese elite.[62]

The ideas of freedom and democracy were basic not only to the Kuomintang elite but to all Chinese politicians and were linked to the Manichaean vision of a heroic struggle against political enemies, no matter who they were. Thus the Chinese elite assumed that "freedom" meant not the freedom to define moral standards subjectively but freedom from oppressors' preventing one from pursuing those universal, absolute moral standards of which one had reliable knowledge. Morality also meant following civilizational virtues such as the repression of egoistic desires, manners, and love of learning. One

Chinese elite supporter of the KMT described the relationship between a sense of morality and the idea of freedom or democracy this way: "The ultimate goal mankind pursues is no more than a state of contentment, happiness, well-being, and the realization of various spiritual values, including ethics, morality, religious faith, and philosophical thought. Democracy is only one among the many means needed to reach the goals mentioned above."[63] For those elite fighting to realize these civilizational virtues, the political repression of opponents not only is compatible with democracy but is the only path to democracy. For this reason, then, KMT members endorsed banning the journals of the political opposition and arresting dissidents. Similarly, the opposition elite were determined to wage a relentless struggle, lasting a lifetime if needed, to bring about a more perfect democratic polity.

Yet the elite moderates of the *dangwai* and skeptical intellectual supporters of the Kuomintang also shared well-developed non-Manichaean values. These shared values originate in the tolerant eclecticism of the ancient historian Ci Maqian (145?–90? B.C.), who believed all schools of thought led to the truth, and in Confucius's emphasis on empathy *(Zhongshu eryi)*. In this context conflicts are resolved by "adopting a harmonious approach, forgiving each other" *(hexie huliang)*. The saying, "It depends on your point of view" *(jianren jianzhi)* is not used to cast doubt on general principles (whether one should avoid selfishness does not "depend on one's point of view"). Moreover, in 1960 Hu Shih had emphasized the need for *rongren* (tolerance) in dealing with the KMT. The elite also shared the Confucianist belief that leaders need "balancing and checking" *(zhiheng)* and should accept criticism.

KMT liberals, critical of their party's autocratic leadership, urged greater openness and tolerance within the party. As early as January 1955 the editors of *Ziyou zhongguo* argued that "KMT representatives should participate in the determination of party policies because, after promulgating government laws, it was necessary for them to participate in local councils where party policies were debated." In addition, they wanted "party discussions to be open" and appealed for greater "tolerance in the party" of a political opposition: "Democratic politics is the absolute respect of the individual's worth and dignity. A democratic political party not only tolerates opposition parties outside itself but tolerates opposing factions within."[64] Repeated appeals from the intellectual elite for political tolerance by the KMT leadership began appearing in journals published in Taiwan and overseas such as *Shibao zhoukan* (China times weekly) and *Mingbao* (Mingbao monthly) After the Kaohsiung incident, even right-leaning journals like *Zhonghua zazhi* avoided harsh attitudes toward the dissidents and their relatives, urging instead that they be treated with respect and emphasizing their lack of judgment rather than any evil proclivity.[65] Even among the opposition there was a tolerant attitude toward the KMT, as exemplified by the actions and statements of opposition politicians like Su Nan-cheng.

### The Amateur View of Political Opposition

Even at the grassroots level, people began tolerating political opposition. In 1972 a book by Gu Ying, titled *An Ordinary Citizen Speaks Out,* represented the thinking of many in Taiwanese cities who were above the laboring class but did not have enough money or education to be securely in the middle class. Gu's outlook combines an emphasis on modernization with tradition-oriented values, respect for the established structure of power and property, and pride in the nation's progress. Gu expresses anger about extremist intellectuals and students who challenge the KMT and threaten the prosperity he treasures, but he speaks with respect and admiration of the dissident professor Yin Hai-kuang. He supports the KMT but does not idealize it, viewing it as run by crafty old politicians *(laojian zhuhua)* more to be admired for their skill than their integrity. Gu adopts not a heroic stance but a humble one, mixing self-interest with service to the community, and he certainly sees no "tide" of events in history moving toward a transformation of society.

By 1977 ordinary citizens had experienced more than a quarter century of voting in local elections. They readily ignored the boastful candidates and approved of opposition candidates if they performed well in office. One observer of the 1977 elections noted that "the voting standards of the people have been elevated, and those candidates engaged in making accusations and scolding their rivals actually produce the opposite result of what they expect."[66] In the race for the Hsinchu city mayorship, the candidates who resorted to vituperative criticism of other candidates lost heavily.[67] This voter behavior was not lost on the opposition. One *dangwai* candidate, Hsu Hsin-liang, was especially pleased by voter support and expressed optimistism after the elections: "Taiwan's society is now most suitable to promote democracy."[68] He credited the government with increasing citizens' awareness: "The government has always been promoting democracy. But I always felt that the speed of democratic progress was too slow. Maybe it was because some people failed to understand that promoting democratic politics was more worthwhile than doing anything else. But democracy is Taiwan's greatest future contribution to China."[69] The public, having been taught in school that there could be no democracy without an opposition, took great pride in exercising their vote. One observer described voting behavior in the November 1977 elections as follows:

Five government elections were held throughout Taiwan yesterday on a fair, clear day with the weather beautiful and warm. The ordinary citizens were equipped with their newly acquired knowledge about democratic politics and local elections. They took pride in their right to vote and were very eager about doing so. This was the most unique event since local elections were held in the province twenty-seven years ago. ... People lined up to vote as early as 7:00 A.M. in most places. At 8:00 A.M. most shops in Taipei had closed for the day. Many workers went to cast their votes before going to work, while the elderly were helped to vote by their grandchildren. Housewives carried their grocery baskets to the voting booths. ... Everyone went to vote. So by noon yesterday, already half of the people had cast their ballots.[70]

Citizen participation and interest in local and supplementary local elections greatly increased during the 1970s. The Taiwanese flocked to the political rallies, and a very high proportion of registered voters actually voted. Voters knew the opposition candidates and understood what they stood for. At the same time, the media began focusing on the election process, eliciting the views of experts to interpret the elections for their readers. By the late 1970s and early 1980s, the media's views of these elections and the activities of the political opposition increasingly shaped public opinion and helped to define how a political opposition should behave.

## The Media's View of Political Opposition

Even in the regulated media of the period there was moderation and tolerance of criticism. The press endorsed local and supplementary elections even when opposition candidates defeated KMT candidates. This attitude surfaced after the November 19, 1977, elections, when more people than ever had voted and more non-KMT politicians had defeated KMT candidates. One journalist described the election's significance this way:

Ever since the elections became so ferociously competitive, I have been attending the most interesting election rallies in Taipei and Taoyuan. I have never before seen such extraordinary rallies. What interested me most was not so much the candidates' speeches but to observe the behavior of the people who participated in these political activities. Their overall passion toward politics demonstrated that the foundation of democratic politics already has been established at the very base of our society. The people now have a long-term view toward democratic politics, and their hope for democracy is no longer just a wish or an ideal. One cannot deny that this is the greatest achievement of the KMT, especially as we confront the totalitarian polity of mainland China. But now we are in the superior position because the mainland cannot attack us by using the same weapon of political democracy.[71]

The media also noted a maturity and enthusiasm among voters that it interpreted as representing a healthy democracy. Not only was political debate morally legitimate, but losing an election was not a disgrace. According to the press, the opposition politicians performed well because the "KMT party workers were selfless in this election, and some nonparty candidates even said it was an unusually fair, just, and open election."[72] Was the regulated press patronizing the opposition? Maybe. But why should the controlled press admit that the KMT had deliberately nominated fewer candidates so as to give more opportunity for the opposition candidates? Did the ruling party fear a loss of legitimacy if the opposition was totally beaten? As if lecturing to those victorious politicians, the press counseled with these words: "Immediately identify with the nation's ideology and its political mission of completing the establishment of the Three Principles of the People on Taiwan. From a political point of view, the opposition should have a spirit of being willing to agree to disagree."[73] By recognizing the inevitability of some KMT candidates' being defeated in the democratic election process, the regulated media now affirmed and applauded opposition victories.

This attitude prevailed in the critical December 6, 1980, election, which had been postponed since December 1978. This election was a milestone, with Taiwan's incipient democracy becoming legitimated in the eyes of the ruling elite. At stake were ninety-seven seats (23 percent) in the Legislative Yuan and seventy-six (6 percent) in the National Assembly. "Of the candidates to the Legislative Yuan, 55 percent were to be picked by the general electorate, 17 percent by women's groups and professional organizations such as farmers and workers, and 28 percent by the Overseas Chinese. Of candidates seeking seats in the National Assembly, 70 percent were to be chosen by the general electorate and 30 percent by women's and professional groups."[74]

The election campaign had begun on November 21, and on December 6, in poor weather, some 65 percent of the eligible voters trooped to the polls. The KMT won sixty-three of the seventy-six seats, or 82 percent, for the National Assembly while winning fifty-six of the ninety-seven of the seats, or 80 percent, in the Legislative Yuan. Nonparty candidates won a slim minority, but several obtained the top number of votes of any candidate running. The press gave the election front-page coverage and canvassed experts and academics for their views. Presidential adviser Tao Pai-chuan stated that "this election is a complete success; I am entirely in favor of the results."[75] Academic Yang Guoshu of National Taiwan University said, "This election showed that our voters have rapidly learned how to vote."[76] Another National Taiwan University professor declared: "The progress in this election indicated greater voter rationality, and the election process was smooth and orderly. The government and the mass media contributed considerable resources to this election."[77] The political scientist Hu Fu admitted: "I was very touched by the cool, rational, sincere behavior of the voters and candidates during this election. . . . Voters and candidates displayed great abilities, and I am optimistic about Taiwan's future democracy."[78] Although the KMT and the opposition could both claim victory, it seemed clear to the media, and certainly to the ruling elite, that as long as elections continued this way an opposition could be tolerated. The media also reviewed the opposition's role as positive and helping "to mend a social wound."[79] It hinted that in the past the opposition had erred in tilting toward Taiwanese nationalism and that in the future "it should take the road of a new political entity."[80] Democracy meant gradualism and never repeating the violence of the Kaohsiung incident.[81]

One political commentator cited three types of opposition politicians who had scored election victories.[82] The first type was represented by politicians like Kang Ning-hsiang, Jiang Deming, and Huang Huangxiong, who advocated a *dangwai* using moderate, constructive criticism of the ruling party. The second type, elected by virtue of their connections to local voters, were politicians in the Kaohsiung area like Yu Dengfa and his faction. The final type was composed of family members related to the political dissidents jailed after the Kaohsiung incident such as Xu Rongshu, Zhou Qingyu, and Huang Tianfu. These three types of opposition politicians had differentiated their political positions from those of their KMT opponents and won voters' support.

At the same time, three groups of nonparty politicians had lost and were not likely to succeed in future elections. Group one consisted of ideological-type candidates like Zhang Zhunnan and Liu Fengsong, who tried to sell voters the idea that the Kaohsiung incident was a heroic epic and that they intended to carry on that tradition of political heroism. Group two contained politicians like Su Zhiyang who referred to their prison sentences as badges of courage and stressed that "politics is the main purpose in our lives" and that "prison is our second hometown." A third group simply resorted to dramatic, shock-type rhetoric. Some candidates appeared on platforms with their lips sealed to illustrate the regime's repressiveness. Voters rejected all three groups because of their political extremism and negativism.

Voters seemed to support opposition politicians only if they behaved in a politically mature way, expressed their political standards clearly, and offered voters a practical message. Opposition politicians like Kang Ning-hsiang and his colleagues succeeded because they proposed the goal of establishing checks and balances in the polity. Opposition politicians who tried to play the "tragic hero" role and lived in the dark shadows of the February 28, 1947, uprising were rejected by voters. Finally, a political opposition that tilted toward Taiwanese nationalism seemed destructive and divisive. Any politician advocating this message stood little chance of taking part in Taiwan's embryonic political market process. As nonparty politicians experimented in different ways to appeal to voters, political candidates realized they had to have a relevant message for the voters. Voters' political opinion was becoming a new force. Voters and the elite would tolerate a political opposition as long as it played according to the rules of the Taiwan political game. For one political power broker, Chiang Ching-kuo, it was becoming readily apparent that these rules would have to be changed.

# PART II

# The Lifting of Martial Law

CHAPTER FIVE |

# Chiang Ching-kuo and the Decision to Democratize

While promoting limited democracy, the KMT gradually lost its sectlike qualities and became a huge, bureaucratic party. By spring 1969 the party's membership at the Tenth Party Congress was nearly one million, or eight times the membership of the Seventh Party Congress in October 1953.[1] The party had also acquired great wealth by investing in state-owned companies and purchasing assets in other enterprises. It was becoming one of the richest political parties in the world, and in spring 1994 it could boast assets totaling US$1.44 billion.[2] The party not only guided government policies but coordinated policy regarding culture and information, women's activities, youth affairs, and the overseas Chinese.[3] The party leadership still valued economic and social modernization without extending preferential privileges to any entrenched group and remained relatively free of corruption and cronyism.[4]

The 1970s were a turning point in Taiwan's economic and social development. In 1965 United States economic and military aid had ended, but the nation now possessed the sources of electrical power, cement, machine tools, chemicals, and production capabilities to sustain economic modernization. The economic policies of the 1950s had enabled households to save and finance the organization of small and medium-sized business firms. Export-oriented reforms in 1959–60 promoted market integration with the world economy. Domestic and foreign demand for goods and services increased, and enterprises responded by increasing the supply of goods and services.

Rapid market integration, intense market competition, and a more equal distribution of wealth narrowed income distribution between poor and wealthy households. Rural migration to the cities peaked, and employment increased in manufacturing and services while falling in agriculture.[5]

Party propagandists rebutted regime critics by praising Taiwan's economic miracle, social stability, and limited democracy. KMT leaders and members, except the party's liberal wing, avoided any discussion of accelerating democracy. But the 1970s brought new anxieties about the nation's security. Instead of communist control over the mainland weakening, its grip was firmer than ever. The nation's staunchest friend, the United States, began seeking détente with the PRC, hoping to use that communist giant to check the growing power of the Soviet Union in Asia and the Pacific. The party's paramount leader, Chiang Kai-shek, was aging (he passed away on April 5, 1975). Could his son Chiang Ching-kuo effectively pilot the ship of state and unify China under the banner of Sunist doctrine? How much longer could the mainlander-dominated KMT control the power structure?

By 1980 all outside appearances indicated that the KMT not only was fully entrenched in power but could not be challenged by any outside force to relinquish its power. The party's leaders seemed frozen by inertia and unwilling to deviate from its governing style and historical mission. With every annual celebration of the October 10, 1911, revolution that created the ROC, there was the same display of military and state power amid islandwide festivities. Political power had smoothly shifted to the hands of Chiang Kai-shek's son, Chiang Ching-kuo, who had assumed the KMT's chairmanship on April 28, 1975, and the presidency on March 21, 1978.

But the political opposition and the KMT ruling party were definitely on a collision course, and their political futures were inextricably entwined. Our narrative now shifts to Chiang Ching-kuo's rise to power and the extraordinary role he would play in Taiwan's democratization. Because Chiang Ching-kuo was a product of mainland China's society and culture, we must try to understand his early life, his career and rise to power in Taiwan, and his way of thinking about Taiwan's political future.

## Chiang Ching-kuo's Early Life

Born on March 18, 1910, in Fenghua county of Zhejiang province, Ching-kuo was the son of Chiang Kai-shek and his first wife, Madame Mao (Fuk-mei). His paternal grandmother raised him as a Buddhist, and like most children of elite families in Zhejiang and Jiangsu, he was sent to Shanghai for better schooling.[6]

According to Chen Jieru, Chiang Kai-shek's third wife, who met Ching-kuo in 1921, he was a "countrified schoolboy" and "well-behaved, quiet, and docile, but far too nervous and ill at ease."[7] "Looking at his slight, boyish figure, swarthy face, and small, darting eyes, [she] knew his silence was due not to rudeness or ignorance but to an extreme sense of shyness, bordering on fear."[8] Jieru urged her new husband to be more gentle toward his son. But Chiang Kai-shek was not persuaded: "Pamper him and make him lose his filial respect for me? Oh, no, no. A small boy must learn to be filial, responsible, and respectful. He must learn discipline. The worst thing for a boy is to be spoiled by his parents. I don't want Ching-kuo to be spoiled and suffer as I did. He must learn discipline."[9] Although Chiang Kai-shek rarely saw his son, when he did he was a stern taskmaster. Like most Chinese sons of strict fathers, Ching-kuo desperately sought his father's approval and grew up fearful of disappointing him. After primary school and high school in Shanghai, Ching-kuo went to a small private school for KMT leaders' children in Beijing organized and operated by the revolutionary classical scholar Wu Zhihui. There Ching-kuo became caught up in the euphoria over the successful Bolshevik revolution in Russia. The communist Li Dachao introduced him to many Russians, several of whom encouraged him to go to Moscow to study, an idea endorsed by his Chinese friends. On receiving a Russian scholarship, Ching-kuo impetuously accepted, eager to observe the Russian revolution firsthand. On October 19, 1925, Ching-kuo sailed from Shanghai on a Russian ship.

Chiang would remain in the Soviet Union until March 1937, when, with Faina Epatcheva Vahaleva, whom he had married in March 1935, and his son Alan, born in December 1935, he left Moscow after twelve years as a hostage of the Russian and Chinese Communists. Having conquered long bouts of depression, Chiang Ching-kuo later recalled that "in the course of human history, there are few persons who toiled so miserably as myself; that means suffering the misery of lacking not only material comfort but a healthy spiritual life as well."[10]

The twenty-eight-year-old Chiang Ching-kuo, now reconciled with his father and believing socialism was failing in the Soviet Union and would fail in China as well, went to Qikou in Zhejiang to read the Chinese classics and rediscover his Confucian roots. He decided to devote his life to opposing communism and not to allow it to beguile and destroy China's youth as it had done to him.

The father sent his son to southern Jiangxi as the deputy chief of the provincial security bureau, where he distinguished himself by hard work, honesty, and diligence. Following in the footsteps of his father, he now embraced Sun's

Three Principles of the People,[11] and he exhorted his subordinates to work hard and serve the people:

In order for the people of southern Jiangxi to have factories, food to eat, clothes to wear, and homes to live in, we are determined to carry out a three year plan for building a new southern Jiangsu based on the Three Principles of the People. We serve only for sacrificing our satisfactions to make it possible for the people to prosper and be happy, and we serve only that the people obtain happiness and a full life.[12]

Under Chiang Ching-kuo's leadership, twenty-four counties developed their industry and improved education and public health, winning him the acclaim of the local elite and popular praise.[13] In 1943 his father appointed him director of the Central Cadres School for the National Youth Corps.

In 1945 he entered the circle of officials surrounding his father and there used his Russian language skills and his understanding of the Soviets to further his country's well-being: he accompanied T. V. Soong to Moscow in early 1945 to negotiate a treaty with the USSR; he served as special foreign affairs commissioner under General Xiung Shihui in Manchuria, and from October 7, 1945, to December 1946 participated in negotiations with Soviet military commanders for the return of Manchuria to Nationalist rule; on December 30, 1945, he traveled to Moscow to meet with Joseph Stalin and V. M. Molotov to speed up the Soviet departure from Manchuria.[14] In 1948 Chiang Ching-kuo went to Shanghai with Wang Sheng and others to revive the city's deteriorating economy. Failing in that mission, he accompanied his father in 1949 to the southwest provinces to organize Nationalist defenses and the government's retreat to Taiwan. In December he and his father left Chengdu and flew to Taiwan.

## Life in Taiwan, 1949–1978

At forty years of age, Chiang Ching-kuo became director of the KMT's Taiwan headquarters and assumed two other duties: serving on the sixteen-person Committee to Rebuild the Party and directing the Political Affairs Bureau in the Ministry of Defense. He devoted his energies mainly to the Political Affairs Bureau, establishing a network of officers who conducted political indoctrination and surveillance of the military. He had begun his ascent to power.

Delegates to the Seventh Party Congress in October 1952 elected Chiang Ching-kuo to the new central committee, and later that same month the party assigned him to build the Chinese Youth Anticommunist National Salvation Corps (Jiuguotuan), which recruited the brightest, most ambitious students to its ranks. In September 1953 he visited the United States for the first time and met high officials including President Dwight Eisenhower. In 1954 he became deputy secretary-general of the National Defense Council. By occupying leading positions in the KMT, the military, and the youth corps, Chiang Ching-kuo had carved out a significant sphere of power and influence.

But his ascent to power was not entirely smooth. The former Taipei city mayor and Taiwan provincial governor in 1952, Wu Kuo-chen, recalls his confrontations with Chiang Ching-kuo, whom Wu charged with abusing his power and causing great harm to the Nationalist government. Wu even complained to President Chiang Kai-shek, but to no avail. Of Chiang Ching-kuo's many departments, his Special Affairs Department (*Ji yaoshi*), which overlapped with Governor Wu's Provincial Security Headquarters (*Baoan silingbu*), seems to have indiscriminately arrested many people and detained them for long periods without proper evidence. Wu argued that "we must have a criminal code to arrest people, and there ought to be legal procedures for searching households" so as to have a government based on law to win the people's respect.[15] Wu also charged that during the 1952 Keelung city elections Chiang Ching-kuo's special agents had arrested nine hundred citizens the evening before voting day. Wu intervened and had them released. Several then informed Wu that they had been arrested because they refused to comply with KMT orders to elect a designated KMT council member to head the Keelung city council.[16] Although he was a graduate of Princeton University and highly respected by American officials at that time, Wu could not persuade President Chiang to restrain his son's activities.[17]

The Wu-Chiang Ching-kuo confrontation did not last long. In 1953, when Wu and his wife were being driven to Sun Moon Lake in central Taiwan, they discovered that vital bolts connecting the car's wheels were missing, thus averting an accident that might have brought death on the narrow, mountainous road. Now convinced their lives were in danger, Wu and his wife left Taiwan for the United States, never to return.

General Sun Li-jen, a favorite of United States military commanders, also opposed giving Chiang Ching-kuo's Political Affairs officials greater power. On August 20, 1955, Chiang Ching-kuo placed Sun under house arrest on charges of collaborating with the Communists and organizing a coup. Other generals who disagreed with Chiang Ching-kuo "had a way of ending up as defendants in corruption cases, commandants of military schools, or ambassadors to foreign countries, rather than commanding troops at home."[18] There was never any question in the minds of party, military, or government leaders that Chiang Kai-shek was grooming his son to be his successor. Few dared oppose him.

As the paramount leader's son, Chiang Ching-kuo was respected and feared. Many were jealous of him or hoped to use him in their climb to power, but he had few friends he could trust and virtually no one to talk to or confide in.[19] In the course of his public career, he often had ruthlessly removed opponents who blocked his way. He was easily wounded by personal slights, and he did not forgive or forget. His manipulation of personnel appointments was notorious, and any person he passed over for a promotion or a better job knew his career was ruined. Chiang Ching-kuo carefully recruited brilliant technocrats and loyalists, but he avoided building any conspicuous power base for himself, and he denied that opportunity to others. Successfully projecting one's power and influence meant that others must respect and fear one rather than being envious and eager to compete. Chiang Ching-kuo knew how to establish that ethos of respect and fear and how to remove political rivals.

## Chiang Ching-kuo Takes Charge

On March 1, 1978, Premier Chiang Ching-kuo reported on the state of the nation to the Sixth National Assembly meeting in Taipei, which had convened to elect a new president. He denounced United States efforts to normalize diplomatic ties with the PRC and castigated the Taiwan independence movement (twin dangers that now threatened the ROC). On March 21, Chiang Ching-kuo received 98 percent of the votes cast by the National Assembly to become the sixth-term president; being also party chairman, he now held the power that had been entrusted to his father since 1950. Finally he had consolidated his power and replaced his father.

During the summer and into late fall of 1978, all signs pointed toward the United States' reestablishing ties with the PRC. The blow came on December 16 when the United States government announced that normalization with the PRC would take place on January 1, 1979. Chiang Ching-kuo immediately announced the postponement of the December 23 elections and placed the nation's armed forces on military alert. Some political opposition leaders expressed their support for the president but urged that elections be held soon:

We understand the government's anguish. The Republic of China exists even though U.S.-China relations have been established. That will not have any real bearing on our affairs. We declare that if elections are restored, it will confirm the government's opposition to a government based on lawlessness and its desire to preserve constitutional rule. We wholeheartedly affirm that the government with courage, can resist the temptation to embrace military rule while showing its determination to promote constitutional government and unify the entire nation in an environment of peace and democracy.[20]

On December 18, Deng Xiaoping spoke to Communist Party members in Beijing on how to develop a "united front" strategy toward Taiwan. Several days later Chiang Ching-kuo set up six committees to review possible policy changes regarding domestic and foreign affairs. On December 25, *dangwai* politicians in Taipei convened a National Affairs Conference. The political atmosphere was tense, and the future was uncertain.

The opposition, sensing the government's predicament, became bolder. On January 22, 1979, a number of *dangwai* held a public rally in Kaohsiung to protest the arrest of Yu Dengfa on charges of being a communist spy. On March 12 some forty *dangwai* met at Yao Chia-wen's law office in Taipei and publicly demanded that the ROC reenter the United Nations and seek a new international status. On May 26, *dangwai* politicians offered their support for the *dangwai* magistrate Hsu Hsin-liang, who just had been censured by the Control Yuan for participating in a public rally for Yu Dengfa. On May 31, Kang Ning-hsiang's new journal *Bashi niandai* (Eighties monthly), critical of the government, appeared. On June 1, *dangwai* politicians established a liaison unit for the Dangwai People's Representatives Office, an organization that tried to coordinate *dangwai* activities throughout the island. Opposition activities continued during the summer, and on August 16 the magazine *Meilidao* (Beautiful Formosa) appeared. On August 19 a group of Presbyterians who had long criticized the government began publishing a weekly magazine. On September 30 the Meilidao Kaohsiung Service Office was established. Then on October 2 some ten thousand persons held a brief political rally to protest the sentencing to prison of Yu Dengfa, then seventy-six years of age. Tensions continued to mount until on December 9 the Meilidao incident erupted in Kaohsiung (chapter 3). These activities made a great impression on Chiang Ching-kuo, who immediately ordered mass arrests of *dangwai* leaders in an effort to crush the Meilidao movement.

The government survived both the international and domestic crises, but that next year Chiang Ching-kuo began suffering from severe diabetes. He now became more reflective about his nation's future and his physical ability to serve as president. What were his feelings and ideas about Taiwan's future as the 1980s unfolded?

## Chiang Ching-kuo's Inner World and Character

Ever since his return from the Soviet Union, Chiang Ching-kuo had pursued a career determined by his father. Deeply venerating his father as the leader of Nationalist China, Chiang Ching-kuo was a driven man, consumed by his father's dream of unifying China and carrying out Sun Yat-sen's will by im-planting Sunist doctrine in Chinese society. He loved his father deeply and feared his disappointment. Evidence of their close relationship can be gleaned from the diary he kept of the momentous events in 1949 in which he recounts how his father expressed great concern for Chiang Ching-kuo's safety during the Sino-Japanese war and how father and son were depressed as Nationalist armies crumbled before the communist advance.

After both fled to Taiwan in 1949, the father became more dependent on the son, and their bonds of mutual respect and devotion grew stronger. In the 1950s, the father's unfulfilled dream gradually became the son's dream: to rebuild the KMT, transform Taiwan into a model society to defend against the Communists, and plan for the day when the ROC constitution again could govern the mainland under the Three Principles of the People.

Therefore, when Chiang Ching-kuo became chairman in April 1975, it was to lead an eighty-one-year-old revolutionary party for which tens of thou-sands members had given their lives. He now seized every opportunity to instruct the nation about its mission. On February 23, 1978, Chiang told the Social Democratic Party and Youth Party members (tolerated by the KMT as clients) and nonparty politicians that their mission was clear: "Today we only have one goal in our ongoing struggle: to oppose communism and to recover our country" (fangong fuguo).[21] But to achieve that goal, Chiang warned, ev-eryone had to guard against external and internal enemies. "Enemies are ev-erywhere, planning all kinds of ways to use any opportunity to divide us. Even some of our own people who have failed to understand the problems of our country have become the tools of the enemies, and they hold opposite ideas from our government" (CCKCC, 14:615). These enemies, the Communists, wanted to take over Taiwan, and the Taiwanese Nationalists, who dreamed of a new Taiwan republic. The only way to deal with them was to ruthlessly enforce martial law while promoting those socioeconomic and political devel-opments that could create the perfect moral society based on Sun's Three Principles of the People. There was no contradiction in Ching-kuo's mind between severely punishing those breaking the law and using state power to transform society.

Chiang Ching-kuo often had justified martial law while promoting democ-racy. When West German journalist Wulf Küsta of Der Spiegel asked Chiang on May 16, 1983, why the ROC had retained martial law for so long, Chiang replied as follows.

It is indeed difficult to be perfect in both ways. On the one hand, we face real threats and severe calamities, but on the other hand we hope that the Taiwanese people can maintain their security, peace, happiness, and prosperity. We also hope to preserve effective political functions for safeguarding our democracy and freedom. But the people of the ROC are determined to maintain their free, democratic life and will not change in that regard. This is the psychological basis for our anticommunism, and that will never alter. Moreover, in world history there has not been a single free, democratic state like the ROC that has for so long confronted an expanding communist totalitarianism. Because of this fact, the ROC relies on law and implements martial law to preserve our nation's security and to prevent the communists from exercising all sorts of subversive activities. (*CCKCC*, 15:63)

Blaming the communist threat to justify long term martial law, Chiang made no mention of the internal threat of Taiwanese nationalism. Therefore, when could a mature democracy ever become a reality? The official doctrine had always advocated the KMT's commitment to establishing democracy and the rule of law but had never set any timetable for a democratic transition. Chiang repeatedly endorsed that strategy and linked it to the grand mission of unifying China, as in his remarks on September 23, 1975, to the Legislative Yuan:

To save our country and our people, we must propagate the spirit of sharing a single boat. We truly believe Chiang Kai-shek's great hope to restore our Chinese culture, carry out the Three Principles of the People, vigorously practice democracy, and recovering the Chinese mainland. All of these tasks still remain to be accomplished. (*CCKCC*, 10:540)[22]

For these tasks to be fulfilled, Taiwan's legislators and people had to develop a spirit of honoring the law.

The era of rule by the individual has passed. Only by staying in the era of the rule of law can we establish a common standard of concepts and behavior to build a new Republic of China. The Executive Yuan submits many proposals to you to process so that they can become law. But the most important task we now face is how to educate the people to obey the law. I feel this task is more important than anything else. We no longer can depend on the power of the police or a single official. If all of us obey the law, our ideal of becoming a law-abiding nation will eventually be realized. (*CCKCC*, 10:453)

Democracy and the rule of law also depended on adherence to the constitution. According to Chiang, "The basic political principles of our nation are to be derived from the Chinese constitution, which now serves as the basis for our building a legal and democratic nation" (*CCKCC*, 10:547). But simply having a constitution did not mean that democracy and the rule of law would automatically be established. All citizens had to exercise patience and tolerance to comply with the rule of law and practice democracy before it became a reality. The KMT and all officials, therefore, must take their duties seriously, and politicians participating in local elections must play by the rules.

We carry a great spiritual burden in order to build truly democratic, lawful society. This obligation requires us to build a true, democratic, and lawful society. Therefore, when we promote democratic elections, we must have great patience and tolerance. Indeed, we can tolerate that which cannot be tolerated. But there is a limit to our tolerance, and everyone must realize that. (*CCKCC*, 10:547)

On February 27, 1976, Chiang informed the Legislative Yuan that he intended to expand the quota of national representatives to be elected in the supplementary elections.

If people ask me if it is now suitable to have the supplementary elections for national representatives, my view is the following. Our people are unanimous in wanting to have a democratic, constitutional political system. This goal is also our unswerving national mission. Whatever we must do on behalf of our constitution and the Temporary Provisions, we definitely must carry out in practice. (*CCKCC*, 10:558)

This breakthrough decision was welcomed by the political opposition and immediately implemented by the ruling party (*CCKCC*, 11:622).

After becoming president in March 1978, he reflected on how improving Taiwan's democracy could unify China. He finally conceived of the idea of peacefully transferring Taiwan's democratic experience to the mainland. On October 10, 1980, he expressed his new way of thinking at a commemoration of the founding of the Republic of China: "Because we are dedicated to recovering our country, we hold to these high ideals: the Three Principles of the People, democratic-constitutional politics, freedom, peace, and happiness. *We want to transmit this kind of lifestyle to mainland China and share this with all the people*" (*CCKCC*, 13:45).[23]

Chiang Ching-kuo now believed that if Taiwan could become the first Chinese democracy, that political development could somehow become a powerful moral force that would find its way to the mainland. Yet when opposition politicians like Kang Ning-hsiang in the Legislative Yuan pressed Chiang for the practical policies to achieve this grand political ideal, Chiang could only say: "We will never relinquish our goal—to carry out and put into practice a democratic political system" (*CCKCC*, 14:258). He reminded Kang that articulating political ideals and selecting the appropriate political means to achieve those ideals were difficult because of Taiwan's international isolation and social divisiveness. "Our ruling KMT, on the one hand, must be concerned about our political ideals and never forsake these; at the same time, we must take into account and really care about those real problems of our country—those domestic and international difficulties that still exist today" (*CCKCC*, 14:258). Chiang Ching-kuo then retreated to his old argument that Taiwan's democracy must gradually evolve:

Over the past thirty years we have been promoting democratic politics in Taiwan. Each year the conditions are different, but the progress exceeds that of the previous year. We need more time to promote democratic political rule. As long as our ruling party has the determination to promote democratic politics, we will continuously try to improve our promotion of democratic politics during this process. Of course, in the areas of law and public administration, we have not yet realized our ideals. We need to make more improvement; therefore, to learn more about democratic politics, the government and the people must learn the rules of politics; the elected council members also must learn about democratic politics. Democratic politics is the politics of the people's will. All of us must learn about political democracy.(*CCKCC,* 14:258)

Although he was unable to convince the opposition politicians that gradual democratization was Taiwan's ideal path, Chiang's plan for democratization was taking form. First, only Taiwan's successful democratization could "build a China of the people, for the people, and by the people" (*CCKCC,* 15:135). Second, under democracy, all competing political parties must obey the rule of law as embodied in the 1947 constitution. Finally, his party could win popular support and stay in power under democracy only if its members were perfect models of moral virtue (for examples, see *CCKCC,* 12:370–72, 416–20, 527–42). He repeatedly stressed that party members should cultivate these moral virtues, as illustrated in his remarks to the party's central committee in 1984:

We want to do too much, and in doing too much, it is hard to avoid making mistakes. But it does not matter if there are some mistakes, as long as we recognize our mistakes. Many mistakes that occur are merely the mistakes of two words: individual selfishness. I believe that we need not fear our enemies and even our difficulties. We only need fear that our comrades do not improve and work for the public good and become selfless [*dagong wusi*]. So long as we have the spirit to improve and work for the public good without selfishness, we will definitely achieve great successes. Today, I want to say something else: our comrades who work as cadres should definitely strive with all efforts to win the hearts of the people, go deep to the bottom of society, unite and cooperate with everyone, and with great diligence really serve the people. (*CCKCC,* 15:127)

Again, Chiang Ching-kuo repeated his oft-stated theme—that only by "offering oneself in a reverential way" to "sacrifice personal enjoyment but enjoy the act of sacrifice" and "renew one's dedication to the people" could the KMT win the people's support and build Taiwan's solid democracy. The KMT must be prepared to participate in elections and demonstrate their high moral virtues to the voters by behaving without selfishness. By serving the people in this way, Taiwan could build a perfect democracy.

Elections are a way of making democracy work, and the progress of democracy [on Taiwan] requires an infusion of elections. Our demand is for real democracy, not a false democracy. Our demand is for China to really form a democratic republic, as our leader Sun Yat-sen always hoped. In this fundamental way, the comrades of our party will participate in competitive elections. First of all, we want to go on record to make it clear that our purpose is to serve the people, and it is not to seek individual power and gain. *Our ideal is to offer ourselves with reverence [fengxian] and reverentially make sacrifices for the people, the party, and the nation. This is the basis for democracy.* (*CCKCC*, 20:44–45) [24]

Chiang Ching-kuo's Confucian-style democracy on Taiwan meant having his party members practice high moral principles. Failing that, the party could never hope to convince the people of the mainland that only the "Three Principles of the People can save China and that communism is dead for China." [25]

Behind this image of the Confucian sage leader was a calculating, ruthless, tough, and pragmatic politician who had adopted a lifestyle many have described as plain *(pingfan),* ordinary *(pingdan),* and down-to-earth *(pingshi).* [26] Most accounts of Chiang stress his sufferings in the Soviet Union [27] and glorify his life, [28] thus minimizing his weaknesses and exaggerating his strengths. Little reliable evidence exists to flesh out the real person, for few individuals were privy to Chiang Ching-kuo. Those who were, like his closest friend in Taiwan, James Wei (Wei Ching-meng), the owner-editor of the English paper *China News,* never recorded their conversations with him.

This much we know. Besides his passion for public service and work, he loved to walk among the people and talk to them at length. [29] On his tours of the island, he visited friends and ordinary people to discuss their lives. He loved to read, especially from Mencius, Sima Guang's *Zizhi tongjian* (Comprehensive mirror for aid in government) of the Sung period, and Zhang Shaofeng, who wrote short stories ruminating about life in graceful prose. As diabetes and failing eyesight crippled him in 1981, he was deprived of his two great hobbies. He imposed his simple, frugal lifestyle on officials, as during the 1972 oil crisis, when he refused to use an air conditioner in his office and insisted that air conditioners be turned off at ministerial meetings. His office, devoid of ornate furniture, scrolls, or vases, had a few pictures of his family, and his desk was perfectly clean.

As early as 1960, he voiced the desire for more Taiwanese in government. He also realized that Taiwan's future political development depended not on a "single, dominant political system" *(yiyuanhua)* but on political pluralism. But how to prepare his party for that outcome? If the Chinese Communist Party could survive the famine of 1959–60 and consolidate its power, surely the KMT could deepen its roots on Taiwan. He began encouraging his colleagues to seek out the best and brightest Taiwanese to promote in the party, government, and military. At the same time, he urged his officials to be courteous, practical, innovative, hard-working, open to ideas, friendly, simple in taste, and devoted to work. He was severe toward high officials but appreciative and kind toward lower-ranked officials *(sha guida, shang guixiao)*.[30]

He also knew when to lightly admonish and when to severely punish. Rather than arrest and prosecute non-KMT politicians involved in the November 19, 1977, Chungli incident, he insisted that Lee Huan, then head of the youth corps, take the responsibility and resign. But after the Kaohsiung incident, he dealt harshly with the *dangwai* activists. Chiang also blocked his subordinates from acquiring excessive power that might subvert his authority. He never allowed any official to hold two powerful positions as he had done (the youth corps and the military's political affairs office). He allowed Lee Huan to be director of the *Jiuguotuan* (National Salvation Corps) but assigned General Wang Sheng to manage political warfare *(Zhengzhan xitong)*. He also demoted General Wang Sheng in 1983, who then directed the KMT's powerful political personnel bureau *(Liushao kang bangongshi)*, to become the ROC's ambassador to Paraguay,[31] thus removing him from power. He could overlook the amorous adventures of his subordinates *(guaren yuji)*, including an official's having a mistress *(hongfen zhiji)*, but he could not tolerate malfeasance in office.[32] He gravitated toward men without ambition like Sun Yun-suan and Yu Kuo-hwa, and they became his premiers.

Chiang Ching-kuo ignored his critics when he believed he was right. In 1974 many party leaders and academics condemned as wasteful his plan of spending huge sums for ten great infrastructure projects. Chiang rebutted them, saying: "If we do not act today, tomorrow we will regret,"[33] and he pressed forward to complete them. Often exhausted and depressed, he complained that political life was "one of the dirtiest forms of human activity."[34] This lonely leader could confide only in James Wei, who always told him the truth, no matter how painful.[35] It was this isolated, powerful strong man—both feared and admired—who dared to turn Taiwan into a democracy.

## Chiang Ching-kuo's Plan of Action

After the December 1983 election, Chiang-kuo began to tolerate the opposition politicians as long as they behaved themselves and did not try to organize a political party. He still ordered the banning of seditious magazines but spared those politicians who did not plot to undermine the government.[36] He was now convinced that Taiwan's democracy was inevitable and part of a worldwide trend. Yet he worried how the opposition politicians might behave under democracy. If they adhered to the 1947 constitution and agreed to China's unification, then the dream he shared with previous KMT leaders could be realized. Their uncertain response was his greatest worry. By now Chiang Ching-kuo believed that building Taiwan's democracy—initiating reforms and lifting martial law—was the only way to vindicate the KMT's efforts on Taiwan and still unify China. Democratization had become the only worthwhile goal in his remaining years.

In 1984 the National Assembly easily elected him to a second-term presidency, and the party chairmanship was his. But if his health deteriorated further so that he could not finish his term and complete his political reforms, who would succeed him to do so?

Back in May 1978, Chiang had picked the technocrat Sun Yun-suan as his premier; the two soon became close friends.[37] They supported the highly criticized ten projects being subsidized by the state at great expense.[38] Both were pragmatic and innovative and favored gradual democratization. Chiang Ching-kuo increasingly relied on Sun to help him manage domestic and foreign affairs.

Born in Manchuria, Sun Yun-suan had graduated in 1934 from Harbin Engineering University's Department of Electrical Engineering. During World War II he managed electrical power plants in Gansu and Qinghua provinces. After fleeing to Taiwan in 1949, he became the chief engineer and general manager of Taiwan Electrical Power, the state's leading source of electrical energy, and upgraded its facilities. He later went to Nigeria as a consultant for that country's national electrical power plant. He increased that plant's electrical energy capabilities by more than 80 percent, and on his return to Taiwan, Chiang selected him to head the Economic Development Cooperation Commission. During the 1970s he became the prime mover of the nation's ten great infrastructure projects. Easygoing and humble in manner, Sun was greatly admired for "saying little but accomplishing much."[39] He quickly became a popular premier for his enlightened administrative style. One *dangwai* leader, the mainlander Fei Hsi-ping, praised him: "Given the legal authority he possesses, Premier Sun has performed most exemplary; regarding all the things he did not do, it was because they were impossible to accomplish."[40] Here was an official and KMT leader even the opposition respected.

In 1983 many thought that Chiang was preparing Sun to be his vice president and successor.[41] Sun gave the key graduation speech at the nation's military academy, which trained the officers for all three services. He met virtually every leading foreign dignitary who visited Taiwan and lectured at the KMT cadres' training institute in the Yangming Mountains. One political observer remarked that "from all of the high-ranking personnel shake-ups that have occurred, there is no doubt that Sun Yun-Suan will be the heir-designate to follow Chiang Ching-kuo. The next vice-president must be Sun Yun-suan."[42]

In political life, however, appearances are not always reality. Although Chiang appeared to be grooming Sun, as March 21, 1984, the election day for the seventh-term president, loomed closer, Chiang was still deliberating on his next running mate and successor, feeling that his grand plan was at stake. Martial law must be lifted. Rules regulating political opposition had to be changed. The new party leader would have to deal with challenges to Taiwan's security from the PRC and from Taiwanese nationalists trying to seize power. Chiang's successor, ideally, should be a Taiwanese who could command the respect of the party, especially its elder leaders, and also win the support of the elite and people. For these reasons, it was unlikely that any mainlander in the KMT had the youth, energy, or experience to be Chiang's running mate. Chiang also realized he first had to convince his party colleagues that a Tai-wanese was the ideal successor. Political power always had resided with the Chiang family, and the party elders, all mainlanders, preferred one of their own. As March 21, 1984, drew closer, rumors became rampant.[43] Many party elders expressed a preference for Sun Yun-suan as vice president.[44] Sun re-cords in his diary that "the rumor is, I will be nominated as vice president and that will bring me fame and fortune." Fearing the strain on his health, Sun wrote: "I have been exhausted these past few years, and we now need new people in this new era who can provide a balance and cultivate political re-form." In early February, Chiang Ching-kuo received Sun in his office and told him: "I will make you work hard for another six years."[45] Hearing these words, Sun realized that Chiang was handing him another six years of the premiership, not the vice presidency. If Sun was devastated by this news, he never revealed it. Chiang had already decided on his successor.

On February 14, 1984, Sun addressed the National Assembly that had con-vened to elect the seventh-term president and vice president. After his speech, *dangwai* assemblyperson An Ruilin rose and loudly said: "Sun only speaks; he takes no action. He does everything he should not do, and what he ought to do he does not do right."[46] Many applauded the critic's forthright remarks, but Sun was devastated. Ten days later, still humiliated and having forgotten to take his daily blood pressure pill, Sun raced to Chiang Kai-shek National Airport to meet his wife. He collapsed early the next day and on February 25 underwent surgery to remove a blood clot from his brain. Chiang Ching-kuo daily visited Sun, who was now paralyzed and confined to bed, to monitor his health.

If Sun was not be be Chiang's successor, then who was? The few competent, experienced KMT leaders capable of being vice president were in their early seventies. Good health was a crucial factor for the nation's leadership. Who could replace Chiang Ching-kuo should he suddenly die? That leader had to have many of Chiang's skills and, above all, be able to deal with the Taiwanese nationalism problem. One astute commentator put the succession issue in exactly those terms: "As to who can succeed Chiang Ching-kuo, that person must have the rectitude of his ideas, possess political wisdom and administrative ability, and have won support from within the party. In reality, the most delicate element for the successor is the problem of mainlanders versus Taiwanese" *(shengji wenti).*[47]

Throughout early February 1984, President Chiang consulted with close friends, advisers, and party elders but never revealed his innermost thoughts.[48] On February 14 the party's central committee held its second plenum to elect a new standing committee and nominate its presidential candidate. The next day, the central committee nominated Chairman Chiang as the presidential candidate. Chiang Ching-kuo then announced in an authoritarian tone: "I nominate Lee Teng-hui [as the vice presidential candidate]."[49] The nation's most powerful politicians applauded politely, but they were stunned by his choice, never dreaming that Chiang had such great trust and confidence in Lee Teng-hui. Why had Chiang nominated him?

Ching-kuo had known Lee, a Taiwanese and a former National Taiwan University professor, since the early 1970s, when he had selected him to advise the ROC government on how to grant development loans to several African states. The two men got along well, with Lee often accompanying Chiang on his island tours. Under Chiang's watchful eye, the KMT appointed Lee mayor of Taipei from 1978 to 1981, at which time he became governor of Taiwan province. To Chiang, Lee was an exemplary official: modest, hardworking, innovative, encouraging to others, without personal ambition and having no male heir to govern as a successor. Chiang particularly liked Lee's candid assessments and loyalty, ingrained by twenty years of Japanese acculturation and education. Thus, on March 16 the First National Assembly elected Chiang Ching-kuo as president; on March 17 it elected Lee Teng-hui as vice president. On May 20 Chiang and Lee were inaugurated at Chungshanlou Auditorium in the Yangming Mountains.

At the end of March 1984, then, the nation was ruled by a powerful but sick president and a sixty-year-old Taiwanese vice president in excellent health but without power. The ruling party still adhered to its mission of unifying China according to Sunist doctrine and never sharing power with an opposition whose leaders wanted immediate democracy and were sympathetic to Taiwanese nationalism. The opposition politicians were weak, divided, and without a party to mobilize voters. There seemed no compelling reason for the KMT to expand democracy or worry about sharing power with a new party.[50] Writing in the fall of 1986, one observer confirmed the existence in 1984 of a "democratic bottleneck" *(minzhu pingjing)*, in which the vector of political forces did not have sufficient momentum to diffuse political power.[51] He analyzed Taiwan's political conditions in 1984 as follows.

The KMT was a huge, powerful, bureaucratic party with extensive influence in the central and provincial government as well as in education, national defense, and cultural affairs. But the party's chairman and nation's president still had not identified a successor. How could this strongman guarantee that a power struggle would not erupt to split and destroy the party? How could constitutional law be revived and a pluralistic polity be created in these circumstances?

How was it possible to lift martial law and restore constitutional law? How was it possible to form a political democracy to accommodate a pluralistic society? Within the KMT different factions and views on these issues prevailed. For Chiang Ching-kuo, the pressure to change never came from outside but originated from the different ideological and interest groups within his own party. . . . As for Chiang, then, how did he exercise and manipulate power to work toward his objective? This was, indeed, a very difficult task.[52]

Finally, our commentator mused: "No doubt a breakthrough from that democratic bottleneck seemed possible, but the capability to do that only lay with the KMT and had nothing to do with the checking and balancing abilities of the *dangwai*."[53] The issue facing Chiang Ching-kuo in 1984 was, How did he intend to initiate democracy when conditions for democratization were still so difficult?

On March 21, 1984, the day after Vice President Lee's inauguration, President Chiang visited Lee's office and talked with him for some forty minutes. At that meeting the president revealed his intentions of carrying out major political reform and said that he expected his vice president to play an important role and to continue those efforts when the president was gone. To ensure political continuity, President Chiang insisted that his vice president learn about every sector of government. From that day on, Vice President Lee not only held hourly meetings each day with the president to discuss affairs of state but visited all branches of government to familiarize himself with key leaders and their problems.[54]

Chiang Ching-kuo had confided in his vice president but in no other top party leaders.[55] The authoritarian, disciplined party chairman Chiang Ching-kuo was the KMT's powerful, paramount leader. If there was to be political reform, only he could accomplish it. His public speeches continued to stress how Taiwan's democratic progress would stir hearts and minds in the PRC. For Chiang Ching-kuo, the issue now was when to enact political reform, which depended only on how quickly his vice president learned the art of governance.

## New Pressures on the Inhibited Political Center

Between 1980 and spring of 1986, the KMT-dominated political center came under increasing pressures from outside and from within. United States pressure on Taipei to improve human rights intensified. On May 31, 1984, Congressman Stephen Solarz, a Democrat, introduced a resolution in the House of Representatives that the ROC lift martial law and improve human rights by freeing political prisoners.[56] On June 23, Senator Claiborn Pell, a Republican, echoed these sentiments. Pressures from Washington never eased.

Similarly, the PRC leadership continued to pressure Taipei to negotiate and adopt its one-country, two-systems formula for unifying China. At the same time, Beijing successfully arranged with Washington to issue the August 1983 joint communiqué to limit United States arms sales to Taiwan.

The greatest pressure on the KMT, however, came from the relentless challenge of the *dangwai* to organize a political party. Before 1980 the *dangwai* had not yet projected a new identity that differentiated their candidates from other independent candidates in the local and supplementary elections. But in the 1980 and 1983 elections the percentage of popular votes for *dangwai* candidates rose from 8 percent to 16 percent, whereas the percentage of voters supporting independent candidates declined from 18 percent to 10 percent but only from 73 percent to 72 percent for KMT candidates.[57] Even so, *dangwai* candidates won only six seats in each of the Legislative Yuan elections of 1980 and 1983 (total Legislative Yuan seats in 1980 and 1983 were 406 and 368, respectively). In fact, some notable *dangwai* politicians like Kang Ning-hsiang, Chang Deming, Huang Huangxiong, and others had lost in the December 1983 elections. This setback forced the *dangwai* to admit that their message had not persuaded the voters. *Dangwai* candidates also had insufficient resources to campaign, and *dangwai* slogans had failed to inspire voters.[58]

But the *dangwai* quickly bounced back. In January 1984 a group of *dangwai* national representatives petitioned Minister Lin Yang-kang of the Ministry of Interior for permission to establish a Public Policy Study Association (Gong-

gong zhengci yanjiuhui). They were refused. On March 11, 1984, Fei Hsi-ping, Chen Shui-bian, and Lin Zhengshe (secretary) launched the Public Policy Association (Gongzhenghui, later expanded and renamed the Association the Association for Public Policy and Strategic Research), under whose auspices they sent a letter to Chiang Yen-shih, secretary-general of the KMT, urging a dialogue between the two sides and explaining that they did not want to oppose the KMT, only to monitor its activities.[59] Arguing that they were anti-communist and patriotic, they vehemently denied the charge made by KMT member Wu Poh-hsiung in the Legislative Yuan that they had behaved unlawfully.[60] When the KMT learned of this new political group, the leaders wanted to close it down; when they received this letter, however, their fears diminished. By September 2, the *dangwai* had obtained permission to have its Public Policy Association.[61] As one *dangwai* writer later explained it:

At first the KMT blocked our efforts to form a Public Policy Assocation. But rather than use martial law to force us to desist, the authorities referred to Article 53 of the Criminal Code. Later the government conceded that if we did not establish branch offices, the *dangwai* could have an association as long as we posted a sign marked Dangwai Liaison Office.[62]

The authorities preferred a compromise solution that maintained the status quo.

In fall 1984 the *dangwai* organized the Taiwan Human Rights Promotional Association and joined with the Dangwai Writers Alliance to celebrate Human Rights Day on December 10, 1984. Dangwai members then elected Yu Ching as director of the Dangwai Public Policy Association on April 26, 1985. In response to the Garrison Command's closing 90 percent of all *dangwai* magazines between January and April of that year, about forty *dangwai* demonstrated in front of the Taipei city council, the Legislative Yuan, and the Control Yuan on May 6.[63] On May 16, fourteen *dangwai* provincial government councilpersons (about one-fifth of the provincial government council) threatened to resign if the government did not enforce its laws governing the provincial government. On August 23 the Dangwai Public Policy Association held a large meeting, followed on September 1 by elections of officers and the formation of a special committee to raise funds. In that same month, *dangwai* activists held meetings to select candidates for the November 1985 elections of the Taiwan provincial assembly, Taipei and Kaohsiung city councils, and district magistrates. In these elections for 191 candidates, the KMT won 146 seats (76 percent) and the *dangwai* won 34 (18 percent), with independents taking the rest. The *dangwai* increased their seats on the Kaohsiung city council from six to ten, and on the Taipei city council from eight to twelve. Through their courage, enterprise, and zeal, the *dangwai* had now become a new force in Taiwan's political life.

In 1985 political prisoners smuggled messages to relatives that appeared in *dangwai* magazines. Writer and activist Huang Hua was now forty-seven and had spent virtually all his life in prison since he was twenty-five. Incarcerated in a military prison on Green Island, Huang began fasting about mid-1985 by refusing to consume more than five hundred cubic centimeters of milk each day. He reportedly told some *dangwai* comrades that "if no party is formed and the Meilidao political prisoners are not released within a year, I will never eat or drink again." [64] In that same prison was Shih Ming-Teh, who began fasting on April 1, 1985. The authorities moved Shih to a military hospital in Taipei for close observation. His weight declined from sixty-three to forty-six kilograms, and he was barely lucid. By July 1 rumors circulated that he was near death, had written a will, and had implored *dangwai* comrades "to form a democratic party as quickly as possible" *(liji zu minzhudang)*. [65]

In this new political climate, *dangwai* members redoubled their efforts to develop a political party. On December 26, 1985, members of the Dangwai Public Policy Association decided on procedures to establish branch offices in other cities. As they witnessed new scandals overwhelming the KMT in late 1984 and 1985, they became bolder. On February 10, 1986, that same association agreed on specific measures to establish branch offices in the central and southern districts but did not take immediate action. Then on March 10, 1986, the association's board of directors decided to set up two branch offices in Kaohsiung. The *dangwai* were more determined than ever to establish their political party.

Another pressure on the inhibited political center was that of Western liberal thought, which had been crystallizing for more than a decade in the minds of many Chinese elite and can be summarized as follows. Most advanced countries in the twentieth century had moved or were moving inexorably toward democracy. A democratic political system was anchored to a constitution that the people and their political parties obeyed. That constitution consisted of rules defining how the people elected their leaders and how their political institutions functioned. The people elected their leaders and representatives through political parties. There were constitutional procedures by which the people could recall and reelect their representatives and leaders, even impeaching them for inappropriate behavior. Political democracy also required the open, fair competition of political parties and a free press. A free press informed the public, evaluated the performance of leaders and representatives, and encouraged critical discussion of affairs relevant to the people's concerns and interests.

These ideas, current in Taiwan's embryonic ideological marketplace of the 1960s and 1970s, were now being widely reflected in the writings of liberal academics like Tao Pai-chuan, a former member of the Control Yuan and a national policy adviser to the president since 1977. Throughout the 1980s, Chiang Ching-kuo often asked Tao for advice. Before 1982, Tao argued that the ROC should adopt more elements of the Western liberal-democratic system,[66] conceding that the KMT had developed a solid, positive political foundation with social stability but warning that if a "dominant party" ruled too long, political conditions would likely worsen.

I believe that Taiwan's democratic future relies on the KMT, which is a single-party monopoly [*yidang duda*]. So far, political and social stability has been good. The KMT does not dominate so harshly as not to allow freedom. But if the present polity continues in its present form for too long, then there will be a misuse of party power; public resources will be used by selfish officials; new political energy cannot be generated; the polity will be moving against the world tide; and bad political habits will be cultivated, and there cannot be any progress. Therefore, we must find new ways for the KMT to develop.[67]

By 1982 Tao believed that Taiwan's polity had reached an impasse, the only way out being free, fair political elections that would select high-quality representatives of the people. In this way, political party competition could check and balance the various administrative organs of the state.[68] Therefore Tao advocated that the KMT begin to promote "real political party politics" and called for a change in the "single-party monopoly" style of political rule. In 1983 Tao went so far as to express hope that the *dangwai* politicians could form a political organization good enough to compete with the KMT.[69]

As discussion intensified among the KMT-backed elite on how to develop democracy in Taiwan, it was obvious to many of them that the ROC polity did not compare favorably with the standards of an ideal democratic polity. KMT spokespersons had no difficulty defending the party's accomplishments—achieving economic development and maintaining social stability—but they could not cite evidence that the polity conformed to the standards of liberal democracy. Moreover, no major KMT leader could rebut the argument that a democracy could effectively replace the single-party ruled polity.[70]

If the KMT failed to rebut the arguments calling for political pluralism and a free press, had those arguments penetrated the top KMT leadership? Leaders like Chiang Ching-kuo and those close to him certainly knew of such political views,[71] but they endorsed the official theory of gradual democratization and

Chiang Ching-kuo's Chinese-style democracy in which only the virtuous elite could represent the people and govern them. They were skeptical whether a larger, critical voice in the polity would improve policy making. Moreover, they did not fear that the people would demand that KMT undertake political reforms it opposed. Official surveys of public opinion throughout the 1980s revealed a remarkably high degree of public support and goodwill toward the ROC government.[72]

Nor were Chiang Ching-kuo and his colleagues nervous about what the *dangwai* politicians might do if democratic reform was not forthcoming. The state's power to crush political opposition was enormous. The government's Security Bureau had informants in the ranks of the *dangwai* and the overseas Taiwan independence movement and thus knew their intentions and activities, which Chiang Ching-kuo followed through weekly reports submitted to him by government intelligence units.[73] Nevertheless, the new liberal thinking about democracy was a force that Chiang Ching-kuo understood, although at moments he was skeptical of its virtues. In late April 1986, when Tao Pai-chuan privately conferred with Chiang Ching-kuo, Chiang told him he was not optimistic that political party competition would be good for ROC governance.[74]

In early 1986 the liberal elite continued their discussion forums to urge party reforms for democratization. At a seminar held on March 28, 1986, one day before the KMT Third Plenum, Yuan Songxi stated, "As for the ruling party, its most serious predicament is our divided country."[75] Recognizing that Taiwan's unique security conditions had required martial law, Yuan then added, "After the Third Plenum, I hope the ruling party will recognize that the people's attitude is to expect some new change." Yuan also hoped that "in personnel appointments, the government will select new people with new ideas and policies."

A leading academic, Yang Guoshu, then urged the ruling party to accelerate democratization by adopting two new directions of change:

First, the party must carry out democratization. Second, the party must gradually develop pluralism. In the past, the Third Plenum meetings always had operated on the basis of doing things from the top to the bottom of the party, and its elections have followed that same pattern. In this way, the party system became more rigid and decayed. Party members are also scattered everywhere, and they can represent the needs of the people. This would make our party more pluralistic and represent different interest groups.[76]

Hu Fu, a constitutional law expert at National Taiwan University, offered this observation: "A society must have a basic consensus at the highest level, and that means on the constitution."[77] He went on to say that the ruling party was forever talking about the Three Principles of the People unifying China; but, he asked, what were the principles to unify groups inside and outside the KMT? Only the constitution could provide the basis for that unity. According to Hu, the "Three Principles of the People must be carried out in the real spirit of the constitution, and if we cannot do that well in Taiwan, we cannot do it on the mainland."

Although aware of the growing demands for democracy from both the *dangwai* and the liberal elements in his party, Chiang had not been able to put his plan for political reform into action because of two unexpected crises that beset the KMT and government in late 1984 and 1985.

On October 15, 1984, the journalist Jiang Nan, author of a soon-to-be-published, supposedly critical, biography of Chiang Ching-kuo, was slain in his garage in Daly City, California, just south of San Francisco. A flood of unfavorable accounts in the United States press criticized the ROC security personnel's surveillance and harassment of Chinese living in the United States. The Federal Bureau of Investigation entered the case, and ROC officials began cooperating in the investigation. On February 27, 1985, ROC authorities arrested three leaders of the underworld Bamboo Gang and brought them to trial; on March 26, 1985, ROC police arrested three Intelligence Bureau officials for ordering the Bamboo Gang members to arrange the killing. On April 19 a military court sentenced the chief of the National Defense Intelligence Bureau, Wang Xiling, to life imprisonment and deputy bureau head Hu Yimei and the deputy of the bureau's Third Section, Chen Chumen, to prison terms of two and a half years.[78] Many critics of the ROC still believed that officials higher up the chain of command, including Chiang Chiang-kuo, had ordered the murder. This scandal's corrosive effects on public and party morale absorbed all Chiang's energy, and he could not consider political reform. Then on February 9, 1985, just as Chiang and the party were recovering from the Jiang Nan scandal, the Shixin (Tenth Credit) cooperative association went bankrupt and countless individuals lost their savings. This new scandal implicated KMT and government officials and revealed the party's unsavory ties to big business.

The scandal had its roots in the 1950s, when Zai Wanzhun and his two brothers, Wanlin and Wanzai, founded the Cathay business empire.[79] By late 1977, their group had twenty-four member firms claiming total assets of close to US$1 billion. Zai used the Shixin to pay high interest for saving deposits and then directed those savings to Cathay's various business ventures, including several highly lucrative urban real estate deals. This strategy expanded

Cathay's wealth, but after another brother, Zai Zhenshou, took over Shixin's management, he recklessly expanded Shixin's loans, which by early 1985 could no longer be paid off because reserves were exhausted. To make matters worse, a number of KMT members who had invested in Shixin and were worried about financial losses tried to influence the Legislative Yuan to revise the Banking Law. That action "would have forced the Ministry of Finance to grant the Investment Trust Companies greater access to short-term funds and broader investment privileges" and possibly have saved the cooperative from ruin.[80] But Shixin went bankrupt before the Legislative Yuan took any action. Therefore, throughout 1985 the party and government tried to clean up this mess and other troubles, so that Chiang still could not consider political reform.[81]

## Chiang Ching-kuo Finally Initiates Political Reform

Chiang Ching-kuo finally acted at the KMT's Third Plenum, March 29–31, 1986. He first affirmed his party's mission and desire for democracy.[82]

The Three Principles of the People definitely can be practiced and carried out in all of China. Taiwan serves as a base to use these principles as the blueprint for building a lasting peace for China and establishing the foundations for Nationalism [minzu], People's Rights [minchuan], and People's Livelihood [minsheng]. Our party advocates practicing "the spirit of making our present world a perfect moral order" [tianxia weigong] and to carry our ROC constitution to the mainland to initiate democratic, constitutional government: do away with dictatorship and class warfare; really implement a way for our people to determine their destiny; return political power to the people; and make them entirely equal before the law.[83]

With the Shixin scandal in mind, Chiang Ching-kuo described how the party had allowed free enterprise to flourish and had protected personal freedoms but that owners and producers had a responsibility to manage their resources to improve all citizens' quality of life. He strongly asserted that social harmony had to be enhanced and special privileges eliminated.

On March 31 the party elected a new thirty-one-person standing committee as its top leaders. Of this number, twenty-seven were former standing committee members and four were new. Of the thirty-one, fourteen were Taiwanese, representing an increase of Taiwanization from 39 percent to 45 percent.[84] With this new leadership in place, Chiang immediately called in Secretary-General Mah Soo-lay and instructed him to establish a twelve-person committee to form six subcommittees for studying how the party should initiate political reforms.[85] On April 9, the twelve-person committee was named.[86] Chiang Ching-kuo had finally acted on his plan for democratization. Unforeseen obstacles in 1984–85 had delayed his plan's implementation. But in late March 1986 Chiang Ching-kuo alone decided the time had come to launch democratization.[87]

# Political Conflict and Lifting Martial Law

On March 15, 1986, at the Legislative Yuan, opposition legislator Fei Hsi-ping asked Premier Yu Kuo-hwa, "As there is no war, why do we still have martial law in Taiwan?" (Fei, born in 1916 in southern Manchuria, had graduated from National Peking University. An ardent patriot, he became a guerrilla leader in the war with Japan. After coming to Taiwan, he served in the KMT but left it in the 1970s to join those opposition politicians demanding rapid democratization.)[1] The premier replied: "On the surface, one can say there is no war, but the PRC has never renounced the use of force against our nation, so there always exists the possibility of war. Therefore, we have martial law to protect the constitution. We are trying to promote democracy and the ideology of democracy and in this way to uphold the constitution in our daily life."[2] Thus the struggle over martial law continued. The regime's top officials defended it; their critics denounced it and the institutions that supported it.

To those living in Taiwan during 1986, martial law never seemed any problem because of the island's unprecedented prosperity and social tranquility. Foreign luxury cars jammed the streets of the main cities. High-rise apartments and office buildings clogged each city's central district. Modern department stores bulged with consumer goods, and boutiques everywhere displayed fashions from Japan, America, and Europe. Middle-class prosperity, not the wealth of a few, drove the booming economy. Having a per capita GNP of US$3,992 compared with only US$964 in 1975, the population now saved 38 percent of GNP compared with 26 percent in 1975.[3] Manufacturing and services absorbed 83 percent of the workforce, and only 17 percent worked in farming, fishing, and forestry compared with 30 percent in 1975. The average household in 1986 spent only 37 percent of its annual expenditures on food, beverages, and tobacco compared with 47 percent in 1975. Interest rates on secured loans had declined from 13 percent in 1975 to 9 percent in 1986. Taiwan's markets had slowly opened to more imports because of American pressures and the appreciating exchange rate of NT$38 per United States dollar in 1975 to NT$35 per United States dollar.

Popular demonstrations were commonplace in South Korea and the Philippines in the mid-1980s, but relatively few had yet occurred in Taiwan. Urban crime slowly increased but was still rare compared with elsewhere in the West. Private associations already championed the interests of the rice farmers, the handicapped, veterans, religious groups, and environmentalists. In this new civil society, these groups distributed their information to the public and to officials. The supply of new information had skyrocketed. More people traveled abroad, and foreign tourists flocked to Taiwan. The island boasted a spanking new international airport, a north-south superhighway, and new harbors and storage facilities.

Thus, when the political opposition publicly demanded the government lift martial law so that real democracy could begin, the argument by Premier Yu Kuo-hwa did not seem persuasive. Certainly a prosperous, socially tranquil society like Taiwan did not need martial law. Its citizens supported their government and its policies and obeyed its laws. People were opposed to communism and supported Sunist ideology. The opposition believed the time had come for martial law to be lifted and political parties to form to check and balance the KMT. According to the opposition, the government was not about to lift martial law soon, so it would be necessary to form a political party even if that meant risking arrest and imprisonment.

The political opposition included radicals and moderates who shared an intense dislike of the KMT, a strong desire to have a political party compete with the KMT for power, and a fervent hope that Taiwan could adopt a Western-style democracy. As young people joined the opposition, they insisted on a new style of political struggle, the public street demonstration. The period between the spring of 1986 and July 15, 1987, when martial law was lifted, was tense and uncertain. Had both sides not respected the law and kept their extremists in check, the transition to democracy might have been derailed.

## The First Opposition Party

While the KMT leadership established committees to study how the "inhibited" political center could be peacefully transformed into a "subordinated" center according to the 1947 constitution, the *dangwai* opposition leaders discussed among themselves how a new party could be formed. They were uplifted in early May 1986 to learn that Hsu Hsin-liang, Xie Congming, Lin Shuichuan, and others had set up the Taiwan Democratic Party in San Francisco on May 1.[4] Through several international telephone conversations, Hsu and Xie told the *dangwai* leaders that they wanted their party to be the bridgehead for launching an opposition party in Taiwan before the year's end. All these activists were on the government's list of criminals to be prosecuted for violating martial law *(tongjifa)*, but they told their comrades they were willing to return to Taiwan and participate in the launching of a new party even if it meant their arrest and imprisonment.[5] At one point in the conversations Xie Congming said, "We cannot have democracy without having an opposition party."

On May 12 an editorial in Kang Ning-hsiang's magazine *Bashi niandai* (Eighties monthly) announced that Zheng Nanrong and other *dangwai* had drawn up a declaration of intent to challenge the *dangwai* to establish a political party for achieving five objectives: establish direct presidential election, reelect all national representatives, abolish martial law, release all political prisoners, and eliminate all restrictions preventing political parties from competing and a free press from forming.[6] The *dangwai* were now putting the KMT on notice that it was only a matter of time before they would act to try to form a political party.

On May 7, at a weekly KMT Standing Committee meeting, Chiang Ching-kuo stressed the need for the party "to have contacts with all elite in society and to maintain social harmony."[7] Aware of the *dangwai*'s plans, Chiang explained that the time had come to make contact with the political opposition and have discussions. He then assembled a delegation of party liberals comprising Hu Fu, Yang Guoshu, Li Hongxi, and Tao Pai-chuan, led by conservative legislator Liang Su-jung, to meet with the *dangwai* on May 10, 1986. Chiang instructed them to negotiate with a "white face" (politely setting forth the KMT point of view) and to reach an agreement that would include the *dangwai*'s not forming a party.[8] Delegations from both sides met in a restaurant, had lunch, and talked for many hours. Liang urged the *dangwai* not to establish a party and to respect the ROC constitution. Both sides agreed that martial law should be abolished, along with the Temporary Provisions, but the *dangwai* delegates would not agree to the Public Policy Association's registering with the police, insisting that their association be accepted just like the KMT.[9] Both groups stated that their differences should be peacefully resolved and that further discussions should be held; yet they had reached an impasse, which two later meetings, on May 24 and June 7, failed to resolve.

Meanwhile, on May 10, 1986, Chen Shui-bian and several young *dangwai* members established a Taipei branch of the Public Policy Association; on that same day the Garrison Command closed Kang's magazine, *Bashi niandai*. On May 19 some two hundred *dangwai*, wearing their symbolic green ribbons and shouting slogans, assembled at Taipei's Dragon Mountain Temple (Lung Shanshih) for a march to the president's office, several miles away, but they were surrounded by more than a thousand police. After some twelve hours of negotiations and tense verbal exchanges, the group peacefully disbanded.[10] For the first time in Taipei, there was a new pattern of political confrontation—*dangwai* politicians eagerly took to the streets to demonstrate their cause and challenged the authorities to stop them. It would be repeated many times in late 1986 and continue through 1987 and 1988. Passionate opposition politicians like Chen Shui-bian called for a new spirit of "strong resistance" *(kangyi)* and publicly exclaimed, "We are not afraid to die; we can even be beaten to death; and we will never retreat."[11]

The government responded by closing down *Penglai* magazine and arresting Chen Shui-bian and several others, arraigning them and sentencing them to eight months in prison. *Dangwai* members retaliated by holding a "farewell for the prisoners" at which some ten thousand supporters contributed money to their legal defense. The *dangwai* now decided to break off their meetings with the ruling party.[12] Then on June 13, 1986, Kang and Lin Zhenzhe formed a Taipei branch of the Public Policy Association and announced a five-year timetable for democratizing Taiwan. Their schedule called for allowing new parties to compete in 1987, lifting martial law in 1988, reforming the constitution in 1989, completing political reform and holding direct elections for a president in 1990, and resolving Taiwan's international problems in 1991. On August 10 a large group of *dangwai* members met at the Jinghua Middle School to discuss establishing an organization that would promote democracy; some participants openly declared that they wanted to form a political party. Kang exhorted the crowd to organize a party this year or miss a great opportunity; he concluded that he was willing to go to prison to create such a party.[13] On September 3, 1986, after a Taipei court sentenced Lin Zhenzhe to eighteen months in prison on a libel charge, Kang Ning-hsiang and other *dangwai* immediately organized a march to the Office of the President; in other cities, the *dangwai* held similar protest demonstrations.[14]

By September, then, the *dangwai* leaders were convinced they must form a party before the year's end. On September 19 a small group of *dangwai* leaders convened and decided to form a committee led by Fei Hsi-ping and made up of Yu Ching, Xie Changting, Yan Xifu, Huang Ershuang, Fu Zheng, and You Xikung to study what kind of name the party should adopt and what its charter and articles should be.[15] After the committee had met several times, it was expanded to include a sixteen-person group that met on September 27, which finally agreed on the party's name, charter, and articles. They vowed that "in order to promote the democratic process and to organize a new party, we will widely solicit those party organizers willing to create such a new party and to establish a committee of party representatives."[16] On the next day, at a meeting attended by about 130 *dangwai* representatives, the group discussed the procedures and the timing to form their party. About 5:00 P.M., Ju Gau-jeng suddenly proposed that "all of the *dangwai* candidates who plan to run in the year-end elections for the Legislative Yuan and the National Assembly will be on the front line, so why don't we organize our new party right now? If we are persecuted, our candidates can refuse to participate in the year-end elections. Such an action of protest will elicit great public sympathy, and the KMT will be the target of great international pressure, especially from the United States."[17] Everyone warmly endorsed Ju's proposal. They agreed on the party name of the Democratic Progressive Party (DPP). That same evening, at a press conference at the Grand Hotel, Yu Ching and Xie Changting, spoke to the press on behalf of the new party. Xie said, "Our party is an open-style, democratic party; it has nothing to do with the overseas democratic party that recently formed. It is open to everyone who shares our views. We will not refer to China or Taiwan in order to avoid the Taiwan-China problem."[18] An opposition party had now formed.

The government-regulated press immediately criticized the action. One newspaper conducted an opinion poll in which almost half of those interviewed opposed this political development; an astonishing 46 percent expressed no opinion on the matter, suggesting enormous political ignorance, apathy, or fear.[19] Another newspaper, pointing out that the new party had not stated its position on Taiwan independence, worried that this event might cause the PRC to use force against Taiwan, which would have terrible consequences for the nation.[20] On October 1 Zhang Jianbang, a Taipei city council member, bitterly denounced the new party: "Normally, if a party has formed, there is a clear plan, but this new party proposes nothing clear and concrete. We are now studying six key political issues and trying to have a dialogue with these people. Yet they still go ahead and form their party. This merely shows their unwillingness to cooperate."[21] The government still took no action. Nor did the new party adopt an aggressive stance. Its top leaders feared arrest at any minute.

On September 30 Vice President Lee Teng-hui talked with President Chiang Ching-kuo about the recent formation of the DPP; Lee recorded the following in his daily journal:

I reported to Chiang Ching-kuo that the *dangwai*'s Public Policy Association had decided to establish a political party at the Grand Hotel. I said that this behavior does not fulfill the requirement of being illegal. Therefore, for the time being, I recommend we should just observe their behavior.

Chiang Ching-kuo then replied, "At this time it is not good to resort to anger and recklessly take aggressive action that might cause great disturbances in society. We should try to adopt a calm attitude and consider the nation's stability and the people's security. Taking these as our goals, we should try to resolve this matter."[22]

Several days later Vice President Lee replaced Yen Chia-kan, who was ill, as chair of the political reform committee established by Chiang Ching-kuo in March 1986. The vice president spoke to the committee as follows: "Mr. Yen is now in the hospital. Therefore, I am chairing this meeting. As for the issue of [DPP] party organization, as long as it does not violate our national strategy and the rules of our constitution, we can move ahead in our secret discussions as far as the issue of party organization is concerned."[23] In effect, the KMT leadership pressed forward in its task to determine how to reform the polity to facilitate democratization.

Chiang Ching-kuo had been instructing the KMT and the relevant government organizations to take no retaliatory action against the DPP. Fully comprehending the president's tolerance of an opposition party, Vice President Lee wrote the following in his journal: "I think that the president is indeed a great and outstanding leader. He repeatedly has emphasized the basic direction for how the party should pursue democracy, and this never has changed simply because objective circumstances have changed. His principle always should be followed."[24] Realizing now that the government intended to take no action to arrest them, the new party's organizers continued their daily meetings. On November 16, DPP organizers announced their first elected chairman, a lawyer named Jiang Pengjian. The sixth of ten children of a Taipei shoemaker, Jiang was educated and trained in law at National Taiwan University and had defended Lin Yixiong and others who had been involved in the

1979 Kaohsiung incident. In 1983, after being elected to the Legislative Yuan, he described himself as "a stupid bird who flies first." On being elected the DPP's first chairman, Jiang declared, "I hope the new party will have openness and tolerance and serve as a real democratic party for the people." Jiang was optimistic that the new party "could garner support because of its high moral standards and its willingness to act."[25]

What were the goals of the DPP, and how was this new party to be organized? Party representatives throughout the island did not meet again until April 16–18, 1988, in Kaohsiung to draft a party charter consisting of eleven chapters and thirty-three articles outlining membership rules, committee responsibilities, party organization, and disciplinary action for violating rules.[26] Delegates heatedly debated "whether party members had the right to advocate Taiwan independence" and whether a statement to that effect should be included in the party charter.[27] On April 17 they finally agreed that "Taiwan independence, as a principle, will not be inserted in the DPP charter."[28]

The party platform consisted of five "basic suggestions" and ten "concrete suggestions." In brief, the party stood for democracy and freedom and criticized the government for not abiding by its constitution and for violating human liberty and rights over the past thirty-five years.[29] The party advocated a polity having the following features: a strong parliament, "a sound system for division of power for checks and balances," healthy party politics, freedom of assembly, freedom of the press, the rule of law, a "neutral and responsible administrative system," and the means to "supervise the government's emergency decrees."[30] The platform also presented detailed discussions for how the party would strive to improve the people's welfare, develop the educational system, allow Taiwan's people to determine the future of Taiwan, develop diplomatic ties with other nations, build peaceful relations with China, strengthen freedom and human rights, reduce the size of the armed forces without diminishing the nation's defense capabilities, promote bilingual education, enhance the study of Taiwan's history and culture, and "tell the people the truth about the February 28 incident and set February 28 as 'Peace Day' to narrow the gap between mainlanders and Taiwan natives."[31] By promoting greater Taiwanese ethnicity and expanding Taiwan's international recognition, this party hoped to elicit more popular support for its nationalistic and democratic goals.

The DPP stopped short of calling for Taiwan to break with mainland China and establish a Republic of Taiwan having a new constitution, flag, and anthem. Yet its platform appealed to Taiwanese sentiments favoring a mixture of liberties, democracy, and Taiwanese nationalism along with state-sponsored social welfare policies giving citizens numerous entitlements.

As for party organization, decision making and authority were consolidated in an executive committee and a central committee very much like those in the KMT, which it had long opposed. Party representatives participated in periodic islandwide congresses that elected their chairman and committee members every three years. The executive and central committees, along with a secretary-general and deputy, managed seven departments in charge of party functions that were responsible for implementing party policies, recruiting members, and mobilizing popular support. Such was the party that opposition politicians had striven for more than a decade to create.

## The Ruling Party Tries to Reform the Polity

In August and September, Chiang Ching-kuo knew of the *dangwai* politicians' intentions, but he merely watched and urged his six reform committees to continue their deliberations.[32] After the DPP had formed, voices inside the KMT urged Chiang to arrest the ringleaders and imprison them.[33] He refused the advice. Instead, Chiang announced on October 2 that the government intended to lift martial law as soon as possible after a new security law had been drafted and approved.[34] On October 5, one week after the DPP formed, Chiang Ching-kuo offered his judgment of this remarkable political event: "The times have changed; events have changed; trends have changed. In response to these changes, the ruling party must adopt new ways to meet this democratic revolution and link up with this historical trend."[35] On October 7, Chiang Ching-kuo granted an interview to Katherine C. Graham, chair of the *Washington Post*'s board of directors, informing her that the ROC intended to lift martial law but that, because the PRC remained a serious threat, the nation must have a national security law.[36]

KMT leaders now debated how to respond to the new political circumstances. Some questioned why the illegal DPP was allowed to demonstrate in the streets and stir up public passions; others worried that the DPP wanted to establish a Republic of Taiwan, an act that might infuriate the PRC and precipitate a military conflict. But Chiang Ching-kuo and his supporters countered these concerns by arguing that the time had come for major political reform and that their party must lead the way under the rule of law. Addressing the central committee on December 10, Chiang called on his party to comply with the law: "There must be a spirit of serious rule of law as the foundation for our society. Our party members must truly carry out these rules. If there is no law, there can be no democracy. The foundation of democracy must be the spirit of obeying the law."[37] Meanwhile, the KMT's first reform group's two committees continued their work to determine how martial law should be lifted and political parties legalized. By September the first reform group recommended that a new national security law *(Anchuanfa)* be drafted into law to replace martial law. Many countries used this law to empower their governments to suppress seditious activities while still practicing democracy. The group also recommended that a new law be approved to govern the registration and conduct of political parties. Passage of these two laws would develop Taiwan's democracy according to the rule of law.

Just as the intellectuals now broke a long-standing political taboo by openly discussing martial law,[38] on October 23 the government announced its intention to draft and approve a new national security law.[39] A draft of this law went first to the Defense Ministry and the Department of Legal Affairs for study and approval. Then the Ministry of Interior reviewed the bill and, after more study and revision, sent the draft law to the Legislative Yuan.

The national security law now became the main issue of KMT concern. When the review and approval process bogged down, Chiang Ching-kuo publicly declared that this law must be passed quickly.[40] In late November 1986 a special KMT committee finally approved the law and sent it to the Executive Yuan for review and approval. The bill lingered there until the end of December, when the ruling party invited Legislative Yuan members to discuss the law so they would support and approve it. The KMT finally agreed that the bill must be openly debated in the Legislative Yuan because it wanted the public to be informed of its content.[41] By early 1987 the national security bill had entered the Legislative Yuan but was strongly opposed by the DPP, who did not trust the government and feared this new security law might limit individual freedom and rights in the name of national security. Debate heated up on March 12 when eight DPP legislators began arguing with three government officials who supported the bill. One DPP legislator said, "What is the reason for having a national security law, and why should it even be a separate issue for making a law?"[42] The stage was now set for a fierce battle over the passage of the security law.

## An Election Takes Place

Before describing the struggle over lifting martial law could be resolved, an important election was to be held on December 6, 1986, for selecting a new quota of national representatives to the Legislative Yuan and First National Assembly. This crucial election was a litmus test for Taiwan's emerging democracy. It would reflect voters' sentiments toward the new opposition party and suggest how they might support it in the future.[43] If voters favored the DPP and elected many of its candidates as national representatives, that outcome might influence the KMT's willingness to push democratic reform in the future. Similarly, by electing more opposition politicians to the Legislative Yuan and National Assembly, their number could influence the passage of laws governing the pace of Taiwan's democratization. Therefore, if the DPP achieved a stunning election victory, KMT conservatives might try to slow down the pace of democratization, perhaps even to reverse it.

On November 14, 1986, top DPP leaders converged on Chiang Kai-shek International Airport to greet seven members of the overseas Democratic Progressive Party that had formed in May. Four of the arriving group did not have visas and were not allowed to leave the aircraft.[44] Police barred the DPP leaders from greeting them. Then on November 30 rumors circulated throughout the island that dissident Hsu Hsin-liang had flown to Tokyo and was preparing to fly to Taipei to participate in the December elections. Several thousand DPP members and supporters went to meet Hsu, but scores of police and military police had sealed off the airport. For some ten hours the crowd laid siege to the airport and tried to crash through the police barrier. Some thirty police cars were badly damaged, stones were hurled, and many were injured.[45] The crowd finally dispersed when news leaked out that Hsu was unable to fly to Taiwan.

The violence at the Chiang Kai-shek International Airport stunned the island's populace. The KMT-controlled press immediately accused the DPP of using violence to achieve its political aims. Many newspaper editorials reported that popular support for the DPP had waned because people now perceived that party as advocating violence. But Kang Ning-hsiang and others held a public meeting and showed videotapes to tell the DPP's story of the airport incident, in effect arguing that it was not the crowd but the local police who had perpetrated the violence.[46]

In early November the DPP began preparing for the December 6 elections. On November 7 the party announced its political goals. The DPP opposed Communist China and all forms of political dictatorship and renounced the use of revolutionary tactics as a means of political struggle. It also urged "that political parties should peacefully compete and work for the prosperity and peace of Taiwan. The future of Taiwan can only be decided by the people of Taiwan in a fair and equitable way under the conditions of freedom and self-determination."[47] The DPP immediately began distributing information on its goals to all candidates to inform them how to compete against their KMT opponents. On November 15 all election candidates registered, and on November 21 campaigning began.[48]

For the first time, a political party supported candidates who opposed KMT candidates in an election. As election campaigning intensified, the DPP was able to hold many more political rallies than when *dangwai* politicians had campaigned separately. The DPP also concentrated its activities in the north, especially in Panchiao township and in Taoyuan district.[49] By late November both parties were clearly articulating their different positions and vigorously criticizing each other. "The KMT criticized the 'new party' as not being politically mature and not offering any principles or ideas for how to promote social progress."[50] The DPP had selected the color green to represent its goals of peace, security, and prosperity. That prompted Jian Yuxiang, a KMT candidate in Taipei, to complain that the DPP "are trying to use the ideology of separatism to destroy social harmony. Their members also use very aggressive tactics to destroy our society's rules merely to further their political aims. Their actions have created a fear of the color green."[51] The DPP candidate Kang Ning-hsiang responded by criticizing the KMT for never having used Taiwanese in government cabinet positions. DPP member Xie Changting also criticized the KMT's forty years of rule as having "controlled all social and political resources to make the political system rigid and corrupt."[52]

In the last days before December 6, both parties sought support for their candidates from the local factions. In this regard, the KMT political machine had more funds as well as close, long-term ties with faction leaders. Aware of their weak party organization, the DPP responded by working more vigorously to elicit voter support. These actions led one observer to say that "this election is a tremendous struggle that not only is between both political parties but is also ongoing within both parties. The candidates attack each other unmercifully."[53] As candidates continually insulted each other, the KMT candidates attacked their DPP opponents by reminding voters never to forget how the DPP "fomented violence at the Taoyuan international airport." The DPP candidates replied that the "police brutally beat up our demonstrators who were peacefully behaving themselves."[54] Reports of vote buying surfaced every day because so many candidates were dispensing gifts and small amounts of money to voters.

On December 6, voters quietly went to the polls and cast their ballots. There were no reports of disturbances. One commentator noted that "never

## TABLE 7
### Results of the December 6, 1986, Supplementary Election for National Representatives

| | KMT (total) | KMT Party Nominees | KMT Self-Nominated | DPP (total) | DPP Party Nominees | DPP Self-Nominated | Youth Party | Social Democratic Party | Nonparty |
|---|---|---|---|---|---|---|---|---|---|
| **Legislative Yuan (73 seats)** | | | | | | | | | |
| Elected seats | 59 | 59 | 0 | 12 | 12 | 0 | 0 | 0 | 2 |
| Percentage | 80.82 | | | 16.71 | | | 0 | 0 | 2.47 |
| No. of candidates | | 75 | 16 | | 19 | 2 | 2 | 1 | 22 |
| **National Assembly (84 seats)** | | | | | | | | | |
| Elected | 68 | 68 | 0 | 11 | 11 | 0 | 0 | 1 | 4 |
| Percentage | 80.95 | | | 13.10 | | | 0 | 1.19 | 4.76 |
| No. of candidates | | 83 | 19 | | 25 | 5 | 3 | 2 | 32 |
| **Legislative Yuan** | | | | | | | | | |
| No. of votes | 4,391,870 | | | 1,641,487 | | | 4,275 | 1,180 | 484,810 |
| Percentage | 66.30 | | | 24.87 | | | 0.36 | 0.012 | 7.32 |
| **National Assembly** | | | | | | | | | |
| No. of votes | 3,932,600 | | | 1,450,967 | | | 9,938 | 2,650 | 666,460 |
| Percentage | 60.20 | | | 22.21 | | | 0.15 | 0.04 | 10.20 |

SOURCE: Zhongguo shibao, December 7, 1986, p. 1.

before in an election have so many resources been used."[55] The KMT-controlled press evaluated the election results as "being more favorable for the ruling party, but the DPP, using considerable resources, has also established a certain defined, organizational base and made a major impression on the public. Both parties have achieved important gains."[56] This evenhanded judgment was based on a reading of the following election results.

Of the total votes cast for the Legislative Yuan supplementary seats, the DPP had won nearly one-quarter of the popular votes and the KMT obtained roughly two-thirds. For the National Assembly supplementary seats, the KMT won three-fifths and the DPP slightly more than one-fifth. Did these results represent a sharp break with the past when *dangwai* candidates ran without any party support? Taking only the Legislative Yuan contest, in 1983 the KMT won eighty-three of the ninety-eight seats, or 84.6 percent, compared with 80.8 percent in 1986; the *dangwai* had won only six seats, or 6.1 percent, compared with 16.7 percent in 1986.[57] This clearly was an increase, but in the National Assembly election for 1980 (no information for 1983), the KMT won 80.2 percent of the seats compared with 81.0 percent in 1986, whereas all independents won only 18.4 percent compared with the DPP's share of 13.0 percent in 1986. Clearly, the DPP had not fared quite as well in the National Assembly supplementary election.

According to National Taiwan University voter surveys undertaken in every election year, their results showed a slight increase in voters who liked the KMT, up to 44.5 percent in 1986 compared with 37.4 percent in 1983.[58] For voters favoring the *dangwai* in 1983, their share was 7.1 percent and increased to 8.9 percent in 1986. Meanwhile, the proportion of "neutral" voters in 1983 was 55.3 percent compared with 46.6 percent in 1986. These results suggest a hard core of *dangwai* and DPP supporters remaining firm between 1983 and 1986 but perhaps increasing slightly, while more voters still preferred the KMT and a substantial number were neutral.

Many interpreted the December 6 election as the climax to a year of tumultuous political events: the KMT leaders had pushed democratic reforms, promised to lift martial law, and agreed to reforms that the political opposition had demanded for many years.[59] There now was a new political opposition party trying to win middle-class support, whereas in previous years its members had only humiliated and ridiculed the KMT leaders and "spit on the KMT flag."[60] In spite of many demonstrations in the streets and at the international airport, social stability still prevailed, according to one commentator: "Taiwan certainly is more and more stable, and this is an admirable trait to observe."[61] But the stage was now set for the political opposition to go to the streets. In their eagerness for democracy, they still did not believe the KMT was sincere in its promise to accelerate democratization. The opposition subscribed to a political culture of mistrust in which those outside the political center were unconvinced that their leaders had any sincere commitment to the well-being of society. The opposition distrusted the KMT and suspected it of always using deceit and tricks to avoid developing true democracy.

## Political Conflict Moves to the Streets

A great debate now began in the Legislative Yuan that pitted a handful of DPP legislators (11) against a huge KMT majority (about 195). The DPP minority insisted that a national security law was not necessary to replace the lifting of martial law and threatened street demonstrations to win public support.[62] Their virulent attack caught many KMT legislators by surprise, for they believed that by openly debating this issue they were demonstrating their tolerance and sense of fair play. Some KMT legislators became angry and threatened rapid passage of the law, by virtue of their huge majority. Most KMT legislators, however, preferred building a consensus so as to project the impression that their actions represented the will of the people.

Many academics also believed that their country required this security law[63] because the PRC had never renounced the use of force against the ROC. After lifting martial law, the government should have some legal provisions in place to protect the nation's security, and such a security law fulfilled a psychological need for protection. But scholars such as National Taiwan University's legal expert Hu Fu and others believed a law was unnecessary, and the political scientist Lu Yali disapproved of the current version of the law, wanting an "ideal, practical law" as a substitute. Kang Ning-hsiang spoke for the political opposition by declaring that the government should lift martial law, abandon its idea of a national security law, and return to the true spirit of the 1947 constitution. Kang too believed that the national security law would restrict human liberties. As politicians were arguing the merits of a security law to replace martial law, political conflict shifted to the streets.

As early as 1980, citizens had begun forming groups to increase government and public awareness of shoddy consumer goods and services and environmental pollution.[64] By 1982 other groups had begun protesting on behalf of aboriginal human rights and women's rights. The reported incidents of social protest rose from 175 in 1983 to 204 in 1984 and 274 in 1985, then increased to 337 in 1986 but doubled to 734 in 1987.[65] Church groups began demonstrating in 1986, followed in 1987 by organized laborers, farmers, veterans, teachers, and the disabled. Closely connected with this social wave of peaceful demonstrations and protests in 1987 were the DPP's street demonstrations, conducted whenever its leaders believed that pressure should be imposed on the political center. Elite writings in early spring of 1987 turned angry over the DPP street demonstrations, warning that these episodes could easily spill over into violence and give PRC leaders the opportunity to use force against the ROC.[66] But such complaints and criticisms did not impress the DPP leaders.

At a meeting on March 29, 1987, the DPP announced that it would stage a large demonstration on April 19 in front of the Office of the President to protest the national security law.[67] In Taipei, apprehension grew as the day approached. When the right-wing Anticommunist Patriotic League declared it would oppose any street demonstration, the DPP announced it was canceling the demonstration. But DPP members like Chen Shui-bian, Fei Hsi-ping, and Ju Gau-jeng protested, and the decision was quickly reversed. Chen Shui-bian then announced that if the KMT did not lift martial law before May 19, "they would march to the Office of the President on May 24 to demonstrate."[68] The security law and its ten articles could be passed in a month; the DPP, therefore, wanted to mount a massive popular street demonstration as soon as possible to force the government to lift martial law without passing the new security law.

Meanwhile the government, hoping that a goodwill gesture would improve the political atmosphere and restore calm, announced that Huang Hsin-chieh and Chang Chun-Chong would be released from prison.[69] Huang and Chang had been leaders of the Meilidao incident, so the DPP welcomed their release but vowed to have the May 24 demonstration anyway. High-level discussions between the KMT's Liang Su-jung and the DPP's Fei Hsi-ping and Jiang Pengjian took place in early May to find means to avoid conflict in the streets.[70] Liang informed them that the KMT would pass the security law and, because it was lifting martial law, the KMT leaders hoped the DPP would not demonstrate. Learning that the DPP still planned to demonstrate on May 19, Liang said that he "hoped relations with the DPP could be normalized and made legal; if both parties can compete, the future of the country will be bright."[71]

In early May DPP member Xie Changting stated that his party planned a public demonstration on May 19 because "we want it [martial law] lifted immediately."[72] In the early hours of the nineteenth, the Taipei police used bales of barbed wire to block off the streets into Sun Yat-sen Memorial Park, where the protest was scheduled to begin.[73] Police also set up barricades and stationed guards around the Office of the President. Military vehicles were positioned around the Judicial Yuan, and twenty-four armed vehicles moved into the park off Chieh-shou Road near the Office of the President. By noon the hot sun was burning down on the rapidly assembling crowd in Sun Yat-sen Memorial Park. Fei Hsi-ping, the leader of the demonstration, began addressing the crowd on the stairs of the Sun Yat-sen Memorial Auditorium in the park. By half past one in the afternoon, some ten thousand people had gathered to listen to Ju Gau-jeng, Xie Changting, Huang Huangxuan, and others make short speeches demanding the unconditional lifting of martial law.

At one point Chen Lizhong, the vice director of the Taipei Police Administrative Division, and three policemen went up the stairs to talk to the DPP leaders. Kang Ning-hsiang asked Chen for a police escort to accompany the DPP legislators back to the Legislative Yuan. Chen said he hoped that there would be only speeches in the park and that then the crowd would disperse. "Please do not go into the streets," he said. Fei replied, "We have no problem controlling this rally." Fei's assistant, Xie Changting, then protested to Chen Lizhong that the police had placed wire, gas canisters, fire trucks with water hoses, and banners cursing the DPP along the nearby streets. Legislator Yu Ching intervened, saying "We do not want to have another incident like the one at the Taoyuan airport [where thousands of protestors hurled stones and other objects at police] last November."

Chen said, "Although I see that many have come only to observe, I also see that you were leading songs to stir up the people. The situation outside is not very stable. If anybody throws stones, somebody will be hurt. I simply hope you will not take your rally into the streets."

Xie Changting replied, "We cannot have a rally? Let me turn this crowd over to you then, and you can manage it. We just want to walk to Xinsheng South Road and then disperse."

Chen answered, "That is going to be difficult!" At that point Fei Hsi-ping suggested, "Let's just walk to Jianguo South Road." But Chen would not agree. Kang Ning-hsiang, realizing they could not reach a consensus, urged Chen to return to his superiors. At ten minutes to two, their discussion ended and the speeches resumed.

A man who had spent more than twenty years in ROC prisons spoke to the crowd: "Twenty years ago I joined Guo Yuxin's party, and I was arrested and put into prison until now. I have been sacrificed and victimized by martial law. I am a living witness of martial law. I am one who was sacrificed. Long live the Taiwanese people!" Others followed him to vent their anger toward martial law. Vice Director Chen then returned, having discussed the situation with his superiors. Fei told Chen that he did not want a street rally but that "we have to let this crowd walk a little after all these speeches." Chen replied, "If you want to walk to rid yourselves of anger, then walk around the Memorial Park. I guarantee that your bowel and urinary movements will be more effective." Yu Ching countered, "Do you think we are here just for gymnastics?" Another DPP leader intervened, "You seem a reasonable fellow; don't bullshit us! The KMT has been here for thirty-five years running our affairs, and we cannot protest for even a single day. Don't be so stingy." Yu Ching looked across the park and said, "You guys have got us totally surrounded. What do you think we are? I hope you don't treat our people as your enemies. We just want to take a walk in the streets."

Chen urged Yu Ching to recognize the seriousness of the current situation. "If you do not march, the newspapers will praise you." Yu Ching replied, "You ask yourself which country could have such a gentle, rational parade as we want to have." Chen retorted, "But which country has police as gentle as I am? The police of other countries beat up their people." About half past three Liao Jiangxiang, the head of the Taipei police force, came to the stairs and sternly addressed Xie Changting: "You are a council member. This meeting is illegal. You know what is legal and what is not. If you violate the law, you alone will be responsible for all the consequences."

Li Ping, the vice deputy commander of the Garrison Command, then appeared and severely admonished the DPP leaders. Looking at the crowd, he said, "If they advance, it will be over my dead body." Another official said, "If they climb over any of the barriers, they will be arrested." Kang Ning-hsiang went to a nearby parked car and talked to the police officials through a microphone: "Why don't you leave and go home? Just ask Mr. Chen to come here and discuss terms with me. I know you like to fight, and your connections [guanxi] with Commander Hao are great. You merely want to suppress us." The crowd echoed Kang's message, but Liao stood his ground.

At quarter after four, Taipei police chief Liao stood on a small traffic island at the intersection of Jenai and Kuangfu South Roads and shouted through a bullhorn, "I want all of you to disperse in ten minutes." Many in the crowd hissed and told him to go away. Kang Ning-hsiang then spoke from a hastily erected platform: "We have the right to stand here and negotiate with you." By five o'clock rain had started, and some of the crowd began wandering out into the street not far from Kuangfu Road, which is adjacent to Sun Yat-sen Park and Memorial Hall. Some people erected a cover over the DPP headquarters at the top of the Memorial Hall staircase, and under it the DPP leaders, many of whom come from other parts of the island, discussed their next move. They had expected to march to the Office of the President and present Chiang with a letter, and they did not want to be disappointed. The leadership had promised a peaceful demonstration. But the KMT sent no high-ranking leader to meet with them, only a two-star general from the Garrison Command.

By quarter after five many students, who were just getting out of school, joined the crowd. As the heavy rain swept into the Taipei basin from the Pacific Ocean, one student sang out, "We can't learn about real politics in the classroom, but it is great that we are in the streets learning it firsthand."

More DPP leaders gave speeches. At half past six Kang, Yu Ching, DPP chairman Jiang Pengjian, and Fei led a huge crowd from the street back to Memorial Hall, heatedly discussing among themselves whether to disperse or continue their protest. Ju Gau-jeng insisted they should stay. Others agreed, arguing that they would lose face if they dispersed. Fei Hsi-ping said, "If we fear losing face, we should never have had this demonstration." One person urged a hunger strike. Party chairman Jiang then stated that they would break up after raising the party flag, the first time it had been displayed in public. At eight o'clock someone shouted for the crowd to disperse, but Yu Ching and others, who already had moved to the intersection of Chunghsiao East Road and Kuangfu South Road, said, "Our supporters are still here; let's march to the railway station!" Police vice director Chen Lizhong then returned, urging them not to do so and suggesting they that use another road to march to the railway station. He promised Yu Ching and Zhou Chingyou, a DPP National Assembly representative, that he would obtain the necessary permission from his superiors. Yu Ching praised Chen, saying he hoped he would be promoted. Chen then ordered Fu-hsing South Road opened so the crowd could march a short distance, after which the demonstration ended and the crowd dispersed. Chen bade the DPP leaders good night and jokingly said, "We have had a gymnastic competition that has been troublesome for all parties concerned."

This major confrontation of the opposition party with the authorities in the streets thus ended without bloodshed. Both sides claimed victory: the DPP boasted that they had held their demonstration and criticized martial law; the authorities were proud that mob violence had not erupted, embarrassing the city and the government. The leaders of both groups negotiated, made concessions, and avoided extreme solutions. More important, each side learned much about the other. The DPP was not well organized, but its leaders and members were responsible and wanted to avoid violence. The police were equipped to deal with large crowds without angering the populace. The DPP's leaders believed that people rallied to their cause because they approved of DPP actions and endorsed their efforts to display heroic, responsible leadership. DPP leaders did not want to break the law and thereby invite the authorities to arrest them. The nation's press welcomed the peaceful resolution of the May 19 political demonstration, as did the police.[74] Chen Lizhong, the vice director of the police administrative unit in the Ministry of Interior, stated:

The main thing is that people obeyed the law. Anyone out of control that day could have broken the law with terrible consequences. To obey the rule of law is the valuable experience everyone gained from the May 19 event.[75]

Xie Changting, the DPP member in charge of that party's social movements, affirmed his party's cause:

While it rained hard, we shared the determination to uphold democratic politics from beginning to end. We held this demonstration to protest forty years of martial law and to express the people's unhappiness about this law.[76]

And Huang Yueqing, a professor of law at National Zhengzhi University, expressed the hopes of many:

I hope this will be the last time there will be this kind of march. This should serve as a lesson to the ruling party. The KMT has launched political reform, but these reforms were not well designed and prepared. No plan for how to deal with demonstrations after lifting martial law has been established.[77]

This would not always be the case. In 1988 there were 1,172 demonstrations in Taiwan, and 43 of them were larger than one thousand persons.[78] After 1989, however, the people of Taipei and other cities became weary of street parades with their traffic jams and the loss of business for merchants; political organizations, then made legal, had become commmplace, so their number greatly declined. Thus, the May 19, 1987, political demonstration became a model the DPP tried to emulate when organizing its public demonstrations.

## The National Security Law Finally Passes

The KMT members of the Legislative Yuan paid little attention to the May 19 demonstration and tried to approve the ten articles of the national security law. On June 5, thirty-eight of the forty-seven members in attendance approved Article 1.[79] The next day a great debate erupted over Article 2, which read:

No person may violate the constitution or advocate communism or the division of national territory in the exercise of the people's freedoms of assembly and association.

The assembly and association mentioned in the preceding paragraph shall be governed by laws to be enacted separately.

The words *violate* and *advocate* enraged the DPP, but to no avail; the KMT majority rammed the article through and approved the wording despite DPP delays, accusations, and abuse.[80] On June 7 Articles 3 and 4, which pertained to entry and exit from the country and how the police should check and monitor such activities, also passed without difficulty.[81]

On June 10 more than one hundred DPP members assembled before the Legislative Yuan in South Chungshan Road, where they clashed with veterans and supporters of the Anticommunist Patriotic League who had assembled there to oppose them. Some DPP members tried to enter the Legislative Yuan but were stopped by police. DPP organizer Xie Changting shouted, "Those who ratified this law are totally without shame."[82] Xie and his supporters then positioned themselves at the Legislative Yuan's entrance and, when KMT legislators emerged or entered, shouted insults such as "You're too old—why haven't you died yet?" Fights broke out between members of the DPP and the KMT.

On June 12, as deliberations over the national security law continued, DPP members and their supporters, along with members of the Anticommunist Patriotic League, who vehemently hated the DPP, again squared off.[83] But this time the police failed to control the situation. By the time enough police arrived, individuals of both camps had seized flagpoles and other objects and had begun attacking each other; many were seriously injured.[84] Although the police managed to break up many fights, the crowd refused to disperse. At one point the Anticommunist Patriotic League people, who had come to intimidate DPP protesters, hoisted their flag, but shortly afterward someone stole it, provoking another altercation. When police ordered the crowd to disperse, spokespersons from both sides said they would not leave until the other group left. This standoff, which aggravated passion and pride on both sides, continued all day. About seven in the evening DPP leaders Kang, Fei, and Yao Chia-wen addressed the crowd, pleading with them to return to their homes.[85] They, too, had no success.

Wang Huazhen, the deputy commander of the Taipei Police Department, tried to negotiate a truce but failed, finally saying, "I will apologize for both sides if only you will leave."[86] Still the leaders and their respective followers refused to disperse. Police chased individuals and beat them with clubs, but it was no use. At eleven that night DPP leader Kang Nang-hsiang returned again, pleading with the crowd to disperse but without success. At midnight, Wang Huazhen began broadcasting to the crowd that he intended to use force if they did not leave.[87] Finally, by two o'clock in the morning, the police had chased and arrested so many people that only a few hundred remained. By three, the street in front of the Legislative Yuan was deserted.

The June 12 violence was the worst since the Kaohsiung incident and lasted longer, even though the Taipei police had not used all their personnel or water cannons, instead relying on persuasion to coax the opposing groups to leave the streets. On June 13, Premier Yu Kuo-hwa angrily said:

Our government has done so much in recent years to promote in a positive way political reform and with tolerance to promote democracy. But some individuals have constantly tried to damage our social tranquility and threaten the security of our country. I am profoundly alarmed by these events. This government has the responsibility to protect the national security, and so it will legally deal with these illegal activities.[88]

Still the KMT and government security personnel took no action against the DPP. The incident became a topic of great argument. Could Taiwan become democratic without tearing itself apart?

The KMT continued to press for passage of the national security law, which had languished in the Legislative Yuan since early March. Legislators had held fifteen major discussions on all but one article of the law, and heated debates again ended in fistfights, name calling, and walkouts by DPP legislators,[89] marking the worst violence that had ever occurred in the parliament, all of it focused on Article 9. The final form of that article read as follows:

Criminal cases regarding civilians who, having been tried or being tried by military courts in areas in which the Emergency Decree had been in effect, shall be dealt with according to the following provisions after the termination of the Emergency Decree:

(1) Where military trial proceedings have not been completed, cases undergoing investigation shall be transferred to a competent (civilian) public prosecutor for investigation; cases pending trial shall be transferred to a competent (civilian) court for trial.

(2) Where criminal judgments have become final, appeal or interlocutory appeal to a competent (civilian) court shall not be allowed; however, where grounds for retrial or extraordinary appeal exist, applications for retrial or extraordinary appeal may be pursuant to the law.

(3) Where final criminal judgments have not yet been executed, or are being executed, they shall be transferred to a competent (civilian) public prosecutor for execution under his direction.

Much of the furor over this article was occasioned by the difficulties of shifting legal cases from the military courts under martial law to the civil court system. The criminal code virtually had to be revised and, most important, the bureaucratic functions of the Garrison Command had to be dramatically changed after the lifting of martial law. The DPP demanded that all people imprisoned under martial law be pardoned and released. The KMT allowed only special cases for pardon and release and remained firm on the wording of Article 9. When Article 9 did pass, the DPP legislators walked out. KMT legislators, along with the elected legislators of the China Youth and Social Democratic Parties, made modest revisions to the entire bill,[90] and on June 23 the bill passed into law.[91]

On June 24, KMT chairman Chiang Ching-kuo addressed the party's central standing committee and expressed his delight in the security law's passage. Lauding it as a great milestone in ROC history, he said that the country could now move into a new era. He did not apologize for the long period of martial law and even said that "martial law actually helped us to achieve our successes in those years." Then he concluded:

Now I must point out that our determination to protect our country's security has not changed and our sincere determination to promote a democratic central government has not changed. Our belief that the Three Principles of the People can unify China also has not changed. We only want to protect the welfare of the people and guarantee the secure future of our country.[92]

Sensitive to the DPP opposition and eager to promote social healing, Chiang Ching-kuo instructed the Executive Yuan to ask the Ministry of Defense to reexamine, case by case, those nonmilitary persons still in prison to determine whether their sentences could be reduced and their civil rights restored.[93] DPP legislators like Yu Ching argued that all political prisoners should be released and their rights restored.

On July 14, President Chiang Ching-kuo issued a special decree that at zero hour martial law should be lifted; on July 15 martial law ended.[94] Premier Yu then ordered that the "National Security Provisional Law under the Period of Extreme Emergency also would take effect on July 15." Chinese democratization had reached a new stage.

DPP National Assembly members demonstrating in front of the Office of the President to demand the reelection of a new national assembly (December 1987).

President Chiang Ching-kuo conducts a memorial ceremony in the Office of the President on New Year's Day, 1988 (Vice President Lee Teng-hui is at extreme right).

Lee Teng-hui inaugurated as president on January 13, 1988.

Assemblyperson Ju Gau-jeng protesting at a session of the Legislative Yuan to demand that all national representatives of the First National Assembly retire (1990).

National student demonstration at the Taipei Chiang Kai-shek Memorial Park to demand the abolition of the Temporary Provisions and to dissolve the First National Assembly (March 1990). The banner identifies the group from Zheng zhi University.

ROC citizens voting in the Second National Assembly election on December 21, 1991.

# PART III

# Political Conflict and
# Partial Reconciliation

# CHAPTER SEVEN

# The First Election after the Lifting of Martial Law

Between spring 1986 and late 1987 Taiwan was rocked by seismic political events. One observer summed it up this way:

Our entire society is in the process of loosening up. Voices fearing to speak out in the past now can be heard. Everyone is trying to discover a new historical point of view. Many sociopolitical groups have formed: students, retired soldiers, women, workers, taxi drivers, and merchants march in opposition to the old ways. There is now a new opening up and great freedom.[1]

"Taiwan was no longer a single corporate society but becoming a pluralistic society."[2] With the formation of a new party and the KMT's tolerance of political opposition, with the lifting of martial law and press censorship, and with the increasing number of street demonstrations, the KMT "inhibited political center" started to dissolve into a "subordinated political center" more susceptible to demands from civil society and political parties. Whether this democratic breakthrough would produce the "quiet revolution" of democratization or revert to authoritarianism was not clear at the time.

Chiang Ching-kuo alone had initiated the democratic process and kept it moving forward. Chiang had created the six committees to determine how Taiwan's polity should be reformed. When the DPP formed illegally, a government intelligence unit had urged Chiang to act and abolish the party, but Chiang had refused.[3] When a KMT reform committee proposed the National Security Law draft containing forty articles, Chiang had amended it to only eleven articles to facilitate its approval into law.[4] When the draft law for people's organizations to form legally was ready for submission to the Ministry of Interior, Chiang inserted the words "political party" into the draft law.

In this tumultuous period Chiang Ching-kuo had worried greatly whether he could "establish a firm basis for popular democracy."[5] More than anything else, he wanted to influence the course of historical events so that democracy would serve "to preserve the prospect and hope for China's unification."[6]

After martial law was lifted on July 15, 1987, the stringent rules governing where and how newspapers printed their daily editions were finally removed on January 1, 1988. With the press free to publish what it deemed correct and worthy, newspapers expanded in size, and new companies began issuing dailies. In October 1986 the KMT finally produced a draft law allowing sociopolitical groups to organize and sent it to the Ministry of Interior for review.[7] Zheng Shuizhi, head of the ministry's Policy Affairs Section, said this law would specify what groups must register, the criteria for evaluating their political charters, and the type of permit to be issued after they registered in a court of law.[8] In early 1987 the ministry sent this draft to the Executive Yuan for review, and by November 5, 1987, the new bill was almost ready for the Legislative Yuan to amend and approve into law.[9]

Another KMT committee also had completed a draft law to compensate the aging national representatives when they retired. The party also was preparing a legal ruling for the mandatory retirement of all national representatives, but that ruling had to be approved by the Legislative Yuan and then the Judicial Yuan. During 1987 Chiang was extremely ill, yet he made every effort to implement these important legal rulings to guarantee that democratization advanced according to the rule of law. But Chiang Ching-kuo did not have much longer to live.

## The Death of Chiang Ching-kuo

According to Hau Pei-tsun, Chiang's illness was graver than most people had realized.[10] His eyesight had deteriorated in 1987, and he often spent long periods confined to bed in his official residence at Tachih. His mind was clear, however, and his memory was excellent.[11] The few officials admitted to his presence included Shen Chang-huan, the secretary-general of the Office of the President; Wang Tao-yuan, head of the Ministry of Defense; Premier Yü Kuo-hwa; and chief of staff General Hau Pei-tsun. KMT Secretary-General Lee Huan and his vice deputy, Ma Ying-chiu, met with the president in the early afternoon of June 13, 1988. Chiang Ching-kuo told them he was worried that the plan to replace the national representatives elected in 1947 was moving too slowly and that it must be approved soon to uphold the 1947 constitution.[12]

At 6:50 P.M. that same day, central committee members filed into KMT headquarters and received the news that Chiang had died at 3:50 P.M. that day.[13] At 7:00P.M. Vice President Lee Teng-hui was sworn in by Lin Yang-kang, head of the Judicial Yuan, and became the seventh president of the ROC. For the first time, a Taiwanese occupied that position.

When DPP member Ju Gau-jeng learned of President Chiang's death, he cried openly. Ju later said that "Chiang was a most respected leader."[14] He praised the late president as a leader who "mixed with the people, projected a friendly image, and was self-restrained." For the first time in forty years, KMT headquarters received a telegram from the central committee of the Chinese Communist Party, conveying to the KMT's central committee condolences on the death of its chairman.

Surprisingly, the country remained calm and even serene. A telephone survey of 1,000 households in Taipei conducted on January 14–15 reported that, of 952 responses, about 70 percent believed that President Lee Teng-hui would be able to handle the presidency; 20 percent were not clear about the future, and 7.8 percent thought real difficulties lay ahead. As for Taiwan's future after the death of President Chiang, 42.3 percent reported that "it was difficult to judge the future because of some uncertainties." The more educated of those surveyed, 41.6 percent, responded that democratization would continue; only 29.9 percent were very uncertain about the future of democracy. In fact, 69.5 percent of those interviewed were optimistic about Taiwan's future; only 16.9 percent were not certain about the island's future, and 3.8 percent were not at all optimistic. As the days passed after President Chiang's death, the public's view of Taiwan's future seemed as follows: "The reason Taiwan is maintaining a peaceful and serene as usual atmosphere is that everyone feels secure and confident about our present circumstances."[15]

Although the island's people remained calm and quite optimistic about their future, Taiwan's leaders confronted an unknown and dangerous future. Ever since the United States had adopted a "one China" policy by recognizing the People's Republic of China as the government of China and acknowledging that Taiwan was a part of China, the ROC had become isolated in the world order. Although President Chiang had courageously initiated an opening-up step with the PRC in late 1987 by allowing Chinese people to visit relatives on the mainland if the PRC granted visitation rights, tensions between Taiwan and mainland China were still high. Could the ROC break out of its international isolation and reach an agreement with the PRC government on their relationship?[16] Could the ROC maintain political stability though its democratic transition? Could political reform continue to achieve a mature democracy? These challenges now faced the ROC's new president, Lee Teng-hui. Who was this leader?

## Lee's Ascendancy to Power

When, on March 22, 1984, Lee Teng-hui became the seventh vice president of the ROC, he had never participated in an election. His rise to power had been swifter than that of any politician on Taiwan.

His humble origins, career, and character would greatly influence the political struggle for democracy over the next decade. Born on January 15, 1923, in the village of Puping in Sanchih township northwest of Taipei city, Lee Teng-hui grew up in a small landowning family that farmed and rented land to tenants. His Hakka ancestors had migrated from Fukien to an area near Tansui city in Sanchih township. Lee's father, Lee Jinlung, had three sons, of whom Lee was the second.[17] The family was not impoverished, but everyone worked hard. As a child, Lee often accompanied his grandfather to the Taipei produce market early in the morning to sell their farm's products. From 1929 to 1935, Lee attended various primary schools, graduating from a Christian middle school in Tansui city. In 1939 he was one of four Chinese students in his class selected to attend Taipei's foremost Japanese high school, the best in Taiwan.[18] In 1943 Lee was admitted to Kyoto Imperial University to study agricultural economics; he graduated in 1946 and returned to Taiwan that same year. From his Japanese education Lee came to admire Japan's leaders for producing the Meiji Restoration, modernizing Japan, and making that small country powerful, respected, and feared. Lee was particularly struck by the Japanese spirit of teamwork, strong desire to achieve, long-term approach to accomplishing goals, and deep respect for personal loyalty and duty. That Lee aspired to these qualities endeared him to Chiang Ching-kuo, who also espoused them.

When Lee returned to Taipei at age twenty-three, he entered National Taiwan University, the country's finest university, as a transfer student. He graduated at age twenty-six and then became an instructor at the same university. In 1951 he won a scholarship to Iowa State University to study agricultural economics. Returning to National Taiwan University in 1953, he became an instructor in the Department of Economics. Regarded as a rising star among agricultural economists, he was employed as an economic analyst by the Joint Commission on Rural Reconstruction (JCRR) and assigned to conduct feasibility studies for its pilot projects in the countryside, which was then suffering severe underemployment and rapid population growth. In the next few years Lee published several articles arguing that Taiwan had experienced a green revolution (productivity increased by new seeds, improved fertilizers, and irrigation) under Japanese rule that the ROC government continued to nurture.

In 1965 Lee received a scholarship to Cornell University; by 1968, at age forty-two, he had completed his coursework and written a Ph.D. thesis that won the American Agricultural Economic Association's prize for the outstanding doctoral thesis in the United States that year. His work explained how increased agricultural productivity had produced a large surplus that taxation and other policies had extracted to finance Taiwan's capital formation and industrialization during Japanese and ROC rule. Lee's ingenious accounting method measured agriculture's annual surplus contribution to Taiwan's capital formation and was highly praised by economists. With his degree in hand, Lee returned to Taiwan as a full professor at National Taiwan University and an adviser to the JCRR.

His educational and professional career put him at the pinnacle of Taiwan's academia and won him international acclaim. On June 2, 1972, while he was attending a conference in New Zealand, the Executive Yuan offered him the position of minister without portfolio.[19] Lee accepted, and the government assigned him to Africa to study ROC aid projects that competed with similar PRC efforts. Lee also had the opportunity to travel throughout Taiwan, increasing his contacts and friendships. In June 1978 President Chiang Ching-kuo made Lee mayor of Taipei city, an office that, like the mayoralty of Kaohsiung, is appointive rather than elective. That appointment stunned many in political circles and aroused jealousy of the young technocrat, who was only fifty-five years old. President Chiang, however, had been observing Lee Teng-hui's performance in the Executive Yuan and saw a man who pursued his work with a diligence, thoroughness, and analytic acumen unusual in officials. With powerful logic and clarity of exposition Lee compelled his committees to do their homework and present careful, reasoned recommendations to the government.[20] Chiang was also pleased that Lee had no political base and did not seem interested in establishing one.

In 1979 Chiang saw to it that Lee Teng-hui was selected to serve on the prestigious, powerful Standing Committee of the KMT. This group of thirty-odd persons, chaired by Chiang Ching-kuo, met each week to decide on policies for the party and government. Lee had been a KMT member for only a decade, and his appointment to this august body again surprised many inside and outside the party.[21] In 1981, Chiang picked Lee to become governor of Taiwan. Tragedy befell Lee in 1983 when he lost his only son to cancer. This tragedy, however, helped convince Chiang that Lee might become his successor; in the Chinese way of thinking, a leader without a son is more inclined to carry out that power holder's legacy than to cultivate power for himself and his family.[22] Thus, a year after the death of Lee's son Chiang decided Lee should become his vice presidential running mate. Lee had now arrived at the penultimate position of political power.[23]

## Lee Becomes the KMT Chairman

Immediately after President Chiang died, KMT secretary-general Lee Huan consulted with his three deputies about the vacant party chairmanship.[24] They finally agreed that the Standing Committee should propose that Lee Teng-hui serve as acting chairman until the party's Thirteenth Congress (in July 1988) could give formal approval. On the evening of January 18, Lee Huan received a letter from Madame Chiang Kai-shek, who wrote that the Central Evaluation Committee, which she chaired, had decided the party should have a collective leadership until the party's Thirteenth Congress. Lee Huan was now in a predicament. On the evening of January 26, Chiang Hsiao-yung, Ching-kuo's third son, telephoned Yu Kuo-hwa and asked him not to propose the acting chairman idea at the standing committee's meeting. Yu also did not know what to do. On the morning of January 27, the party leaders discussed the matter and decided to follow the original plan of making Lee Teng-hui the acting party chairman. Later that day, at the standing committee meeting chaired by Yu Chi-chung, discussion centered on various issues but not the vacant chair. Finally James C. Y. Soong asked to speak. Although Soong was only the deputy secretary-general and still very young, without speaking privileges, acting chairman Yu allowed him to address the group. Soong, after expressing his extreme unhappiness that a decision on the chairmanship had been delayed, said, "For our party and for the country, the damage will become worse each day if a decision is not made, and we must do this for the sake of Chiang Ching-kuo." Soong then left the room. Discussion on the issue ensued, and soon a vote was taken to make Lee Teng-hui acting party chairman until the Thirteenth Congress. What appeared as a major political crisis caused by the intervention of Madame Chiang had been averted, and the way was now clear for Lee to take over the chairmanship. Several days later Soong accompanied the new party chairman to visit Madame Chiang and mend fences. Madame Chiang said, "I did not object to having a Taiwanese as party chairman. . . . I only hope Lee will do a good job."

For nearly forty years the Chiang family had dominated Taiwan's politics.

When Chiang Ching-kuo died, received wisdom contended that "no one can believe a president could serve and not have the name Chiang."[25] Transferring power to a Taiwanese was unthinkable, and the atmosphere became tense as the nation's elite watched and waited. The newly confirmed president quickly took the reins of power and began a series of personal visits: first to members of the Chiang family to express his sympathy and promise to uphold the late president's legacy; next, to KMT elders to seek their advice; then to government advisers and evaluation commissioners; then to top military leaders to ask for their support, promising in return his respect and help; and finally, to the nation's front lines on the offshore islands to praise the troops for their fighting spirit.[26] After a month had passed, Lee undertook a series of quick trips to cities and towns to call on local leaders and ask for their support. He thus conveyed the image of a party chairman and president who not only cared about the nation's leaders and ordinary people but deeply venerated a dead leader and promised to carry on his policies.

But difficulties now intruded: Taiwan was in the grip of a mainland China "fever," with many demanding that the government abandon its "no contact" policy with the PRC. The government had to decide whether to be represented in the upcoming Asian Games; an agenda for the Thirteenth KMT Congress had to be developed; and the old national representatives continued to be a problem for the party, for the DPP used the issue to mobilize popular sentiment against the government. While dealing with these problems in 1988 and 1989, President Lee also dealt with administrative matters. On June 1, 1988, he replaced Yu Kuo-Hwa, an effective but unpopular premier, with Lee Huan and promised more decisive action from the Executive Yuan. He extended General Hau Pei-tsun's term for another year as chief of staff. In late 1988 he announced that a new fighter aircraft would be named after Chiang Ching-kuo.[27]

Meanwhile, he planned how to expand national elections and replace the old representatives. He supported a new law mandating handsome retirement stipends for all national representatives who retired voluntarily. At the first year's commemoration of Chiang's passing, January 13, 1989, Lee extolled the late president's achievements and vowed to carry on his mission of unifying China under the Three Principles of the People. By spring 1988 most KMT members scored Lee's performance as commendable, and it appeared that a majority of the old national representatives in the powerful National Assembly would vote him in as the eighth president of the ROC in March 1990.[28] Only the DPP criticized President Lee, calling his new cabinet members "amateurs leading the experts."[29] But on July 8, 1988, the Thirteenth KMT Congress confirmed Lee as party chairman.[30] By now a new political market process was taking form.

## A New Political Market Process Evolves

Taiwan had long experienced an economic market process comprising small and medium-sized enterprises as well as large-scale companies that competed in domestic and world markets. The ROC government regulated that economic market process but allowed households the freedom of choice to be active in the market. The nation also had a limited ideological market process under martial law (chapter 3). All ideologies except Marxism, Leninism, and socialism competed. What Taiwan still lacked was a mature political market process that practiced democracy.

A political market process allows for interest groups and individuals, through political parties, to articulate their demands and compete for power. Political parties try to satisfy those demands by promoting candidates who compete in elections to become representatives and leaders. Voters express their political preferences by voting for party candidates based on some mixture of political idealism and selfish interest. Once elected, political representatives and leaders use their power to pass laws and allocate public resources to satisfy their voters' demands. This political market process is supposed to satisfy the greatest number of voters in a democracy that guarantees freedom and individual rights, free, competitive public media, competing political parties, and a healthy civil society. These rules, embodied in a constitution, also establish checks and balances within government, and govern the turnover of leaders and representatives through routine free, open elections.

In 1989 Taiwan's political market process rapidly evolved, but democracy was still perceived as an ideal. Without a constitution, democracy was impossible. The 1947 constitution, frozen since 1949, first had to be reactivated by abolishing the Temporary Provisions. Then the constitution had to be amended to apply to Taiwan's political realities rather than those of mainland China as its framers had intended. But constitutional reform was impossible until the aging national representatives from mainland China had been replaced and new representatives from Taiwan elected to the Legislative Yuan and National Assembly. To remove these obstacles, the KMT and the government had to draft a reform strategy. Could they count on the support of the DPP?

The DPP and KMT had no practical experience of cooperating to promote political reform. Each distrusted the other. The parties did not even communicate with each other. The DPP resented the KMT's great wealth and power, especially its domination of the national and provincial governments and its control over the electronic media. Nor did the DPP trust the KMT's sincerity about pushing political reform because of its shared culture of mistrusting political authority. The KMT shared that same culture because its members believed the DPP only wanted to establish a Republic of Taiwan and opposed building a democracy to unify Taiwan and the Chinese mainland.

The ethnic cleavage between Taiwanese and mainlanders, which had moderated in recent decades because of expanding middle-class prosperity, urbanization, and educational opportunities, could worsen if parties fiercely debated Taiwan's political future. But people now valued their freedom of speech, and Taiwan's political future became a political issue polarizing society along lines of ethnicity, social class, and ideology. The elite began quarreling among themselves about how to remove the senior national representatives and undertake constitutional reform.

Moreover, could the KMT and DPP avoid factionalism and remain unified and strong enough to complete those necessary political reforms for democracy? In the KMT, young and old liberals favored rapid democratization, but conservatives wanted to maintain the ruling party's status quo and feared the DPP wanted only to make Taiwan politically independent of China. The conservatives' enthusiasm for democracy was merely gilded by rhetorical appeals to high-sounding moral principles. But by summer 1989 there were already signs that factions were emerging in both parties.

In the DPP, politicians like Huang Hsin-chieh, Chang Chun-hong, and Xu Rungxu had aligned with Lin Zhengjie to form the Beautiful Taiwan Alliance (Xin meilidao liuxi), which was supported by many lower-level provincial and government officials.[31] This group wanted to expand the DPP's influence in the provincial assembly and city councils. Its strategy was "to use the locales and regions to surround and strangle the political center" (yi difang baowei zhongyang). The other principal faction, called the New Tide (Xinchao liuxi), was led by individuals like Chou Yiren, Liu Xushui, Li Yiyang, Yao Chia-wen, and others who believed the party should try to mobilize mass support for its goal of establishing a Republic of Taiwan under a new constitution, flag, and anthem. They advocated that their party should conduct protests and street demonstrations to build public support for a political transformation of Taiwan.

Within the KMT, there were young party members, highly educated mainlanders who made their homes in Taipei, like Lee Shen-fong, Chao Shao-kang, and Yü Mu-ming, who had established the New KMT Alliance [Xin guomindang lianxian]. This group argued their "original purpose for forming this alliance within the party was to help KMT candidates in the December 1989 elections, and they had no other purpose in mind."[32] They worried that, with so many new laws and so many new candidates planning to compete, their party needed a new image to win these elections. Lin Shengfeng made the point that their group only wanted political reform, and so they had conceived of this idea to express their hopes for the KMT. But many in the KMT did not accept that argument and worried that a new faction was beginning to form in the party.

The year 1989 was critical because the first regional-city elections were to be held under new legal conditions. By January 11, 1988, the Legislative Yuan already had passed the Law on Assembly and Parades during the Period of National Mobilization for Suppression of the Communist Rebellion. That law granted people the right to hold public meetings and marches on condition that there be no anticonstitution protests, no advocacy of communism, and no calls for dividing the ROC. On January 20, 1989, the Legislative Yuan then passed the Law on the Organization of Civic Groups, which allowed new political parties to register and compete in elections. By summer both the DPP and KMT had registered as legal parties and scores of new parties were registering to compete in the December 1989 elections. On January 26, 1989, the Legislative Yuan also passed the revised Law on the Election and Recall of Public Officials and the Law on the Voluntary Retirement of Senior Parliamentarians.[33] The former set forth rules for how parties must compete in elections. The latter outlined the terms under which the senior national representatives would be compensated when they retired. In this new political marketplace, political life was never going to be the same.

## A Great Debate Begins

In early November 1989, Lin Yixiong, one of Taiwan's best-known DPP members, toured the island, speaking to large audiences about Taiwan independence *(Taidu)*.[34] On November 22, Guo Beihong, a political dissident who had secretly returned to Taiwan from the United States, appeared at a political rally in Taipei; he eluded a dragnet of police by slipping into a large crowd.[35] That same day, campaigning began for the December 2 local and national elections. The press immediately began discussing the pros and cons of establishing a Republic of Taiwan and redrafting the 1947 constitution.[36] All political taboos had now disappeared.

The pro argument asserted that an independent Taiwan did not threaten the PRC and that for the first time since 1949 peace between the two governments could be affirmed.[37] The PRC, busy with its "four modernizations" and resisting democratization, would never risk attacking Taiwan. Moreover, by forming a new republic the people of Taiwan would demonstrate that they were in change of their island's destiny. A newly elected National Assembly would reduce defense expenditures, freeing funds for economic and social development. Establishing a new constitution would reflect the political realities of 1989: Taiwan under the 1947 constitution was like a "little child wearing oversized shoes [*xiang xiachai chuan daxie*]."[38] An independent Taiwan also could enter the United Nations and join the community of nation-states on an equal footing. Hungary had changed its name from the People's Republic of Hungary to the Republic of Hungary, so why couldn't Taiwan do the same?

Those opposed argued that the ROC's political system aimed at eradicating communism from the China mainland; changing the country's name and altering the constitution violated that great mission. Because Communist China now faced severe crises, the ROC had the opportunity to achieve its historic mission. The ROC government, by promoting democratic elections and creating a harmonious society, had capably guided the nation's destiny. The military would never intervene in the polity, and the government upheld the law. An independent Taiwan, in contrast, would invite the Chinese Communist navy to blockade the island and paralyze its economy. Moreover, even the United States limits personal freedom in order to protect national security. The 1947 constitution was the law of the land, and the majority of the people favored it. Finally, the PRC would prevent Taiwan from entering the United Nations, from changing its name, and from opting for independent rule.[39]

This new debate and the return of exiled dissidents added drama to an already supercharged election. Foreign interest was also keen. United States congressman Stephen Solarz and members of his staff came to Taipei to observe the elections. By November 25, there were 105 correspondents from around the world in Taiwan, with some 200 expected by election day.

These elections were significant in other ways. First, the KMT's standing committee decided to hold a primary election from June 22 to July 22 to give rank-and-file members the power to nominate candidates for the first time in its ninety-five-year history.[40] On primary day, party voters found a complicated ballot, and the experiment led the KMT to regard "primaries as advisory, not conclusive, in selecting candidates," but this represented another small step toward democracy as other parties quickly followed its example. Second, the elections determined whether the transition to democracy would be peaceful and stable. Finally, the elections also would signal whether public opinion affirmed the existing constitution and political structure or preferred the goals of Taiwanese nationalism. Because of its great importance, this election quickly took on the character of a small war. Party candidates mapped their campaigns like battlefield maneuvers; they mobilized their forces, devised their tactics, and attacked their enemies to snatch the spoils of war.

## The Spoils of War

The spoils of this war were seats having political power and influence. A fierce struggle now broke out among some forty political parties, with more candidates competing for the available seats: 69 for 16 county magistrate seats and 5 city mayorships; 302 for 101 Legislative Yuan seats; 148 for 73 Taiwan provincial council seats; and 203 for 99 Taipei city, Kaohsiung city, and mountainous district councils.

Both the KMT and the DPP had more candidates running than either party had endorsed because many powerful clans and local groups had decided to nominate candidates.[41] All parties now regarded these races as crucial for future grassroots political party building. With 101 Legislative Yuan seats vacant, the DPP needed only 20 more to introduce legislation, which would be a major triumph. More non-KMT seats would enable the opposition parties to form coalitions with KMT members who would be more eager to satisfy local constituents than to comply with party demands. If the DPP won more votes, that meant more political power in the central and provincial governments. For the moment, the political elite did not consider long-run political reforms but concentrated their energies on this election.

## Preparations for War

All parties had to register their candidates by July 15, 1989. The KMT, with its alleged two million members, had registered 557 candidates; the DPP, with a membership of about seventeen thousand, registered 204.[42] To choose these candidates, each party held primary elections. But primary elections caused enormous confusion and controversy in both parties. In the KMT, primary election campaigning lasted only ten days, with voting taking place on different days because not all parties registered their candidates in time. Only about 5 percent of the voters turned out.[43]

The July primary, however, elevated local KMT politicians' morale.[44] For the first time, some party candidates admitted they belonged to the KMT and defended their party's performance; many local KMT members even supported these candidates in spite of their party's refusal to endorse them. An independent spirit swept the KMT rank and file, and they campaigned more vigorously for their nominees than in any previous election, although the party withheld endorsement.

The primary election also caused major headaches for the DPP. Ju Gau-jeng wanted to run for a second term in the Legislative Yuan, but the DPP nominated Huang Erxuan. These two politicians represented two factions then taking form in the DPP: the New Tide, trying to mobilize the lower social strata and intellectuals to transform the existing political system,[45] and Beautiful Taiwan, the brainchild of Chang Chun-hong, Lin Wenlang, and Xu Minde, which supported Ju Gau-jeng and backed a strategy of improving public welfare (upgrading transport, reducing environmental pollution, and providing more social services).[46] Both factions tried to project political maturity, sensitivity to voters, and assistance for small and medium-sized enterprises.

Ju Gau-jeng called the New Tide faction a "malignant tumor" and threatened to leave the DPP if it did not register him in the primary.[47] Many businesspeople declared they would withhold financial support from the DPP if Ju was not registered, and some in the DPP supported Ju because they wanted to reduce the New Tide's influence. In the end, the DPP decided to support Ju but not nominate him. Ju won the primary and then ran for the Legislative Yuan to represent Yunlin county.

The DPP's political strategy, "using the localities to surround and strangle the center," aimed at winning at least 35 percent of all votes cast[48] and capturing at least twenty-one county magistrate and city mayor races.[49] Winning ten district seats would expand the DPP's political base, force the KMT to share power, and begin the restructuring of Taiwan's polity. The DPP targeted key county magistrate races like Taipei county, where it ran Yu Ching, a popular politician, against the KMT nominee, Li Xikun, an unknown professor from National Taiwan University. Party leaders now shifted more resources to this race and several other major contests.[50]

To counter the DPP, the KMT planned to strengthen its ties with local factions and their power holders.[51] But the primaries, and the KMT-nominated candidates they produced, often angered those local party candidates who wanted to run and believed they could win. In August and September the party sent Secretary-General Soong and President Lee Teng-hui's father, Lee Jinlung, around the island to urge nonendorsed KMT candidates to withdraw. The KMT then drew up election combat zones: areas where it had lost a race for county magistrate or city mayor and where more resources were needed to recover those seats; areas in which the KMT encountered strong DPP and other opposition but had a two-out-of-three chance to win; and areas where KMT surveys showed its popularity to be strong.[52]

Meanwhile, in early September the DPP assembled its candidates running for county and city offices in Panchiao and formed an alliance association. For several intense hours, they reviewed all the sins of the KMT, from leaky public housing to the February 28, 1947 uprising.[53]

## Waging War

By late November, political warfare raged all over the island. The warring parties tried to win votes by establishing links with local patrons and their clients or by discrediting their chief opponents and drawing attention to themselves. (Both strategies required candidates to raise enormous sums of money.) Election laws forbade television campaigning, but candidates found other ways to win votes. The candidates' headquarters alerted voters to their opponents' flaws and their own superior qualities. In the weeks before election day, many candidates circulated rumors, humiliated and attacked their opponents, and wooed voters with visits, gifts, and bribes.

Never before had a Taiwan election been reported in such detail. You Xikung, the DPP candidate running for county magistrate, was alleged to be affiliated with the underworld (liumang) because of a particular tattoo on his chest.[54] This rumor so angered You that at one public rally he opened his shirt to show that he had no such mark.

In the Hsinchu county magistrate race, Fu Zhongxiong, the KMT candidate, called on his DPP opponent, Fan Zhengzong, to "open the skylight and speak the truth" (dakai tianchuang shuo lianghua). He accused Fan of talking like a "matchmaker" who tried to marry an incompatible man and woman, never making up his mind on any issue, and even of being a fornicator (fangshi).[55] Fan rebutted Fu by saying that the KMT had dumped Fu into a race he knew nothing about and that he should return to Taichung county and work as a KMT party hack.[56]

In the crucial Taipei county magistrate race, KMT candidate Li Xikun tried to humiliate Yu Ching by accusing him of being a Japanese sympathizer. He insinuated that Yu "really wanted the Japanese to come to Taiwan to help him become elected, and in the future [if Yu was elected], Mr. Yu might personally have to travel to Japan for consultation." Yu Ching described his opponent as a professor without any political experience and out of touch with the local people.

In the race for the Legislative Yuan in Kaohsiung city's south district no. 2, Xu Xiaodan, a woman, ran against Wu Demei, another woman, and Liu Hongzong, a man. The Labor Party candidate, Xu, achieved notoriety when she shocked the public by baring her bosom in the Legislative Yuan. In one of the campaign posters she appeared nude from the waist up; in her left hand were flowers representing love and peace, and in her right hand were burning political posters symbolizing her desire to rid Taiwan of the "dark elements of politics."[57] As this race heated up, so did the rhetoric. At one point Liu Hongng produced a poster with the words "one piece to counter two points" (yitiao dui liangdian), meaning that Xu Xiaodan "might have two breasts, but Liu had something else that could take care of her."[58] Xu called Liu a "low-grade golden ox" (xialiu di guang jinniu) and attacked Wu Demei as cowardly. Some candidates even purchased foreign diplomas to elevate their social status.[59] Others asked prominent academics and intellectuals to endorse their candidacy. Some 160 National Taiwan University professors and Academia Sinica scholars publicly declared: "We support Yu Ching to become magistrate of Taipei county."[60] Another candidate kicked off his campaign by commissioning a troupe to perform a traditional lion dance at his campaign headquarters, hoping it would bring him good luck.[61]

Wealthy candidates hosted lavish banquets or bought votes. In Chung-ho district of Taipei county, the KMT candidates Li Xikun, You Mingcai, and Jiang Shangjing ran for county magistrate, Legislative Yuan, and provincial assembly, respectively. They purportedly prepared seven thousand banquet tables for voters between November 17 and November 26.[62] The DPP strongly protested but then hosted two thousand tables. These examples were repeated in every district.

Most candidates for the Legislative Yuan solicited money from businesspeople to pay for their costly campaigns. One businessman said that "when he wants a small favor from a legislator, it costs NT$100,000 [US$3,846], whereas a 'big' favor costs between NT$500,000 [US$19,230] and NT$1 million [US$38,461]."[63] Some former legislators admitted these donations made it possible for them to recover all their campaign expenses.[64] Critics called these legislators "golden oxen" (jinniu) for blatantly soliciting such support.[65] The Americans who observed the elections were horrified to learn that a candidate for the Legislative Yuan spent as much as NT$30–80 million (US$1.15–3.07 million).[66] By November 28, some 176 violations had been reported during the first nine days of campaigning (November 17–26). But only nineteen were prosecuted (another twenty were reviewed by the local election commissions).

Some violence did occur. Chen Yuanji, a candidate for the Legislative Yuan from Tainan city and a former KMT member, joined the China Democratic Party because he had not been endorsed. On November 5, four men attacked Chen and broke his left leg, fractured several ribs, and inflicted severe head injuries, confining him in the hospital for several months.[67] Chen continued his campaign in a wheelchair. Chen Yongyuan, another candidate for the Legislative Yuan in Changhua county, was gunned down on November 6 by four armed men in a taxi. Firing at least eleven bullets, they sped away, leaving Chen paralyzed from the waist down.[68] These events led some to suggest that candidates wear bulletproof vests.[69]

## The Struggle for Hearts and Minds

What were the key issues in this election? The DPP offered a broad platform of political and economic reform. It urged voters to break the 30 percent voting barrier so their candidates could acquire power.[70] The party advocated self-determination for the people, complete reform of the National Assembly, and direct voting for the nation's president, the provincial governor, and the mayors of Taipei and Kaohsiung.[71] It also wanted to share tax revenues more equally between central and local governments, to reduce taxes, to privatize more national enterprises, and to use the country's foreign reserves for the people's benefit. It also proposed a national health plan and more spending to protect the environment. Finally, it called for an independent judiciary and an end to political abuses.

Meanwhile, the KMT reminded voters that forty years of successful rule had guaranteed the nation's security, made the country prosperous, preserved social stability, and improved the people's life chances. The KMT projected itself as the party of maturity and experience, with talented leaders and officials able to govern the country in the future.

Two leading politicians sharply defined their respective parties' goals and achievements.[72] Wu Den-yih, KMT magistrate of Nantou county, argued that, although Taiwan had been ruled by the powerful Chiang family under martial law with numerous political taboos discouraging open debate, those conditions no longer existed. If the island had a peaceful election, it would affirm forty years of successful KMT rule. Wu admitted that the KMT's successful modernization had created new problems: Taiwan had order but lacked security (*zhian buan*); the environment had been preserved but lacked adequate protection (*huanbao bubao*); Taiwan had transport but needed more (*jiaotong butong*).[73] Wu asked voters not to judge Taiwan's conditions by the standards of advanced countries because that would be unfair; Taiwan should be evaluated by the progress achieved over the past forty years.

Wu offered three standards. First, had the people's life chances expanded and had they been educated to become good citizens? Second, had the military intervened in the governance of society? Third, had economic development made the people better off? Using these standards, Wu judged that the KMT had been successful but that it still had much to do and could not relax. Wu felt that the one great problem facing the KMT was that its successes had produced a surfeit of wealth but that the mindless pursuit of wealth had eroded some traditional Chinese cultural values. He lamented that the KMT had not kept the country on a firm course, balancing prosperity with responsible citizenship and high moral standards. Win or lose this election, the KMT must build a model polity by providing efficient, moral, and enlightened governance.

He also recommended that the nation's foreign exchange reserves should be supervised by a responsible committee and not registered in the accounts of particular individuals.[74] Only an experienced and mature KMT could serve the people of Taiwan in the future. Wu charged that although the DPP had gathered many to its embrace, far too many lacked the proper qualifications to govern. Moreover, the DPP's leadership consisted mainly of intellectuals and few middle-class people, appealing mostly to the intellectuals, the lower class, and marginal groups. The KMT had build good, solid foundations. People might complain that "iron cannot become steel" *(hentie bucheng gang)*, but "iron is not soft."[75] Wu concluded that the KMT might not be perfect but that it had built a good foundation in Taiwan and, with popular support, encouragement, and an ever-watchful eye, could perform even better.

Ju Gau-jeng, the DPP candidate from Yunlin county running for the Legislative Yuan, admitted that considerable progress had taken place under KMT rule but charged that it had been achieved by an excessive reliance on national security laws, which allowed the KMT to perpetrate many political crimes and violate human rights.[76] Moreover, economic growth had not been balanced: infrastructure lagged behind development. Imbalance also plagued the educational system, with not enough topflight universities in the south. If the military had never played a role in Taiwan politics, it was because the Chiang family had close ties with both the security and military establishments. The Legislative Yuan could not account for how the Ministry of Defense spent its money.[77]

Therefore, Ju argued, the polity must be restructured, and only the DPP could do that, by reforming the National Assembly and the judiciary. The

DPP did not want to just monitor the KMT; it wanted at least 35–40 percent of the votes to share power with the ruling party. The KMT need not fear that the country would be poorly governed at local levels because DPP politicians had proved they could perform as well as or better than KMT politicians: consider Yuchen Yuoying, the magistrate of Kaohsiung county, and Chen Dinghan, the magistrate of Ilan county. To achieve political reform and have a ruling political party concerned with people's human rights, welfare and social justice, Ju urged Taiwan voters to vote DPP.[78]

More women campaigned than ever before.[79] The DPP nominee Yuchen Yuoying ran for Kaohsiung county magistrate; Wu Demei was running for the Legislative Yuan from Kaohsiung city with the support of her husband's family, the Ju lineage. Zhang Wenying ran for Chiai city mayor and Zhang Boya ran for the Legislative Yuan. Some women ran on behalf of husbands who had been imprisoned or otherwise victimized by the KMT. Most were nominated by the DPP. Zhou Qingyu ran for Changhua county magistrate; Xu Rongshu, for Taichung city mayor. Ye Zhulan, whose husband, Zheng Nanrung, the editor of a dissident journal, had burned himself to death rather than allow the government to close him down, ran for the Legislative Yuan for Taipei; Zhou Huiying ran for the Taiwan provincial council from Taipei County. Zhang Wenying from Taichung city had been imprisoned because of her connection with Shih Ming-teh, then in prison. Suhong Yuejiao from Yünlin county, the wife of Su Dongqi, who had been imprisoned for sedition, ran for the Legislative Yuan. Ling Lizhen, running for city council of Kaohsiung, was the wife of Ling Hongxuan, who had been punished for his role in the Meilidao incident. Other women politicians, mostly mainlanders, were supported by the armed forces and various veteran associations; Shen Zhihui (from Taichung city and running for the Legislative Yuan), Zhu Fengzhi (Taoyuan county), Xiao Jinlan (Kaohsiung county), and Wang Sujun (Pingtung county). The KMT also supported several Taipei women for the Legislative Yuan.

Were the candidates appealing to an informed electorate? A poll taken in early September revealed that nearly 90 percent of the voters knew about the county and city official elections and that 28 percent of the voters would support the KMT, with only 4 percent supporting the DPP.[80] A later poll revealed that only 13 percent supported KMT candidates, while 7 percent supported DPP candidates.[81] Voters were definitely informed but more and more uncertain of their preferences.

However, a survey of 1,800 persons (1,680 responded) undertaken in the summer of 1989 in twenty-one districts and cities found that only 7.9 percent believed the DPP was becoming a better party, 24.5 percent reported the DPP was behaving badly, and 20.0 percent felt the party's image was satisfactory. But only 8.9 percent really wanted to support the DPP, 30 percent supported the KMT, 25 percent had no opinion for or against either party, and 13 percent did not like either party.[82] These findings are similar to those reported in September showing that slightly less than 10 percent strongly favored the DPP and slightly less than 30 percent, the KMT. The large middle group of uncommitted, neutral voters would make up their minds at the last moment. In future elections, this large middle group greatly influenced election outcomes.

As election day neared, more polling detected voter indecision. About half the voting populace expressed no intention of voting. Only about 10 percent seemed to have attended political rallies to listen to candidates' speeches, probably because the press reported the election in great detail. Some polls predicted that voter turnout would be lower than in previous elections.[83] On November 30 and December 1, campaigning intensified as candidates drove through the crowded streets of Taiwan's cities appealing for votes. Some DPP members claimed to have captured a truck carrying gifts of soap and spices for KMT voters.[84] Voters all over the island formed betting pools, totaling millions of NT dollars, for their favorite candidates.[85] Another voter survey conducted on December 1 claimed that widespread voter indecision still prevailed: for every hundred voters, only twenty-five had decided how to vote; another twenty had decided their votes during the early and middle campaigning period; some fifteen would decide only one day before voting day; another ten would decide on voting day; and the rest would not vote at all.[86] On December 2, a perfect day, a low voter turnout seemed unlikely.

## The Outcome

The polls opened at 8:00 A.M. and closed promptly at 5:00 P.M.; 12,600,810 persons were eligible to vote. The National Police Administration, warning the public to refrain from violence,[87] had secretly installed cameras at polling stations.[88] The Prosecutor's Office of the Taiwan High Court ordered that a district prosecutor be stationed at all major police departments. Contrary to predictions, voters turned out en masse, with 72 percent of the eligible voters going to the polls, a ten-year high.[89]

Calm prevailed except in Hsinying city in Tainan county, where three thousand supporters of DPP candidate Li Zongfan surrounded the county government office and charged, "destroying furniture, wrecking computer equipment and smashing windows"[90] after Li Zongfan complained of ballot rigging. A ballot count later proved that the KMT candidate, Li Yaqiao, had defeated Li Zongfan, who had confused the vote count at his station with that of another station.[91]

On December 3 the election results were clear: The KMT had won fourteen of the county/city races; the DPP, six; and an independent, one seat. This was the first time a political opposition had won so many districts. The KMT had won seventy-two seats for the Legislative Yuan and the DPP twenty-one; for the county and city council races, the KMT won 101 seats and the DPP 38.[92] Of the total votes cast in the races for county and city magistrate and mayor, the KMT had won 52.7 percent, the DPP 38.6 percent, and other parties 8.7 percent.[93] The races for Taipei and Tainan counties had been close: Yu Ching, the DPP candidate from Taipei county, had 626,333 votes to 622,248 for Li Xikun, the KMT contender; in Tainan County, Li Yaqiao, the KMT winner, earned 243,766 to 234,237 for Li Zongfan.[94] The total number of DPP votes amounted to 29 percent of the total votes cast for winning candidates, with the KMT winning 65 percent and other parties gaining 6 percent (see table 8). Of the share of total votes cast, 59 percent went for the KMT, 30 percent for the DPP, and 11 percent for other parties.

In the first open election, with many legally registered parties competing, the KMT had been challenged by candidates from thirty-nine parties. The

TABLE 8
*Results of the December 2, 1989, ROC Elections*

| | KMT | DPP | Other parties | Total |
|---|---|---|---|---|
| County and city officials | | | | |
| County magistrates | 3,271,314 | 2,551,352 | 451,029 | 6,273,695 |
| City mayors | 586,110 | 273,764 | 186,722 | 1,046,596 |
| Total | 3,857,424 | 2,825,116 | 637,751 | 7,320,291 |
| Percentage of total votes cast | 52.69 | 38.58 | 8.73 | 100.00 |
| Legislative Yuan | | | | |
| District | 4,519,629 | 2,334,597 | 833,495 | 7,687,721 |
| Occupational and other categories | 920,229 | 279,619 | 229,725 | 1,429,573 |
| Total | 5,439,858 | 2,614,216 | 1,063,220 | 9,117,294 |
| Percentage of total votes cast | 59.67 | 28.67 | 11.66 | 100.00 |
| Taiwan provincial council | 4,566,033 | 1,868,609 | 876,943 | 7,311,585 |
| Percentage of total votes cast | 62.45 | 25.56 | 11.99 | 100.00 |
| Taiwan city councils | | | | |
| Taipei | 824,038 | 275,569 | 80,276 | 1,179,883 |
| Kaohsiung | 407,667 | 136,513 | 64,265 | 608,445 |
| Total | 1,231,705 | 412,082 | 144,541 | 1,788,328 |
| Percentage of total votes cast | 68.87 | 23.05 | 8.08 | 100.00 |
| Grand total | 15,095,020 | 7,720,023 | 2,722,455 | 25,357,498 |
| Percentage of total votes cast | 59.11 | 30.23 | 10.66 | 100.00 |

SOURCE: *Shijie ribao*, December 3, 1989, p. 8.

KMT won nearly 60 percent of the total votes cast instead of its usual 66.6 percent or more. The ruling party also won roughly a three-to-one ratio of the seats over the DPP in all three races. With freedom of the press, enormous sums spent by all parties (the KMT spent the most), and intense political campaigning for nearly a half year, the KMT victory still seemed impressive. In many authoritarian regimes that moved toward democracy since the 1970s, voters had frequently rejected the old ruling parties, but not in Taiwan. Despite decades of iron rule, a decisive majority continued to support the old ruling party. Moreover, in the January 20, 1990, elections popular support for the KMT was even stronger; the KMT won 69.83 percent of the 842 races for county and city council seats and 85.11 percent of the 309 races for mayor of the units just below county government.

The press, however, concluded that the KMT had suffered a stunning defeat,[95] and leading KMT leaders apologized for their party's not winning the customary 70 percent of winning votes, or 66.6 percent of the total votes cast. James C. Y. Soong immediately visited the seven counties where the KMT had lost magistrate and mayor races and vowed to the party rank and file that the party would win back those areas in four years by building a new grassroots network.[96] Soong argued that even though many voters had perceived the KMT as not solving the country's problems, forty years had to pass in Japan before the Liberal Democratic Party could successfully deal with housing, labor, and environmental problems. He exhorted the party faithful not to despair, saying that "we should be responsible for our defeat but should not feel defeated."[97] Some KMT members in the Legislative Yuan criticized the KMT's election strategy and complained that the party should have held its Third Central Committee Plenum much earlier to map out better election policies. On December 6, KMT party chairman Lee Teng-hui also lamented the election outcome, declaring that "we must say it was a defeat; because of the decisions made by all the voters, we cannot say the election outcome was unexpected or an accident."[98] He urged the party to reform even more. Some KMT supporters believed that the party now had to accept the DPP as a legitimate opposition party.[99] One commentator reflected that, like so many citizens, he now worried about the country's political future: while the KMT was the party of the "bribe," the DPP was the party of "violence."[100] He complained that few candidates mentioned the lofty ideals of the Three Principles of the People; they only worshiped money. The KMT must improve society's morality and revitalize itself to be a role model for the country. This political advertising by the elite merely indicated that the Chinese elite of all political persuasions still shared a widespread cultural propensity for mistrust.

Such lamentations and frustration expressed by the elite over voters' and candidates' pursuing their self-interests revealed an unrealistic, utopian view of democracy. Rather than applaud the generally compliant, enthusiastic, peaceful behavior of voters and candidates in Taiwan's first real democratic election, many elite only worried about the dark aspects of Taiwan's evolving political market process.

As KMT leaders and their supporters gloomily appraised the election outcome and planned for the future, so too did the DPP make its plans. In an interview with journalists, DPP secretary-general Chang Chun-hong stated that the KMT should now treat the DPP as a party equal to the task of governing the ROC rather than regarding it as a mortal enemy.[101] After demanding more respect for the main opposition party, Chang declared that those county magistrates and city mayors who had won election seats would form a DPP alliance that would make new personnel appointments and plan how to reorganize the First National Assembly to directly elect the country's president and vice president. He also urged both parties to embark on coalition politics by having the provincial, county, and city councils cooperate to solve the country's problems. Chang wanted the DPP to become stronger so that the nation could have two major political parties capable of checking and balancing each other. When asked about the DPP's "New Tide Alliance," Chang admitted he did not know whether his party would include the goal of an "independent Taiwan" in the party's constitution but insisted that the issue be publicly discussed. He noted that of the thirty-two DPP members belonging to the "New Tide Alliance," voters had elected twenty. The DPP also announced that seven county magistrates and mayors would form an alliance to implement the party's strategy of "using the localities to surround and strangle the center," a strategy that could succeed only if the DPP built a strong base to elect local politicians, influence government personnel appointments, and divert more state tax revenues to the localities.[102]

Taiwan had experienced its first local election without martial law in which many political parties, including a major opposition party, had opposed the KMT for the first time. Shelley Rigger's recent study of this election reveals that powerful factions in different districts that previously had supported the KMT shifted their support to DPP candidates for reasons of self-interest rather than ideology.[103] According to Rigger's analysis, local factions undermined Li Xikun's bid to become Taipei county magistrate, and other examples for Tainan and Kaohsiung counties indicate a similar pattern. Powerful factions, in other words, had accounted for voter defections that allocated support to the DPP rather than the KMT and vice versa. In another sense the 1989 elections marked a major watershed: new politicians had appeared; candidates spent more money than ever before; old political taboos had been jettisoned. The voters had not embraced Taiwan nationalism, although they had an opportunity to do so. Many neutral voters had finally voted for the DPP to enable the DPP to compete with the ruling party and force it to perform better.[104] Voters also had elected DPP politicians because they belived they could serve as effective public servants and satisfy their self-interests. Yet a majority of voters had still voted for the ruling power, believing in that party's ability to serve the people. Taiwan's voters had rejected extremists positions. Even many United States observers conceded that Taiwan had taken a giant step toward democracy.[105]

# CHAPTER EIGHT

# Democracy's First Crisis

As 1990 began, the KMT still approved of Lee Teng-hui's management of party and government, and nearly seven of every ten voters backed the ruling party. The public and most elite looked on political party competition as healthy because it challenged the ruling party to perform better. Street demonstrations had become commonplace, and the media had a field day, investigating politics with a fervor never before seen in this society. The public as a whole had not embraced Taiwanese nationalism, even though the issue had been heatedly debated before the December 1989 elections, but it had embraced democracy, since 70 percent of the voting population had voted.

But many KMT mainlander leaders worried whether their party, led by a Taiwanese, would remain committed to the goal of unifying China under the ROC constitution. The opposition elite were frustrated by the lack of dialogue with the ruling party on how to expand national elections for government representatives and top leaders. The KMT still had no formal communications with the DPP and other parties. The Office of the President still held enormous power under the Temporary Provisions, and the opposition was divided between restoring and amending the constitution or redrafting that document altogether.

As political power shifted from an older generation of leaders (over seventy years of age) to a younger generation, political tensions were on the rise, involving nothing less than how to reform the ROC political structure that had been governed by the KMT for four decades. The KMT offered no vision for how Taiwan's democracy should develop. Chiang Ching-kuo had never articulated his vision of democracy with any clarity except to embellish democracy with the idealistic human conditions that "everyone must work for the public good and become selfless" *(dagong wusi)*. Lee Teng-hui still had not presented to his party or the nation any vision of how Taiwan's democracy should be developed. The democratic breakthrough launched by the late President Chiang between 1986 and 1988 could collapse at any time like a dam, allowing the backed-up floodwaters to swirl over the debris of Taiwan's political institutions. Since 1987, urban disorder had become more widespread, culminating in the May 20, 1988, demonstration by the Farmers' Rights and Interests Association, led by Lin Guohua, which shut down much of the city from early afternoon until early evening. These public demonstrations increased in 1989 and continued into 1990.

In this new atmosphere the elites debated Taiwan's development options: the DPP wanted rapid removal of the aging national representatives and direct elections for the nation's leaders and national representatives, but the party was split over whether to amend or redraft the 1947 constitution; the KMT wanted an orderly, procedural removal of the old national representatives and amending of the constitution according to law. The majority of the KMT, still conservative, also preferred that the National Assembly indirectly elect the president and vice president.

The two parties were definitely on a collision course. With tensions between the DPP and KMT already running high, the election of a new president and vice president in the spring of 1990 was likely to set the stage for dramatic conflict between the two parties. And such a conflict might cause division within the ruling party to initiate a political crisis that could even prompt the military to restore order. Speculations of this sort were commonplace and reflected the fragility of Taiwan's democracy.

The public, meanwhile, was also apprehensive because of the large number of public demonstrations taking place and its concern that Taiwanese nationalism might provoke the PRC leadership to use military force to unify China. Therefore, when the National Assembly convened for the eighth time in Taipei during February and March 1990 to elect a new president and vice president, attention was riveted on it, for in that critical period, all the issues above would likely be addressed. Meanwhile, the mainland leaders in the KMT wanted a vice president they could trust to work with President Lee and restrict his power if need be. All circumstances were now in place for this young democracy to face its first crisis.

## The ROC Presidential System

Although a political market process was evolving for the first time, democracy was still limited because Taiwan's people could not directly elect their leaders and national representatives. Direct national elections had never been held in Taiwan. According to section 3 of the ROC's 1947 constitution, the National Assembly elects the nation's president and vice president every six years, subject to recall. This body also amends the constitution and votes on proposed constitutional amendments submitted by the Legislative Yuan. Between the spring of 1948 and 1984, the mainlanders dominated the first National Assembly, which had convened seven congresses to elect a president and vice president and to deliberate on other affairs of state (see table 9). The number of National Assembly members had declined since 1948, when the first congress was convened in Nanking to elect Li Zongren as vice president and Chiang Kai-shek as president. This assembly continued to be an ardent supporter of the Chiang family, electing the father to five terms and the son to two terms.

The power vested in the ROC president, who also served as chairman of the ruling party, was enormous, especially after the constitution was frozen in 1948. The president was the supreme commander of the nation's armed forces; he appointed the most important government and military officers, including the cabinet, the governor of Taiwan, and the mayors of Kaohsiung and Taipei cities,[1] and he influenced the agenda for legislation. From Chiang Kai-shek, between 1949 and 1975, to Chiang Ching-kuo, between 1978 and 1988, and now to Lee Teng-hui, the constitution's normal checks on the president's power had never existed.

The political opposition, which had rejoiced after the lifting of martial law, now set its sights on expanding national elections for Taiwan's representatives and leaders. Between 1987 and 1989 many political prisoners had been released, including Huang Hsin-chieh, Yao Chia-wen, and others who had been major figures in the Kaohsiung incident. To their ranks came many dissidents from abroad who not only realized that a new political era had begun but wanted to play a role in political change. The reentry of these personalities into the opposition mainstream greatly strengthened the DPP leadership but also factionalized it, as already pointed out.

For over two decades the *dangwai* had criticized the National Assembly because its representatives had never been elected from Taiwan and did not represent the Taiwanese people. Moreover, those representatives were aging, were unable to perform their duties, and received more privileges than they deserved. After the 1950s, the number of assembly representatives declined

## TABLE 9

Seven National Assembly Congresses, Their Representatives' Attendance and Membership, and the Number of Votes Cast for ROC Presidents and Vice Presidents

| Representatives | | | President | Votes cast | Percentage | Vice president | Votes cast | Percentage of total | KMT chairman |
|---|---|---|---|---|---|---|---|---|---|
| Total No. | No. attending | Percentage attending | | | | | | | |
| First Congress (March 9–May 1, 1948: Nanking) | | | | | | | | | |
| 3,045 | 2,841 | 93.30 | Chiang Kai-shek | 2,430 | 88.88 | Li Tsung-jen | 1,438 | 51.55 | Chiang Kai-shek |
| Second Congress (February 19–March 25, 1954: Taipei) | | | | | | | | | |
| 3,045 | 1,578 | 51.82 | Chiang Kai-shek | 1,507 | 95.62 | Chen Cheng | 1,417 | 90.25 | Chiang Kai-shek |
| Third Congress (February 20–March 25, 1960: Taipei) | | | | | | | | | |
| 1,576 | 1,521 | 96.51 | Chiang Kai-shek | 1,481 | 98.08 | Chen Cheng | 1,381 | 91.76 | Chiang Kai-shek |
| Fourth Congress (February 19–March 25, 1966: Taipei) | | | | | | | | | |
| 1,488 | 1,446 | 97.18 | Chiang Kai-shek | 1,405 | 98.46 | Yen Chia-kan | 782 | 54.92 | Chiang Kai-shek |
| Fifth Congress (February 20–March 25, 1972: Taipei) | | | | | | | | | |
| 1,374 | 1,344 | 97.82 | Chiang Kai-shek | 1,308 | 99.39 | Yen Chia-kan | 1,095 | 83.78 | Chiang Kai-shek and Chiang Ching-kuo |
| Sixth Congress (February 19–March 25, 1978: Taipei) | | | | | | | | | |
| 1,248 | 1,220 | 97.36 | Chiang Ching-kuo | 1,184 | 98.34 | Hsieh Tung-min | 941 | 79.14 | Chiang Ching-kuo |
| Seventh Congress (February 19–March 24, 1984: Taipei) | | | | | | | | | |
| 1,064 | 1,036 | 97.39 | Chiang Ching-kuo | 1,012 | 99.02 | Lee Teng-hui | 873 | 87.30 | Chiang Ching-kuo and Lee Teng-hui |

SOURCES: See *Guomin dahui tongji huibao* (1984), pp. 8–9, 15–16; *Di yici guomin dahui di liuci huiyi tongji* (1978), p. 13; and *Zhunghua minguo nianjian* (1985), pp. 162–65.

TABLE 10

Changing Age, Political Affiliation, and Residential and Educational Profile of Seven National Assemblies

(Selected Years)

| | 1973 | 1978 | 1983 | 1984 | 1985 | 1987 | 1988 |
|---|---|---|---|---|---|---|---|
| *Total* | 1,411 | 1,263 | 1,085 | 1,067 | 1,018 | 964 | 917 |
| Male | 1,203 | 1,068 | 902 | 885 | 842 | 795 | 755 |
| Female | 208 | 195 | 183 | 182 | 176 | 169 | 162 |
| *Age distribution* | | | | | | | |
| Under 40 | 24 | —[a] | 8 | 7 | 6 | 10 | 9 |
| 40–49 | 24 | — | 35 | 34 | 34 | 43 | 37 |
| 50–59 | 250 | — | 33 | 32 | 30 | 33 | 37 |
| 60–69 | 701 | — | 231 | 193 | 167 | 106 | 9 |
| 70–79 | 345 | — | 546 | 520 | 479 | 463 | 422 |
| 80–89 | 63 | — | 213 | 257 | 278 | 282 | 289 |
| Over 89 | 3 | — | 19 | 24 | 24 | 27 | 33 |
| *Party affiliation* | | | | | | | |
| KMT | 1,182 | 1,084 | 933 | 918 | 883 | 830 | 788 |
| Youth Party | 75 | 62 | 53 | 52 | 48 | 46 | 43 |
| Democratic Socialist Party | 44 | 37 | 31 | 30 | 25 | 25 | 24 |
| Other | 110 | 80 | 68 | 67 | 62 | 63 | 62 |
| *Residence* | | | | | | | |
| In ROC | 1,294 | 1,152 | 994 | 976 | 930 | 880 | 837 |
| Outside ROC | 117 | 111 | 91 | 91 | 88 | 84 | 80 |
| *Educational background* | | | | | | | |
| Overseas study | 229 | 203 | 159 | 153 | 142 | 148 | 139 |
| University | 709 | 646 | 585 | 577 | 553 | 529 | 503 |
| Special schools | 159 | 147 | 116 | 116 | 112 | 102 | 99 |
| High school | 69 | 58 | 57 | 56 | 56 | 45 | 44 |
| Military academy | 182 | 154 | 119 | 117 | 109 | 97 | 92 |
| Police academy | 20 | 19 | 16 | 15 | 14 | 14 | 13 |
| Training class | 17 | 16 | 13 | 13 | 13 | 13 | 11 |
| Self-study | 25 | 20 | 20 | 20 | 19 | 16 | 16 |

SOURCES: See *Guomin dahui tongji huibao* (1984), pp. 35–38; *Di yici guomin dahui di liuci huiyi tongji* (1978), pp. 136–38; and *Zhunghua minguo nianjian* (1973, 1983–85, 1987–88).

[a]Data omitted in original source.

because of death and retirement (see table 10). In 1969 the KMT initiated the supplementary quota election for national representatives to take place with the triennial local elections. By 1988 there were eighty-one Taiwan-elected representatives (most of them KMT members) in the National Assembly—too few to challenge the mainlander majority even had they wanted to. The KMT senior representatives in that body had voted almost unanimously for President Chiang Kai-shek and his son, Chiang Ching-kuo, with some opposing the various Taiwanese vice presidents (see table 9). Most National Assembly members were male and resided in Taiwan. More than half possessed a college or university degree. By 1990 there were 753 assembly members, and it took 377 to elect the president and vice president.[2] Most KMT mainlanders approved of Lee's performance, and thus the mainlander-dominated National Assembly seemed likely to elect the first Taiwanese as the ROC's president. The key question was: whom would the National Assembly elect as vice president?

## The Kuomintang Nominates a President and Vice President

Although numerous political parties had sprung up since 1986, none of them could nominate a presidential or vice presidential candidate because they had no influence in the National Assembly. Most assembly members belonged to the KMT and sympathized with its goals. But in early 1990 more politicians and elite than ever before were demanding that National Assembly members resign so that newly elected representatives from Taiwan could reconstitute that body, amend the constitution, and empower the people to elect the president and vice president. But the majority of National Assembly members refused to resign, declaring that they had been duly elected in 1947 by all the Chinese people and that they would carry out their responsibilities to the bitter end. In February 1990, then, public attention focused on whom the KMT would nominate because that ticket would surely be endorsed by the National Assembly.

President Lee had proved to be an extremely popular president. Public opinion surveys gave him approval ratings of 80 percent or higher. Although the KMT's endorsing his candidacy was taken for granted, his running mate was an unknown quantity. Premier Lee Huan was often mentioned as a desirable candidate.[3] A mainlander who worked well with Taiwanese, Lee had helped Chiang Ching-kuo recruit talented young people for the KMT during the 1970s. Many young and old politicians in the KMT, the National Assembly, and the opposition parties perceived Lee as being "middle of the road" in his political views and respected him. James C. Y. Soong, Chen Li-an, and Chien Fu were other frequently mentioned candidates. The candidate who attracted the most public attention, however, was a military general named Chiang Wei-kuo, long believed to be the son of Chiang Kai-shek.

In December 1989, a rumor spread that Chiang Wei-kuo was actively seeking the vice presidency. By mid-January new rumors indicated that President Lee not only would ignore Chiang but would bypass Premier Lee as well.[4] These speculations were fueled by Chiang Wei-kuo's public comments. In early February, while visiting the United States, Chiang said, "It will be the free will of the National Assembly representatives to elect me as president or vice-president; I shall accept the will of the party, the will of the constitution, and the will of Heaven."[5] When asked by a reporter why he had made such a statement when former president Chiang Ching-kuo had declared that no member of the Chiang family would ever serve as president or vice president, Chiang Wei-kuo denied that Chiang Ching-kuo ever made such a statement. Chiang Wei-kuo's remarks caused a great sensation in Taiwan because many believed he was seeking the party's nomination.

Speculation over President Lee's running mate mounted until February 11, when the party chairman announced his preferred candidate.[6] At eleven o'clock that morning, the KMT's central committee did something unprecedented: it began discussing how to vote for the president and vice president. The central committee had always voted by standing up (approval) or sitting down (disapproval). But some party members, worried about Chairman Lee's nomination, proposed a secret ballot rather than the traditional standing or sitting.

The debate became heated, and many central committee members took the podium to defend their positions. Premier Lee Huan, who favored the secret ballot, argued for "first approving the method of voting and then deciding whom the party would nominate as president or vice president."[7] Secretary-General Soong countered, saying, "This body used the method of standing in the Chiang Ching-kuo era, and it is the traditional way we have always elected a president; only a few people have recently expressed strong feelings to disturb the party and want the secret ballot. Everyone should use the responsible approach of standing. Only by standing can you express whom you want to support and whom you do not want to support."[8] Chang Yu-sheng, the director of the Pacific Cultural Foundation, opposed Soong, saying that a high official had called him the night before and asked him to "support the procedure of standing up. I did not agree with his request. Moreover, who are they trying to manipulate? Do you want me to say their names? If you have the courage, let's have a secret ballot."[9] And so the debate continued, finally being determined by a show of hands in the early afternoon. The first vote of the 180 central committee members was 97 in favor of standing up and 79 opposed; in a second vote 99 voted against the secret ballot, and 70 voted for it.[10] Chairman Lee arrived at 2:30 P.M. and announced that his running mate was Li Yuan-zu. Except for one person, the central committee members stood, approving the slate of Lee Teng-hui for president and Li Yuan-zu for vice president

Li had been trained in West Germany as a lawyer, had served as president of National Zhengzhi University, and had been a minister of education and a judge in the military courts. Even with his impressive career, Li had kept out of the public eye, and consequently he was not well known. Mild-mannered and reticent, Li Yuan-zu belonged to no political faction. But just as he had no enemies, he also had few friends. At this time, most people did not realize that President Lee had appointed him because of his constitutional and legal expertise.[11] The president wanted Li's help to plan constitutional reform that would consolidate Taiwan's democracy.

High-ranking individuals in both the KMT and the government, however, viewed Chairman Lee's choice of vice president with alarm. Premier Lee Huan and Minister of Defense Hau Pei-tsun, bitter because the party chairman had not consulted them, also wanted to know the chairman's plans for the nation's future, especially toward the PRC, and believed he had excluded them from his inner circle. Many party elders now feared they might not be able to control the chairman and that mainlander political aspirations would no longer be assured, as in the past. Supporters of Premier Lee and Minister Hau began maneuvering in the National Assembly to select a new slate of candidates to oppose the KMT's nominees, meaning that, for the first time, there was no guarantee the National Assembly would automatically approve the KMT's choice of president and vice president. Their activities were immediately opposed by Lee's supporters in the party, so that for the first time since 1949 the KMT began to divide.

## Opposition Mounts

Refusing to consult with Minister Hau Pei-tsun, Premier Lee Huan, and others, Chairman Lee kept his choice of a running mate secret until the day he announced his choice, and his choice infuriated many top party leaders. Although Secretary-General Soong and others had persuaded the central committee to follow the traditional voting procedure, the president would now pay for his independent manner and political decisiveness.

The day after Lee nominated his running mate, Premier Lee Huan's supporters in the National Assembly began mobilizing the one hundred signatures necessary to propose Lin Yang-kang for president and Chiang Wei-kuo for vice president.[12] Lin, a highly respected and experienced Taiwanese, had served as Taiwan's provincial governor and premier and was president of the Judicial Yuan. He was popular in the south and could count on strong business support. Chiang Wei-kuo, a native of Chekiang province, chaired the National Security Council. Many National Assembly elders preferred Chiang because of his strong commitment to unifying China under the 1947 constitution. The ticket had the ideal ethnic balance, and momentum to support it rapidly grew among the National Assembly representatives.

Assemblyman Deng Jie, who had long-standing connections with the security and military branches and was popular with other representatives, assiduously gathered the one hundred signatures necessary to nominate the new ticket.[13] Deng Jie argued that the contest represented "a struggle between democracy and dictatorship," in which dictatorship (*ducai*) referred to President Lee, who had abused his presidential power. Moreover, said Deng Jie, "with the Lin-Chiang ticket there will be real democratization and the unification of China. This is a ticket that no one can refuse, not even the two nominees themselves."[14]

The president and his running mate, Li Yuan-zu, were severely criticized. For the first time since 1949, an ROC president was sharply and bitterly criticized in public, not by the opposition, but by members of his own party. On February 13, KMT member Chang Yu-sheng publicly complained that a faction in the KMT wanted too much power, that the party was not democratic, and that factional infighting was widespread.[15] He blamed the chairman and his secretary-general for this sorry state of affairs.

Two weeks later, on March 1, Lee Shen-fong, a KMT member of the party's New United Alliance faction, said, "The fact that the ruling party had to have a provisional committee to get the president and vice president elected was not legal."[16] He also complained that a "strong man [running] party affairs was passé, yet Lee Teng-hui still behaves like a strong man, because he makes the major decisions himself."[17] According to Lee, the party chairman and president had become a lonely, dictatorial leader, isolated from the people and poorly informed by his advisers.

On that same day, another party member of the same faction, the young legislator Chao Shao-kang, attacked President Lee for not displaying strong leadership and for selecting narrow-minded people for high government and party posts. He complained that the president had failed to make his policies clear to the people, thus losing their support. Chao charged that "when Lee Teng-hui was sworn into office as president, Hau Pei-tsun, Chiang Wei-kuo, and Lee Huan had supported him, but now they oppose him."[18]

Those criticizing Lee Teng-hui began referring to the key members led by Chairman Lee Teng-hui, Secretary-General Soong, and other standing committee and central committee members and the "mainstream" (zhuliu pai) group and those party members led by as the Lee Huan, Hau Pei-tsun, and others in the standing committee and central committee as the "nonmainstream" (fei zhuliu pai) group. These two groups did not divide exclusively along ethnic lines, nor did they reflect any particular ideological and policy position. But KMT conservatives, elders, many younger party members, and the New United Alliance increasingly sided with the nonmainstream faction to oppose Lee Teng-hui and the party's mainstream faction, who supported Lee. This cleavage now spilled into the National Assembly and threatened its proceedings.

On March 2, at the Chungshanlou Auditorium, Deng Jie stated that Lin and Chiang had agreed to be drafted for a new ticket, and he had already secured more than the one hundred signatures needed to nominate them.[19] A strong tide now ran in the National Assembly to elect Lin as the eighth president of the Republic of China and Chiang as vice president. If the assembly elected Lin and Chiang, it would be perceived by the opposition and many in the KMT as a conservative restoration trying to reverse democratization. The DPP-elected representatives in the National Assembly and Legislative Yuan now prepared to engage in a battle with KMT national representatives, although they were greatly outnumbered. The DPP also began organizing street demonstrations to mobilize public support against the First National Assembly.

## New Strains

The opening ceremony for the Eighth Congress of the National Assembly began at 10:00A.M. after 719 members were bused to the conference hall (33 were absent).[20] The assembly's secretary-general, Irwine W. Ho, opened the congress and nominated the ninety-four-year-old Xue Yue as the assembly's ceremonial chairman. Two DPP representatives immediately shouted, "We protest!" Zhang Guimu, another DPP representative, rushed to the podium and tried to turn off Xue's microphone while screaming that Xue Yue was not qualified to be congress chairman. Various elders then began shouting, and the DPP's Xu Meiying, a woman, and some supporting onlookers whistled loudly. Secretary-General Irwine W. Ho shouted, "Let us maintain the conference rules."

Suddenly a score of policemen entered the hall and seized the four DPP delegates (Cai Shiyuan, Huang Chaohui, Su Jiaquan, and Lo Meiwen), who had been loudly denouncing Xue Yue, and removed them from the hall while they kicked, cursed, and screamed, breaking one of the side glass doors as they were ejected. Secretary-General Ho then called the body to order and asked for a show of hands for Xue Yue. Xue was elected by a large margin. Supported by two colleagues, Xue slowly advanced to the podium, only to be blocked by DPP representative Hong Qichang. Police intervened and assisted the aged Xue to the podium. Irwine W. Ho then called for the national anthem to be sung, but midway through, Hong Qichang pushed over a large vase, sending it crashing to the floor. Xue Yue now began to read the assembly oath, but so slowly that Ho had to complete it. At that point eight DPP delegates rushed to the platform and hoisted a large black cotton banner with characters reading, "If the old representatives take their oaths, that means the death of the constitution." By now it was 10:30, and President Lee Teng-hui had arrived to address the assembly. The eight DPP members, as President Lee began to speak, stood up and shouted that their colleagues had been removed and demanded that the president do something. President Lee smiled and asked them to "please sit down." They sat down in front of the podium.

Meanwhile, the four DPP representatives who had been removed from the hall were placed on two separate buses and driven around the Yangming Mountains. The bus carrying Cai, Huang, and Lo eventually returned to the Chungshanlou Auditorium. On leaving the bus, Huang took an umbrella and shattered the bus window, and Cai whistled loudly without stopping. Huang then seized a brick and hurled it at the glass window of the conference hall's front door, shattering it, and cried out, "Whoever damages my reputation, I go all the way. This is my character." (The bus transporting Su Jiaquan had mysteriously disappeared.)

Inside the conference hall, President Lee had been addressing the assembly, but he stopped when he heard the altercation outside. The police then formed a human wall to prevent Huang Chaohui from entering the hall. The president finished his speech at 10:50; at 11:30 a luncheon began, with members taking their seats at nearby tables.

Huang and Cai were then allowed to rejoin their companions inside the hall. As the luncheon progressed, President Lee moved from table to table, toasting the assembly members. At 11:40 the ten remaining DPP members rose and called to the president in the Taiwanese dialect, instead of the national *guoyu* language, complaining that Su Jiaquan had not been allowed to return to the conference hall. President Lee ignored their comments and continued his rounds.

Assemblyman Huang Chaohui then stood on a chair and loudly cried, "Now I am counting to ten, and if Su Jiaquan is not immediately returned to this hall, I will begin to overturn these banquet tables!" Having counted to ten, he grasped the tablecloth of a nearby table, pulled it, and overturned the table, sending glasses of wine, plates of food, and bowls of soup, fish, and meat flying. Huang then overturned six more tables. Pandemonium broke out as aged assemblymen slipped in the food and people began screaming.

Security guards immediately grabbed the stunned president and whisked him into a side room, where one old assemblyman remarked, "This is horrible. What are you going to do about it?" The old assemblyman then said to Secretary-General Li Yuan-zu of the Office of the President, "If you cannot solve this problem, we will not support you." Li Yuan-zu did not speak, but President Lee answered in a firm voice, "I can solve this problem! I can solve this problem!"[21]

## Polarization and Reconciliation

As these events show, the political opposition's strategy had become violent. From their perspective, not only was democracy incomplete and progressing too slowly, but their members in the National Assembly were too few to make any difference. Therefore they had to resort to violent confrontation to arouse public passions to oppose this unjust, undemocratic institution. Too much political power was still concentrated in the National Assembly, and its members refused to step down and allow the election of Taiwanese representatives. The opposition now decided to use the tactics of humiliation and violence against the KMT representatives to arouse public indignation. The altercation on the opening day of the National Assembly's Eighth Convention was a shot across the bow of the mainlander-dominated power structure. Outnumbered in the main organs of the central government, the opposition, led by the DPP, now risked arrest in a a desperate effort to remove mainlander senior representatives from office so that direct elections for Taiwan's national representatives could be held.

The February 19 upheaval at the National Assembly was the talk of the island for many days. Many praised Huang Chaohui as a hero and glorified him as an advocate of democracy. Others, appalled at such behavior, wondered aloud whether such antics truly represented democracy. Many assembly delegates were now convinced that President Lee was too "soft" and "incompetent" to serve as president of the ROC at such a critical time and considered voting for the Lin-Chiang ticket. The February 19 affair further polarized the KMT.

Recognizing the serious challenge to his nomination from the KMT assemblymen and the threat of violence by the DPP directed at the political center, and stung by mounting press criticism of his indecision, President Lee turned to political brokering to end the KMT's factional power struggle. On March 2 he announced the formation of a small committee of respected party elders—Huang Shao-ku, Shieh Tung-min, Yuan Shou-chien, Li Kuo-ting, Chiang Yen-shih, Chen Li-fu, Ku Chen-fu, and Ni Wen-ya—that would mediate between the two factions.[22] Ni Wen-ya, a former chairman of the Legislative Yuan and husband of Finance Minister Shirley W. Y. Kuo, had links to leading figures in the mainstream faction, whereas Huang Shao-ku reputedly had links to those prominent in the nonmainstream faction.[23] President Lee wanted to end party factional strife quickly and obtain the assembly's approval of his party's presidential ticket.

At 4:00 P.M. on March 3, the eight-man group met with President Lee at his home to discuss how to avoid confrontation in the National Assembly and ensure President Lee's election. At the meeting, which lasted two hours and twenty minutes, President Lee expressed deep regret for the "political confusion" and listened to various elders criticize him for not selecting talented people and not consulting with top officials.[24] President Lee defended his actions, explaining that he had selected a vice president who understood constitutional reform and could help him reform the ROC polity by adhering to the 1947 constitution. Finally, Lee hoped that the elders could persuade Lin and Chiang to withdraw their names. The team decided on three arguments to get Lin and Chiang to renounce their candidacy: (1) the Lin-Chiang ticket violated KMT party discipline and unity; (2) it endangered the unity of the KMT party; and (3) because the party had nominated President Lee and his running mate, Lin and Chiang must withdraw their candidacy.[25] On that same day, Lin and Chiang went to a large luncheon, attended by some two hundred National Assembly members, where toasts could be heard of "Long live Chiang Wei-kuo" and "Long live the Republic of China."[26]

On March 5, Chiang Yen-shih took the lead and invited Shieh Tung-min, Hau Pei-tsun, Lin Yang-kang, and Chiang Wei-kuo to lunch with the other seven elders at the Taipei Pinkuan. Chiang had served in the Joint Commission for Rural Reconstruction and had been KMT secretary-general under Chiang Ching-kuo. He not only was friendly to President Lee but was highly respected among the party elders as brilliant, fair-minded, and able to achieving consensus under the most difficult of conditions. Acting as chairman, Chiang Yen-shih outlined President Lee's opinions on how the ROC could achieve stability and solve the election impasse.[27] For the next four hours the group discussed the president's handling of ROC participation in the 1989 Asian Development Bank meeting in Beijing; the role he played in the exit of the KMT director of organizational affairs, Kuan Chung (then still deputy secretary-general); and his selection of Li Yuan-zu as vice president.[28] Everyone finally agreed that, to reconcile the conflict, four goals had to be achieved: a collective leadership must be established; a working dialogue between the top leaders must begin; President Lee must clearly articulate his views on constitutional reform; and he must outline his policy toward mainland China. Some opined that President Lee should not chair the KMT because the party's chairman should be separate from the presidency and that the party needed a new secretary-general.[29]

President Lee answered his critics in a speech on March 7.[30] He promised to elicit the views of experts to consider a constitutional reform that would conform to "the spirit of the country." Defending his dual role of president and KMT chairman, President Lee insisted that he intended to consult with others about the efficacy of holding these two offices simultaneously and to act accordingly. He reiterated his strong commitment to unifying China, and he denounced those who used the slogan "democracy" to advocate an independent Taiwan, disturb social harmony, and destabilize the political order. Lee vowed to suppress their activities. Finally, he declared he would adopt an "attitude of selfless dedication to the public good" *(dagong wusi taidu)* and rely on institutionalized procedures *(zhiduhua)* to select the best personnel, rather than presidential cronies, to run the government. The president was fighting for his political life. His speech received an unenthusiastic reaction and persuaded only a few.[31] DPP member Ju Gau-jeng expressed his displeasure at the president's failure to offer any concrete details. KMT legislator Chao Shao-kang said that "the contents of his speech still left much to be desired to satisfy the expectations of the people" and that the president had "focused only on principles and not on how to take concrete action."[32] Hau Pei-tsun gave the president no support, saying only that he had no opinion and belonged to no faction, that, as defense minister, he would not obey any party's decision, and that his only intention was to loyally serve the government. Meanwhile, those in favor of the Lin-Chiang ticket continued to mobilize support within the National Assembly. Lin and Chiang publicly stated that they were not actively competing to be nominated but that they would accept a nomination if the National Assembly so decided.[33]

The mediating efforts by Chiang Yen-shih and the other elder statesmen so far had failed to break the impasse. Yet Chiang Yen-shih continued to shuttle back and forth between key elder statesmen and their contacts in each faction to build a consensus that would persuade Lin and Chiang to withdraw from the race. Shieh Tung-min, a former vice president and a Taiwanese, held talks with Lin Yang-kang.[34] Some felt that resolving the crisis depended on President Lee's giving up his chairmanship of the KMT and limiting his power. Behind the scenes, many Taiwanese business persons and various elite contacted Lin Yang-kang and urged him to step down.[35]

On March 9, with the deadlock still persisting, President Lee tried a new tactic. He said, "It is rare in a democratic society to have two factions of a single party running for the presidency, but as long as there is unity and peace, that contest cannot harm the country and the party."[36] He was in effect telling his opponents that he would allow the election contest to be played out in the National Assembly. The mood of many top government officials became gloomy. On that same day Wang Chien-hsüan, vice minister of the political affairs section of the Economics Ministry, declared that, because there was no longer any authority in government to carry out policy, he felt helpless and feared for the future. After serving in government for twenty-eight years, Wang decided to resign.[37] Although many elite like Wang now were experiencing a sense of what Thomas A. Metzger has called the "Confucian predicament"—a state of great anxiety caused by the shared perceptions that existing "negative" circumstances are becoming worse and worse because of great moral failure and that without dramatic actions all is lost[38]—the key elite were ready to accept Chiang Yen-shih's compromise solution.

On March 9 the mediating efforts of Chiang Yen-shih, Shieh Tung-min, and other KMT elders, who had held extended discussions with Lin Yang-kang, finally paid off. On that day Lin publicly withdrew his name from the presidential contest.[39] The next day Chiang Wei-kuo announced that he would not run for the vice presidency.[40] President Lee met privately with both men to express his gratitude and best wishes. Those in the National Assembly backing Lin and Chiang, however, were not to be deterred and vowed to fight on to elect the pair.[41] Political brokering had ended the crisis. The factions had reconciled and agreed to the Lee Teng-hui and Li Yuan-zu ticket, paving the way for the National Assembly to elect the KMT candidates.

The severity of this elite struggle was unprecedented in KMT history since 1949. Its resolution gravely affected the personal relations and morale within the KMT leadership. Lee Huan and Lee Teng-hui, who had effectively cooperated before, could no longer work together, and Lee Huan would soon retire from political life. Many party elders, frustrated and embittered by the sudden turn of events, would also retire. In effect, the conservative mainlander elite had lost their bid to retain power within the KMT. No longer able to control this Taiwanese president and party chairman as they hoped, they had to work with him, but some continued to wage a rear-guard struggle to influence government policy, yet their days in power were numbered. New challenges now arose from the opposition elite and their supporters.

## A National Crisis

Had Lin and Chiang not stepped down, National Assemblyman Deng Jie and others, who had mobilized many in the assembly to support them, could well have maneuvered the assembly's election of Lin and Chiang; on March 15, Deng had announced that "all together we have obtained 140 Assembly signatures on behalf of the Lin-Chiang ticket, and we will not reveal their names."[42] But Deng now admitted defeat and said he no longer intended to seek support for the Lin-Chiang ticket (four days before, vigorous efforts had commenced in the National Assembly to elicit support for the Lee-Li ticket).[43] National Assembly representatives now addressed the recent attacks of the political opposition. On March 14 the National Assembly leadership issued a circular to twenty-seven DPP representatives informing them that they could not participate in the congress because they had not taken the assembly oath correctly. (On opening day, eleven DPP representatives had refused to say "the people of the ROC" and had insisted on saying "the people of Taiwan" [*Taiwan renmin*]. Another sixteen KMT representatives from Taiwan, when taking the oath, had insisted on using the Western calendar instead of referring to the Republic of China periodizing, which began in 1912.)[44] The ROC judiciary declared their oaths invalid, and those representatives were denied their rights in the National Assembly and informed that they could not participate in the assembly's proceedings.[45]

On that same day, the assembly's First Examination Committee, meeting for only twenty-four minutes, approved four recommendations for the National Assembly to adopt; in effect, strengthen the assembly's power: revise the Temporary Provisions; instruct the National Assembly to meet annually instead of once every six years; increase each assembly representative's monthly salary from NT$52,000 (US$1,925) to NT$200,000 (US$7,407); and authorize the National Assembly to veto laws passed by the Legislative Yuan.[46] (Between 1947 and 1972 the National Assembly had held five meetings to approve the Temporary Provisions' eleven articles.[47] The First Examination Committee wanted to retain Article 7, which allowed the assembly to use its power to change laws, but it recommended that Article 8 be altered to allow the assembly to meet once each year instead of waiting for the president to convene the assembly.)[48] By disciplining the DPP representatives and possibly approving the committee's four recommendations, the National Assembly gave the distinct impression that it was trying to enhance its power. At least the elite and ordinary people throughout Taiwan thought so,[49] igniting a firestorm throughout Taiwan. Outrage fulminated from all quarters. DPP leaders tried to obtain support from the Legislative Yuan to reinstate their sixteen assemblymen. Liberal KMT leaders, angry with the assembly, tried to do the same, but to no avail.

The DPP then decided to muster popular support for their deposed representatives. Several hundred members marched to Chungshanlou Auditorium to demand that their party's representatives be allowed to join the congress. A wall of police blocked their efforts, and after some party stalwarts repeatedly hurled their bodies against the police, they sat down in front of the police line, refusing to move.[50] The next day, the DPP again marched to Chungshanlow Auditorium, only to be blocked by a thousand riot police.

Angry KMT members called on President Lee on March 15 to demand an end to the "constitutional revision farce" in the National Assembly.[51] On March 16, fourteen DPP leaders and party representatives of the National Assembly, including DPP chairman Huang Hsin-chieh, tried to stage a sit-down protest in front of the Office of the President.[52] Military police quickly dragged them away.

On March 14, students at National Taiwan University (NTU) began assembling in small groups on campus.[53] By March 16, hundreds of NTU students in a frenzy of moral outrage over the National Assembly's actions, called on other university students to gather at the Chiang Kai-shek Memorial in a large-scale sit-down demonstration.[54] Students at universities in Taichung and Tainan cities also began demonstrating. On March 17 the students already assembled at the Chiang Kai-shek Memorial in Taipei were joined by students from more than a dozen universities and colleges.[55] For the first time in forty years, a large-scale student movement, involving some twenty-two thousand students, had broken out. Taiwan's students, inspired by Chinese students in

Beijing in spring 1989, now decided to organize a student boycott of the National Assembly, very much as Beijing students had organized a similar demonstration against the CCP at Tiananmen Square. The ROC government made no attempt to disband the students.

Slogans like Organize Mass Boycotts! Cut Classes! and Refuse to Pay Taxes! began reverberating throughout society. The situation was becoming explosive, with violence likely if the authorities tried to force the students to return to their classrooms. Editorials appeared in the press denouncing the National Assembly. The Legislative Yuan met and vowed to cut off funds to the National Assembly.[56] Public opinion had suddenly turned against the National Assembly, as revealed by opinion polls taken by newspapers and by the Research, Development, and Evaluation Commission of the Executive Yuan.[57] A national crisis was brewing.

## Resolving the Crisis

On Saturday afternoon, March 17, as thousands of students congregated in Chiang Kai-shek Memorial Park, President Lee Teng-hui appeared on all three ROC television channels to appeal for calm and patience.[58] He said that the National Assembly would be cautious, eschew any reckless action, and act responsibly in its decision making. He predicted that the assembly would abide by the will of the people, and he promised the nation that democratic reform would continue.

The president's speech did not deter the students, whose resolve stiffened over the next few days as many promised to sit in for the entire week until the National Assembly dissolved. Many vowed to undertake a hunger strike. By March 18, some thirty thousand students and other people had clustered around the Chiang Kai-shek Memorial.[59] A sea of posters and banners had also appeared at the memorial with such slogans as Down with the Thieves in the Yangming Mountains! Nothing like this had ever occurred in Taiwan's history. The students remained calm and orderly. The government still did not intervene. Meanwhile, the National Assembly had taken the measure of the public's anger. On March 18 it published a declaration explaining the rogue committee's actions: the committee had reflected the views of only a few representatives and not the will of the entire assembly; the proposal to meet once a year had nothing to do with the assembly's power to initiate and approve new laws; the committee's proposal to revise the Temporary Provisions had not been approved, and only the assembly would do that; finally, more detailed discussion would follow about these four recommendations. This declaration did little to soothe public anger or persuade the students to return to their classrooms.

On March 19 President Lee offered a new proposal; he promised to convene a Conference to Decide the ROC's Destiny (Guoshi huiyi) in June. The president described the conference as representing all walks of life in Taiwan; participants would discuss the nation's future and try to reach a consensus on how to resolve the nation's problems.[60] On that same day, the National Assembly overwhelmingly rejected the recommendations passed by its First Examination Committee.[61] The National Assembly had backed down.

Yet the students, the last obstacle to restoring national calm, refused to budge, and on that morning of March 20 many began a hunger strike.[62] President Lee now sent his education minister, Mao Kao-wen, and the director of the Research, Development, and Evaluation Commission, Ma Ying-chiu, with a personal letter urging the students to protect their health and return to their schools. The students were still not persuaded. Meanwhile, the president met with several groups of student leaders and tried to placate them. The next day, President Lee repeated his intention to press forward with his conference. He repeated that serious issues faced the nation and vowed that views from the full spectrum of society would be represented to deal with the problems facing the nation.[63]

On March 21, the National Assembly voted for a new president: of 668 ballots cast, 641 went for Lee Teng-hui, the eighth president of the ROC.[64] Lee expressed his gratitude, promising to push for democratic reform and improve the society and economy. The next day the students began leaving the Chiang Kai-shek Memorial, having spent more than 150 hours peacefully demonstrating against the National Assembly.[65] On that same day, the assembly elected Li Yuan-zu the eighth vice president of the ROC, giving him the highest share of votes ever accorded a vice president, 602 ballots out of a total of 644 cast.[66] The crisis had ended.

Taiwan's democracy now entered a new, critical phase. The DPP-led opposition, emboldened by its successful struggle to delegitimize the National Assembly, now wanted to accelerate the democratization process. But that opposition still did not have the legal means to compete for national political power as long as the Temporary Provisions remained in place, freezing the constitution, and the senior representatives still held power by controlling the National Assembly and Legislative Yuan. The DPP and the KMT still had no formal contacts with each other. How, then, could the DPP-led opposition work within the framework of the law to reform the constitution, if the KMT did not offer a vision and plan for constitutional reform? The issue of constitutional reform also laid bare the ethnicity problem *(shengji wenti)* and the issue of Taiwan nationalism. Taiwan's political elite were still divided and unable to agree on how political power should be used. In both the ruling party and the DPP factions now competed, to divide the elite even more. Under these conditions, if factional disagreement shifted to the streets in the form of competing popular demonstrations, it was a recipe for disaster for Taiwan's fragile democracy. The key issue facing the new president was how to encourage the elite to settle their differences and work together, play by the rules, and agree to work for constitutional reform. In other words, how to forge an elite alliance or pact so that orderly constitutional reform could pave the way for removing the senior representatives and establishing elections for Taiwan's national representatives and leaders. Elite support for this political reform also had to be connected with some nationally agreed-on plan for the unification of China, or else the ruling party might lose its legitimacy to govern.

# CHAPTER NINE

# Achieving a Partial
# Political Settlement

The March unrest originated in elite disagreements and public passions, but there was no substantive public dissatisfaction directed toward the reform of the constitution, as confirmed by two public opinion polls at that time: of the elite sample, 86.4 percent believed that the ROC was experiencing a constitutional crisis, but of the general public sample only 47.3 percent believed such a crisis existed.[1] To restore elite confidence in the polity and the prospects for reform, on March 21, 1990, President Lee appointed Chiang Yen-shih to convene a National Affairs Conference to decide the country's destiny.[2] On April 2, Chiang Yen-shih stated that "President Lee considered the National Affairs Conference to be for the entire country, neither for a political party nor for a small political group. It was not a meeting to strike a political deal."[3]

But elite suspicion of the president's plan ran deep, reflecting that political culture of mistrust that afflicted virtually all of the Chinese elite. Some believed that the president was trying to promote Taiwan independence and had abandoned the KMT's mission. Still others suspected him of currying favor with the mainlander power groups to strengthen his personal power. These suspicions of the president's intentions continued right up until the National Affairs Conference convened in late June, attesting to that widely shared elite skepticism toward the political center. Such suspicion, however, has always characterized the way the Chinese regarded their leaders. If President Lee wanted elite support for his National Affairs Conference, he had to entice the major players to take his proposal seriously and support it. Given the traditional distrust between the ruling party and the opposition and the absence of any formal communication between them, the president risked having his conference discredited and never held, an outcome certain to weaken his authority even more.

## The National Affairs Conference

By March 28, Chiang Yen-shih and his colleagues had drawn up a tentative list of twenty-five names for the National Affairs Conference's preparatory committee (table 11).[4] Most invitees were less than sixty years old, and KMT members were overwhelmingly from that party's liberal wing. At least half the members were non-KMT, representing business, academia, the opposition party, and nonparty circles. President Lee ordered that a special post office box be established so that anyone could express his or her views to the preparatory

TABLE 11

*Members of the National Affairs Conference's Preparatory Committee*

| Name | Occupation | Party Affiliation |
|---|---|---|
| Wang Yü-yun | National policy adviser to president | KMT |
| Wang Tih-wu | Chairman of board for *Lianhebao* | KMT |
| Tien Hung-mao | Scholar, University of Wisconsin | None |
| Chiu Hungdah | Scholar, University of Maryland | None |
| Lü Yali | Scholar, National Taiwan University | None |
| Yü Chi-chung | Chairman of board for *Zhongguo shibao* | KMT |
| James C. Y. Soong | Secretary-general of KMT | KMT |
| Wu Feng-shan | Head of nonparty organization | None |
| Shih Chi-yang | Vice premier | KMT |
| Hu Fu | Scholar, National Taiwan University | None |
| Kao Yu-shu | Senior adviser to president | None |
| Chen Yongxing | Businessman | DPP |
| Chen Changwen | Lawyer | KMT |
| Tao Pai-chuan | Scholar, national policy adviser to president | KMT |
| Kang Ning-hsiang | Politician | DPP |
| Huang Hsin-chieh | Politician | DPP |
| Chang Chun-hong | Politician | DPP |
| Huang Shicheng | Government official | None |
| Huang Yuejing | Scholar | None |
| Chang King-yuh | President of National Zhengzhi University | KMT |
| Zhang Boya | Head, Health Department | None |
| Ku Cheng-fu | Businessman | KMT |
| Cai Hongwen | National policy adviser to president | KMT |
| Chiang Yen-shih | Secretary-general of Office of the President | KMT |
| Hsieh Shen-san | Head of United Workers' League | KMT |

SOURCE: See chapter 9, note 4.

committee.[5] Then on March 29 a special telephone hot line was set up to encourage people to express their opinions to the committee.[6] On April 8 the government revealed that the Executive Yuan would appropriate NT$20 million (US$740,740) for the National Affairs Conference.

On March 24, Chiang Yen-shih scheduled the preparatory committee to convene on April 4 at 10:00 A.M., but it did not meet until April 14 at the Taipei Pinkuan.[7] President Lee addressed the committee members by exhorting them to carry out their work with fairness, impartiality, and diligence while maintaining high professional standards. After deciding the time, place, and topics, the committee consulted with ninety-five scholars and met with some five thousand overseas Chinese and another five thousand youths in Taiwan.

By May 5 the committee had drawn up rules for selecting the National Affairs Conference's 120 delegates,[8] and a seven-person committee, headed by Chiang Yen-shih, had reviewed the possible delegates' social status, professional standing, and general knowledge. President Lee then selected twenty members; each member of the committee selected two persons; another twenty-five were chosen from various segments of society. On May 18 President Lee sent out the personal invitations to the chosen delegates.

The president then clarified the purpose of the National Affairs Conference: "This National Affairs Conference takes no partisan position to advance any definitive conclusions at this time. The people can say anything they want, such as how long the premier should serve or how the constitution and polity should be reformed. The people's opinion, after all, serves as the foundation for politics." He then emphasized that "only through stability and unity can we build the foundation for all kinds of reform."[9] Chiang Yen-shih followed, insisting that the president believed that the National Affairs Conference was "most certainly being endorsed by the people."[10] But the suspicious elite were still unconvinced of the president's sincerity.

On May 14 President Lee met with nine university presidents and told them that he had no intention of limiting the conference's topics and that any issue could be discussed.[11] On June 23 Cheyne J. Y. Chiu, the president's spokesperson, stated that "if there are any consequences from this conference, it will not be the doing of the KMT."[12] "The National Affairs Conference had no preconceived political agenda," but if there was a consensus, political reform might follow.

But the press still suspected that President Lee intended to use the National Affairs Conference to pursue his political agenda. On April 29, when the president said that "the constitution need not be fundamentally changed, and we

TABLE 12
*Profile of National Affairs Conference Participants*

| | No. | Percentage |
|---|---|---|
| Kuomintang veterans | 34 | 26 |
| Kuomintang liberals | 15 | 12 |
| Intellectuals, scholars | 22 | 17 |
| Business people | 4 | 3 |
| Democratic Progressive Party members | 13 | 10 |
| Former political dissidents or political prisoners | 12 | 9 |
| Media representatives | 7 | 5 |
| Members of religious groups | 3 | 2 |
| National Assembly representatives | 10 | 8 |
| Other nonparty elite | 5 | 4 |
| Unclassified attendees | 5 | 4 |
| TOTAL | 130 | 100 |

SOURCE: Compiled by the authors from the official conference list of those who attended the opening session. For a complete list of invited delegates and those who attended, see *Guoshi huiyi zongjie baogao* (Complete conclusions reported from the National Affairs Conference), no. 1 (1990), pp. 1–2, unpublished.

can simply add new articles," the press vilified him. President Lee's associates denied that he was up to anything and averred that he was only expressing his personal opinion.[13]

On June 24 the procedures for convening the National Affairs Conference were made final, with 150 delegates invited from all walks of life (table 12) (130 actually attended).[14] The next day Chiang Yen-shih announced that a conference standing committee would review the conference findings and report to the Office of the President.[15] The elites' response to the president's conference was mixed.

## Elite Responses to the National Affairs Conference

Many opposition politicians and liberal KMT members now wanted to abolish the Temporary Provisions, end the "period of suppression of communist insurrection," and retire the "senior representatives."[16] But the more radical among them wanted to restructure the polity. The intellectual Chen Fangmin, for example, wanted the conference "to reform the political system and provide a blueprint for restructuring the character of the state." He predicted that "if the KMT only wants to use the National Affairs Conference to mollify a single party—the DPP—and to cool down the current crisis, then this conference will not succeed. The tensions in society will worsen, and this conference will be the greatest political hoax perpetrated by the KMT since it arrived on

Taiwan."[17] Other elite worried that if the conference failed, it would ruin the chance for real political reform. Zhang Minggui, a political scientist from National Zhengzhi University, doubted the efficacy of a National Affairs Conference because it seemed to lack legitimacy and did not have a moral mandate from the people.[18] Another scholar, Yang Taixun, worried that "if the National Affairs Conference did not produce any concrete results, the people would lose their faith in the KMT."[19]

Some scholars argued that the National Affairs Conference should include "constitutional and political reform and policies toward the mainland," as well as "basic human rights," because "a major issue for this conference should be to build into our democratic system the preservation of human rights so that the development of Taiwan's society and polity can be made a reality."[20] Overseas scholars like Chen Wenyen charged that the National Affairs Conference could never achieve political reform because it was solely the president's idea: "How dare the president propose a national conference in the name of the Taiwan people?"[21] Chen doubted that the Office of the President could hold a fair conference, and he charged the president with having a hidden political agenda that this conference was supposed to promote.

But by early June some intellectuals, after careful study, began endorsing President Lee's conference and admiring his courage. Chen Zheming hoped the conference would identify areas of "consensus" for future reform.[22] But Professor Hu Fu, a distinguished expert on constitutional law, withdrew from the conference only a few days before it convened,[23] saying: "I do not know what the results will be from holding this National Affairs Conference. Its results might have nothing to do with constitutional reform and only reflect political struggle. Therefore, I am withdrawing."[24] This conference, he added, is "a soccer game in which one does not know where to kick the ball."[25]

Li Hongxi, Hu's departmental colleague, believed that popular demonstrations had produced the National Affairs Conference, not the KMT's leadership. Moreover, he did not trust the KMT members who organized the conference, and he doubted whether enough reform-minded delegates would be invited.[26] Yang Guoshu, a social scientist at the Academia Sinica and a liberal, also refused to attend, claiming that those few scholars invited "were like a small vase of flowers [huaping] with no opportunity to be seen and heard."[27] Yang believed the major parties would cut a deal at the conference because everyone was "already divided into two parties. You belong to either one side or the other, and there is no chance to be independent."[28]

Just as many liberal elites were skeptical of this conference, so too were the opposition elite. When DPP leaders heard President Lee propose the National

Affairs Conference, they set up a committee to select their delegates to participate according to the proportion of votes their political party had won in the December 2, 1989, election.[29] This committee recommended that if the KMT fielded more representatives than it was entitled to, the DPP should boycott the conference. Central committee member Chen said, "We don't care if we don't participate in this conference. It could turn out to be just another endless affair with all sorts of opinions and viewpoints. The DPP should make a complete study of how to prepare this conference and develop its position on constitutional reform."[30]

From the start, the DPP had feared that the KMT would dominate the National Affairs Conference and that the president was insincere about reform. On March 29, 1990, Chiang Yen-shih met with DPP chairman Huang Hsin-chieh to discuss setting up a preparatory committee. They agreed that impartial and public-spirited persons *(gongzheng renshi)* should be appointed to such a committee.[31] After the meeting, Chiang Yen-shih said, "Both sides have agreed that the National Affairs Conference is a good idea"; DPP chairman Huang said that he "hoped it would be a success." Their conciliatory meeting paved the way for President Lee's inviting Chairman Huang to the Office of the President on April 2, the first time that the ruling party's leader had even formally met with the main opposition party's leader. Given the powerful, Manichaean currents of distrust, this meeting was a breakthrough for political reconciliation.

Huang and Lee, both men of simple origins, got along well at their first meeting. Chairman Huang later told reporters that the president was a "daring, candid, and courageous man. He could not do a satisfactory job at first because the old political system had tied his hands, and he had no way so far to be his own person. But if he can truly respect the people and run in a real popular election, the DPP party will vote for him."[32] Huang proved his political skills by fielding a tough question on where he and his party stood on "unification with China" and an "independent Taiwan":

Many say that if there is no Taiwan independence, we cannot gain any respect. This is false. The main problem for Taiwan is that it has not become a truly open and democratic society. If we can achieve that goal, then we do not have to do anything more. . . . The people on both sides of the Taiwan Straits really do not understand each other. We need the means for better interaction with each other, so that after a long period of time there will be better understanding. Then we can talk about unification.[33]

Huang believed that the president sincerely "wants reforms" but that "he must take full responsibility, because he represents all the people. As for myself, I represent only the opposition party and those our party represents."[34]

But Huang's party was not united about participating in the National Affairs Conference. On April 3 former DPP chairman Yao Chia-wen criticized his party for not demanding more credit for promoting political reform: "I feel that yesterday's meeting was a success, but the real credit for that should go to the DPP's leadership meeting of March 26 and the decision taken at that time, as well as to our party's standing committee meeting, insisting that reform issues should be clearly sorted out so that the national conference will not ignore our party's aims."[35] Yao doubted the president was sincere about convening a fair conference and felt it would take at least two years to reform the entire political system. How could this conference bring about political reforms? Other DPP members, including Wu Nairen, felt the same way.[36] The party appeared to be splitting along factional lines over participation in the conference. Then, on April 3, Chiang Yen-shih invited four DPP members— Chang Chun-hong, Chen Yongxing, Wu Nairen, and Zhang Junxiong—to join the preparatory committee.[37] The DPP declined.[38] Chiang Yen-shih again invited DPP members to join,[39] and on April 10 the DPP agreed but nominated Huang Hsin-chieh, Chang Chun-hong, Chen Yongxing, and Kang Ning-hsiang.[40]

The DPP leaders still disagreed on whether to join the conference, with Chen Yongxing saying that "if the DPP wishes to withdraw from the battlefield of the National Affairs Conference, that is indeed regrettable. Whatever Chairman Huang and others decide, I will still participate in the National Affairs Conference even if that means I do not have the support of my party. In such a case, I will withdraw from the party."[41] Wu Nairen scolded Chen, and debate continued, with Chang Chun-hong, the DPP's secretary-general, saying, "I feel we should stay on the battlefield and get as much as we can out of our efforts."[42] On May 15, Chairman Huang lashed out, saying that if the New Tide faction wanted to oppose Premier Hau and President Lee, they should do so but without making any further trouble for the DPP.[43] On June 2 the DPP's standing committee met and approved (eighteeen to thirteen) the party's participation in the National Affairs Conference. Both Shih Ming-Teh, just released from prison, and Hsu Hsin-liang, who had already returned to Taiwan, supported the conference. Thus the strong doubts shared by top DPP members about President Lee and his intentions had faded by mid-June.

Having decided to participate, the DPP began preparing its constitution to replace that of the ROC and, by June 20, had produced a draft to present at the upcoming National Affairs Conference.[44] On June 28 the DPP joined the conference. Had President Lee and Chiang Yen-shih failed to convince the DPP to join the National Affairs Conference, the DPP would have boycotted it, and there would have been no elite rapprochement.

Meanwhile, a KMT team studying the Lushan Conference of 1936 (Lushan huiyi) and the Political Consultative Conference of 1946 (Zhengzhi xieshang huiyi) for lessons the party could apply to the upcoming conference[45] concluded that the Lushan Conference had forged a strong consensus to oppose Japan and wage war if need be. But the 1946 conference had not achieved a consensus on other issues, and it had accomplished little. The KMT team feared that the June conference would follow the pattern of the 1946 conference and that the KMT would be blamed.

Premier Hau Pei-tsun countered: "This national conference is only to gather information and elicit diverse opinions; it is definitely not a meeting to produce new laws, nor does it have any power to 'enforce' or 'set definite limits' for reform."[46] Chiang Yen-shih pointed out that "diverse views exist within the KMT about the national conference's purpose, and party members disagree about the question of reform; some want only more enlightenment *[kaiming]*, while others demand reform *[gaige]*."[47]

The KMT, like the DPP, was not unified. In late June an internal KMT survey indicated great disagreement over the conference.[48] Of 750 questionnaires sent out, only 126 members responded, suggesting that most had not expressed their views because they feared offending those party leaders supporting the conference. Of the less than one-fifth who had responded, some 90 percent believed that the party should first agree on what the conference ought to achieve so that this consensus could then be used to mobilize support for political reform. These same respondents also wanted to abolish the Temporary Provisions, to terminate the "period of suppressing the communist rebellion," and to amend the ROC constitution but not draft a new one. Respondents were divided over government policy toward the PRC: half stated that the government's current policy was too conservative and imprecise; the other half agreed with it. On June 19 the KMT leadership stated that its conference representatives would ask only to amend the constitution, abolish the Temporary Provisions, preserve the current government structure, and elect a new national assembly while retaining its powers.[49]

Leading businessmen had been invited to the conference, but the billionaire Wang Yung-ching, head of the Taiwan Plastics Corporation, declined, saying that when he had previously attended a government-sponsored conference on economic reform, he had felt "cheated."[50] Wang typified many Taiwanese businesspeople who doubted that this conference could produce satisfactory political reforms.

Cheng Wenlong, a leading pundit, suggested that the National Affairs Conference must be based on the "will of the majority of the country's citizens and must nurture their aspirations."[51] Cheng doubted that such a conference, with several hundred representatives meeting for only three to five days, could produce any concrete results or break "the political logjam." Others also felt this conference could not achieve any practical results. Xie Xuexian, executive secretary of the China Youth Party, believed that in such a conference "each person would just speak his own mind" and that no consensus could be reached.[52]

On May 13 some thirty-odd scholars and policy experts who had rejected both the KMT and DPP positions proposed a reform platform of simplifying Taiwan's administrative system and unifying the National Assembly and Legislative Yuan. They also demanded that all the country's top leaders be directly elected by the people and that the PRC and ROC explore cooperation.[53]

On April 22 the Presbyterian Church announced three recommendations it was sending President Lee Teng-hui: abolish the Temporary Provisions, establish a basic law to replace the present constitution, and free all political prisoners.[54] The church's leaders vowed that if the president did not act on these recommendations, they would mobilize their members and demonstrate against the conference. The Association for the Homeless even drafted a letter to Premier Lee Huan demanding that the National Affairs Conference discuss rising land prices and the shortage of housing.[55] Xie Xuexian condemned the conference as a tool of the KMT and the DPP that would give them special political power.[56]

By mid-June a rising tide of criticism and alarm made it seem that the conference might never be held. DPP chairman Huang Hsin-chieh declared that "if the National Affairs Conference cannot reach a satisfactory consensus regarding political reform, we will not hesitate to withdraw from it."[57] Chen Yongxing, who had been eager to represent the DPP on the preparatory committee, stated that "if the National Affairs Conference does not meet the people's expectations, the DPP will withdraw and hold its own conference. The present list of representatives is already dominated by too many right-wing scholars."[58] Xuan Yiwen, a woman in the Youth Party, believed that "a lot of people would just talk about a lot of things."[59] She predicted that it "is not going to have any influence on future historical events" and therefore she would not participate.

To silence his critics, President Lee invited a number of overseas Chinese, six of whom had been on the government's blacklist and thus not allowed in the country, to attend the conference. Shortly before their arrival in Taipei, the government had arrested Chen Zhaonan, a leading dissident who had formed a party in the United States aimed at overthrowing the ROC government. Chen had been released on bail, and his lawyer now demanded that charges against him be dropped. On June 24, before the judiciary reviewed his case, four overseas delegates to the conference, Wu Fengpei, Yang Meixing, Wang Guirong, and Chang Fu-mei, held a press conference at which they called for his immediate exoneration and threatened to boycott the conference if their demands were not met.[60] They tried to see President Lee to ask him to order the judiciary to drop all charges against Chen.[61] The president refused to see them, but Secretary-General Chiang Yen-shih met with them for ninety minutes and persuaded them to await the judiciary's decision, explaining that the Office of the President had no authority to intervene. He urged patience; the group relented and attended the conference.

President Lee even invited Peng Ming-min, the most famous dissident since 1949, to attend the conference. Peng had been arrested in 1964 for sedition, released pending trial, and then fled, ending up in the United States, where he spent more than twenty years denouncing the KMT as an immoral, illegal group undermining democratization and economic growth. Tien Hung-mao had met with Peng in Los Angeles in May and informed ROC officials that he might be willing to return to Taiwan for the conference.[62] After President Lee extended his invitation to Peng, the island was awash with speculation about Peng's return. Wu Feng-shan and Huang Hsin-chieh even went to the United States to plead with Peng to return to Taiwan. Peng then wrote to Li Ao, a journalist and KMT critic, listing seven conditions that would have to be met before he would participate. The most important was that the judiciary's Prosecution Office apologize for its treatment of him some twenty years before. He also demanded that the office's top official meet him at the airport, but without shaking hands. The judiciary officials reacted swiftly.[63] They had merely followed the law and had no reason to apologize to Peng; Peng did not respect ROC law, but if he returned they would close his case after some questioning. Peng declined Lee's invitation, but two years later he returned to Taiwan; in 1995 he joined the DPP, and in early 1996 he ran as the DPP candidate for the ninth-term president of the ROC.

## The National Affairs Conference Begins

On June 28, 1990, the National Affairs Conference opened with a salute to the ROC flag, in which DPP member Hsu Hsin-liang refused to participate.[64] President Lee opened with a brief address stressing two themes: the ROC "will have a healthy, complete, and all-round constitutional system," and "there will be a unified China."[65] Only 136 of the invited 150 representatives showed up because 14 had refused to register.[66] (Eight leading elite, formerly invited, did not participate.)[67]

Participants were divided into five groups that met for three days and discussed five similar issues. On the fourth day (a rest day) the five chairpersons assembled and approved each group's minutes. Open discussions were held in the final three days, and on July 4 the conference ended with a banquet hosted by President Lee.

Never in Taiwan's history had this many individuals of different political views gathered to discuss political reform. Fully aware of the electric atmosphere and the potential for violence, each group's chairperson had been instructed to allow all arguments and to refrain from soliciting resolutions from the floor.[68]

Vice Secretary Cheyne J. Y. Chiu of the preparatory committee called a press conference after President Lee's opening address to announce that the conference would make no "preliminary deals" to resolve political disagreements and emphasized that the president had no intention of forcing his agenda for reform on the conference.[69] The government feared that the public regarded the conference as a vehicle of political deal making instead of a forum in which all political views could be expressed and a consensus reached about political reform.

Early in the evening of the first day, delegates from the DPP, nonparty affiliates, liberals, scholars, and overseas Taiwan representatives held a press conference in room 306 of the Grand Hotel to express their unhappiness.[70] The DPP members blasted the conference as getting nowhere and being out of touch with the people. Chang Chun-hong insisted that the conference must solve the current constitutional crisis. Yao Chia-wen denounced the conference as just an exchange of opinions and feared there would be no resolutions for popular ratification. Xie Changling feared that the conference was degenerating into a "big festival" (da baibai) and that the KMT delegates "shared the same view of postponing constitutional reform until after 1992." Overseas representative Chang Fu-mei proposed a public survey to determine if the people wanted the National Assembly representatives retired immediately. Hsu Hsin-liang said that the people would be disappointed if the conference turned into nothing but a report for President Lee, and that only the people had the power to influence this conference. Fearing that their reforms might not receive serious attention, DPP representatives circulated their proposals the next day.[71] But the unhappiness expressed by these opposition delegates soon dissipated.

The television news later that same evening showed political opponents who for years had insulted and attacked each other shaking hands and smiling at a banquet: President Lee smiled and chatted with Hsu Hsin-liang; Premier Hau Pei-tsun conferred with the overseas dissident and delegate Wang Guirong; KMT secretary-general Soong talked with DPP member Yao Chia-wen, one of the New Tide faction.[72] At that evening's dinner party hosted by Premier Hau, DPP chairman Huang Hsin-chieh moved among the tables, smiling and toasting the various representatives. When he arrived at the tables of some younger KMT officials, he bantered with them, saying that "in the future, all of you will become state ministers, and if I do not make friends with you now, there will be no chance in the future."[73] Chinese banquet conviviality was turning old enemies into friends. When overseas representative Wang Guirong told Premier Hau that "we overseas representatives are afraid of the military intervening in politics," Premier Hau replied, "Do I look that way to you?" and warmly toasted Wang. Hsu Hsin-liang and Premier Hau then toasted each other. Hsiao Wan-ch'ang, minister of economics, and Chang Chun-hong embraced; Economic Planning Council chief Shirley W. Y. Kuo and Yao Chia-wen, imprisoned for his role in the Kaohsiung incident, reminisced about their old teachers and their student days. The ice had been broken.

On the next day, discussion focused on whether conference resolutions should be ratified by the people and whether political representation should be reapportioned in the voting system. Hsu Hsin-liang argued that "reforms must be initiated right away or else it will become a serious problem of whether reforms can occur at all." KMT representative Zheng Xinxiong countered that "we must take into account political stability" and said that the KMT's actions "were responsible and not conservative." Overseas representative Kao Ying-mao wanted political reform, not legal reform. Wu Feng-shan, head of the *Zili wanbao* (Independent evening news), described the Taiwan political system as a house in which the basic structure was rotten and only the occupants' holding it up prevented its collapse. Liao Shuzong said that "the fact that all dissidents from overseas have returned is an admission of the total failure of all past reforms, and if that was not recognized, this conference could not be successful."

KMT secretary-general Soong commented that "this National Affairs Conference's basic spirit was for all people to say what they believed important to reform the ROC polity. If persons withdrew from the national conference, they were the losers and it was regrettable they could not express what was on their minds."[74] According to Soong, this forum was "a battle for wisdom."

Responding to this, Chang Chun-hong said that "he and Hsu Hsin-liang had withdrawn from the KMT party because they believed that party was a dictatorship without any opportunity for democracy to flower." But he admitted that he "still loved the KMT and did not want to see that party dissolved."[75] He feared that if the KMT became too weak, the DPP "would become a single-party dictatorship, and I would have to withdraw a second time." His impromptu statement shocked many DPP members but was atoned for by Kang Shuimu: "To hear the DPP party secretary-general talk about withdrawing from his own party is a very damaging statement, and I hope that the reporters here will not take his comments seriously."[76]

The second day's session brought the issue of Taiwan-mainlander tensions to the surface. Overseas delegate Chang Fu-mei charged that some people had lived in Taiwan for forty years but their hearts were still on the mainland. Zheng Xinxiong, KMT director of the Commission on Mainland Affairs, retorted that he had lived on Taiwan for forty years and that, though he loved Taiwan, he still "believed that the future of China was on the mainland" and urged his colleagues not to judge mainlanders "through eyes of hatred."[77]

Taiwan politicians who had long opposed the ruling party mixed easily with younger KMT leaders. They appeared relaxed outside the formal sessions and respectfully debated with KMT leaders while expressing their appreciation of the KMT's political reforms.[78] As one local politician put it, "the KMT today is an opponent you can talk to." The overseas delegates, many of whom had been on the government's blacklist, were increasingly critical of the KMT and the government and appeared tense and uncomfortable when speaking with KMT leaders. Said one, "We are in a race in which, for the DPP, all that matters is how to win."[79]

On the third day, July 1, a vote was called for the resolution proposing the direct election of the president. The resolution carried, convincing most opposition politicians to remain at the conference and not withdraw as they had threatened on the first day.[80] By now the different political groups had made clear their political reform proposals.

The DPP and its supporters wanted rapid, far-reaching political reforms:[81] All senior assembly members must retire by the end of 1990, and the National Assembly and the Examination and Control Yuans must be abolished. A National Assembly election for some 120 to 150 members should be held no later than July 31, 1991, to represent all citizens living in areas under ROC governance. Moreoever, the president should be directly elected by the citizens living in Taiwan. The president should appoint a premier, take charge of foreign policy and defense, and have special powers to handle national crises. There should be elections for the provincial governor and Taipei and Kaohsiung mayors before July 31, 1991. Local governments should manage and collect tax revenues for their own police forces and education systems. Taiwan should be restructured into six provinces with two politically autonomous metropolitan centers. The Temporary Provisions should be abolished, and a constitutional reform committee should be set up in two months to draft a constitution for the people to ratify. As for mainland China, relations should be based on the principles of equality, peace, pragmatism, and mutual benefit, but constitutional reform must be enacted before considering how to unify China. Trade and investment with the mainland should not be expanded until both sides agreed and signed a peace treaty, and the security of Taiwan should not be endangered. Finally, a China mainland affairs committee should be established with a Taiwanese director.

The reform package offered by the KMT stressed amending the constitution[82] and said that the National Assembly should elect the president but have no power over the legislature. All senior representatives should be given a resignation deadline. A new national assembly of eighty members should be elected to initiate political reforms. Popular ratification of reforms was unworkable, since Beijing would interpret it as promoting Taiwan independence. The KMT wanted to study electing a Taiwan governor.

The KMT representatives also wanted the Office of the President, the cabinet, the premier, and the legislature to remain intact.[83] They also compromised, agreeing to change the Examination and Control Yuans but to retain their functions in a different form.[84] Yet they were unwilling to change the current system of local governance. The KMT, feeling that the time was not ripe for direct talks with the Beijing regime, wanted to create an informal unit to regulate traffic between the two territories.[85] Both sides agreed with President Lee in his inauguration address when he said that only when the PRC promised to renounce the use of force against Taiwan and begin to liberalize its society and polity would the ROC negotiate with it.

These elite were amicably interacting and discussing political reform. KMT secretary-general Soong and DPP secretary-general Chang agreed to ask President Lee to set up a consultative group for constitutional political reform and try to implement some of the general agreements reached at the conference.[86] Several DPP leaders even proposed that, if the KMT agreed on a direct presidential election within three or four years and elected a National Assembly, the Taiwan provincial governor, and the Kaohsiung and Taipei mayors, the DPP would not insist on rewriting the constitution.[87] Huang Hsin-chieh went so far as to say that if President Lee agreed to direct presidential elections, the three-to four-year time limit need not apply.[88]

Hearing that political reform would eliminate their power, the senior representatives responded angrily, threatening that "we still hold the power of veto and will use it if conditions demand."[89] Some scholars still insisted that the National Affairs Conference did not truly represent the full spectrum of reform views.[90] Yang Guoshu asked, "Where are the lawful resolutions and source of power in this national conference? This gathering was not about changing the law but to provide information for the president and the chairman of the conference's preparatory committee."[91] The KMT, under pressure, had to promote political reforms; by inviting overseas dissidents to attend and allowing Hsu Hsin-liang to participate, Yang admitted, it had created a harmonious atmosphere that signaled the beginning of a new political environment. Yang also acknowledged that all opposition politicians were now perceived as equal with the KMT delegates and that many old political taboos had been swept aside. Hu Fu confirmed Yang's views but noted that the conference had "degenerated into a two-party affair, and the intellectuals had no role to play on the political stage."[92] Elite political reconciliation had begun, but could it continue?

## The National Affairs Conference Ends

On July 2 a secret session of leading members of the KMT and DPP as well as the conference chairman and nonparty representative Wu Feng-shan was held in room 646 of the Grand Hotel.[93] The DPP delegates agreed to withdraw their demand that constitutional reform be ratified by the people in exchange for a KMT promise to elect a new president through direct popular vote.[94] At least three more secret meetings between these party leaders occurred that day.[95] Rumors of these meetings leaked to other conference delegates, who vociferously complained of being left out of the political bargaining. Some even threatened to withdraw in protest.[96] They criticized these discussions as tarnishing the conference's image and devaluing its importance.[97] Jin Yaoji, provost of the Chinese University of Hong Kong, presented a declaration signed by ten scholars demanding that the two political parties explain why they were engaged in secret political negotiations and threatening to withdraw if they refused.[98]

Meanwhile, conference group discussions focused on procedures for direct presidential elections;[99] Wu Feng-shan and other delegates optimistically reported that the day's deliberations had produced a consensus that "the president will be directly elected by all the citizens."[100] The media became euphoric about this new consensus, some describing it as "an unimaginable achievement."[101]

DPP members immediately began discussing whom to field as a presidential candidate. Hsu Hsin-liang commented that he wanted Huang Hsin-chieh to run for president.[102] Huang replied that it would cost about NT$5 billion (about US$185 million) for him to be elected; he had no desire to run for president and merely wanted to sit at home in peace, drink tea, and chat with close friends.[103]

When asked about the KMT's participation in direct presidential elections, President Lee Teng-hui declared that he did not oppose them in principle but that "if they were held in the next five years, he might try to participate in such a historic event, but only if the law allowed him to do so."[104] Some DPP members urged that direct elections be held as soon as possible, while others held out for first creating an electoral college.[105]

Meanwhile President Lee, joined by Chiang Yen-shih, dropped in on the various groups and listened impassively. Neither commented on the conference discussions, fearing they might be either misquoted or misunderstood. On July 3, Chiang Yen-shih finally declared that a gradual consensus was emerging between the two parties' delegates on how to elect a president but that any agreement would have to be approved by the scholars and the conference body.[106] He insisted that debate was a healthy way to exchange views and that even if conclusions were not reached, it was important to communicate with one another.

Scholars who had not participated continued to complain that the intellectuals had not played any positive role and that political reform through political bargaining was morally wrong. Hu Fu asserted that the "KMT had given in a lot to the DPP, but that was just for their own benefit."[107] Hu feared that "the Republic of China [Zhonghua minguo], might even be discarded as a by-product of crass political bargaining." Hu spoke for many intellectuals when he said: "Everyone talks about the people's voice being heard at this national conference, but have they really had any voice at all? The scholars have been just like a political vase. Only a small group of people will derive any benefit from the conference, and those benefits will go only to those political bargaining agents, not to the scholars!"[108] Hu and other scholar-intellectuals believed they could serve as better architects of political reform than the politicians. As their voices became louder over the years, their skepticism and distrust of politicians increased. The view that only scholar-intellectuals could remain above the political fray, untarnished by selfish interests, was widely shared by the elite.

Meanwhile, differences over how the constitution should be reformed had not been resolved. KMT delegates Guo Renfu, Yao Xun, Li Nianzu, Ma Ying-chiu, and Chiu Hungdah argued that "restructuring the constitution is an act of destroying the constitution, and besides, that action is extremely dangerous and very expensive."[109] The opposition reformers Huang Huangxiong, Qiu

Cuiliang, and others believed that "the request for a new constitution matches with the requirements of our new democratic movement. If we do not restructure the constitution, our political and economic system will be adversely affected." [110] KMT delegate Ma Ying-chiu countered that "any new form of a constitution would be opposed by me and many others. Our constitution is only in crisis; we do not have to abolish it. If that is done, it will be very difficult to reach any consensus to have a new constitutional draft, and even a new draft might not be as good as what we have now." [111] But DPP adviser Hsu Hsin-liang insisted that "after forty years the people now wanted the constitutional crisis resolved." [112] Hsu also scoffed at President Lee's comment that the conference had reached a consensus on constitutional reform: "The president must be joking." But the American economist Cheng Chu-yuan countered that "President Lee asked us to participate and to offer suggestions; he said he would try to carry out our requests, but whether he will do so is his decision alone." [113]

On the conference's final day, July 4, behind-the-scenes bargaining between leaders of the two major political parties and other delegates produced several areas of important political consensus. [114] First, there was general agreement on a popular, direct election of the ROC president and the governor of Taiwan province, although delegates refrained from outlining how that would be achieved. Second, they agreed that all senior representatives should be retired, but again no details or time schedule were mentioned.

The conference chairpersons of all five groups proposed to President Lee that a consultative group on constitutional reform be established after the conference ended. [115] DPP chairman Huang Hsin-chieh concurred, urging that the group also serve as a "watchdog" over the government to make certain that the "intentions of the National Affairs Conference" were carried out. [116] Chiang Yen-shih said that the president would study the final conference reports and then present a timetable for "concrete political reform." [117] President Lee seemed to favor a "consultative group" and declared that "whatever is beneficial to the country should be done." [118] But on July 6 the Office of the President announced that it would not set up such a committee because the agreements reached at the National Affairs Conference could be accomplished. But on July 9 the Office of the President reversed itself, announcing that a committee for constitutional and other reforms would be set up in the Kuomintang. [119]

DPP chairman Huang Hsin-chieh praised President Lee's decision "because the president realizes that the National Affairs Conference has produced consensus. Therefore, I am not worried. Let President Lee make these reforms, and let's just see what happens." [120] But others in the DPP felt that "strong opposition" to constitutional reform existed in the KMT and that a KMT committee would do nothing. [121]

The conference concluded on the evening of July 4, when President Lee hosted a huge banquet for all the conference delegates at the Grand Hotel. He toasted all members three times, thanking them for their hard work, wishing them good health, and asking them to join him in a toast for the welfare and prosperity of the ROC. [122] President Lee then toasted Huang Hsin-chieh, the DPP chairman. Chairman Huang, with his new friends Chang Fu-mei, Chang Chun-hong, and Huang Huangxiong, then toasted President Lee. Former dissident Hsu Hsin-liang went up to President Lee and offered him a toast. With these expressions of friendship and goodwill, former enemies parted and the conference disbanded.

## The Elites Agree to a Settlement

Although many opposition politicians claimed that the National Affairs Conference was successful and owed much to their historic struggle, [123] others believed the conference had produced more harm than good. Nan Fangshuo pointed out that the old wound *(shengji chingjie)* between mainlanders and Taiwanese had been opened. [124] Hou Lichai felt that the conference had exacerbated the differences between the many political groups and that the political crisis had worsened rather than improved. [125] Political pundit Sima Wenwu charged that the National Affairs Conference was a cruel hoax: Just because President Lee created a committee in his party to act on the conference's general agreements did not mean reform was forthcoming:

The KMT itself is a party much in need of reform. Therefore, if the KMT is responsible for promoting political reform, one can see what will likely take place. In particular, if someone like Lin Yang-kang [head of the new reform committee] is responsible for proposing reform policies, they will be totally against the spirit of the National Affairs Conference. The KMT reform committee is actually a step backward for constitutional reform. [126]

The political philosopher Hu Chiu-yuan dismissed the National Affairs Conference but worried that it might send a signal "to challenge Communist China to not fear war." [127]

But the DPP, which had mobilized enormous public sympathy for its goals and forged links with overseas scholars and nonparty representatives, was elated by the conference's success. [128] The party had planted the idea of citizens' electing their president and provincial governor as well as a new national assembly. The DPP was elated that the conference had forced the KMT to promise reform, feeling that the widespread agreement reached at the conference would elicit public support and oblige the KMT to press for political reform in the future. Xie Changting a popular DPP member just elected to the Legislative Yuan, exulted that "the National Affairs Conference had produced better results than I had expected because of the several areas of consensus actually reached." Even the Meilidao coalition under Huang Hsin-chieh was euphoric, believing their party had forced the rapid reform of the National Assembly and the direct election of a provincial governor and the president.[129] Most important, the DPP established formal lines of communication with the liberal KMT elites and forged links with other politicians and overseas representatives.

After the conference President Lee, in an address to the KMT's central committee, thanked the party for its support and said he wanted the conference results studied and the agreements reached at the conference translated into policies. Various party members then expressed the opinion that the conference had produced much better results than they had expected: it had "helped to elevate the prestige of the ruling party" and set the stage for further political reform;[130] "there would only be constitutional revision and not the creation of a new constitution."[131] They also promised that the party would broaden its contacts with the academic community. Party elder Chin Hsiao-i opined that "the KMT party must continue to achieve consensus and in all possible ways persuade party members to carry out the consensual decisions reached at the National Affairs Conference."[132]

Reactions in the Legislative Yuan were mixed. Yao Yingqi, Huang Zhuwen, Chen Shui-bian, and Xie Changting applauded the conference results and said that their colleagues' opposing it would have been "slapping your own face" *(zuda erguang).*[133] They believed that the consensus reached at the conference represented the "will of the people." But Chao Shao-kang said that he had "never expected the conference representatives to display such exaggerated self-importance and to try to override the authority of the president and the Legislative Yuan."[134] Lee Shen-fong said that the "Legislative Yuan should not be responsible to the National Affairs Conference. The legislature's sole purpose was to serve the people. The National Affairs Conference only has been a means of allowing certain actors to acquire political advantages. The scholars' views have been ignored, and democracy has been twisted."[135] Liang Su-jung, head of the Legislative Yuan, claimed that "the KMT has been duped by the DPP" and lamented that if "the KMT cannot deliver now, then the DPP will become the ruling party."[136] Opposing direct elections for the president,

Liang believed that the DPP was the big winner and had led the KMT around by the nose. "The DPP only wants to pull down the president and reelect a new one. Such an election will ruin the country." [137] Former premier Lee Huan believed that "the National Affairs Conference marked the beginning of a new era in Chinese democracy, and we ought to affirm that point." [138] Other KMT elders dismissed the conference as having no practical value; "it was merely a huge, unnecessary expense and a waste of time." [139] Political tensions and worry about Taiwan's polity had deepened in spring 1990, but by mid year those tensions had moderated and optimism had rebounded about Taiwan's political future. President Lee's conference had successfully produced an elite settlement. Taking the initiative and using Chiang Yen-shih, Secretary-General Soong, and others as political brokers, President Lee had reached out to the political opposition, even casting his net overseas to those in the Taiwan independence movement, to assemble all elites and talk about political reform. Deep suspicion had clouded Lee's efforts, but he and his colleagues persevered. The president managed to coax the DPP chairman to come on board; along with his supporters, he brought the party to the conference table. Although prominent intellectuals bolted at the last moment, fearful of being pawns in a political power struggle, most of Taiwan's important elite had attended the conference.

Significant differences still separated the ruling party and the political opposition, but major areas of consensus were reached: the senior representatives must retire; elections would be held to replace them; and the constitution would at least be amended. For the first time, the issue of popular elections for the nation's leaders was openly discussed, and a remarkable consensus emerged that in the near future democracy must adopt this course. The conference established the framework for formal contacts to be developed between the ruling party and the political opposition's leading party, the DPP. New momentum for political reform had been generated by this elite gathering, and for the first time since martial law was lifted, the prospects for democracy looked bright. But the KMT and DPP political differences regarding Taiwan's future democratization were still very deep, and the consensus achieved by both parties still reflected only a partial political settlement, as the political events in the next chapter will show.

# PART IV

Constitutional Reform and
Elite Convergence

# CHAPTER TEN

# Preparing for Constitutional Reform

The partial settlement reached between the KMT and the opposition politicians initiated political bargaining and a willingness to play by the political rules. Although a core of opposition politicians wanted a new constitution of their making, their belief in Western democratic principles discouraged them from resorting to radical action. They realized that without popular support they had little chance of redrafting the 1947 constitution and creating a Republic of Taiwan. Most elites in political life now approved of gradualism and wanted only to revise the 1947 constitution.

Having brought the DPP and other dissidents into Taiwan's political mainstream, President Lee now could turn to political reform. He faced major problems: how to terminate the tenure of the senior national representatives, expand national elections, carry out the KMT's mission of unifying China, and reform the KMT to win elections. Solving the first problem required restoring the constitution and amending it to accommodate to Taiwan's political realities. Resolving the remaining problems meant obtaining a popular mandate for democratic reform and foreign policy without alienating public support and reforming the KMT while retaining political power.

## Retiring the Senior National Representatives

Criticism of the senior representatives had begun with the *dangwai* politicians in the late 1970s and 1980s and was now endorsed by most elite. The KMT had supported the National Assembly until 1988, when its leadership became attuned to political reform and the necessity to replace that body.[1]

Early in 1988 Lee Huan and Ma Ying-chiu called a meeting with leading National Assembly senior representatives to discuss a retirement program. The meeting began with the senior representatives severely criticizing the KMT, demanding that the party "restore martial law to stop the violent activities of the DPP."[2] One representative, Hou Xikai blasted Lee and Ma, saying, "How can you encourage the senior representatives to retire! Who will elect the president?"[3] Lee and Ma listened to their tirades and their threats not to retire unless the PRC took over Taiwan or the island became an independent republic.

In early 1989 some National Assembly representatives announced their retirement, but others declared that "it was all right for them to retire, because they have not been active."[4] In March 1989, the ROC government sent retirement forms to all senior representatives.[5] By early July some 150 had responded, saying they intended to step down, but a group of diehards wrote them insulting letters declaring that "if you retire, you will not be fulfilling your duty." One senior representative complained that he had received so many telephone calls urging him not to retire that he became ashamed and changed his mind.[6] Relatives who depended on their salaries also pressured these representatives not to retire.[7]

Political tensions over the retirement issue worsened. On July 20, 1989, Cai Shiyun, a DPP central committee deputy secretary and a national assemblyman, took a batch of retirement forms to the Chungshantang Building's fifth floor in Taipei's Hsimenting area,[8] where many senior national representatives typically spent the day playing chess, drinking tea, and chatting. When Cai began distributing the forms, pandemonium broke out with voices screaming: "God damn it, who do you think you are, you little bastard?" Cai responded, "You have been here forty years, and you no longer have any right to represent the Chinese people." Someone screamed, "Hit him! Call the police and take him away!" Another cried, "I will never retire, and what are you going to do about it?" One elderly female representative pounded the table with her fist and shouted, "Who do you think you are?" Cai left after distributing his forms. This altercation attracted public attention, and some voices urged moderation. Some elite also worried that when President Lee Teng-hui addressed the general meeting of the National Assembly, he might, by urging retirement, provoke many senior representatives whose goodwill he needed to be reelected.[9] In the late summer of 1989, however, as pressure mounted, more representatives did retire, including Sunzhen Shuying the ninety-eight-year-old daughter-in-law of Sun Yat-sen, and Wu Hongshen, the uncle of Taipei's mayor, Wu Po-hsiung.[10]

## Phasing out the First National Assembly

The events of March 1990 galvanized the public to demand that the remaining senior representatives step down. The KMT had already initiated legislation to grant handsome early retirement benefits to senior representatives if they resigned. In addition, the party had planned a legal maneuver to compel them to retire by a definite deadline. In these efforts they were backed by the opposition. On April 3, 1990, the entire central committee of the DPP unanimously voted that the National Assembly representatives should retire before September 1990.[11] On the following day DPP legislator Chen Shui-bian, other politicians, and numerous KMT members introduced a resolution in the Legislative Yuan to request that the Council of Grand Justices in the Judicial Yuan interpret the role of the senior representatives according to existing law.[12] This request called for a strict interpretation of the constitution's Article 28, sections 1 and 2, and Article 6, sections 2 and 3, of the Temporary Provisions to justify prompt retirement.[13]

As the legal machinery began to move, Irwine W. Ho, the secretary-general of the First National Assembly, declared that "he did not want to be secretary-general for very much longer, and because the president and vice president had just been elected in March 1990, he wanted to step down."[14] Then, on June 21, 1990, the Council of Grand Justices decreed (in court case 261) that by December 31, 1991, all senior representatives in the central government must step down.[15] (In 1954 that body had ruled that the national representatives in the central government could serve indefinitely; that same body now moved full circle, abolishing the former law.) Undismayed, a group of senior representatives signed a petition protesting the grand justices' decision and declaring that they were being thrown aside after all their years of service (guohe cheqiao).[16] According to Ho, however, only a small minority of representatives believed they had been betrayed.[17]

The KMT continued to try to persuade the holdout senior representatives to retire. Throughout late 1990 and early 1991, top KMT officials including President Lee and Secretary-General Soong personally urged each senior representative to accept voluntary retirement. The press continued to criticize, scold, and ridicule those senior representatives who refused to comply with the legal ruling,[18] claiming they did "not even care whether the KMT expelled them or not."[19]

On February 26, 1991, President Lee ordered the National Assembly to convene in April 1991 to amend the constitution for electing a second-term national assembly.[20] The Office of the President instructed the 619 senior representatives to meet in Taipei to ensure that a quorum (450) would attend.[21] The stage was set for a momentous meeting.

The president wanted the assembly to abolish the Temporary Provisions, terminate the state of insurgency with the Communists, and approve new articles for the 1947 constitution for electing a new national assembly. If the president's plan succeeded, all senior representatives would retire by year's end except those few elected from Taiwan. On March 29, 1991, then, 604 representatives registered for the last meeting of the First National Assembly.[22] The events of the first day's meetings revealed that the KMT and DPP were not cooperating to amend the constitution. But the KMT took full charge of restoring constitutional governance and amending the constitution.

On April 8, 1991, as delegates filed into the main hall of the Chungshanlou in the Yangming Mountains, some DPP and KMT representatives began arguing. The DPP delegates, still bitter toward the senior representatives, accused their opponents of being unqualified to attend the meeting.[23] When President Lee arrived to deliver the opening address, eight DPP representatives in two teams held up two banners reading "Political Blackmail Is Not Allowed" and "The Old Representatives Have No Right to Revise the Constitution." When a squad of police came to remove them, they screamed and used foul language. Many old representatives smiled and clapped for the police while reporters snapped pictures. One commentator remarked, "This opening ceremony was even more raucous than a street market." After order was restored, President Lee read his prepared speech, "never even twitching an eyelid."

On April 9, assembly members nominated a chair committee to manage their proceedings. Ye Jingfeng, responsible for the selection process, began quarreling with several DPP representatives, and a fight erupted, with people slapping and striking each other. The police formed a human wall to protect Madame Ye, who announced the eighty-five persons to serve as the chair committee. Following procedural rules, KMT members dominated that committee. Frustrated by their inability to have delegates on the chair committee, DPP representatives screamed, "Why don't you just take over the entire ratification process?" DPP representative Wu Zhilang marched up to the platform, took a bundle of flowers from one of the large vases, and threw them into the audience. On April 11 another fight broke out between KMT and DPP representatives over the seating arrangements in the conference hall.

Thereafter calm prevailed, and the KMT majority controlled the ratification process. The assembly agreed to abolish the Temporary Provisions and end the state of communist insurgency. On April 22 it approved ten new articles to the constitution that outlined the procedures for nominating and electing members to the second-term National Assembly, the Legislative Yuan, and the Control Yuan.[24]

The violence at the final meeting of the First National Assembly had dismayed and shocked the public, and many wondered if perhaps the Chinese did deserve an authoritarian political system. Others feared that the young people might want to solve political problems with violence. But some elites offered diverse explanations for the opposition's obstructionist political behavior and why the political settlement achieved at the June–July 1990 conference had been only partial.

Lu Yali, a professor of political science at National Taiwan University, stressed that political polarization had been ongoing for many years, leaving the DPP frustrated and isolated from the political process. Yang Guoshu theorized that the DPP felt helpless *(wunai)* in the political arena, causing its members to behave irrationally. Certain KMT elite questioned the DPP's sincerity, claiming that the party, wanting to establish a Taiwan Republic with a new constitution, insisted on redrafting the constitution. Moreover, many DPP politicians resorted to violence because they wanted name recognition. KMT legislator Hong Shaonan sympathized with the DPP's frustration but pointed out that such behavior only united the KMT. Zhang Junxiong, a DPP legislator, argued that the KMT shared the reactionary outlook of Liang Sujung, a diehard who had long chaired the Legislative Yuan using procedural rules that enabled the KMT to steamroller the minority DPP. Another DPP member, Lin Zhengjie, claimed that the two parties lacked effective channels of communication and, when DPP members tried to compromise with the KMT, they were condemned by radicals in their own party who did not believe in compromise or bargaining with the KMT. The radicals wanted to establish a new constitution and ratify it by a popular vote. Faced with this dilemma, the DPP lost patience. Lin gave the DPP the following advice: "Speak out for what your effective power allows you to say, and set realistic goals to be achieved; have a bottom line for negotiating with the ruling party!"[25]

The *Zhongguo shibao* (China times) also held a discussion forum with three assembly representatives: Chen Xian (KMT), Wu Zhelang (DPP), and Zhao Changbing (a participant in KMT constitutional reform discussions procedures).[26] Chen led off by pointing out that, at the recent National Assembly meeting, about 84 percent were senior representatives, of whom about 80 percent were calm and patriotic. Chen claimed that only a minority opposed phasing out the first-term National Assembly and electing a second-term National Assembly to revise the 1947 constitution. But Wu Zhelang countered that at least 95 percent of the senior representatives were isolated from the people, out of touch with the changing times, and in the assembly only to receive benefits. Wu condemned them for opposing the recent Judicial Yuan decision, insisted they had no right to revise the constitution, and criticized the KMT for allowing the senior representatives to stay in power so long. Zhao Changbing, emphasizing that all political parties must participate in constitutional revision, argued that the final meeting of the first-term National Assembly was a major advance toward constitutional revision. With the removal of the senior representatives and an election scheduled for the second-term National Assembly, the nation would have a new political institution to revise the 1947 constitution. These examples of disparate elite political thinking revealed disagreements but an acceptance of the constitutional reform process.

## Further Strengthening of Human Liberties

Article 100 had been part of the national criminal code for more than half a century and regulated "domestic criminal violence." In brief, the article stated that "if any person behaves as if he or she *intends* to destroy the national polity, steal or take over national property, use illegal means to change the nation's constitution, or actually carries out these intentions, then that person has committed a crime of domestic criminal violence."[27] The Garrison Command frequently invoked Article 100 to charge critics of the regime with endangering the nation's security and to imprison them for varying terms. As dissidents returned from abroad, the government tried to arrest them on criminal charges under Article 100.

Critics of this law, especially the DPP, complained that Article 100 was imprecise and violated free speech and other freedoms. As Taiwan's democracy progressed, the judiciary found it difficult to interpret this article in the light of the new freedoms being acquired by Taiwan's citizens after the lifting of martial law. Clearly, the article needed to be abolished or revised.

By the late spring of 1991, KMT politicians like Chao Shao-kang and Huang Zhuwen were insisting that Article 100 be revised. On May 16, Chao, Huang, and forty-five other legislators in the Legislative Yuan proposed that if Article 100 was used to charge individuals with the intention of creating domestic violence, that charge "seriously invades the freedom of thought and speech of another person, which are guaranteed by the constitution."[28] Those legislators urged that Article 100 be revised, and they voted to refer the matter to a special judicial committee of the legislature. DPP legislators like Chen Shui-bian demanded that Article 100 be abolished.

The KMT, faced with these demands, feared a major revision of the criminal code, a task the party regarded as immensely difficult.[29] But on May 20 the judicial branch of the government began reviewing how Article 100 might be revised.[30] Their actions produced strident debate in the Legislative Yuan and the press over whether Article 100 should be abolished outright or revised as a new article in the criminal code. Legislator Huang Zhuwen advocated revision, arguing that "if somebody wants to blackmail or force the president to carry out illegal political reform, only Article 100 can be used to prevent such action."[31] Other individuals advocating revision stated that "if we abolish Article 100, the freedom of speech will be expanded, and that greatly facilitates democratization. But that development can lead to a situation of any political party supporting whatever goals it wants. That means granting an enormous opportunity for any kind of political party to form."[32] As politicians quarreled about revising or abolishing Article 100, the issue became fiercely politicized along party lines in the Legislative Yuan. The KMT's Huang Zhuwen asserted that "the main argument is about the meaning of any criminal act to create public disorder, and that act must be precisely defined to eliminate ambiguity. That means a lot of discussion and building a consensus through three readings to produce a law that everyone can accept. This should be the appropriate procedure."[33] DPP legislator Chen Shuibian countered that "we always have wanted to abolish this article. All nonviolent political action falls within the scope of freedom of speech and should be protected by the constitution."[34] The KMT finally agreed that the article should be revised, but as a major concession to the DPP, because for more than six decades it had depended on that article to arrest and imprison the regime's critics.[35] Scholars soon joined the debate and urged a consensus.[36]

Meanwhile a new group of activists calling themselves the Alliance to Abolish Article 100 began demonstrating in front of the Legislative Yuan to persuade legislators to abrogate Article 100 once and for all. Because this group consisted of well-known politicians and scholars, the Office of the President sent Chiang Yen-shih and James C. Y. Soong to meet with its leaders to explain the government's position and urge a peaceful end to the demonstration.[37] The debate continued to rage.

To break the deadlock in the Legislative Yuan, the Executive Yuan formed a committee, chaired by the deputy vice premier, Shih Chi-yang, to study Article 100. This committee conferred with legal scholars at National Taiwan University and elsewhere to find a compromise.[38] Meanwhile, the government arrested Li Yingyen and Guo Peihong, two dissidents who had just returned from overseas, by using Article 100. The DPP immediately declared that the article ought to be abolished. The Alliance to Abolish Article 100 also joined the fray, urging the DPP to break off discussions with the KMT and demand that Article 100 be abolished. On September 24, DPP legislators physically prevented Premier Hau from presenting his administrative report to the Legislative Yuan. On September 27 a similar altercation occurred in the Legislative Yuan over the fate of Article 100.

The battle over Article 100 began on March 1, 1992, when two versions of it made their appearance, coming from the judiciary.[39] The Executive Yuan held eight committee meetings to study and revise the two proposals. On May 15 the Legislative Yuan approved the third reading of the revised article. Of the fifty-seven legislators present, forty-five approved, with ten DPP legislators still pressing to abolish the article. The new article clearly defined "domestic upheaval" [neiluan] and included the following statement: "If there is no act of violence and no threatening behavior, there will be no punishment."[40] The new article also required proof of threat and the commission of violence before charges and arrest could take place. The KMT had acceded significantly to the demands of the DPP to modify the original law.

Under the new version of Article 100, political dissidents Zhou Chaolong and Huang Hua were immediately freed from prison, as were Chen Wanzhen and five other dissidents who had belonged to an organization to build a new Taiwan (Taijian zuzhi), which advocated Taiwan independence. Huang Hua had been arrested three times under the old Article 100 and imprisoned for a total of twenty-three years and eight months for writing about his hope for Taiwan independence. On his release, Huang said: "Ideals are more important than life itself."[41]

For some, the struggle to revise Article 100 marked the beginning of a new age in Taiwan, one in which the people never again need fear the "white terror" of the 1950s, when merely a critical word brought arrest and imprisonment. Some complained, however, that the information media were still rigidly controlled by the government and that public television should freely provide information. Those advocating freedom of speech went on record as saying that "we expect to see a more peaceful society, and we expect to see the end of any use of inadequate or inaccurate information. We also expect to see

Taiwan's political conditions become more open and free."[42] Democratization after 1986 reflected this new reality.

## A New Strategy for Unifying China

Meanwhile President Lee, in tandem with his constitutional reform, had moved to develop a new China unification strategy. For many decades KMT leaders had expressed their intention of recovering the mainland but had provided no concrete guidelines for achieving it. Even Chiang Ching-kuo remained silent except for repeatedly announcing that building a perfect democracy in Taiwan would someday provide the basis for China's unification. On September 16, 1987, Chiang Ching-kuo, in a bold initiative, informed the central standing committee that he wanted to appoint Lee Teng-hui, Yu Kuo-hwa, Ni Wen-ya, Wu Po-hsiung, and Irwine W. Ho to examine the rules banning travel between Taiwan and the mainland. That committee submitted a report on October 14 to the central standing committee proposing that the rules be adjusted. After the Executive Yuan drew up new regulations, on October 15 Interior Minister Wu Po-hsiung announced the lifting of the travel ban, and on November 2 the Red Cross began accepting applications from Taiwanese to visit relatives on the mainland. In early December 1988 the ROC agreed to allow Taiwanese stranded on the mainland since 1949 to visit their families and relatives. In the summer of 1989, public school faculty members were permitted to visit the mainland. By May 1989 more than a quarter of a million people had visited the mainland, and a mainland "fever" was in vogue.

Chiang Ching-kuo's reform now opened new avenues between Taiwan and the mainland and helped ease tensions between the two sides. On August 18, 1988, the Executive Yuan established the Mainland Affairs Council to manage the evolving informal relations between Taiwan and the mainland, and thereafter trade and exchanges of people between the two sides increased by leaps and bounds. The KMT elders approved of these developments, and some like Chen Li-fu even wanted the government to finance large-scale modernization projects if the PRC would abandon communism. Building on these developments, on October 1, 1990, President Lee set up a National Unification Council under the Office of the President, comprising leading elite across the political spectrum as well as representatives from business, academia, and the professions. The president even invited Kang Ning-hsiang from the DPP to participate, and after much agonizing Kang accepted. The president gambled that if the council agreed on a strategy for unifying China, the KMT elders and conservatives would support it, satisfied that their chairman was sincerely carrying out the party's historical mission, and that the political opposition would also support it. By including Kang Ning-hsiang on this council, President Lee hoped to persuade the DPP to support the council's recommended guidelines. New ROC policy guidelines toward the PRC would also strengthen the president's hand to push domestic political reform.

On February 23, 1991, after many weeks of deliberation, the National Unification Council, which the president chaired, agreed on a framework for the unification of China. The Executive Yuan approved it on March 14, 1991. This framework postulated that a unified China must be democratic, free, and equitably prosperous and have the following characteristics: political democratization, economic liberalization, social pluralization, and a Chinese cultural renaissance. China, it was agreed, was now divided into two areas, both of which made up the territory of China, each territory being governed by a different political entity, with neither side having effective jurisdiction over the other area. The guidelines proposed that China's unification take place according to three developmental phases. In the first, exchange and reciprocity must occur based largely on private sector exchanges between the two sides. Second, mutual trust and cooperation promoting direct postal, transport, and commercial agreements must acknowledge the sovereign basis of the other side. The third phase would involve consulting and cooperating to create a political framework for unification that would reflect the will of the people in Taiwan and on the mainland. The council's guidelines were acceptable to all Taiwan's political parties. On July 16, 1992, the Legislative Yuan endorsed these guidelines by passing the Statute Governing the Relations between the People of the Taiwan Area and the People of the Mainland Area to facilitate the exchanges dictated by the first phase of the guidelines. By mid-1991, then, President Lee had further consolidated the elite settlement achieved in 1990.

The president was now ready to implement the ten articles that the National Assembly had approved at its sixth plenary meeting on April 22, 1991. These articles had been added to the 1947 constitution in accordance with Article 27, paragraph 1, item 3, and Article 174, item 1. They called for electing the second-term National Assembly by year's end, electing a new Legislative Yuan before January 31, 1993, and the Provincial Assembly and municipal councils' electing members of the Control Yuan before January 31, 1993. In a single stroke the president, by expanding national elections, guaranteed that the mainlander senior representatives would be replaced. The national polity would never be the same. By abolishing the Temporary Provisions, the president had restored constitutional law and reduced his power, but new articles amending the constitution granted him the authority to determine security policies and to establish the National Security Council and the National Security Bureau. But perhaps more important, the president had unilaterally ended the state of war with the China mainland, further easing tensions across the Taiwan Straits.

## Electing the Second-Term National Assembly

Electing the second-term National Assembly involved only Taiwan voters, not those of the Chinese mainland. A critical political turning point had now been reached. The island's political future was at stake and with it the future of the KMT's role in Taiwan's democracy. If the forthcoming election allowed the political opposition to control more than one-quarter of the National Assembly seats, the KMT could not control constitutional reform, and power would begin to shift to the political opposition.[43] If an impasse over constitutional reform occurred, the KMT risked an internal split, and open conflict between Taiwan's political elite was very likely. If the opposition controlled the constitutional reform process, it could call a national referendum to draft a new constitution. For the first time since 1949, public opinion suddenly became a powerful force influencing constitutional reform and the island's political future.

In spring 1991, all political parties agreed on the election procedures for the second-term National Assembly: divide Taiwan and its offshore islands into fifty-eight districts, from which a total of 225 candidates would be elected to the new assembly according to a plurality of votes for each candidate; choose 20 more assembly representatives on a quota basis from the overseas Chinese according to the number of votes won by the competing parties from the fifty-eight election districts; and finally, choose another 80 assembly representatives to represent women, aboriginal groups, and various professions, again by the number of votes won by competing parties from the fifty-eight election districts.[44] This made for a new National Assembly of 325 representatives.

The KMT hoped its superior party machine could nominate enough candidates in each of the fifty-eight districts to give it an overwhelming majority. The DPP, although lacking the resources to field candidates in all fifty-eight election districts,[45] was confident enough to field candidates in at least half those districts and hoped to become a significant minority. The KMT planned to nominate at least 192 candidates, more than 2 candidates for each district, hoping that its nominees could win at least three-quarters of the 225 elected assembly seats. The other parties, which had reluctantly agreed to the fifty-eight election districts because they preferred fewer districts, pinned their hopes on fielding enough candidates in key districts to deprive the KMT of at least one-quarter of the 225 seats.[46]

As part of its election preparations, the KMT leadership concentrated on party reform. In May 1991 the KMT's central committee approved a just-concluded three-year reform plan study.[47] That plan called for reducing party expenditures in personnel costs by NT$60 million (US$2.4 million) and cutting party workers—reforms affecting at least half the membership. The party was to be streamlined by combining bureaus and departments and reassigning tasks to a much-reduced party bureaucracy. By September a partly reformed KMT was poised to win votes. A seven-member KMT team convened in late September to review its nominees for all fifty-eight districts[48] and consulted with top party leaders, party elders, and younger party officials.[49] In October another special screening committee evaluated and approved[50] a list of 192 nominees.[51] Their average age was forty-five, with 140 candidates under forty-nine. Twenty-three percent of the nominees held M.A. and Ph.D. degrees; 165 (85 percent) were male and 27 (15 percent) were female, all of them entering politics for the first time.

The KMT also assiduously checked the list of overseas Chinese (twenty seats) and the national nominees for the eighty nondistrict seats. For the overseas Chinese the party consulted with its overseas Chinese community networks to compile a list of outstanding people in different regions of the globe.[52] Nominees had to be over twenty-three years of age, be recognized in their occupations and communities, and have made major contributions to the KMT. Turning to the island's fifty-eight election districts, KMT secretary-general James C. Y. Soong and other high-level party leaders toured the island several times, conferring with local party bosses to build network support for its nominees. These candidates quickly established their headquarters and made ready to wage the election war.

The meticulous, carefully planned preparations of the KMT were not matched by the other parties. Without efficient local party machinery, funding, and staff, the DPP and other parties had to target their resources on the densely populated cities. By August 28 the DPP had drafted a new constitution it hoped would persuade voters to elect enough of its candidates to revise the 1947 constitution.[53] To advertise this dramatic act, the DPP news office announced that the DPP "was really a party for Taiwan independence"; that theme was heatedly debated throughout the island in the coming months but condemned by the KMT and leading government officials.[54]

By early September the DPP planned to nominate between 99 and 104 candidates, hoping to win at least one-quarter, if not more, of the 225 seats. But the DPP had split into three factions: the moderate Meilidao (Beautiful Formosa), the largest group, led by Hsu Hsin-liang, who had spent the previous six months touring Taiwan to find candidates; the more radical New Tide (Xinchao liuxi), led by Wu Nairen, who looked for candidates with a strong sense of Taiwanese identity who might lead the party in the future; and a new extremist wing called Taiwan Independence Alliance (Taidu lianmeng).[55] Many of these radical dissidents had lived in the United States and had just returned to Taiwan, making it difficult for them to obtain party and local support. The deepening factional struggle in the DPP threatened to splinter the party.

The DPP's central committee met on October 12–13, 1991, and made three important decisions:[56] it chose as its chairman Hsu Hsin-liang, who polled 180 votes more than second-place Shih Ming-teh; it added a new article to its party charter calling for the establishment of an independent Republic of Taiwan; and it voted for a new central executive committee, giving the Meilidao fourteen seats, with sixteen seats divided between the other two factions. The moderate Meilidao faction had been losing ground, prompting former DPP party chairman Huang Hsin-chieh to say in mid-November that if the three factions could not be unified, the DPP might split and form a new but stronger party.[57] Huang believed that the people wanted an opposition party in Taiwan but that DPP factions merely wanted to oppose the ruling party for opposition's sake. Huang complained that when the DPP formed, it had a membership of more than twenty thousand, which had since dropped to about fourteen thousand.

Trying to downplay DPP factionalism, newly elected Chairman Hsu said: "The DPP will actively promote the principle of a Republic of Taiwan, and it will try to win the support of the people by democratic means. In the next two years, the chairman hopes to elevate the DPP to become the country's ruling party." Chairman Hsu alluded to Shih Ming-teh as his old "battlefield comrade" who would provide advice, and he dismissed fears that the PRC would take aggressive action against Taiwan because of the DPP's declaration in favor of an independent Republic of Taiwan. Hsu promised to improve the DPP's political image, appealed for more "economic openness" and more democracy, and resolved to promote the "concept of a Taiwan Republic."[58] This new DPP leadership's optimism persisted throughout the election campaign. As late as December 18, just before the election, Hsu boasted that "international opinion favors the DPP, and if the people could vote today, the

DPP could win 30 to 40 percent of the seats. In a few more days, the DPP should be able to capture 50 to 90 percent of the vote."[59]

A third party, called the China Social Democratic Party, or CSDP (Zhonghua shehui minzhu dang), was led by former DPP firebrand Ju Gau-jeng.[60] This party, whose members wore yellow suits with red ties, hoped to win at least 12 percent of the vote, and it offered a third choice to candidates unhappy about the two major parties.[61]

By the end of November, then, 471 candidates had registered to compete for 225 National Assembly seats; another 136 candidates from five political parties had registered for 80 nondistrict seats; and 30 candidates from the KMT, DPP, and CSDP had been nominated for the 20 available seats representing the overseas Chinese community.[62] As in the December 2, 1989, election contest, the press again referred to the upcoming election as a "war."

## The Campaign Begins

By late October, then, all parties had staked out their positions to the voters.[63] The DPP pledged that its elected candidates would draft a new constitution for creating a Republic of Taiwan but with no prospect for China's unification. The party's slogan was Draft a Constitution for an Independent Taiwan (Taidu zhixian). The KMT countered that the DPP was playing with fire by emboldening the PRC to attack or blockade Taiwan. The KMT pledged to maintain the status quo and informed voters that voting for KMT candidates meant reform (gexin), stability (anding), and prosperity (fanrong). The KMT wanted only constitutional revision and to elect future presidents by an electoral college instead of a direct vote, as demanded by the DPP.[64]

Each party mapped out a campaign strategy to communicate its position to the voters. The KMT divided Taiwan into twenty-three campaign areas and dispatched high-ranking party officials from the government to visit each area to confer with the local political machine.[65] Premier Hau and high officials visited these areas to support KMT candidates. James C. Y. Soong and Chen Jingzhang also visited and conferred with all 221 candidates at their election headquarters.[66] The party also tapped the immense prestige and influence of a popular president who campaigned for candidates with local elites.[67] Stressing its candidates' educational achievements, wealth, and high social standing, the KMT blanketed large cities with handbills and advertisements. In small locales, the party cultivated its candidates' image to match up with area concerns and issues.[68]

In November public polls showed that 56 percent of the voting-age population did not view the election as important. The KMT then began working even harder to get its message to the voters.[69] The party widely advertised its candidates: famous legal scholars like Su Yunqing of Zhengzhi University, Xie Huichi of Shifan Normal College, and Li Nianzu of Dongwu University,[70] well-known religious leaders like Xing Yun from the Fuguanshan monastery near Kaohsiung, the Buddhist monk Wu Ming, and the Taoist leader Guo Zhongxin from the Zhinangong Temple. But the KMT refused to nominate any candidates from such radical religious groups as the Yiguandao.[71]

Possessing few resources and nominating only about half as many candidates as the KMT, the DPP concentrated mainly on Taipei and Kaohsiung[72] but recruited campaign workers from Taipei, Changhua, Pingtung, and Hualien counties.[73] The party also recruited the Taiwan Professors' Association (Taiwan jiaoshou xiehui), whose members expressed contempt for the old National Assembly, referring to that institution as "having been rotten." Zhengzhi University professor Shao Zonghai supported the DPP because "the reason the Ming dynasty fell was that the intellectuals simply remained critical but never took any action."[74] Plagued by deep splits in the party, having few disciplined workers, and with a leadership divided over how to project the party's vision for change, in the final weeks of the campaign the DPP struggled to convey its message.[75]

The other parties had even fewer resources than the DPP and greater difficulty in projecting their message to voters. The platform of the China Social Democratic Party (Zhonghua shehui minzhu dang), written in abstract, academic language the ordinary citizen found difficult to comprehend, asserted that "we are personalistic liberals" and "our party strives for world peace, revival of nature, human dignity, and social justice."[76] Party chairman Ju Gau-jeng was an electrifying speaker who had led street demonstrations and provoked fights in the Legislative Yuan as a DPP member, but his party was visible in a few cities and nowhere else.

For the first time in Taiwan the government permitted free public campaigning on television, but only between 9:05 and 9:35 P.M.[77] The Central Election Commission required each party to submit its campaign tapes to make certain each party "adhered to the terms of the ROC," which meant that any slogans advocating an independent Taiwan or abrogating the ROC constitution were deleted.

The KMT submitted eight films. One, titled *Your Old Friend*, portrayed the KMT as evolving with a prospering Taiwan. The film urged viewers to regard the KMT as a trusted friend and vowed that the party would march with the people of Taiwan into the future to score even greater achievements. Another

KMT film, titled *The Chinese KMT Has the Ability to Manage Crises*, showed how the party handled international and domestic crises. The DPP's film emphasized the benefits of directly electing the president and vice president. The CSDP's film depicted the poor life of Taiwan's farmers, fishermen, and aboriginal people to highlight the party's concern for the socially deprived. A film by the People's Non-Political Alliance (PNPA) argued that the time had come for a political change.[78]

Many people did not watch this television campaign, and some of those who did misunderstood which party stood for what.[79] A telephone survey found that only 18 percent of those polled watched the program; of those polled, about two-thirds viewed the political advertising from beginning to end.[80] Half the households reported that they did not believe such political information would influence how they voted. More than half the voters did not know what the election was about. Nearly 60 percent of those polled reported that they did not understand the various categories of electing candidates, particularly the nondistrict quota concept.[81]

On December 7, political rallies commenced. The KMT again sent its top officials across the island in a last great effort. Premier Hau visited a water utility, informing the workers that "it is conceivable, but not right now, that only after communism on the China mainland has been discarded and democracy established, we can unify."[82] The premier went on to say that an "independent Taiwan" might risk the security of the island's twenty million people and urged everyone "to reflect on whether the KMT wanted chaos or stability."

President Lee pledged his backing for KMT candidates and called for reports on preelection conditions. James C. Y. Soong and other leaders toured the province again, urging a get-out-the-vote effort because December 21 would be "the critical day on which you can choose revolutionary reform or revolution, stability or chaos, and prosperity or stagnation." The DPP, meanwhile, sent its candidates to the street to rally voters; one nominee even went down on his knees to appeal to passersby to vote on his behalf. The PNPA and the CSDP appealed, "Do you want the KMT to speed up democratic reform? Do you want the DPP to abandon violence? The PNPA and the CSDP offer a new choice, a new hope."[83]

Several days before the election, however, a new poll revealed that nearly half the voters were still undecided about how to cast their ballots.[84] Furthermore, support for the KMT had increased from 40 percent to 56 percent, and the DPP's support had increased from 5 percent to 7.2 percent. That left about one-third of the voters undecided. The KMT was guardedly optimistic, hoping for 75 percent but expecting only 65 percent. The CSDP hoped to win eight seats, and the PNPA predicted a win of ten to fifteen seats.[85]

Meanwhile, campaign costs, including buying votes *(huixuan)*, became an issue. Candidates hired famous entertainers to appear at their political rallies. In Panchiao city popular starlet Bai Pingping attracted large crowds for a KMT candidate, while a block away fewer than seventy people listened to a DPP candidate speak. Ye Zimei, an exotic movie actress from Hong Kong, supported another candidate's campaign. A candidate in the Sungshan section of Taipei hosted a large dinner party for voters, but when he spoke, all eyes were riveted on the nude young woman he had asked to sit on the platform.[86]

Candidates also spent huge sums for tables of food; voters came, ate, and left, followed by others.[87] Many candidates illegally paid middlemen large sums to round up votes. A candidate in Taichung city gave ward officials *(lichang)* funds to give to potential voters.[88] Some candidates hired shady lawyers, accountants, and judges to distribute funds to potential voters. Candidates also sent stationery, calendars, pens, cosmetics, and cash to voters. The Bureau of Investigation discovered a village in southern Taiwan where candidates hosted parties at which the villagers were given a red package containing money *(hongbao)*; the candidate who gave the largest amount received all the votes of the village.[89] Mr. Liu Zhengwen, a KMT candidate for Taipei, stated:

There are still nine more days before voting, and a voter's ballot now costs roughly NT$300–500 [US$12–20]. One still cannot be sure that money will really buy votes. In the 1950s you could depend on 40 percent of the votes you had paid for; in the 1960s, about 30 percent; in the 1970s, about 20 percent; and in the 1989 election, 10 percent. For this election, it might still be 10 percent.[90]

An average KMT candidate spent some NT$10–20 million (US$400,000–800,000), and if the campaign struggle intensified, that sum could rise to more than NT$30 million (US$1.2 million.[91] Taipei candidate Zhou Jindi remarked that candidates in his district were ready to spend NT$30 million (US$1.2 million) to buy votes.[92] Another candidate disclosed that he had scraped together NT$5 million (US$200,000), but when it came time to start campaigning, that sum had already been spent. It was said that if a candidate spent less than NT$50 million (US$2 million), that person would lose the election; if one spent at least NT$100 million (US$4 million), then victory was more certain.[93]

Charges of vote buying did not move the public, which regarded it as typical of the election culture of recent decades and doubted that the authorities could police election violations. Yet the Taiwan High Court Prosecutor's Office reported on December 17 that it was examining 134 such (alleged) violations.[94] The authorities charged sixty-two candidates with violating campaign rules and fined several.[95]

On the final day of campaigning, December 20, President Lee appealed to the citizens for "their sacred vote."[96] DPP chairman Hsu Hsin-liang, who had been averaging four hours of sleep a night during the campaign, spent the entire day visiting all his party's candidates in a taxicab.[97] Chairman Ju Gau-jeng of the CSDP, reputedly the hardest-working chairman, rose at 4:00 A.M. every day. On this last day, Ju moved throughout the Taipei district, where his third brother was a candidate. Su Yufu, chairman of the PNPA, admitted that he was totally exhausted, but he made the rounds one last time on behalf of his party's candidates.

On December 21, with a light rain falling over much of Taiwan, President Lee informed the people that "this is a historic moment, and I hope everyone will participate."[98] Polling booths around the island opened promptly at 8:00 A.M. and closed at 4:00 P.M. People assembled at their assigned polling booths, confirmed that their names were correctly registered, obtained ballots, voted, and departed, with no reported incidents of violence or other irregularities. The election results were reported on islandwide television by 10:30 P.M. and in the press the next day.

## Election Results

Of the 325 National Assembly seats, the KMT won 254, more than the 75 percent it needed to dominate the constitutional revision process.[99] The DPP won 66 seats, far less than the 25 percent it needed for a strong voice. The CSDP won no seats, but the PNPA garnered 3. Of the 225 seats in the fifty-eight districts, the KMT won 179, the DPP, 41, and the PNPA, 3; of the 80 nondistrict apportioned seats, the KMT obtained 60, the DPP 20, and the other parties none; for the overseas Chinese seats, the KMT won 15, the DPP 5, and the other parties none. Of the 13,083,000 people registered, 8,638,622 voted, a participation rate of 68.32 percent (see table 13).

The seventy-eight delegates elected from Taiwan for the first-term National Assembly retained their seats in the second-term National Assembly; the new institution now had 403 seats, of which the KMT claimed almost 79 percent and the DPP about 18 percent.[100] The assembly's new composition meant the KMT would determine constitutional revision.

The day after the election, KMT secretary-general Soong called a press conference to announce that "on this day the citizens of the Republic of China can be most proud." Soong went on: "The election results really show that

TABLE 13
*Results of the December 21, 1991, Election for the Second National Assembly*

| Party | Votes (%) | Seats No. | Seats Percentage | Composition of Assembly Seats | Composition of Assembly Percentage |
|---|---|---|---|---|---|
| KMT | 71.17 | 254 | 78.15 | 318 | 78.91 |
| DPP | 23.94 | 66 | 20.31 | 75 | 18.61 |
| People's Alliance | 2.27 | 3 | 0.92 | 3 | 0.74 |
| China Social Democratic Party | 2.18 | 0 | 0.00 | 0 | 0.00 |
| People's Nonpolitical Alliance | 0.44 | 2 | 0.62 | 7 | 1.74 |
| TOTAL | 100.00 | 325 | 100.00 | 403 | 100.00 |

SOURCE: Nan Fangshuo, "Xuanju jieguo xianshi Taiwan zouxiang wending" (The results of the election reflect that Taiwan is moving toward stability), *Jiushi niandai* (Nineties), no. 264 (January 1992): 50.

the people are the biggest winners. They want stability, and they expect the ruling party to continue to be responsible, within the current stability and prosperity of the country, and produce more reform and achievements." He concluded that "the Republic of China proudly demonstrates to the world that the Chinese people can pass the test of democracy and create an even better democratic society in the future." Ma Ying-chiu, another young, high-ranking party official, stated, "Really, God and good fortune have favored us" and predicted that the election outcome would "have a decisive influence on Taiwan's future development."

DPP chairman Hsu also called a press conference and complained that the "DPP could not effectively deal with the KMT's massive election bribery." Hsu downplayed the voting results, saying that the "DPP actually was not defeated; it just did not advance forward; the seeds for Taiwan independence were planted during the deep winter, and they will mature slowly." Returning to his theme that the KMT had bought the election, he remarked that the "DPP candidates were newcomers, they were not well known, and they lacked experience. But their loss had nothing to do with their political views." Insinuating that the DPP had advanced poor candidates, Hsu unwittingly cast aspersions on his own leadership capabilities. Former DPP chairman Huang Hsin-chieh defended Hsu, arguing that he had only recently become the party's chairman and had not had enough time to prepare a strong campaign. But he admitted that the people had not been able to accept the idea of a Taiwan Republic. Even DPP candidate Lin Zhuoshui lost after he recommended that his party amend its charter to demand an independent Republic of Taiwan.[101]

Many commentators explained the KMT's landslide victory in these terms: DPP factional strife produced its radical platform; small election districts limited the DPP's ability to campaign for votes; KMT candidates had greater wealth; the DPP's shrill political slogans frightened middle-class voters.[102]

Others pointed out that the KMT had skillfully mobilized the nation's military and civilian associations to vote for KMT-backed candidates.[103] The DPP and its supporters blamed KMT vote buying as *the* single most important factor tipping the election in the ruling party's favor.[104] Parris Chang (Chang Xu-zheng), an American professor who had led a team of United States observers to study the election, also believed the KMT had bought the election.

The big victory for the KMT in this election is not the party's victory, but it is the triumph of paper money, with the inscription of Sun Yat-sen and Chiang Kai-shek on the 500- and 1,000-dollar notes shipped by truck to the south to bribe each area in the most massive way. This example of election-buying has no precedent in former elections. Without such bribery, the margin between the KMT and the DPP would have been much closer, like a 45 or 50 percent difference. In the past, the KMT had always promised that it would conduct a clean campaign, but they could never deliver on their promise.[105]

The irony is that, in the December 2, 1989, election, vote buying had also reportedly occurred on a massive scale. But when the KMT lost ground in that race, no one complained of vote buying. Moreover, in areas like Taipei, where middle-class voters predominated and opposed vote buying, the DPP hoped to perform well and failed. Its severe defeat in Taipei was probably caused by its radical call for a Republic of Taiwan, which most middle-class voters rejected.

One commentator stressed that the Taiwan voters simply had rejected the DPP's radical message and greatly trusted Lee Teng-hui. DPP member Kang Ning-hsiang, interviewed after the election, remarked that the election had been significant in several ways: all views were now expressed in the political marketplace; no ethnic conflict had surfaced between the younger generation of Taiwanese and the mainlanders; and, finally, there was President Lee's influence: "Without his charismatic and powerful role, the election outcome might have been different." [106]

The DPP leaders met to take stock. Although severely defeated because of poor campaign tactics and planning, the opposition party agreed to continue to play by the rules and try to win voter support. The central committee began preparing for the important December 1992 Legislative Yuan and Control Yuan elections by revamping the party machine, interviewing voters, and evaluating party members.[107] Committee members admitted their organization did not link the party center and the grass roots as well as the KMT did. The party intended to find better candidates and instruct them in how to win elections. "Maybe," one mused, "it is a disadvantage for the DPP to advocate Taiwan independence, or else the KMT's candidates would not have won the number of ballots they did." [108] The leadership also concluded that their party must unite with mainstream Taiwan society and find effective means to counter the election message of the KMT. Before election day, one DPP candidate had promised that if he lost he would shave his head; he kept his promise.

What did the voters think? A telephone survey by the *Zhongguo shibao* reported that of nine hundred people polled on December 22, 19.3 percent were very satisfied with the election outcome, 60.9 percent were satisfied, 7.6 described themselves as not too satisfied, and 1.7 percent were very unhappy, with the rest unknown. Thus, if this small survey was at all valid, [109] four-fifths of the voting populace were satisfied with the election. The *New York Times* reported that

several days later, on December 21, the people of Taiwan voted and gave a 71 percent landslide victory to the Kuomintang. The election was marred by vote-buying, a Taiwan tradition, but it was nonetheless an astonishing victory for the Nationalists. It also marked a milestone in Taiwan's transition from autocracy to democracy. [110]

After more than forty years, a political institution dominated by mainlander politicians became one of representatives from Taiwan and its offshore islands. Few had predicted the KMT's stunning victory; the voters had rejected the DPP's appeal for a radical transformation of Taiwan's polity. Vote buying had been rampant but less so in the Taipei region, where the KMT victory was most apparent.

## The Calm before the Storm

After the party's landslide victory, KMT leaders confidently promised that constitutional reform would move forward. In early January 1992, President Lee reminded the people that "in the past year, everyone worked hard to help the government get through a difficult period; this year will be the year for constitutional reform, and I hope everyone will do their best to cooperate." [111]

But what kind of constitutional reform should the second-term National Assembly produce? And what did the elite and public think about constitutional reform? On January 3, Chen Shouguo, a journalist, commented that "implementing constitutional reform has never been so close at hand and so obvious to the people, but the direction of such reform is unclear." Chen then posed a problem: "If direct election [of a president] is the DPP's only purpose and the DPP regards that as the key to its success, then popular election in fact constitutes democratization. But we are ignoring the design of our political system. Constitutional revision then becomes most worrisome." [112] Chen had put his finger on a critical issue: directly electing the nation's top leaders might require considerable constitutional revision, which in turn might question the legitimacy of the ROC government. At a seminar several days later political commentators discussed whether it was necessary to have a National Assembly if its functions replicated those of the Legislative Yuan. If both institutions could initiate laws and ratify them, what was the purpose of the National Assembly? [113]

Simmering below that concern were two problems that the KMT had not resolved but that the DPP had resolved by virtue of its new constitution. First, the KMT must decide whether the nation's leaders should be directly or indirectly elected. Second, should the government adhere to the current five-power governance system of the Executive, Legislative, Judicial, Examination, and Control Yuans or opt for a different system?

By the end of February 1992, the KMT and DPP's positions on constitutional reform had crystallized as follows.[114] The KMT wanted the second-term National Assembly to meet before May 20, 1995, and indirectly elect a president and vice president for a four-year term instead of the six-year term of the past. It also wanted minimal constitutional revision to allow the president to nominate members for the Judicial, Examination, and Control Yuans and empower the National Assembly to confirm or reject those nominees. The KMT wanted the National Assembly to meet once a year to hear the president's report, discuss affairs of state, propose recommendations, revise the constitution, and ratify any constitutional laws proposed by the Legislative Yuan. In addition the KMT wanted Legislative Yuan and National Assembly members to serve a single term of six years and allow one-quarter of the National Assembly members to recall the president. If two-thirds of that membership approved, recall would become mandatory, and, if more than half of the Control Yuan members proposed to recall the president and over two-thirds approved, then recall would be mandatory. Finally, the KMT wanted Article 113 of the 1947 constitution to be enforced to allow the people to elect Taiwan's provincial governor.

The DPP wanted to abolish the National Assembly and have direct elections of the president and vice president, who would serve a single term of four years. The DPP also preferred a government with a president, parliament, and judiciary. The president could be recalled if more than 10 percent of the qualified voters petitioned and more than 50 percent voted for recall; the judiciary could also impeach the president. The Taiwan provincial government and its governor would be abolished.

Although the two parties were at odds on constitutional reform, some political experts urged the KMT to negotiate with the DPP so that ROC democracy could move forward, but they never called on the DPP to initiate negotiation and compromise.[115] Leading intellectuals, supported by the media, insisted that the KMT take the lead and compromise with the DPP.

The KMT tried to project an image of unity, but in reality its members were divided over how to elect a president and vice president and what role the National Assembly should play. Some KMT delegates at the 1990 National Affairs Conference had advocated direct presidential elections. But party elders and conservatives did not agree. Therefore, when registering the Second National Assembly delegates on January 1, 1992, Ma Ying-chiu emphasized that the ruling party had "not yet determined what methods it would propose to elect a president. It all depends on the people's will [minyi]."[116] Despite internal dissension, the KMT still publicly endorsed the "indirect" method of electing the president.

On January 21, some DPP and KMT National Assembly delegates argued heatedly over whether the nation should adopt direct or indirect presidential elections.[117] The KMT delegates demanded the election of a third-term National Assembly and insisted that each party's nominee for that election should express a preference for the party's presidential and vice presidential nominee; the voters would simultaneously elect an assembly delegate and their party's president and vice president. In the KMT's view, third-term National Assembly representatives would later cast their predetermined ballots for the presidential and vice presidential candidates. The DPP delegates rejected that proposal and supported direct election. Each party would nominate a president and vice president ninety days before the current leaders' term expired; a majority of the popular vote would then elect the president and vice president. (This procedure eliminated electing a third-term National Assembly.) These public debates indicated that the KMT wanted the indirect election process and a modest revision of the constitution.[118]

On February 22 the KMT and DPP agreed to meet to discuss the upcoming constitutional reform convention and other political matters.[119] Both parties also agreed on negotiating procedures but did not publicize them. Then on March 4 the KMT reopened discussions about which election procedure it should adopt.[120] With that development the calm unity that had prevailed in the ruling party shattered.

# Reforming the Constitution

Taiwan's political elite now interacted more closely than ever in an effort to agree on how the constitution should be amended to elect the nation's representatives and top leaders. But the ruling party had long been divided over how to elect the president and vice president. These differences had not surfaced when the party struggled to win the December 1991 election for control of the second-term National Assembly. But when the ruling party's delegates prepared to attend the assembly's spring 1992 convention, they became manifest.

If the party agreed on direct presidential elections, what would become of the National Assembly, the nation's most powerful political institution that amended the constitution and elected the president and vice president? Allocating power to the Legislative Yuan or initiating another arrangement to amend the constitution raised the question of how the polity should be structured and should function. Ruling party elders and conservatives did not want the polity and constitution radically altered. They expected to use the constitution to unify China and the National Assembly to preserve KMT power. Therefore they strongly opposed direct presidential elections.

But KMT liberals and political opposition members believed that Taiwan's democracy must be based on direct elections. To realize that goal, they agreed that some modification of existing political institutions was necessary, but there was little agreement on how that should be done. The political dispute that rocked the ruling party in March 1992 threatened to divide it and dissipate its power. Closely connected with this new crisis was the issue of whether the political opposition would continue to play by the rules of the game if the KMT somehow resolved its differences and dominated the constitutional revision process. Would the opposition boycott the National Assembly and resort to street demonstrations to win public support for its goals?

## The President Initiates a Debate

At a meeting on March 4, President Lee and some high-level government and KMT officials agreed that direct elections should be given serious consideration, and the president immediately urged the party to discuss the issue.[1] The news shook Taiwan's political world. Lee Huan, an older, out-of-power KMT official, declared that he did not understand the KMT's sudden shift on constitutional reform and remarked that this policy change "would make it difficult to maintain Taiwan's five-power polity, because how could there be a direct election of a president and still retain the National Assembly? It was all very strange [qiguai]." Vice Premier Shih Chi-yang stated, "I did not know until now [March 7, 6:00 P.M.]. I had not received any news on this matter."[2] KMT officials Wu Po-hsiung, Chen Li-an, and Hsu Shui-te refused to comment. But Kao Yü-jen, chairman of the board for China Television, admitted that opinions were divided within the KMT on how to elect the nation's leaders. What had been perceived as a united front in the party for indirect elections no longer existed.

Chiang Yen-shih, secretary-general of the Office of the President, tried to dispel the confusion:

At first we adopted the indirect election procedure to maintain political stability and obtain the support of the overseas Chinese so that we could not be criticized for electing a president of Taiwan. Having direct elections really means electing a Taiwan president. Although our party's committee had proposed indirect election, the voice for direct elections always had been present. We simply are studying this alternative. In reality, President Lee is a leader who looks at the entirety of China as a major concern. He wants to use the China mainland as the means for promoting our economy. In the past, many suspected him of wanting only to promote Taiwanese independence. That is incorrect. He has his mission. He wants to be the torchbearer of contemporary Chinese history.[3]

The dispute over constitutional reform divided the KMT.[4] KMT politician Huang Zhuwen liked the idea. KMT legislator Yü Mu-ming disagreed: direct elections meant abandoning the five-power polity and being forced to accept a three-power government. Hu Fu, KMT a legal expert, complained that "instead of debating what kind of a political system we want, we go about it in the reverse way by debating which election method we want."

The *Lianhe wanbao* (United evening news) criticized direct elections.[5] Xing Zhiren, dean of Zhengzhi University Law School, worried that if the KMT made direct presidential elections the centerpiece of constitutional reform, it meant radical reform. Xie Ruizhi, professor of public administration at Taiwan Normal University, pointed out that directly electing the president would destroy the ROC's five-power polity and averred that "such a change was too great." Li Nianzu, a lawyer and member of the Second National Assembly, posed this question: "If we elect a president by popular vote, what happens to the National Assembly, the Executive Yuan, and the premier? Will we also abolish the Control and Examination Yuans, and if so, how will there be adequate checks on presidential power?" Yang Zongseng, director of the National Library, argued that Taiwan must have an educated citizenry and worried that opulence and violence might influence future elections: "Therefore, would not the direct election procedure more likely cause instability? Moreover, we must still worry about the communist threat."

The DPP welcomed the KMT's decision to consider direct elections, expressing delight at the turnabout.[6] DPP party leaders had always advocated abolishing the National Assembly, and they appealed to the public to support direct presidential elections. They acknowledged that the KMT was finally in accord with the world trend of democracies' directly electing their leaders. On March 8 President Lee tried to calm the political storm.[7] He pointed out that constitutional revision was difficult and complex and that, as in the past, he intended to stand above the fray and work hard to promote democracy. He merely wanted the KMT to reflect the people's will.

Some KMT politicians immediately called President Lee's decision to reopen the direct election issue a political maneuver to consolidate his personal power. Kuan Chung, former KMT deputy secretary-general and now chairman of the Foundation for Democracy, evaluated Lee's sudden decision this way:

For the past two years the ruling party has emphasized constitutional revision, and for the past eight months it has advocated indirect election. Suddenly, in the past two days, it has shifted its position to support direct elections. This is incompatible with democratic procedures. I do not object to President Lee's wanting to make such a change and even wanting to increase his power, but such action involves the constitution. Our constitution is 100 percent supportive of the cabinet system. If we want to change to direct election of the president, then the entire constitution must be greatly revised. It not only is unnecessary to do that, it is unwise and very dangerous.[8]

Kuan Chung spoke for many enemies and critics of the president.

Meanwhile, KMT heavyweights Lin Yang-kang, Chiang Yen-shih, Cheyne J. Y. Chiu, Wu Po-hsiung, Lien Chan, James C. Y. Soong, and Chen Jinrang came out in favor of the proposal. But KMT stalwarts like Lee Huan and Ch'iu Chuang-huan opposed direct election. Premier Hau steered a middle course, explaining that "constitutional revision should not be radical. If we change to a direct election system, our constitutional articles must be changed accordingly, and that would mean the entire constitution might have to be changed. Therefore, we should move with caution." [9]

Meanwhile, DPP leaders speculated on the implications of the uproar for constitutional revision to allow for direct election of the president. [10] Former chairman Huang Hsin-chieh remarked that the KMT might not have decided how to revise the constitution, and that even if direct election took place, he lacked the qualifications to become president. DPP chairman Hsu Hsin-liang stated that it was too early to decide who would run for president. Shih Ming-Teh remarked that direct election, should it become the law, was something he had always believed would take place. Finally, KMT officials Ma Ying-chiu and Shih Chi-yang, who had frequently discussed indirect elections before the National Assembly election, refused to speak to the press; they were too embarrassed by their party's sudden change in position. [11]

## Confrontation and Consensus in the KMT

Why had the president reconsidered direct election of the president when the party had publicly supported electing that official indirectly? Vice President Li Yuan-zu's advisory committee on constitutional reform, which had met 165 times during the year, with some 4,500 persons attending, favored indirect elections. His committee drew up the following guidelines: avoid revising constitutional articles, maintain the five-power constitution, add articles if required. [12] President Lee admitted that he knew his vice president's committee had been studying the advantages and difficulties of both election procedures. [13] But, he said, when he campaigned in December on behalf of his party's candidates, his meetings with local leaders convinced him that there was no popular support for indirect elections. [14] President Lee then met with various scholars and leading officials from Kaohsiung and Taipei who worried that many KMT candidates running for the December 1992 Legislative Yuan election might lose if the party did not endorse direct elections. From these meetings President Lee decided that the party should discuss both election procedures and reach a consensus before the second-term National Assembly convened on March 25, 1992. We do not know whether President Lee consulted with his vice president before making his decision. Someone high up in the party then informed the press, which reported the chairman's sudden decision to have the party debate the method of presidential election.

On March 9, 1992, proposals for direct and indirect election procedures were submitted to the central committee for review and discussion.[15] At that meeting, lasting nearly eight hours, KMT members first agreed that the Third Plenum, set for March 14–15, must decide which election procedure KMT delegates of the second-term National Assembly should support. Then they urged party unity. But at one point, tempers reached the boiling point. Defense Minister Chen Li-an turned to Vice President Li Yuan-zu and said, "Li Yuan-zu did not prepare the two plans carefully to present to the central committee so that it could make a rational decision."[16] The vice president replied, "We arranged for the central committee members to meet and discuss our study group's proposals, but unfortunately you were not there. Retract what you just said." Chen did not respond.

Former Taiwan governor Shieh Tung-min then stated that "the fewer changes made in the constitution, the better." Technocrat policy maker Li Kuo-ting followed: "I have never understood politics, but I feel that our country has a five-power constitution and four levels of governmental administration. When we talk about constitutional revision, we must also take into account the China mainland, and therefore, we should not radically alter the constitution."[17] Ch'iu Chuang-huan said, "In last year's elections, a majority supported indirect elections. The party has always advocated indirect elections, and that is what I believe and still believe in." KMT elder statesman Shen Chang-Huan concurred: "The ruling party has long leaned toward indirect elections. I do not understand, and I am surprised there has been a sudden change in direction; it will harm the unity of our party."

Other central committee members voiced different points of view. Lin Yang-kang argued that "one ballot will be a vote for a single candidate, but voting indirectly means casting a ballot for three candidates: the National Assembly candidate as well as the president and vice president. Suppose a voter does not like the assembly candidate but approves of the president—how can he make a choice?" Foreign Minister Chien Fu added that "the direct election is a worldwide democratic tide and will strengthen the power of the president and the people's will. It will positively improve our international position." But Xu Lilung who favored indirect elections, asked, "What is the people's will [minyi]? When the KMT advocated the indirect election last year and won 71 percent of the popular support while the DPP, supporting direct election, only won 23 percent—that is a definitive, legal expression of the people's will that cannot be violated."[18]

After much heated discussion, they still had failed to reach a compromise and had to agree to continue the debate at the Third Plenum. Ten central committee members supported indirect elections, and fifteen advocated direct elections, with the rest neutral.[19] No consensus had been reached. Although many were reluctant to criticize the chairman for not following the recommendations of his vice president's committee, President Lee undoubtedly realized that many party leaders were frustrated by debating a policy that seemed to have been predetermined by the vice president's committee and then reversed by the president at the last moment. On the one hand, many privately blamed Chairman Lee for not consulting in advance with party elders and others about his new view. The chairman, on the other hand, did not believe he had sufficient time to persuade party leaders to reconsider the party's options. Therefore, before the March 14–15 Third Plenum at the Chungshanlou Auditorium, an atmosphere of heightened tension prevailed; party consensus had broken down and been replaced by bitter confrontation. Uncomfortable with disharmony of views, many now feared that the KMT might split.

The Third Plenum focused on three issues: selecting the procedure for electing a president and vice president; deciding whether to allow the president to nominate members to the Control Yuan, subject to the approval of the National Assembly, or to follow the old practice of allowing urban councils to elect these same members; finally, after resolving the first two issues, providing guidelines for KMT members of the second-term National Assembly.[20]

On March 12 the media called for KMT leaders to avoid factionalism and eschew personal gain and power; they also denounced certain nameless individuals as "criminals of the KMT and the country" while insisting that "the KMT must build a democratic elector system in its party and substitute that for feudal forms of politics." They finally urged "selecting the best leaders having a point of view worthy of being elected."[21] By admonishing the top leadership to avoid making serious political mistakes, the media tried to influence this critical debate.

On the day before the plenum, KMT secretary-general James C. Y. Soong informed the press that the KMT had yet to agree on a method for electing the president and vice president. At the June–July 1990 National Conference, Soong had assembled a small group to study national elections, which had agreed to adopt America's indirect election method. But the party had never concurred. Soong explained that election methods were still being reviewed within the party and that many different opinions existed. To calm fears, he said:

Although I must sincerely admit the KMT has advocated indirect elections in its literature, we did this because the public did not understand this method, and we were
trying to educate our party. In our last election, the method of electing a president
was not a major issue. Everyone worried about Taiwan independence. Had the KMT
supported direct elections, it would have misled the public. The ROC is no longer in
the shadow of "Taiwan independence," and there is now more opportunity to think
about direct elections.[22]

Direct elections could be interpreted as promoting Taiwan independence even
though many KMT members opposed that outcome and favored directly
electing a president.

On the evening of the March 11, 1992, four party heavyweights (President
Lee, Premier Hau, secretary-general Chiang Yen-shih of the Office of the President, and Soong) dined together to discuss how to resolve the party's crisis.
The group finally agreed that the ROC's five-power structure must be maintained but that a system of direct elections should be promoted. This action
did not mean taking the road of "Taiwan independence" because the ROC
could adhere to the constitution and the five-power system no matter how
the president was elected.[23]

But rumors circulated about this meeting's outcome. One held that no
consensus had been reached and that the Third Plenum would have to resolve
the crisis. Another contended that Premier Hau had expressed no view on the
election issue, but that was proved false the next day when he went before the
Legislative Yuan to state that as a private individual he preferred indirect election. DPP member Chen Shui-bian asked Hau how that voting system could
reflect the will of the people. Hau replied: "What is the people's will [minyi]?
Are public surveys indicative of the people's will? I believe that popular elections like that held late last year really demonstrated the popular will. The
majority of votes won by the National Assembly candidates really reflected
the people's will."[24] Hau preferred indirect election but agreed that his party
should promote direct elections.

At 9:00 A.M. on March 14, Chairman Lee opened the Third Plenum, emphasizing that the KMT would always be united with the people. He urged
party central committee members "to work hard at promoting a spirit of
peace and use practical ways to create a 'new age' for the ROC."[25] Some party
elders then attacked the policy of direct elections. Chen Li-fu, eldest senior
adviser to the Office of the President, warned, "There is nothing under heaven
that is so important; there are only fools trying to make trouble." He noted
that the political process so far had performed well but that some individuals
were trying to change everything.

We must realize that at present this is a period of political constitution and not one of political tutelage. How can the party draft such a policy as direct election and ask the National Assembly to adhere to that policy? The direct election approach would require abolishing the National Assembly, which has the right to elect the president. How can we have the power to do that? This plenum has no right to decide such a policy. The present political system is quite adequate, as is our economy. Why does the KMT want to make trouble for itself? Why must we please those who are against us?[26]

Wei Yung, a political scientist and former government official, agreed with Chen: "The KMT has forgotten what kind of a political party it is. Any proposal to revise the Constitution should be submitted to the National Assembly for their decision, and we cannot tell them what to do."

Former premier Sun Yun-suan presented another point of view: "I believe the main concern should be not to decide how to elect a president but to avoid splitting the party. The people want security and harmony, but if our party divides, we must apologize to our founding father. We should return to our five-power constitutional principles and avoid splitting so easily." The party elders and their supporters feared dividing the party on the presidential election issue.

The arguments above indirectly attacked the party chairman, but arguments defending direct elections followed. Only after much spirited debate did Chairman Lee urge party members to agree on a constitutional revision plan to present to the National Assembly. His plan also proposed that any unresolved issues be decided at next year's fourteenth party congress.[27] But Lee's proposal angered National Assembly delegate Shao Zonghai, who stood up and shouted, "What about the question of procedure?" Lee stood his ground and replied, "You are here only to observe, not participate." Shao insisted on proceeding to the podium, but security guards grabbed him and led him, still audibly complaining, to his chair. Taipei KMT branch head Chien Han-sung had to take Shao out of the meeting and calm him down. Then James C. Y. Soong rose and said, "The purpose of our meeting is to give a proposal to the National Assembly. Should we give others an opportunity to speak to this point?"

Wang Sheng rose and said, "I have a different opinion about our party's rule 7. If you put your name on the ballot, that gives people the impression the party wants to control voting. I propose changing the rule to a blank ballot for voting." Kuan Chung added, "The party central committee must build a consensus, but we should first have a thorough discussion. We also ought to obey our party's rule 15, which is to submit a request for speaking and that a person be approved by the chairman to be allowed to speak." After more discussion, Soong rose to calm the situation: "There is no set way to vote [for these proposals]. Everyone can register to speak according to order."

Bitter discussion continued to focus on which election proposal to adopt for the National Assembly. At one point, legislator Yü Mu-ming asked Chairman Lee if he could speak; Lee replied, "Say as much as you want." Yü asked the National Assembly delegates to remain calm and abide by the rules, bringing hisses from many. Yü said, "There is no big deal about you representatives. We elected you," and turning to Chairman Lee, he said, "They also are hissing at you." Lee replied, "Go ahead and speak. Do not be afraid of them."[28] That exchange brought laughter. The barbed exchanges continued, often mixed with mordant humor, until noon, when the session ended for lunch.

The next day and a half of meetings followed the same pattern of arguments and accusations. At midnight on March 16, the party reached a compromise and drafted a brief statement to the effect that the party had not split but that no action would be taken to change the election procedure in the constitution until May 20, 1995, to allow for the ninth presidential election in March 1996. According to Lee, the party had openly debated the election issue and party democratization had advanced.[29] Lin Yang-kang, who had vigorously advocated direct election, concluded, "Since no consensus has been reached about how to elect a president, the National Assembly should not discuss this issue."[30]

On March 25, Chairman Lee explained why he had reversed his party's endorsement of indirect election and kindled debate on direct election. Lee said:

I had talked with the people [late last year], and I learned much about their views. I came to the conclusion that many people wanted direct election, and so I encouraged both election methods to be openly discussed at the Third Plenum. Some see direct election as representing Taiwan independence, and there is no reason for alarm about that view. We follow the ROC constitution, and the president will be elected according to that constitution and will represent the ROC. There is no reason to fear that direct election will bring about Taiwan independence. There is no market for Taiwan independence. The DPP was soundly defeated in the last election, and any party advocating Taiwan independence will be defeated by the voters.[31]

Although Chairman Lee and some top party leaders had wanted the direct election method and could have won enough votes to pass the measure, many KMT elders and top leaders disagreed, arguing that this political reform was too radical and might require radical constitutional change. Chairman Lee did not press for a vote; instead, the party compromised by postponing the matter. Within the next three years, the party leadership hoped to find a way to elect a president and vice president, maintain the five-branch government, and perhaps retain the National Assembly.[32] Finally, the plenum granted the president the power to nominate Control Yuan members, to be approved or rejected by the National Assembly.

On the same day, party secretary Soong publicly declared that the KMT had agreed to wait until May 20, 1995, one year before the election of the ninth-term president, to decide how to elect the president.[33] The political discussions captured the public's attention, and the media mentioned little else. One poll found that if the election for president were held at this time, Lee would win by a landslide.[34] The president had increased his popularity and forced his party to accept the prospect of a democracy based on direct presidential elections.

## The National Assembly Convention

The 325 newly elected National Assembly members joined another 78 who had been elected in supplementary elections for a grand total of 403. The KMT had 320 delegates, the DPP 74 (DPP delegate Li Zongfang had died April 1, 1992), the Alliance of Political Parties 6, the Nonpolitical Alliance Party 2, and the Chinese Social Democratic Party 1. Although strongly opposed to the National Assembly, the DPP still agreed to play by the rules. On January 1, 1992, the DPP, in preparing for the National Assembly convention, agreed to press for direct election and for a deputy secretary-general's seat in the assembly's chair committee.[35] DPP leaders realized they had to cooperate with the other parties to effect constitutional change (it took 81 delegates to support a motion, and the DPP had only 74). Disagreements between the party's two leading factions had become evident by mid-January, with the Meilidao faction insisting on leading the delegates and the "New Tide" faction threatening not to comply.[36]

On February 15, DPP National Assembly delegates held a three-day meeting to map out their strategy. Wu Feng-shan argued that "indirect election is too complicated, and direct election is the simple way to elect a president. The ruling party is not likely to lose and need not fear such an election procedure."[37] The DPP thus agreed to make direct election its major objective for constitutional revision.

The DPP also threatened demonstrations if the constitution was not redrafted. On March 2, a group of DPP delegates transported between three hundred and four hundred party members to the hometown of Taiwanese KMT standing committee member Ch'iu Chuang-huan to protest his support for indirect elections.[38] Learning of this demonstration, some fifteen hundred of Ch'iu's local supporters assembled to protect his residence. DPP cars carried placards reading Ch'iu Chuang-huan Has No Principles and Ch'iu Chuang-huan Is the Shame of Chang-hua County! Police restored order, and the incident quickly ended. A week later, the DPP welcomed the KMT's decision to debate the method of electing the president, but many were stunned to learn that some KMT top leaders, including the president, favored direct elections.[39] Former DPP chairman Huang Hsin-chieh noted: "Although Taiwan no longer has a political strongman, the fact that President Lee can change his mind in only a day to support direct elections demonstrates a way of using political power that cannot be ignored." Huang then said, "If the KMT Third Plenum vetoes direct elections, the DPP will organize a mass demonstration."[40] DPP chairman Hsu Hsin-liang, during a visit to Washington, D.C., with twenty-four associates, said, "The Taiwanese people should decide their own fate, and the DPP will never compromise on this issue [of directly electing a president]. No strong force will determine the future of Taiwan without a consensus expressed by the people."[41] On the eve of the National Assembly convention, the rival parties viewed constitutional reform very differently.[42]

## The Second-Term National Assembly Convenes

The second-term National Assembly conducted its business in six stages.[43] During March 20–25, a preparatory committee drew up rules and the assembly elected a chair committee to manage the convention. Between March 26 and April 1, the assembly elected a secretary-general and two deputies who, with the chair committee, set the agenda and rules for the assembly's work. During April 2–10, government officials presented reports and suggestions for constitutional revision. From April 11 to April 27, the assembly evaluated the first reform proposals. From April 28 to May 8, the assembly discussed the evaluation committee's judgments. For the rest of May, the assembly deliberated over the second and third proposals and finally added ten articles to the constitution. Although the KMT had the votes to amend the constitution, elite disagreement over the constitution was severe and portended future factionalism over the nation's constitution.

### Conflict

Before the opening ceremony on March 20, 1992, the DPP announced that its delegates would take the assembly oath separately from the other delegates.

The party also stipulated that the oath taking would use solar rather than lunar dating for the founding of the Republic of China and that no national flag should be in the chamber.[44] The DPP delegates' refusal to take the same oath as the other delegates infuriated the KMT delegates.[45] The next day DPP delegates monopolized floor discussion and frequently disrupted assembly proceedings. KMT delegates now agreed that as few assembly chair committee positions as possible should be given to the DPP, infuriating the DPP delegates, who had expected that one of their delegates would become a deputy secretary-general.[46]

When President Lee arrived at the conference hall, the DPP delegates were wearing green cotton ribbons or purple vests stamped with the slogan Direct Election of the President (zongtong zhixuan). When the president began to speak, DPP delegates in the back rows stood up holding green cloth banners with slogans such as Abolish the Black List, Abolish the National Assembly, Redraft a New Constitution, and Direct Presidential Elections in 1993. One DPP delegate even waved a flag reading Taiwan Independence Alliances. At one point the president exclaimed: "To revise the constitution, we rely on the idea of an ever brighter nation's future, and our foremost goal is to increase the prosperity of our people and to set aside our differences for seeking unity and to create a great, brilliant, new era."[47] But as soon as the president completed his address, several DPP delegates rushed to the stage shouting, "Direct public elections!" All DPP delegates also refused to attend the first assembly luncheon.

## The Conflict Heats Up

During March 20–23, DPP delegates frequently took over the podium, placing chairs and tables there, sitting and smoking, and sometimes hurling their microphones,[48] forcing KMT delegates to move below the podium. The chair committee even had to vacate the podium to manage assembly proceedings. Angered by the KMT's insistence on managing the assembly, DPP delegates resorted to vituperative, often violent behavior. The KMT delegates, by virtue of their superior numbers, elected the assembly's chair committee on March 24.[49] The KMT obtained twenty-six of the thirty-three positions; the DPP received six, not enough to have any influence in assembly affairs.

On March 26, DPP delegates several times marched to the podium and grabbed the microphone away from the speaker. KMT delegates then shouted, "Don't speak! Step down!" At one point, KMT delegate Wang Baichi called the DPP female delegate Su Zhiyang a bitch, which produced an uproar from the DPP delegates, followed by shouts and screams from KMT delegates. Ms. Su demanded that Mr. Wang apologize; he replied by saying, "Those who scolded me are bitches [maren di shi biaozi]."[50] An eighty-seven-year-old KMT delegate entered the fray, shouting, "If you want to brawl, why don't you go outside and fight?" A DPP delegate shouted, "Why not supply a bottle of Yanglode drink to everyone to cool off?" Chen Chongguang, who owned that soft drink company, replied that he would have his company deliver a hundred bottles to "cool off the assembly delegates." But DPP delegate Huang Hsin-chieh jokingly said, "Just send over the Yanglode so they will fight more, drink more, and fight more." Said Chen, "That would be disappointing if things were like that. But this chaos is normal and nothing to get excited about."[51]

By March 28 the situation had become so volatile that the KMT delegates established a six-person committee to mediate the violent outbreaks between the two parties.[52] The KMT delegates worried that the assembly's proceedings were receiving a bad press and that public opinion might turn against the National Assembly. But KMT legislator Huang Zhuwen blamed the DPP for the uproar:

This behavior is very similar to the disorder in the Legislative Yuan. But that occurred because DPP members disrupted KMT members' speaking. In the Legislative Yuan, the senior legislators were still there, and the composition of membership was not healthy. The DPP members were elected, but Legislative Yuan senior legislators had not been elected. In this National Assembly, however, everyone has been elected, and the senior legislators are no more. The DPP delegates should reconsider their tactics so as not to alienate the public.[53]

Politician Ye Jingfeng added:

The DPP uses violent protest as a "right," but there is also the right of the speaker. The DPP excessively resorts to their "rights," but these should be moderated. The National Assembly also spends a lot of the taxpayers' money, and so far the outcome of the assembly has been dismal. Delegates should productively contribute and not constantly disrupt the proceedings.[54]

Some assemblymen like Huang Zhuwen blamed the KMT for not being tolerant of the DPP and making the National Assembly meeting a success: "If the KMT does not improve the assembly procedures, there will be problems in the future. Matters should be resolved when the confusion becomes worse."[55]

These appeals for tolerance did not persuade, and vituperative behavior continued throughout the next few months. When DPP delegates became angry, KMT delegates responded in kind. As a consequence, all reform proposals submitted by the DPP delegates were summarily tabled by the KMT; all proposals submitted by the KMT were in turn subjected to angry attack by DPP delegates.

## The Legislative Yuan Enters the Fray

On April 13, parliamentarians in the Legislative Yuan began reviewing the National Assembly's budget. Legislator Lee Shen-fong angrily described how the National Assembly wanted to expand its power and attacked its members for trying to create a permanent chair committee (yizhang). "They can do everything they want except to change a woman into a man. Persons like Wang Ying-chieh should be discarded like a pile of garbage."[56] The next day Wang Ying-chieh took the podium in the assembly and said, "If I am garbage, then Mr. Li is a cockroach."[57] He was roundly applauded.

Seeing themselves attacked, DPP and KMT assembly delegates set aside their differences and began reviling the Legislative Yuan. Delegate after delegate took the podium to denounce the parliament; one delegate announced that "if National Assembly delegates were pieces of garbage, then the Legislative Yuan was a garbage container." Throughout the morning of April 13, delegates took turns denouncing Lee Shen-fong and the Legislative Yuan.[58]

Lee Shen-fong then said if certain conditions were met, he would apologize to Wang:

I will go up to Yangming Mountain to apologize to Mr. Wang under these conditions. First, the National Assembly will cease its endless squabbles. Second, assembly delegates will not try to monopolize the revision of the constitution. Finally, that the National Assembly will obey the Supreme Court's ruling 282 and interpret that to mean they will not ask for a salary. If these conditions are met, I will personally go to the Yangming Mountain and apologize to the second-term National Assembly as well.[59]

Assembly delegates ignored Lee Shen-fong's challenge and mounted one of their own.

On April 27, at a session of the first evaluation committee, assembly delegates passed five proposals:[60] the National Assembly would establish a budget office; the Legislative Yuan and the assembly would review each other's budgets; the assembly would annually convene a thirty-day meeting to listen to reports from the president and other officials about national affairs; the assembly would establish a permanent chair committee with a deputy chair position; assembly members should not serve in the ROC government.

When the Legislative Yuan met the next day, its members were appalled by the ambitious five-point plan. One muttered, "It's crazy and a joke." Some said that National Assembly delegates were responsible only for constitutional reform and that expanding their power would produce another political crisis. Legislator Zai Bihuang said: "They are treating national affairs like a game. They are causing more conflict with the Legislative Yuan. Their actions will inevitably make many people realize that the second-term National Assembly should be abolished." Another legislator, Chen Kueimiao, stated: "We should look upon the second-term National Assembly as trying to expand its power from all points of view and try to figure out where that body is going and what its proper role should be. What power do they really need? Moreover, the ruling party should really reflect on this state of affairs."[61] Xie Changting added that the assembly's proposal for mutually reviewing assembly and parliamentary budgets was "against the constitution."

The assembly's proposals elicited a response from KMT secretary-general James C. Y. Soong, who warned delegates to "exercise prudence and reflect before you raise your hand to vote."[62] Nor did the Legislative Yuan's criticisms cease. On April 28 one legislator said, "If the National Assembly feels so good [about expanding its power], they should watch out they do not contract AIDS." Delegate Wang Wenzheng retorted, "As their hearts are full of thoughts about AIDS, how can they pass a law without AIDS. Such sick people cannot live for too long in this world."[63] DPP delegate Cai Shiyuan said, "The old thieves have left and now here come the new thieves."[64]

An incident of verbal abuse had snowballed into a major confrontation between two branches of government and encouraged the National Assembly to augment its power. On April 17 the DPP delegates decided to walk out and demonstrate to pressure the KMT to reverse its decision to postpone constitutional reform.

*Confrontation*

KMT delegation leader Shieh Lung-sheng now realized that his most difficult task in the National Assembly was not negotiating with the DPP but trying to achieve consensus among KMT delegates to affirm his party's plan for constitutional revision.[65] As early as March 18, some KMT assembly delegates, resentful at being a tool of the ruling party, had wanted to establish a coalition that included DPP members to press for direct presidential elections. DPP delegate Huang Hsin-chieh welcomed that move: "I do not care if a KMT delegate heads this coalition as long as there are more people in our coalition."[66]

This move alarmed the ruling party, which quickly instructed its delegates not to establish a permanent chair committee. On May 15 the KMT delegates, resentful of being strong-armed by their party, tried to form a quorum and proposed a motion to disperse.[67] At 4:30 P.M., KMT loyalists tried to table the proposal for a permanent chair committee pushed by the independent KMT delegates, producing a howl of protest. The next day the leader of the KMT delegates sponsoring direct presidential elections told his colleagues not to sign the new proposal for abolishing a permanent chair committee. Guo Bo-cun, a KMT delegate, stood in front of the Chungshanlou Auditorium handing out leaflets urging his delegates not to rubber-stamp the KMT's proposal and to have "a little backbone" *(you yidian guqi)*.[68] The KMT delegates supporting their party's platform failed to round up the required 268 signatures to meet that day.

Still another group of KMT delegates insisted that their party desist from tabling the request for a permanent chair committee because they wanted the National Assembly to have the right to review the Legislative Yuan's budget and vice versa. Eager to punish the Legislative Yuan members for not respecting the National Assembly, they also wanted to reduce legislators' terms from three to two years. The actions of independent-minded KMT delegates finally forced KMT secretary-general Soong to plead with reporters not to report this new debacle and to "allow KMT delegates in the assembly to have some 'face.' "[69] President Lee finally intervened by inviting the entire KMT assembly delegation to his office for tea and urging them to settle their differences peacefully and not expand the assembly's power. He reminded them that a complete constitutional reform should not be accomplished at this meeting because they still had four more years to serve.[70] The president's request and the humility he displayed to the delegates persuaded most of them to abandon their demand for a permanent chair committee, but many were still adamant that the terms for Legislative Yuan members not be extended.[71] The KMT was now assured that its delegates would obey the party but not endorse a four-year term for legislators. Their strong opposition compelled the KMT leadership to set aside that controversial reform article until next year's meeting.[72]

But then the Nonpolitical Alliance Party delegates withdrew from the assembly, complaining that the KMT delegates had treated them like dirt by denying all their proposals.[73] Despite this momentary setback, the majority of KMT delegates agreed to abandon their demand for a permanent chair committee, discuss the presidential election issue at a later time, and add eight new articles to the constitution. Political passions had divided assembly KMT delegates and produced strife between the assembly and the Legislative Yuan.

Uncivil behavior in the National Assembly had discredited that institution for the voters. Ironically, both KMT and DPP delegates had contributed to the public's negative view of the National Assembly's political worth.

## The DPP Abandons Constitutional Reform

The DPP central committee had met on March 28 to plan its strategy for the National Assembly convention. Its two-pronged approach was to cooperate with KMT delegates who favored direct elections while mobilizing the public to pressure the KMT to do the same. Deputy Chairman Shih Ming-teh complained that "the fact that President Lee did not push for such elections meant that he failed in his responsibility; the KMT is losing power to behave responsibly and revise the constitution."[74] According to Shih, the DPP must become the vanguard for constitutional reform.

In late March the DPP, which had failed to co-opt many KMT delegates and increasingly found itself isolated in the assembly, established a committee to plan a large public demonstration for April 19.[75] The party hoped to draw 100,000 persons from around the island to support direct presidential elections. The April 19 demonstration was to be led by Huang Hsin-chieh and party stalwarts Hsu Hsin-liang, Yao Chia-wen, Chen Yungxing, Hong Qichang, Cai Tongrong, and others. Some central committee members urged the party to line up many social groups to guarantee the demonstration's success and requested party delegates in the assembly to propose constitutional reforms that might appeal to those same groups.[76]

On April 16, DPP delegates, fed up with KMT delegates' control of the assembly, set off the biggest turmoil since the convention began; a few people were even hospitalized.[77] On April 17, Huang Hsin-chieh led a group of assembly DPP delegates to the Office of the President to demand an audience with President Lee to discuss direct presidential elections. Military police did not allow the group near the building.

On the evening of April 18, the DPP held a meeting at the Taipei Municipal Athletic Center in which party leaders advocated direct presidential elections and led the audience in song. The party hoped to draw thirty thousand, but fewer than ten thousand assembled. On April 19 at 2:00 P.M. some five to six thousand people marched from the athletic center along Tun Hua North Road in the rain.[78] The group consisted of DPP members, friends, and members of the Taiwan Medical Alliance. Several hours later, the marchers returned to the Athletic Center after having caused enormous traffic delays.

On April 20, slightly fewer than ten thousand persons met at the Taipei

Municipal Athletic Center and marched along Tun Hua North Road, led by twenty team leaders in cars and trucks; eleven National Assembly female delegates held banners reading One Person, One Vote for the Direct Election of the President.[79] Among the marchers were four hundred to five hundred persons from the Kaohsiung and Pingtung areas and groups representing various parts of Taiwan. Many marchers wore colorful uniforms. One car had microphones that DPP legislator Xie Changting used to speak to the crowds along the street, apologizing for the inconvenience this demonstration might cause and justifying it on these grounds:

The KMT has postponed direct presidential elections in the National Assembly because of its inner party struggle. Everyone should stand up and use his or her voice and power to struggle for the rights of the people and to make a future for the younger generation in order to create new conditions for Taiwan democracy.[80]

Others also spoke to the crowds as marchers and vehicles slowly but peacefully moved from one street to another, finally dispersing at the Taipei city railway station in downtown Taipei.

On Wednesday, April 22, Hsu Hsin-liang told reporters that the DPP was willing to call off the demonstration if the KMT would get the National Assembly "to agree to fair and just discussions and ratification [of articles] to make a perfect constitution."[81] Hsu wanted the demonstrations to continue until Saturday to signal the ruling party that the DPP meant business. He blamed the activities in the National Assembly on the KMT power struggle:

It is clear that President Lee supports direct presidential elections, but his desire is not strong enough nor his will determined enough to implement direct presidential elections. The current situation within the KMT does not allow President Lee to have that determination.[82]

DPP leaders quarreled over whether to continue the demonstrations: Chang Chun-hung argued that when a demonstration draws the maximum crowd, that is the time to desist; Hsu Hsin-liang wanted to mobilize more people, fire up the masses, and exert greater pressure on the KMT.[83]

On the evening of April 22, rain again fell as demonstrators convened at the Taipei city railroad station, where a large stage had been erected. DPP assembly delegates Wang Xuefeng and Su Jiachuan led the audience in song. There were speeches from those who had been imprisoned under the old Article 100, banning seditious behavior. At 9:00 P.M. Hakka and aboriginal leaders asked the crowd to support direct presidential elections. Presbyterian Church ministers also spoke. And so it went until 11:30 P.M., when Taiwan city chief of police Zhuang Hengdai announced that "the police so far have not taken action in order to avoid injuring people in public places. I simply hope the DPP leaders will disperse the people peacefully." By midnight the railroad station was empty.

Although Chen Yungxing said, "The DPP will definitely not allow the KMT to succeed in their plan of carrying out a one-party constitutional revision,"[84] a majority of its party leaders finally agreed to end the demonstrations and return to the National Assembly. The lackluster crowds mobilized by the three-day demonstration had convinced the party leadership that it was time to rejoin the political process. In the early afternoon of April 29, then, DPP delegates filed into Chungshanlou Auditorium and began criticizing KMT delegation leader Shieh Lung-sheng and delegates supporting indirect presidential elections.[85]

How did the media evaluate the DPP withdrawal and reentry into the political process? Conservative pundits criticized the DPP delegates, complaining that "they do not respect and recognize the country they live in"[86] and pointing out that the DPP party was immature, irresponsible, and disrespectful of the constitution. Others commented that the DPP never took the trouble to inquire what the *people* wanted when it demonstrated. DPP delegates were also accused of always blocking the efforts of others in the National Assembly, and when they could not have their way, taking to the streets. Critics also said the DPP was a party that took action without any reason *(wufeng qilang).*[87]

Liberal commentators agreed that the DPP had overestimated popular backing for its platform and had failed to adopt a constructive, rational plan in the National Assembly.[88] Its inferior numbers gave it little bargaining power, and its delegates merely fomented altercations and discredited their party. One commentator put it bluntly: "The people are really fed up because the DPP does not do a good job at revising the constitution and merely goes to the streets to demonstrate. That behavior gives the people a bad image of the DPP."[89]

Another observer, Zhang Zuojin, chief editor of the *United Daily News* and *United Evening News,* noted that the DPP delegates had used abusive language and physical violence in the National Assembly and that DPP female delegates had used their high-heeled shoes to overturn tables. Moreover, he charged that they "had not done one constructive thing" even though they had excellent qualifications.[90] Although the DPP had raised the public's consciousness about political corruption, the tragedy of the February 28, 1947, uprising, and the necessity to reelect the national representatives, the DPP delegates still relied on their old tactics of using their fists and taking to the streets, suggesting they had learned little in recent years. This barrage of media criticism seemed to reflect some decline in elite support for the DPP.

## The Constitution Is Revised

The National Assembly convention lasted seventy-three days and cost about US$14.0 million.[91] Delegates to the 402-person assembly submitted 155 proposals to revise articles in the constitution and another 141 recommendations for new articles related to social welfare, education, military affairs, public administration, aboriginal matters.[92] Only about one-quarter of the 155 reform proposals passed a first reading. Only 21 articles passed the review, evaluation, and ratification of a second reading, which KMT members further amended and reduced in number. By May 18, KMT delegates had approved 8 new articles that were then ratified by the assembly.[93] But in early May, because of the split between KMT delegates and opposition from non-KMT delegates, the process stalled. To break this impasse, party leaders intervened on at least four occasions.

First, after a number of KMT delegates refused to attend assembly meetings, making a quorum impossible,[94] the party asked its delegates to reside in one hotel so they could be bused to the convention hall to guarantee a quorum.[95] Second, the KMT delegates who had agreed to carry out constitutional revision met early in May to devise a strategy to block other KMT and non-KMT delegates opposed to revision and wanting to establish a permanent chair committee and review the Legislative Yuan's budget. President Lee had to invite disgruntled KMT delegates to his office to urge them to adhere to their party's platform.[96] Third, on May 4, President Lee called a meeting of top-level party and government officials, including Shieh Lung-sheng, who led the KMT assembly delegates, to his office to work out a plan to make certain that enough KMT delegates would approve the party's constitutional reform package.[97] (This high-level group also wanted to reduce the twenty-one proposals agreed on in the assembly to nine.) Fourth, the party insisted that the KMT assembly delegates give up their demand to reduce the Legislative Yuan's term of office from three years to two. By persuasion, threats, and pleading, then, the KMT finally mobilized enough of its assembly delegates to approve eight additional articles to the 1947 constitution.[98]

Those eight articles fixed the period for the third-term National Assembly delegates at four years; stipulated the second-term National Assembly must meet before May 20, 1995, to again revise the constitution; reduced the future president and vice president's terms to four years and allowed them to serve a maximum of two terms; permitted the president to nominate, and the second-term National Assembly to confirm or reject, members of the Judicial, Examination, and Control Yuans; separated the elections of the provincial and county officials from those of the provincial and county assembly elections; and committed the government to modernizing the economy, protecting the environment, and promoting women's rights.

Party chairman Lee Teng-hui praised the second-term National Assembly's performance, calling it democratic, and said that the results corresponded to the KMT platform of the Third Plenum, that the government's five-power structure had been preserved, and that all major reform issues had been included in the eight new articles.[99] On the evening of May 28, Chairman Lee hosted a dinner party for 240 assembly delegates and pointed out that this was the first time in forty years that the National Assembly had engaged in a process reflecting the will of the people. He concluded:

Many different opinions were expressed, but that is normal. This was not a one-party constitutional revision, because one person from the Social Democratic Party, Huang Zhaoren, attended every session. His presence meant this was not a simple one-party revisionary process. Now, Mr. Shieh Lung-sheng says there is no limit to the chairman's liquor supply, so just drink to your hearts' content.[100]

On this jocular note, President Lee congratulated the second-term National Assembly delegates for completing their difficult task.

Other KMT leaders echoed President Lee's view, but the popular response was cool. A survey of 813 persons by the *China News* gave the National Assembly a rating of only 55 out of a possible 100.[101] At least one-quarter of those polled said they were unhappy with the single-party revision of the constitution, but more than half were disappointed by the DPP's behavior at the National Assembly. A telephone survey revealed that 70 percent were dissatisfied with the National Assembly's performance; only 30 percent expressed any confidence in what had been achieved.[102] Some 21 percent had no confidence at all in the National Assembly. This survey never disaggregated the nearly three-quarters of the sample who were unhappy with the assembly's results and therefore never explained why a majority of citizens believed the National Assembly had been a failure.

Elite assessment was also critical of the second-term National Assembly. Scholar Tien Hung-mao pointed out that the KMT delegates had not tried to negotiate with the opposition party and that little substantive reform had taken place: the National Assembly still existed; the five-power system of government had not been altered.[103] According to Tien, KMT leaders had not pressed for major constitutional reform because they wanted to avoid splitting the party. He cited a problem for the future: if the National Assembly approved direct presidential elections but its members insisted on preserving the assembly for the purpose of recalling the nation's top leader, such action scarcely justified preserving that institution.

But some took exception to this negative view. KMT secretary-general Soong emphasized that any consensus was remarkable. "To have different opinions is a phenomenon of democracy. No matter how much they argued, did they not reach harmony and consensus in the end?"[104] According to Soong, consensus was the greatest achievement of the assembly: hadn't its members transcended their vituperative behavior and agreed on concrete constitutional revisions?

Some constitutional experts argued that constitutional reform should have focused on which political system was most suitable for Taiwan and then chosen the election procedure most appropriate for that system. The political scientist Yang Taixun asserted that the government depended on the strong cabinet system and that this system was incompatible with direct presidential elections.[105] Zhou Yangshan, a constitutional expert, argued that the polity should conform to the cabinet system as designed in the 1947 constitution and avoid exaggerating the president's role.[106] Zhou and Hu Fu feared that a direct presidential election system would create great instability in the polity.[107]

Other intellectuals insisted the ROC democracy would be "perfect and complete" only when the top leaders were directly elected by the people to represent the people's will. Invoking this standard, they concluded that constitutional reform had been subverted. Since the National Affairs Conference of 1990, many believed that constitutional reform had been predicated on the direct election of the president, and the spring 1992 constitutional reform did not fulfill their expectation. Then the second-term National Assembly's "constitutional revision became the process for linking KMT conservative and local elite groups so that the liberal forces never had any chance to express their opinions."[108] The KMT did the same to its delegates. Finally, President Lee, who had advocated direct presidential elections, was poorly served by his advisers' urging him to postpone such elections. Although the president deserved praise for his political reforms, it was far better to abolish the National Assembly and have direct presidential elections.

In July 1992 some intellectuals published a new journal containing their evaluations of the second-term National Assembly. They strongly criticized the assembly and the ruling party's actions. Professor Zhai Songlin blamed the assembly for not strengthening individual rights such as free speech or protecting life, property, and so forth. Professor Zhu Xinmin complained that the ruling party had no comprehensive framework for revising the constitution and that political-legal experts never played a major role in the assembly's activities. Professor Chen Yujun offered four key points: the DPP did not recognize the ROC and its constitution, possessed no moral responsibility to preserve the constitution, and wanted to destroy it; the KMT failed to utilize its constitutional reform experts; KMT experts never offered any clear, suitable constitutional reform proposals; ROC political leaders did not understand the significance of political, constitutional principles. Chen claimed that the nation's leaders used the constitution issue only to expand their power, carry on power struggles, and pursue selfish ends. Professor Chen Zhiqi complained that scholars had been ignored in the constitutional reform process.[109] And so the litany of criticism continued.

Some scholars and members of the medical community also expressed their disappointment with the National Assembly's results. A group of university professors calling themselves the Association for Purity (Zhengshe) were furious at the assembly's performance and urged other academics to express their indignation.[110] Another campaign, launched with a thousand signatures from professional and academic groups, condemned the National Assembly as a "worthless institution" and vowed to collect more signatures to send to the Office of the President.[111] Within several days some fifty-two groups had organized to elicit one million signatures on a petition condemning and abolishing the National Assembly.[112] But that summer the elite and intellectuals turned their attention to other issues.

Despite the elite's lukewarm affirmation of constitutional reform, there was to be a national election to replace the Legislative Yuan. Political momentum for direct presidential and vice presidential elections continued to grow. The fate of the National Assembly was uncertain. Enough elite had agreed to constitutional reform to move the democratic process forward. Although the DPP and the other parties had interrupted the assembly and even walked out, they still participated in the process. The majority of politicians had persevered and played by the political rules. All actors in political life now prepared for the new elections that would determine this democracy's future. As democracy advanced, political disagreements became sharper and more numerous, giving the impression of great confusion and mounting tension in Taiwan's political life.

# CHAPTER TWELVE

# Resolving Political Disagreements

The preceding five chapters examined in depth the resolution of disagreements associated with key events that shaped the evolution of Taiwan's early democratic breakthrough from the lifting of martial law until the Second National Assembly's first meeting to amend the constitution. The events that occurred between the summer of 1992 and spring of 1996, the expansionary phase of democratization, will not require the same in-depth study because they resemble those of the previous period: political disagreements were resolved by the same process of leadership and political brokerage, bargaining and public discourse, and compromise and agreement that had been used between fall 1989 and spring 1992.

By early summer 1992, then, Taiwan's elites had crossed a major political divide, and democracy had survived. No political parties or groups had resorted to nondemocratic means to resolve disagreements or suppress conflicts, for fear of losing legitimacy in the eyes of other elites and the voters. Chairman Lee had weathered the factional struggle within his party and initiated a political settlement between the KMT and the opposition that produced an exchange of information and cooperation for more political reform. Voters had elected a new National Assembly and given the ruling party a mandate to guide constitutional reform. Despite its defeat in that election, the DPP participated in the first round of the new assembly's reform process, although protesting the KMT's management of that process. Chairman Lee had prevented his party from amending the constitution to legitimize the indirect election of the president and vice president. These and other examples represented the resolution of political disagreements and a growing tolerance of political differences. New official, intellectual, amateur, and public media political advertising made people more trustful of their political leaders, more tolerant of different political views, and more willing to play by the rules of democracy.

In that next period of political change, from summer 1992 until spring 1996, Taiwan's elites continued to disagree, but democratization continued. In this important transition period, the power formerly concentrated in the inhibited political center gradually dispersed into civil society, and competing political parties and nongovernment organizations began imposing their demands on an evolving subordinated political center. This new subordinated political center has thus far mediated six types of political disagreements that will undoubtedly characterize the ROC's polity in the years to come, including disputes over constitutional reform, within government, within political parties, over election competition and corruption, between civil society and government, and over foreign policy. It is to these disagreements and how they were resolved that we now turn.

## Constitutional Dispute and Reform

A constitution defines how a government can allocate its political power and limit that power on behalf of its citizens. In 1787–88 America's elites and citizens fiercely debated the revision and approval of their new constitution.[1] Similarly, Taiwan's elites heatedly debated the 1947 constitution; a majority preferred revision while a minority wanted to draft a new constitution. By May 1992 the KMT majority in the First and Second National Assemblies had added 18 new articles to the 1947 constitution, which initially had 175 articles in twelve chapters. Between April and July 1994 the Second National Assembly approved 10 articles to replace the former 18 new articles and thus changed the balance of power within the ROC polity.

A Chinese legal expert once described the undergirding of the 1947 constitution as "the spirit by which our nation thoroughly carries out and utilizes the constitution as the highest guiding principle for the polity. The basic spirit of our national constitution is that of democracy, having the means of election and recall, approval, and administrative accountability, all designed to adhere to the fundamental spirit of democracy."[2] The KMT subscribed to this view.

The opposition, however, saw the constitution as imposed on Taiwan's people without their consent. It was not surprising, then, that in April 1991 the DPP's leadership authorized a committee to consult with scholars and draft a new constitution. Between late April and mid-June 1991 this committee prepared a new constitution having ten chapters with 104 articles. Its preamble stated that, because of the "changes in time and space, the present adoption of the ROC constitution is no longer appropriate for the current time and circumstances that prevail on Taiwan, the Pescadores, Matsu, and Quemoy."[3] This draft also defined the rights and duties of Taiwan's citizens and mandated that the state must protect the environment, not sacrifice it to economic growth. Other rules outlined a three-power system of governance similar to that of the United States: a president elected by the people and in charge of the executive branch, a parliament of 120 elected members, and an independent judiciary. The DPP constitution abolished the National Assembly and the Control and Examination Yuans. The DPP publicized this new constitution in its fall 1991 campaign for the Second National Assembly, but it failed to win popular support.

The majority of Taiwanese wanted to amend the 1947 constitution but could not agree on how it should be done, disagreeing over whether to change the complex checks and balances of the 1947 constitution as described by our Chinese legal expert:

> The constitution contains the unifying functional principles for the central government. Our constitution's basic spirit is based on the cabinet system. For example, the tasks of the president and premier of the Executive Yuan are separated; the premier requires the approval and ratification of the Legislative Yuan and is responsible to that body. These are the procedures by which the basic spirit of parliamentary governance operates in this cabinet system.[4]

This cabinet system, through Article 37, allowed the executive head of the cabinet to countersign laws and mandates promulgated by the president, thus ending the president's authority. The KMT liberals who supported President Lee did not approve of Article 37 and wanted the president to have control over the cabinet, but KMT conservatives, disliking President Lee, wanted to retain Article 37. This issue was intensely debated within the KMT in spring 1994 before the fourth session of the Second National Assembly convened on April 29.[5]

On April 23–24, a majority of KMT central committee members, led by Chairman Lee, defeated their conservative opponents and added eight new amendments to the constitution. They included the direct election and recall of the president and vice president, no countersigning of presidential decrees (eliminating Article 37), creating the posts of assembly speaker and deputy speaker, and extending legislators' terms from three years to four.[6]

When the Second National Assembly convened for the second time, DPP delegates demonstrated against President Lee's opening speech on May 2, delaying it for twenty minutes. As in the past, they protested KMT control of the assembly as well as its proposal to allow overseas Chinese to vote for the ROC's president and vice president. The DPP insisted that only citizens residing in Taiwan should vote.

In the following weeks KMT solidarity began to disintegrate as disagreements over the amendment to curtail the premier's countersigning power resurfaced. But KMT leaders managed to mobilize enough delegates to abolish Article 37, only to encounter fierce DPP resistance to the second reading on July 5. DPP delegates filibustered, banged their shoes on tables, and blew whistles to protest the KMT's demand that one-third of the assembly's delegates constitute a quorum. DPP delegates argued that "the constitution mandates a two-thirds quorum for both discussions and votes, while the KMT side said this applie[d] only to votes."[7] The KMT majority prevailed, and the second reading approved twenty-two amendments, one of which said that overseas Chinese could return to Taiwan and vote in a presidential election if they were ROC citizens.

Meanwhile, a June 1994 poll reported growing public dissatisfaction with the Second National Assembly, probably because of the bitter fights in that body. Of 1,015 persons surveyed, 42 percent thought the assembly should be abolished and 62 percent were unhappy about the assembly's performance.[8] Aware of the growing public anger, on July 29 the assembly concluded its third reading and passed ten articles to replace the eighteen amendments previously added.[9] The ten included electing a Third National Assembly, electing the president and vice president, electing the Legislative Yuan (it failed to approve a four-year rather than a three-year term), Judicial, Control, and Examination Yuan appointments, remuneration for National Assembly and Legislative Yuan representatives, local governance, state obligations to citizens, and affirmation of laws governing the rights and obligations between the peoples of the PRC and the ROC. (The DPP, however, had walked out of the second and third readings and never participated in the approval of these ten amendments.)

Amended Article 2 gave the president the power to appoint personnel or remove them from office without the premier's countersignature, nullifying Article 37, as long as the National Assembly and Legislative Yuan concurred. But as the amended constitution now reads, if the president's party loses control of the Legislative Yuan and that body disapproves of the president's premier, the president must consult with the legislature. If no agreement can be reached, then gridlock could paralyze the government. In the elections held between late 1992 and mid-1996, the KMT's power in the Third Legislative Yuan and the Third National Assembly declined, creating the conditions for possible gridlock.

On March 23, 1996, voters elected a Third National Assembly of 334 delegates. The KMT won 183 seats, giving it almost 55 percent of the delegates, with the DPP winning 99 seats and 30 percent of total delegates, the New Party (NP) winning 46 seats (13 percent), and other parties winning a total of 6 seats (2 percent). The KMT no longer had the majority to guarantee having the two-thirds votes required to dominate the assembly as in the past. This election outcome signified the ascendancy of coalition politics in political life, and if such coalition politics cannot produce any consensus, amending the constitution will be difficult.

The KMT wants further constitutional reform to give the president the power to dissolve and reelect a new legislature if that body does not approve of the president's choice of cabinet head. The DPP wants to abolish the National Assembly or merge it with the Legislative Yuan and to hold a plebiscite to approve or reject a new constitution. How the political parties will negotiate to achieve their goals is not clear. Future constitutional reform will reveal how political disagreements are to be resolved and the polity governed.

## Disagreements within Government

During February–March 1990 two opposing groups formed within the KMT—the mainstream group (those supporting Chairman Lee) and the nonmainstream group (those supporting Lee Huan, Hau Pei-tsun, and other party seniors who opposed the chairman). The nonmainstream group included military personnel and their supporters, those who disliked the KMT chairman and his leadership style, party seniors (particularly mainlanders), and young mainlander politicians calling themselves the New KMT Alliance. This anti-Lee coalition resented the chairman's reluctance to consult with top party leaders, his initiation of policies they did not agree with, and his selection of personnel. Lee's opponents complained that he hungered for even more power. In early 1993 Premier Hau Pei-tsun resigned, silencing the leadership of the nonmainstream group, but the two groups continued their struggles until Lin Yang-kang and Hau Pei-tsun left the KMT on November 15, 1995.

To gain insight about one of the most powerful senior members in the KMT, let us briefly examine Hau Pei-tsun and his career. In the 1950s and 1960s, Hau Pei-tsun had steadily advanced through the military ranks, becoming chief of staff of the armed forces. Hau had served under Chiang Ching-kuo and, like Chiang, believed in the separation of politics and business.[10] Patriotic, energetic, and commanding great respect from the military officers under him, General Hau shared the Sunist vision and professed strong loyalty to Chiang Kai-shek and his son. On May 29, 1990, President Lee replaced Premier Lee Huan with Hau in order to remove one of his most formidable opponents, who had persistently tried to block his policies. Hau resigned from the military and, as premier, began mobilizing the police and other agencies to address Taiwan's problems with law and order and urban traffic. His successful efforts in these areas made him immensely popular; in November 1992 some 55 percent of those surveyed in a Gallup poll said that "they have a positive impression of the work of Hau's cabinet in managing the economy, improving the standard of living for the people, and monitoring law and order."[11] Having now removed Hau from the military, President Lee began appointing officers he believed would serve him loyally.

But disagreements between the president and Hau soon surfaced. The premier wanted to appoint his cabinet members and did not always seek the president's approval.[12] On January 3, 1991, Premier Hau opposed having the National Security Bureau, a powerful intelligence agency, placed under the National Security Council, which the Office of the President controlled. Vice President Li Yuan-zu, who obtained party approval for the transfer, overruled Hau.[13]

In February 1992 the president angered Premier Hau during the debate over direct or indirect elections for the ROC president and vice president.[14] At a meeting with the premier, Lee asked, "How do you feel about the issue of electing a president?" Hau replied, "Well, they are about the same." Lee then asked, "Do you agree with having direct elections?" Hau answered, "Well, they are about the same."[15] Later, an extremely annoyed Hau learned that the president had interpreted his comments to mean that the premier favored direct presidential elections.

Some months later, Finance Minister Wang Chien-hsüan resigned after President Lee opposed Wang's proposal to increase a value-added tax on property transactions in which the property had greatly appreciated. Premier Hau had supported Wang and was furious at the president.[16]

In subsequent months Hau interfered in the military appointments made by the Office of the President because he believed he knew the candidates in question better than the president did.[17] Controversy again erupted in October 1992, when DPP legislator Tian Zaiting asked Premier Hau whether the commander of the armed forces would attack the people if there was a vote to change the name of the ROC to the Republic of Taiwan. Hau replied that "it is unthinkable that the commander of the three services of the armed forces of the Republic of China would take no action when seeing the name of the Republic of China being dropped."[18] His remark created a great stir in the media, which the president did not welcome.

In November 1992 the president, having lost faith in his premier and supported in December by the newly elected Second Legislative Yuan, suggested that the cabinet members submit their resignations for approval by the newly elected Second Legislative Yuan. Premier Hau's cabinet balked. In early January the press revealed that Premier Hau held a meeting at his private residence with high-ranking active and retired military officers,[19] setting off rumors of a possible military coup.

On January 13, 1993, a letter from legislator Ju Gau-jeng appeared as an advertisement in many newspapers.[20] This letter strongly defended Premier Hau and castigated President Lee. Ju accused the president of discrediting the Chiang family, ignoring the welfare of the farmers, and failing to consult with other leaders. Blaming the recent power struggle in the KMT on Lee's failed leadership, Ju wrote, "Excessive lust for power and giving orders without proper regard for channels or areas of responsibility are the root causes of your poor relations between you and several premiers." Haughty, shrill, and acerbic, Ju's letter reflected the Chinese political style that seeks to humiliate and discredit. Ju thus hoped to mobilize public opinion and force President Lee to cooperate with party seniors like Hau Pei-tsun and Lee Huan.

In an effort to take advantage of the Ju letter, Hau made overtures to elicit the president's backing for another term as premier. But Hau had underestimated the president's resolve. In what was probably one of their last exchanges in their official capacities, the president said, "You want to resign and then you do not want to resign. That is all right. If you think you can continue to work, then go ahead and work. If you want me to openly declare my support for you, I cannot do it."[21]

Thus on February 4, 1993, Premier Hau and his cabinet resigned.[22] Lee regarded Hau and other nonmainstream coalition leaders as "interested only in prestige and being excessively pretentious. They are out of touch with the democratic trend. Their kind of political culture can only make the country regress. If Taiwan is to progress, we have to 'destroy the politics of face.' "[23] Hau went to the United States for a speaking tour, during which he frequently criticized his former commander-in-chief. President Lee displayed no emotions (buli bucai)[24] but never again met privately with Hau.[25] Once Lee initiated his reforms, his indifference toward the party seniors aroused their antagonism,[26] but the president had the upper hand.

President Lee now turned to the Taiwanese Lien Chan, a friend from their days at National Taiwan University and an experienced official with a doctorate in political science from the University of Chicago, as the next premier. They began working to elevate the ROC's international status.[27] Premier Lien visited a number of countries in June 1994, and his cabinet published a white paper in July outlining the government's new policy toward the PRC. Their warm cooperation removed, at least for the moment, any serious friction between the government's top leaders. But struggles for power between KMT leaders will likely reemerge when the party must nominate a candidate for the tenth-term ROC presidency to be decided in the year 2000.

## Disagreements within Political Parties

### The KMT

When Chiang Ching-kuo launched political reform in the spring of 1986, he also wanted internal party reform, but nine months later it had yet to begin, mainly because the leadership focused on enacting a law to protect national security after lifting martial law.[28] In May 1987 Chiang asked Pan Chen-cheu, head of the party's work organization, and Li Zaotian, head of provincial party headquarters, to draft an internal party reform plan.[29] Still no reform followed. A few in the KMT worried about party reform as a new source of tension in the party.

What was done in the past is no longer correct to do. The KMT always has been a revolutionary party. But if you are going to turn the party into a democratic one, the old cadres will not agree. They still have a sense of strong mission and are willing to sacrifice themselves for the party. We must change this behavior as well as the revolutionary concept in order to become a democratic party.[30]

Could the KMT reorganize and democratize without splitting? Although Chairman Lee followed in Chiang Ching-kuo's footsteps, he adhered to a different vision of democracy than did Chiang. Should the KMT be reorganized into a party capable of winning votes and satisfying the people or merely preserving the old ideology of building a model Taiwan based on the Three Principles of the People to transform the mainland? Advocates of the old ideology wanted gradual democratization based on minimal constitutional reform, gradually expanding elections, and indirect elections of the president by the National Assembly as well as closer ties with the PRC. Proponents of a revitalized party wanted rapid democratization by constitutional reform, direct election of the nation's leaders and national representatives, a "pragmatic foreign policy" *(wushi waijiao)* to enhance the ROC's international status, and guidelines approved by a bipartisan national council and the Legislative and Executive Yuans to unify China only if the Chinese people in both Taiwan and mainland China concurred.

Closely connected to these competing party goals were how party members evaluated their chairman's leadership style. Lee's critics complained that he was not a "real Chinese" and that he wanted to lead the nation toward "independence," separating Taiwan from the mainland. They complained that he never consulted with senior party members, preferring the "yes" people who did his bidding. Calling Lee "the supreme leader" *(ducai)*, they accused him of amassing power so he could impose his will on the party. Lee's supporters countered that he was promoting "real" democracy and challenging the PRC leaders to reform their society.

At the Thirteenth KMT Congress in July 1989, conservative elites and functionaries closed ranks to resist reform. On the issue of changing the party's name, this alliance insisted that the party retain its title of "revolutionary democratic" rather than being called a "democratic party." Fearful of splitting the party, Chairman Lee and his liberal supporters decided not to bring the issue to a vote. Lee did allow Kuan Chung, deputy secretary-general, to say that the party must become a "democratic party" to win future elections if it wanted to retain power[31] and to introduce primary elections.

Although James C. Y. Soong defended this experiment, arguing that "our party must try to combine theory with the popular will so that our party's politics will match up with the real needs of the people,"[32] the primary election experiment flopped. This led to Kuan's being fired (Kuan and Soong never got along).[33]

In April 1991 Chairman Lee began reorganizing the KMT, trimming its bureaucracy of more than nine hundred persons, merging the Overseas and Domestic Work Committees, consolidating other departments and committees, eliminating many deputy director positions, and cutting the staff of the Yangmingshan cadres training academy.[34] The party also agreed to raise some NT$35 billion (about US$1.4 billion). (Upon realizing that this sum would draw public criticism, the party shifted party-owned enterprises' assets to this endowment.)[35] In 1992 the party created a "special affairs management committee," whose members rotated and were supervised by Soong, who urged all party elites, including elders out of power, to consult with one another.[36]

Meanwhile, party leaders and members unhappy with Chairman Lee's reforms supported the New KMT Alliance's efforts to radically revise Article 100 of the criminal code, which Lee and his party supporters only wanted amended. This Alliance also tried to nominate its candidates for the 1992 Legislative Yuan election, supported Hau's reappointment as premier, and over Chairman Lee's objections, pushed for appointing more nonmainstream faction delegates to the August 1993 Fourteenth Party Congress.[37] Chairman Lee, however, defeated the New KMT Alliance efforts and tightened his control over the KMT.

In 1992 and 1993 the KMT's image took another turn for the worse. The press blamed Taiwan's money politics on the "KMT's strategy to consolidate its regime[38] and the party's vote buying on President Lee and Premier Hau for nominating rich people to be election candidates."[39] The press also castigated the KMT for being unable to distinguish "between party and state or between party and government" in the handling of its affairs.[40] Critics took the KMT to task for blocking the publication of new information about the Chiang family and for censoring individuals who wrote about their trips to the PRC.[41] In early 1993 the press reported that the KMT had sanctioned indiscriminate arrests and killings in the 1950s. KMT legislators were also accused of trying to pass two bills that would reward their rich supporters and weaken the DPP's growing influence.[42] Media pundits blamed the KMT and the government for Taiwan's environmental deterioration, high taxes, the widening gap between rich and poor, and the shortage of fresh water.[43]

On August 10, 1993, just before the KMT's Fourteenth Congress, New KMT Alliance members formed the New Party (NP), with polls showing that one out of three voters supported such a move. They did not want to be blamed for the KMT's declining public support.[44] NP spokesperson Chao Shao-kang cavalierly declared that the KMT "will collapse by itself"[45] and complained that the KMT refused to give up control over the electronic media, that the party was undemocratic, and that its chairman never listened to their suggestions.[46] But KMT elder Lee Huan criticized the breakaway action: "Once a split in our party occurs, it is the same as handing power over to the DPP." According to Lee, "the way to go is [for everyone] to work for the improvement of the party."[47] DPP leaders immediately praised the NP, hoping that "it will play a larger role in political life and not merely criticize the KMT" and promised to "stand ready to work with the NP to build a better democracy."[48]

The founders of the NP were Chao Shao-kang, Yü Mu-ming, Li Ching-hua (son of Lee Huan), Zhou Chuan, Chen Kueimiao, Lee Shen-fong, and Wang Chien-hsüan. Their plan was to "use the parliament as the center, use the will of the people as the path to follow, and use elections as the instrument of action; these are the democratic elements of our party."[49] They described the

KMT as a "defeated, corrupt party, aligned only with money" and condemned the DPP for being "irresponsible in its statements."

When the KMT's Fourteenth Congress convened, Kuan Chung, a critic of the chairman, worried that "in the past five years, party reform efforts have amounted to nothing, and the reasons are that the power struggle within the party has worsened and party members have lost confidence in achieving the party's revolutionary tasks."[50] Another Lee critic, Chu Songqui, said:

If only Chairman Lee can behave like a real leader and exhort the party to unify, everyone will respect his call to arms *[denggao yihu]*. This is what a true democratic political leader should do at this critical juncture. If our leaders indeed can be sincere and tolerant of each other for the sake of their country, then by our salvation and self-strengthening efforts and by the principle of mutual trust, all our problems can be reasonably resolved.[51]

These repeated attacks on the party chairman revealed that an angry opposition still existed in the KMT. Before the Fourteenth Party Congress convened, Chairman Lee took unusual measures to ensure that his agenda would be approved.

In addition to the delegates normally eleted to the party's congress, Chairman Lee had invited seven hundred KMT government officials to be congress delegates.[52] Many KMT members criticized his action, but they could do nothing. On the evening before the congress convened (August 16, 1993), Chairman Lee admitted that reforming the KMT had been difficult but said that the "KMT wants to build a true democratic party and a democracy in the 'Taiwan area.'"[53] Two days into the congress, debate focused on whether the party should elect a small group of vice chairpersons to assist the chairman, an idea opposed by the chairman and his supporters, who feared it might limit his power. In the voting later that morning, 1,007 votes supported the proposal, 91 votes short of the necessary two-thirds majority.[54] Many delegates then voiced their disapproval, some running to the podium to make speeches. When the congress adjourned for lunch, Chairperson Ch'iu Chuang-huan and Hsu Shui-te, Xian Shenshan, and Chiang Yen-shih met with Chairman Lee to discuss the next move. To avoid further party splits, the group decided to accept the vice chairperson group.

When the congress reconvened, Lee urged the congress to "establish the vice chairman system to improve the party, and [said that] this decision should be determined by all party representatives." A resounding voice vote confirmed its approval.[55] The congress immediately elected four vice chairpersons—Vice President Li Yuan-zu and Premier Lien Chan, who supported the chairman, and Hau Pei-tsun and Lin Yang-kang, who opposed him,[56]— and agreed that the party chairman should nominate future vice chairpersons, who would then be confirmed by a secret vote. On that same day, for the first time in party history, the congress cast secret ballots for a new chairperson: of the 2,086 eligible representatives, 2,043 cast ballots, and Lee Teng-hui received 1,686, or 82 percent,[57] making him the undisputed KMT leader. The congress also approved a proposal that the party name be changed to a "democratic KMT."

After the congress, disagreements between Chairman Lee and Vice Chairmen Lin and Hau escalated. Party planning for the upcoming election for the Third Legislative Yuan on December 2, 1995, led to the final split. On November 11, Liang Su-jung, Xu Linung, and Lin Yang-kang asked Hau Pei-tsun to be Lin's vice presidential running mate for the March 23, 1996, presidential election. After consulting with his family, Hau joined Lin at a press conference on November 15, where they declared that they would help NP candidates win seats in the upcoming parliamentary race but said nothing about competing in the race for president and vice president.[58]

Repeatedly saying that "they still adhered to the KMT's true mission in a pure, sincere, and loyal way" *(zhentong Guomindang)* but that "they strongly opposed Chairman Lee's leading the party down the road of "Taiwan independence,"[59] on November 18 Lin and Hau were in southern Taiwan, appearing alongside NP candidates to ask for voter support. At the year's end, however, Lin and Hau had decided to campaign for the March 1996 presidential elections as the NP's presidential and vice presidential candidates.

The Lin-Hau defection further weakened the KMT, as more party members either joined the NP or voted for it. (In April 1996 the KMT announced that Lin and Hau would not be reinstated in the party even if they apologized and asked to rejoin it.) In 1996 more reports of political corruption further tarnished the KMT's image. Many contended that the KMT's chairman behaved like a dictator, refusing to employ capable officials and catering to the superrich.[60] Some 69 percent of KMT members were now Taiwanese (the rest were mainlanders), and most of the top leaders were Taiwanese. Chairman Lee had consolidated his grip on the party. His chief opponents had been driven out of the party or had left on their own. Offering a new vision of Taiwan's democracy as early as April 23, 1994, Lee had declared that Taiwan's ideal democracy was "sovereignty residing in the people" *(zhuquan zaimin),* an expression never before uttered by a KMT leader.[61] Thereafter, many party and government leaders repeatedly used this expression to refer to Taiwan's democratization.

## The DPP

Many *dangwai* politicians had suffered arrest and imprisonment for challenging the KMT to build democracy.[62] But after 1986, when political prisoners were given amnesty and released, the DPP's representatives in the Legislative Yuan and the National Assembly staged violent episodes and led street demonstrations.[63] Too few to affect the voting in either body, DPP legislators like Ju Gau-jeng became famous for making "Rambo-like" assaults on the speaker of the Legislative Yuan and disconnecting his microphone. Others like Chen Shui-bian led street demonstrations, some of which turned violent and caused him to spend eight months in jail. Although most Taiwanese did not support the DPP, some saw these DPP politicians as heroes with a go-for-broke style. After 1991, as more elections were held, the DPP desisted from street demonstrations and concentrated on winning political power through the ballot box. By December 2, 1995, that party had won 32 percent of the seats (54) in the 164-delegate Legislative Yuan, and by 1996 its membership was about seventy thousand. It was the foremost opposition party challenging the KMT, whose membership in 1995 was 1.9 million, down from 2.6 million in 1993.

The year 1989 marked a turning point for the DPP as some of its leaders for the first time declared their support for a higher goal than Taiwan's democratization: to establish a Republic of Taiwan with a new constitution affirming Taiwan's separation from mainland China. In late 1990 the Taiwan Professors' Association, a private group formed to support the DPP, advocated that Taiwan become independent from mainland China.[64] The DPP began splintering into various factions, two being paramount: Formosa, the majority group, which insisted that the party embrace democracy and improve the people's welfare, and New Tide, which demanded Taiwanese independence as its main goal and resorted to street demonstrations if elections proved unsuccessful. Between 1990 and 1994, Formosa faction leaders Huang Hsin-chieh and Hsu Hsin-liang chaired the DPP, using their leadership skills to patch up differences between the factions and maintain party unity. Between May 4, 1994, and March 25, 1996, Shih Ming-teh, who had served twenty-five years in prison for his political beliefs, was DPP chairman. Shih announced that he wanted "to march on the road to become the ruling party and achieve his goal of becoming an independent Taiwan and building a new nation."[65] Now that this DPP leader had made Taiwan independence the centerpiece of the party's election campaigning, let us examine how that happened and why the KMT acquiesced.

During the 1980s the political opposition had campaigned only on the platform of building democracy based on competing political parties, constitutional reform, and elections. Although adhering to democratic rules—holding primary elections to nominate their candidates, electing delegates to party congresses, limiting the chairman to two years with one renewal, requiring the party leader to consult with the central executive committee—the DPP was a tightly controlled, disciplined party. Combining party discipline with democratic procedures enabled the DPP to expand its party base quickly. But then DPP elites began to disagree over their goals and the means to achieve them.

Factional struggle came to a head at the DPP's fifth plenum, October 12–13, 1991, in Taipei. The issue that triggered it was introduced on September 25 by Lin Zhuoshui, a New Tide proponent and a former teacher, who proposed that an article be inserted into the DPP charter proclaiming Taiwan independence as a party goal.[66] On October 11, DPP members Chen Shui-bian, Huang Hsin-chieh, and Chang Chun-hong, fearing that if New Tide members did not have their way they would leave the party, decided to amend the wording of the proposed article.

Chen Shui-bian presented the following compromise measure to the DPP plenum:

Any person or any political party can propose different principles, but it is not correct to say that what we advocate, we insist that the people must accept. The final decision always must depend on how the citizens of Taiwan will vote on an issue. The DPP platform is *one* choice for the future of Taiwan. As for asserting a particular principle, this is a matter solely of free speech.[67]

The factions approved, adding the following to the DPP charter: "The residents of Taiwan will decide on their destiny, and the Taiwan people will vote on whether to establish a Republic of Taiwan and redraft the constitution."[68]

At 6:00 P.M. on October 13, plenum delegates elected a new chairman, casting 180 ballots for Hsu Hsin-liang (Shih Ming-teh received only 63 ballots).[69] Plenum delegates then agreed that the DPP must win elections to become Taiwan's ruling party; it would resort to violence only if the KMT struck a deal with Beijing or denied the DPP a lawfully elected office.[70] Party members also agreed that candidates could emphasize Taiwan independence to win voter support. Thus the competing factions agreed to disagree so as to preserve DPP unity and avoid violence.

KMT leaders, outraged by the DPP's decision to make Taiwan independence a party goal, immediately held meetings to consider legal action. James

C. Y. Soong opined that the matter should be adjudicated by the government's Administrative Public Affairs Department. KMT legislators finally drafted a statement proposing that President Lee should admonish the DPP, that the government should render a "swift, clear, fair judgment on this matter," and that all political parties should "consider their nation's benefits when they take action." Admonishment, however, was the extent of the KMT's reaction, which indicated that the KMT felt that the DPP's action was a matter of free speech and that Taiwan, being a democracy, ought to practice free speech.

Having little wealth and dependent on public contributions, the small DPP worked hard to expand itself. In the 1989 local elections, the DPP could support candidates for only a little more than one-quarter of the available seats. But in November 1993 the DPP was able to compete for nearly half the seats available; in Taichung city, for example, twenty DPP candidates ran for forty-three seats.[71] The DPP began using the KMT strategy of appealing to local factions[72] because its candidates believed they were ideologically superior to the KMT candidates.[73]

The DPP also began practicing coalition politics. In the spring of 1993 the newly elected DPP members of the Legislative Yuan worked with disaffected KMT members to pass a "sunshine" bill mandating that government officials must disclose their wealth and place it in a trust while in public office. KMT legislators at first opposed the bill but backed it after public support mounted. The bill passed with a codicil allowing government officials time to establish their trusts. On May 2, 1994, the DPP in the National Assembly tried to convince KMT delegates to oppose the KMT proposal allowing overseas Chinese who were still ROC citizens to return to Taiwan to vote but was unsuccessful.

The DPP also insisted on the formula of "one China, one Taiwan," although 50 percent or more of Taiwan's voting population favored the ROC government's position that there is only one China and that Taiwan is part of China. The "unification of China" guidelines, developed by a national commission created by President Lee in October 1990, stipulate that unification cannot occur until economic and political reforms in the PRC have made the two Chinese societies more equivalent in wealth distribution, freedom, and democracy and that the people on both sides of the Taiwan Strait approve.

Those in the DPP who favor an independent Taiwan believe that the majority of Taiwan's people will support that view when they realize that democracy can survive only if Taiwan is independent of the Chinese mainland. Those in the DPP who agree with the government's position on unification of China believe that only the DPP, not the KMT, can build a "true" democracy on Taiwan. The DPP also emphasizes protecting the environment and providing social welfare to citizens through government spending. The DPP's economic, political, and international goals are thus very different from those of the KMT and have put the two parties on a collision course. Before mid-1996 the factional struggles within the DPP had not yet split the party because the factions still adhered to the consensus reached at the 1991 DPP congress.

The DPP's defeat in the March 23, 1996, presidential elections (it received only 21 percent of the popular vote) set off great debates within the party. Xie Changting, the DPP vice presidential candidate, stated that the party's primary election method and factional struggles had contributed to its defeat. Party leaders began wide-ranging discussions of the DPP's future strategy and goals. In the past the party has experienced election setbacks and then held intraparty debates, with factions agreeing to disagree but helping the party win elections. Uniting these factions to expand the DPP's influence so that it can become Taiwan's ruling party will be difficult if its members continue to establish new parties, as some did on August 18, 1996, when they formed the Taiwan Independence Party (Jianguodang), dedicated to "building the island into an independent, sovereign state."[74]

## The New Party

When Chao Shao-kang, Lee Shen-fong, and others—all members of the KMT—announced on August 25, 1989, that they were establishing the New Alliance, it signaled a new kind of faction within the KMT. These young mainlanders, highly moralistic and intensely ideological, embraced the KMT's mission as advanced by Chiang Kai-shek in the early 1950s; their goal, they said, was to oppose "all those who unlawfully acquired illegal gains," and they invited everyone who shared their views to join them.[75] Advocating a reform of Taiwan's political life, they pledged "to link politics with incorruptible behavior" (qinglian canzheng). For the next four years these youthful Alliance members mounted a steady barrage of criticism at the party chairman and his policies. They complained that Lee let the country drift toward "Taiwan independence" and raged against the businesspeople who gave hefty financial contributions to the party.

Foremost in their group was the outspoken young politician Chao Shao-kang. Born in Su county of Honan province on November 16, 1950, Chao grew up in Taipei, earned a B.A. in agricultural engineering at National Taiwan University, and received an M.A. in mechanical engineering from Clemson College in South Carolina. His fiery speaking style helped him get elected twice to the Taipei city council and three times to the Legislative Yuan. Chao, who also directed the nation's Environmental Protection Agency, by the early 1990s was one of the best-known politicians on the island.

When the KMT refused to appoint any New Alliance members to high party positions, in May 1993 they declared that some of them intended to run in the local elections at year's end.[76] The stunned chairman quickly sent a team of party seniors—Chiang Yen-shih, Hsu Li-te, and Hsu Shui-te—to ask that they withdraw from the elections in exchange for occupying four to six seats on the party's central committee. The young turks refused and made up their mind to leave the KMT and form a new party.

In 1993, Chao Shao-kang's friend, Professor Ding Tingyu of the sociology department of National Taiwan University (who managed the Taiwan Gallup poll), drew up a poll of islandwide voting preferences. The July results revealed that public dissatisfaction with the KMT and DPP was great enough that if a new party were to form, it could win 30 percent of the popular votes. The majority of these voters, more educated, cosmopolitan, and under forty years of age, were most likely to support such a political party.

Heartened by this survey, bitter toward the KMT's leadership, and frustrated by political trends they strongly disapproved of, on August 10, 1993, at a well-attended press conference, Chao Shao-kang and others explained why they had left the KMT to form the NP. First, the party chairman had abused his power by inviting seven hundred elected KMT officials to participate in the Fourteenth Party Congress. Second, they felt that KMT members, rather than the central committee, should elect the party chairman. Finally, claiming they were "destroying one party in order to build a party" *(huidang zudang)*, they vowed that their "democratic political party, the NP, will use the parliament as the core, use the people's will to determine the direction, and use elections as the instrument of action." They promised voters "to reform the polity, stabilize the current political situation, and check and balance the two major political parties" *(gexin zhengzhi, anding zhengju, zhiheng liangdang)*. The founders of the NP described the KMT as a "political party that never reflects on its defeats and has become corrupted by money" and they labeled the DPP as "being irresponsible in its public statements, and a political party consumed with hatred and trying to take advantage of provincial sentiments." Adhering to lofty moral standards of political evaluation, these young leaders offered the people very different options from those of the DPP and the KMT.

## Elections and Political Disagreements

After legal reform and political pressures had forced the old national representatives to step down in December 1991, constitutional reforms paved the way
for the four national elections held between late 1992 and mid-1996, thereby
institutionalizing the national election process, just as local elections had been
institutionalized by the 1960s.

The political parties vigorously competed in these national elections, which
included two elections to replace the Second and Third Legislative Yuans; the
election of the Third National Assembly; the first election for the Taiwan
provincial governor, along with the Taiwan provincial assembly, Kaohsiung
and Taipei city mayors, and their city councils; and the presidential and vice
presidential election (see table 14). These elections reflected a new phase of
democracy and the redistribution of political power.

It is important to note, first, that voters felt the significance of these elections. Voter turnout in all elections was well above 70 percent, with a high of
almost 77 percent for the election of the Taiwan provincial governor, the Taiwan provincial assembly, the Kaohsiung and Taipei mayors, and their city
councils.

Second, the KMT's ability to win votes and dominate the Legislative Yuan
and National Assembly and local elections had begun to decline. If we scruti-
nize election outcomes for the Legislative Yuan between 1972 and 1986, in
which a small number of legislators were voted into the First Legislative Yuan,
we observe that the percentage of votes won by the KMT ranged between 73
percent and 67 percent, or an average of 73 percent for five such elections.[77]
But in the 1992 and 1995 elections for the Second and Third Legislative Yuans,
the KMT's share of votes had declined to only 52 percent and 46 percent,
respectively, with an average of 49 percent. A similar trend is observed for the
National Assembly elections.

The KMT dominated that body until the March 23, 1996, election, when it
won only 55 percent of the seats compared with the 75 percent or more it had
held in previous years.

Finally, the KMT monopoly over local government offices, which had begun to decline in the 1980s, continued to do so. In the 1981 and 1989 elections,
the KMT won 53 percent of the popular vote and then fell to 47 percent in the
1993 local election compared with the DPP's 41 percent, which had risen from
13 percent in the 1985 election to 38 percent in the 1989 election. If this trend
continues, the DPP's long-term strategy of "winning over the local government to surround the political center" will have succeeded.

Third, the DPP's ability to attract votes seemed to level off at about 30 percent but fell dramatically in the March 23, 1996, presidential election when PRC military exercises and a strong KMT election bid convinced voters they could not entrust the DPP with power. As in the past, when Peng Ming-min and Xie Changting made independence a key issue in the first presidential race, they lost badly, as did DPP candidate Chen Dingnan, who ran against James C. Y. Soong of the KMT in a four-way race for the December 1994 Taiwan provincial governorship. The DPP's Chen Shui-bian campaigned on his qualifications for Taipei mayor, rather than emphasizing the independence issue, and won 44 percent of the votes in a four-person race. In local elections, DPP candidates have refrained from campaigning on the Taiwan nationalism issue, concentrated on issues germane to voters' interests, and performed better.

Finally, NP candidates have fared better than expected in national elections because they have capitalized on a strong urban voting base, particularly in northern Taiwan, and the growing unhappiness of educated young voters with the two major parties. NP candidates won enough seats in the Taipei and Kaohsiung city council elections and the Third Legislative Yuan and Third National Assembly elections to play an important role in coalition politics. Whether this third party can survive remains to be seen.

These political parties and their candidates have definitely staked out their positions, giving voters clear choices. Nowhere was this more evident than in the campaign for the ROC's March 1996 presidential elections. In addition to holding presidential debates on February 25 and March 9, on March 17 the Central Election Commission held a nationally televised debate between the four competing presidential teams, in which each team, after drawing lots for the order of speaking, spoke for thirty minutes and answered questions from the audience, a first in the island's history.[78] (Vice presidential rivals debated on March 3.)

Lin Yang-kang led off. Speaking in Taiwanese and Mandarin, he emphasized that the current crisis with the PRC was the fault of President Lee Teng-hui. If Lin were elected, he would go to Beijing and develop a dialogue leading to an agreement *(guoxie)* between the two states. Lin stressed the character flaws of President Lee, pointing out that, as a young student at National Taiwan University, Lee had belonged to a Communist Party cell and betrayed his cell members in exchange for his life.

DPP candidate Peng Ming-min argued that he alone understood the suffering of Taiwan's people. He attacked the leadership of Lin and Hau and said that he intended to bring Taiwan into the world order. Speaking only

TABLE 14

Results of Four National Elections Held between December 19, 1992, and March 23, 1996

A: Legislative Yuan Elections

| Political party | Second Legislative Yuan (December 19, 1992) | | | Political party | Third Legislative Yuan (December 2, 1995) | | |
|---|---|---|---|---|---|---|---|
| | No. of seats | Percentage of seats | Percentage of votes | | No. of seats | Percentage of seats | Percentage of votes |
| KMT | 102 | 63 | 53 | KMT | 85 | 52 | 46 |
| DPP | 50 | 31 | 31 | DPP | 44 | 33 | 33 |
| Other (Social Democratic Party and Nonparty) | 9 | 6 | 16 | NP | 21 | 13 | 13 |
| | | | | Independent | 4 | 2 | 8 |
| TOTAL | 161 | 100 | 100 | TOTAL | 164 | 100 | 100 |
| Average voter turnout = 72.2% | | | | Average voter turnout = 74% | | | |

B: Presidential, Vice Presidential, and Third National Assembly Elections

| Candidates and party | President / Vice President (March 23, 1996) | Political party | Third National Assembly (March 23, 1996) | | |
|---|---|---|---|---|---|
| | | | No. of seats | Percentage of seats | Percentage of vote |
| Lee and Lien (KMT) | 54 | KMT | 183 | 55 | 50 |
| Peng and Xie (DPP) | 21 | DPP | 99 | 30 | 30 |
| Lin and Hao (NP) | 15 | NP | 46 | 14 | 13 |
| Chen and Wang (independent) | 10 | Independent | 6 | 1 | 7 |
| | | TOTAL | 334 | 100 | 100 |
| Average voter turnout = 74% | | | | | |

C: Taiwan Governor, Provincial Assembly, Kaohsiung-Taipei Mayor and Council Elections (December 3, 1994)

| | | | Taiwan Provincial Assembly |
| --- | --- | --- | --- |
| Candidates and party | Taiwan Governor (percentage of votes) | Political party | Provincial council members |
| James C. Y. Soong (KMT) | 56 | KMT | 47 |
| Chen Dingan (DPP) | 38 | DPP | 24 |
| Ju Gau-jeng (NP) | 4 | NP | 2 |
| Independent | 2 | Independent | 6 |
| TOTAL | 100 | | 79 |

| Political Party | Kaohsiung Mayor (Percentage of votes) | Taipei Mayor (Percentage of votes) | Number of Kaohsiung City Council Members | Number of Taipei City Council Members |
| --- | --- | --- | --- | --- |
| KMT | 54 | 26 | 23 | 20 |
| DPP | 39 | 44 | 11 | 18 |
| NP | 4 | 30 | 2 | 11 |
| NP | 3 | 0 | 8 | 3 |
| TOTAL | 100 | 100 | 44 | 52 |

Average voter turnout = 76.8%

Taiwanese, he stressed that his party would build a "green" society on Taiwan, purify Taiwan's politics, and make Taiwan an independent nation. The president, he said, did not really love Taiwan, and the KMT had become increasingly corrupt.

President Lee, speaking in both Taiwanese and Mandarin, listed the key qualities necessary to be president: honesty, the ability to endure harsh criticism, and courage. He promised to preserve the different lifestyles of Taiwan's people and build a grand community *(shengming gongtongti)*. He wanted to strengthen Taiwan's democracy, which he defined as "sovereignty belonging to the people" *(zhuquan zaimin)* and repeated that he would continue to be sensitive to the PRC's demands and try to establish cooperative links with that society. He expressed tolerance toward his enemies and critics.

The final candidate, Chen Li-an, spoke only Mandarin and blamed Taiwan's new crisis with the PRC solely on President Lee, who "has never admitted that he is a Chinese."[79] He promised to clean up Taiwan's politics, which he called corrupt owing to President Lee's bad management. He envisioned Taiwan becoming the Switzerland of the Asian Pacific and its people as ethical, honest, spiritual, and prosperous. He warned Beijing's leaders not to follow the United States and Japan, which he described as interested only in profit.

The last few weeks of this four-candidate race saw the island blanketed by a blizzard of flags, leaflets, and media advertisements. On the walls of some five- and six-story buildings in Taiwan, painted pictures showed President Lee and Premier Lien smiling and beseeching voters to support them. The rhetorical harshness of Chen Li-an and Lin Yang-kang's criticisms of President Lee were matched by the vitriolic comments Peng Ming-min offered about Lin and Hau as well as President Lee. (Such invective might have worked in President Lee's favor, since he was also being vilified by Beijing's leaders.) Lee mainly campaigned in central and southern Taiwan. Projecting an image of toughness and courage, he urged that voters not be intimidated by the PRC rockets being fired near Taiwan and the large-scale military maneuvers on the nearby Fukien coast.

In the period leading up to the election, some 60 percent of Taiwan's voters were still undecided. But on election day, 74 percent of the registered voters went to the polls and gave President Lee and his running mate, Lien Chan, 54 percent of the popular vote, a powerful mandate.

In all the national elections, preelection polls showed that nearly 50–60 percent of the voters were undecided, that 30–40 percent favored the KMT, and that 10–20 percent were for the DPP.[80] All three parties tried to establish links with retired military personnel and their dependents, target subethnic constituencies in the cities, and win voters through the mass media, handbills, and public rallies. The DPP candidates copied their KMT competitors' vote buying and working with local factions; many DPP candidates exuded a blunt, tough style in defense of "Taiwanese interests" and an independent Taiwan. KMT candidates tried to convince voters that their future depended on the same experienced leadership that had already delivered prosperity and stability. NP candidates stressed that they intended to purify politics of corruption and bring clean government to Taiwan. How changed were national elections after the December 1991 election for the Second National Assembly!

In the fall of 1992, a magazine poll concluded that "voter satisfaction with both the KMT and the DPP has risen slightly over the course of the last three years. The KMT satisfaction index rose 3.9 percent compared with last year, while that of the DPP jumped 9.3 percent."[81] As already mentioned, in the spring and summer of 1993, the press negatively evaluated the KMT's rule over Taiwan and, by listing the government's NT$ billionaires, showed that the KMT was more aligned with the wealthy than was the DPP.[82] As the November 1993 local election drew closer, political experts predicted the KMT would suffer a major defeat. One commentator said that "if the KMT does not heighten its vigilance, it is absolutely possible that half of the country in Taiwan will turn 'green' [DPP] from 'blue' [KMT] overnight."[83]

In July 1993 the Central Election Commission ordered that officials of the same party could no longer head that commission *and* the local election committees, thus restricting the KMT's influence.[84] With the formation of the NP in mid-August, the November 1993 local elections became a three-party contest. The NP campaigned to eliminate money from politics; the DPP attacked the KMT's poor performance and corruption while promising more welfare. As the election drew closer, the press predicted a DPP victory.[85]

Realizing the critical importance of this local election and hoping to reverse the KMT decline, President Lee began campaigning for KMT candidates, the first time the nation's president and ruling party chairman had ever appeared in shirtsleeves before crowds. Lee's popularity and enthusiasm helped many a KMT candidate to win who had been on the verge of defeat. The KMT won fifteen mayoral and country magistrate seats in the November 27, 1993, election, although its share of voter support fell to 47 percent (from 52 percent in 1989).[86] The DPP managed to hang on to six country magistrate seats, the same number it had won in 1989. The DPP had expected to win more, but its share of voters rose to only 41 percent (from 38 percent in 1989), not enough to displace the KMT. The KMT lost voters in the Taipei region to the NP.

On January 29, 1994, more than 73 percent of the eligible voters cast their ballots for county and city councils and for mayors and chief executives of small cities, townships, and villages. As in the past, the KMT won an overwhelming majority. The DPP, however, increased its share of seats on councils to 11 percent (from 6 percent in 1986) and to 7 percent for executive positions (from 2 percent in 1986), a modest advance over an eight-year period.[87] The DPP's share of all votes cast in this election, however, was only 15 percent compared with 31 percent in the Legislative Yuan race of 1992 and 41 percent in the election for magistrates in late 1993. Although the DPP had not performed as its members had expected, they were given a new campaign issue.

In February 1994 there were revelations of massive vote buying in the January 29 election, and by mid-March more than 250 criminal indictments had been handed down. Government investigators interrogated some 1,750 people and brought charges against roughly one out of every five of the 858 council members elected in January; the newly elected speaker of Taoyuan county was arrested on his return from a trip overseas.[88] But many in the DPP and the NP criticized the government for failing to produce clean elections and for not arresting more KMT candidates allegedly involved in the vote buying. On March 18, 1994, the DPP announced that it would expel more than ten party members accused of bribery in the January 1994 elections.[89]

Between 1993 and 1996 complaints of political corruption increased, focusing on large contributions by businesspeople to political parties, especially the KMT. The press charged that construction companies with government contracts to build Taipei's rapid transit system produced inferior overhead rail facilities. The judiciary also blamed the construction companies for corrupting local and nationally elected politicians. But by 1996 fewer than half those the government charged with corruption had been found guilty and punished. Adjudication of these cases continued.

## Interest Groups, Party Politics, and the Government

In the 1980s and early 1990s private groups for the first time pressed for legislation and policies favoring their interests. Taiwan's new wealth and vibrant civil society encouraged this activity, as did the democratic transition. Although many examples could be cited, the following case clearly illustrates how such new demands on the political center have politicized society.

In 1980 the government-owned Taiwan Power Corporation proposed building a fourth nuclear power plant to meet Taiwan's future energy needs, but not until May 1992 did the Legislative Yuan consider a budget for this project (US$4.2 billion over the next seven years).[90] DPP legislators strongly opposed the idea, and the project was delayed until the early summer of 1994. On June 22, 1994, the Legislative Yuan was to conduct the first reading for a budget for the power plant. But a coalition of citizens representing the Alliance for Protection of the Environment (Huanbao lianmeng), Kung Liao hamlet, where the plant was to be built, and other environmental protection groups assembled at the Legislative Yuan to protest.[91] In the meantime, DPP legislators argued that the risks for people and the environment were too great; KMT legislators countered that government surveys proved the project was safe and should be built; NP legislators urged that alternative proposals be considered because the debate had become a "face saving," "emotional" dispute.[92]

The next morning, June 23, DPP legislators offered a new argument, claiming that budgeting funds seven years in advance was illegal. But in the afternoon KMT legislators rammed the proposal through in sixteen minutes and enraged the DPP legislators.[93] On July 1, 1994, some politicians appealed for calm, rational discussions of whether to build more nuclear power plants in Taiwan. Legislator Hung Hsiu-chu viewed the dilemma as follows:

I regret this issue has caused such severe disagreement, and we still do not fully understand what this issue is all about. We base our judgments on one-sided opinions. Those supporting the project believe our economy will be ruined if the nuclear power plant is not constructed. Those opposing the project claim that if it is built, future generations of people will be destroyed. These are two extreme views. There have been many arguments advanced to persuade and convince people. Yet there should be some better way to carry out our negotiations and communications with each other. Both sides have never used any rational procedures to discuss the issue of whether to abolish or approve this construction project.[94]

On July 12, the Legislative Yuan concluded the third reading and approved constructing a fourth nuclear power plant.[95] The DPP, refusing to affirm this outcome, complained of the lack of public support for the project and urged foreign companies not to bid on it. Lin Yixiong, a former provincial assemblyperson, began a hunger strike outside the Legislative Yuan. Yu Ching, the DPP Taipei county magistrate, stated that he would not issue a construction permit. Thousands of antinuclear protestors gathered outside the Legislative Yuan. Riot police arrived and arrested several protestors, but a number of cars had already been damaged. This rancorous disagreement finally ended, but public passions had been inflamed, causing another strain in the polity.

## Foreign Policy and Political Disagreements

Since 1950, Taiwan's ruling party always had claimed that Taiwan and its off-shore islands were part of a divided China and that only the ROC constitution and government represented China. After the ROC government withdrew from the United Nations in 1971, most nations switched their diplomatic ties to the PRC, which refused those states the option of simultaneously retaining their ties with the ROC. When the United States broke diplomatic relations with it in December 1978, only thirty-odd nations recognized the sovereignty of the ROC.

By the fall of 1990, President Lee realized that political disagreement in Taiwan might worsen over the government's foreign policy, especially toward the PRC, and that if such dissension occurred within the KMT, the chairman's support for constitutional reform and democratization would melt away. How could he reconcile the KMT goal (that Taiwan be unified with mainland China) with the DPP goal (that Taiwan must eventually become an independent Republic of Taiwan) and establish a democracy that allowed for serious disagreements over foreign policy?

Again, the president turned to consensus-building tactics. In September 1990, President Lee formed a six-person committee of KMT leaders with orders to create a National Unification Council that would draft guidelines for a mainland China policy. After receiving the committee's recommendation, on October 7, 1990, President Lee appointed twenty-eight officials, professionals, and businesspersons to serve on the National Unification Council along with another twelve scholars. In late October the council convened with President Lee in the chair, and it continued to meet until February 23, 1991, by which time the council's guidelines had been accepted by the KMT, approved by the Legislative Yuan, and tacitly approved by the DPP and other opposition parties.

The guidelines called for China's unification when democracy, freedom, and equality of wealth existed in both Taiwan and mainland China. But the peoples of both sides of the Taiwan Strait also had to agree that unification was in their mutual interest; that disagreements must no longer prevail; that they respect each other, be willing to protect basic human rights, and share a common culture; and finally, that the procedures and timing for unification be appropriate. These developments were to be achieved in three phases: a short-term phase of exchanges and reciprocity, a medium-term phase of mutual trust and cooperation, and a long-term phase of consultation and unification. No fixed time schedule was set.

The DPP did not participate in this process, although President Lee had invited Kang Ning-hsiang to serve on the National Unification Council. After agonizing for a time Kang accepted the president's invitation, but as a private citizen. DPP members thereafter snubbed him and refused to nominate him for any high party post, believing he had betrayed the party's mission. Nor did the DPP think very much of President Lee's National Unification Council. When Huang Hsin-chieh learned of the plan, he muttered that "it was nonsense." After the guidelines appeared, many DPP members declared that insisting "China must be unified" misled the people because only the residents of Taiwan had the right to determine their future and "why should Taiwan and mainland China be unified anyway?"[96] Some also feared that "unification" meant that "China mainland would swallow up Taiwan."

Just as the DPP condemned the guidelines, so did scholars and officials in Beijing, as witness the following:

— Seeking the rights and interests of the Taiwan people is false, but claiming to want unification while being independent is Taiwan's real goal.
— To establish democracy and freedom for a unified China is false, but imposing the Three Principles of the People on mainland China is Taiwan's true intention.
— Achieving mutual exchange and benefits is a false objective, while establishing the one country, two systems is a true goal.
— Unifying China in three stages is a false objective, while buying time to wait for mainland China to change is Taiwan's real goal.[97]

Mainland authorities thus interpreted the unification guidelines as a cruel hoax imposed on China by Taiwan's insincere, clever leaders. They charged that the guidelines were not designed to truly unite China because they revealed an excessive concern for the rights of the Taiwan people.

The guidelines had failed to assuage the deep-seated fears of Beijing's leaders as well as those of the DPP, who wanted Taiwan to become an independent nation. But President Lee's consensus-building efforts had not been in vain. The majority within and outside the KMT supported the guidelines, and the Legislative Yuan affirmed them as the principles for the Executive Yuan to develop policies for ROC-PRC relations.[98] Most citizens regarded these principles as a sensible compromise because of the chasm that still separated these societies, derived from their different living standards, customs, and sentiments.

Meanwhile, the ROC government tried to upgrade the nation's status in the world community. In January 1990, using the designation of the Taiwan-

Penghu-Kinmen-Matsu Tariff Area, the ROC government applied for admission to the General Agreement on Tariffs and Trade (GATT). The PRC government agreed as long as China was admitted ahead of Taiwan. In the late summer of 1992, the ROC government mobilized nine nations to support the ROC's application for entry into the United Nations and appealed to that body to adopt the principle of "one country, two seats." The government repeated its efforts to enter the United Nations in 1993 and 1994.

Despite deep mutual distrust between the leaders of Taipei and Beijing, from 1990 until mid-1995 relations between Taiwan and mainland China steadily improved: trade increased, Taiwan's businesspeople invested in the mainland, tourism expanded, and communications grew. Unofficial meetings took place, and both sides even established quasi-official units to mediate disputes across the Taiwan Strait. This détente never involved official contacts, but an atmosphere of goodwill and optimism ensued.

Then in 1994 two events made Beijing's leaders doubt that Taiwan's leaders, President Lee in particular, were sincere about unification. In April President Lee granted a private interview to a Japanese journalist named Shima Ryôtarô of the *Shûkan asahi* (Asahi weekly). President Lee told Shima, "I feel the pain of our inability to do anything for Bosnia. And having been born in Taiwan, I also felt pain for not being able to do anything for Taiwan's people."[99] Then the president said:

Until now, those who held power in Taiwan were always from outside Taiwan. But now, I can bluntly say the following. Even the KMT was an outside force. It was the only party that could govern the Taiwanese. We must make the KMT into a party for the Taiwanese people. Those who are now in their seventies were never able to feel secure, and we do not want that to happen to our children.

The president also identified with the aspirations of the Taiwan people:

I have no gun, only a weak fist. I do not even have any support within the KMT. Yet I have endured all kinds of conditions until now, because I carry the feelings of the people in my heart. The Taiwanese people expect me to act, and I am now trying to take action.

Finally, the president compared his efforts to make Taiwan democratic and modern to the trials of Moses in the Bible:

We have now entered a new era in Taiwan. Even Moses and his people suffered, but Moses and his people still were able to leave Egypt. Thus, when we think about the Taiwanese people and their sacrifices regarding the February 28, 1947, incident, I can only conclude that my role is like that in the exodus from Egypt.[100]

The reactions from Beijing were swift. Li Jiaquan, a leading Taiwan expert, called President Lee arrogant and out of touch with the true feelings of the Chinese people of the mainland. The president was not even a "real Chinese" and in his heart schemed how to lead Taiwan down the road to "independence."[101]

The second event occurred on July 5, when the ROC's Mainland Affairs Council published a white paper responding to the PRC's white paper of August 31, 1993.[102] Taiwan argued that the ROC government had been the only legitimate government of China since 1911, and that since October 25, 1945, it had governed Taiwan. The ROC government still adhered to the "one China principle" but stated that two political entities *(liangguo zhengzhi shiti)* governed different geographical territories that made up China. The white paper argued that both entities should treat each other with respect and peacefully resolve their differences.

Then in early May 1995, the United States Congress voted to invite President Lee to visit the United States, and later his alma mater, Cornell University, invited him to speak at its commencement ceremony. On May 22, President Bill Clinton concurred with Congress, and on June 7 President Lee arrived in the United States to speak on June 9 at Cornell University. He emphasized that his visit was "a private trip" and hoped that "all nations can treat us fairly and reasonably and not overlook the significance, value, and function we represent."[103] He went on to say that "some say it is impossible for us to break out of the diplomatic isolation we face, but we will do our utmost to demand the impossible."

The reaction from Beijing was delayed, but on July 8 the PRC announced that it would undertake missile tests near Taiwan; between July 21 and July 27, the PRC military fired missiles 150 kilometers north of Taiwan. On August 15 the PRC held another round of military exercises off the Fukien coast, including the testing of antiship missiles. In the same two months, the PRC government carried out an intensive propaganda campaign in the press, maligning President Lee and accusing him of having violated the "one China principle" and advocating "Taiwan independence." Again, two weeks before the March 23, 1996, elections in Taiwan, the PRC fired missiles within some fifty miles of the large ports of Keelung and Kaohsiung and followed up with military maneuvers on the Fukien coast.

Cross-strait relations thus deteriorated after the summer of 1995. As tensions increased, many sold their stock in Taiwan, driving stock prices to an all-time low, and there was some panic buying of food. President Lee's political enemies accused him of bringing the two Chinese states to the brink of war.

President Lee stood his ground during the March 1996 elections, projecting to the voters the image of a heroic leader capable of enduring criticism and leading the nation. He insisted that China could be unified only according to the National Unification Council guidelines. He urged the people to support him as the only leader qualified to lead the country. The voters gave the president a powerful victory, but many in Taiwan continue to worry whether their government can resolve the crisis with mainland China.

President Lee's policy of building bipartisan support to craft a mainland China policy had received the support of almost all elites within Taiwan. But the events of 1994–95 convinced Beijing's leaders that Taiwan's leaders were neither sincere nor serious about long-term unification, and they now threatened to use force to unify China. Reestablishing the détente that had existed between the two Chinese societies from 1989 to 1995 was a new challenge for the ROC government. Meanwhile, the KMT's vision that China can be unified according to the guidelines clashes with the DPP's vision that Taiwan must become an independent republic. These opposing visions, not likely to be resolved soon, will be the true test for the survival of Taiwan's democracy.

# CHAPTER THIRTEEN

# Conclusion: The Evolution of the First Chinese Democracy

Democracy had been discussed in Taiwan as early as the 1950s, but replacing authoritarian rule with democracy was never inevitable. The political center's power holders could have maintained the same authoritarian rule that now exists in Singapore and the PRC in order to continue their hegemonic party rule. But political life in these three Chinese societies in the mid-1990s could not be more different: in Taiwan, liberty flourishes, the people hold their leaders and political parties accountable through elections, and access to information is free and open; in Singapore and the PRC, the state severely limits human liberty, sovereignty does not reside in the people, and information is controlled.

Our narrative of Taiwan's democratization shows four patterns of political change evolving and interacting to reshape the relationship between Taiwan's political center and its civil society. Previous scholarship has confirmed some of these patterns but has neither emphasized their interaction nor explained what made Taiwan's democratization similar to yet different from that of other democratizing nations.[1] These patterns are the following:

— A ruling party willingly engaged in a top-down, guided democratic process and tolerated an opposition-driven, bottom-up approach to democratization. These political developments eventually converged, without extremists in either the ruling party or the opposition resorting to excessive violence or sabotage, to become a democratic polity. (Tai-

wan is unique in that the ruling party tolerated the evolution of a political opposition and the prospect of sharing power or the risk of losing it
when it had the power to control society indefinitely.)[2]

— Some in the ruling and opposition parties internalized ideological-political cultural adjustments that fit with the practice of democracy.[3]
(Again, what is unusual in Taiwan is that Chinese political culture facili-
tated those adjustments so that powerful leaders and elites embraced
ideas and values that were more compatible with the practice of democracy than with autocracy.)[4]

— Local elections, established in 1950, were institutionalized by the 1960s,
and the national elections, commencing in the 1970s, were institutionalized by the mid-1990s. (Again, Taiwan stands out because, after decades
of practicing various degrees of democracy, voters did not replace the
ruling party with the opposition party.)[5]

— The ruling elites initially adhered to constitutional rule without practicing it, but their commitment to democracy and pressure from the opposition made it possible to amend the constitution and practice democracy. (Again, Taiwan is unique in that the opposition politicians, who
despised the constitution and wanted to draft a new constitution for
establishing a different democratic polity, participated in a constitutional reform process over which they had very limited influence.)[6]

These four patterns of political change show that the key requisites for
democracy—a responsible opposition, a political culture compatible with democracy, competing political parties participating in free elections, and respect for a constitution—now exist in Taiwan. As long as the extreme minority
committed to drafting a new constitution plays by the rules of democracy,
and as long as the PRC does not try to destroy it, there is a high probability
that Taiwan's democracy can survive. These political changes elucidate the
development of the first Chinese democracy.

## The Era of the Inhibited Political Center

Between 1949 and 1986 a single party, the KMT, ruled Taiwan through its
penetration of the government and control of the military, the security forces,
and the bureaucracy and thus dominated the economy and the society. (We
call this projection of political power an "inhibited" political center.) Humiliated by its defeat on the mainland by communist forces, by 1952 the KMT had
regrouped and concentrated enormous power to itself. Behaving more like a

religious sect than a political party, the KMT tried to build a society on Taiwan according to the ideas of its founder, Sun Yat-sen. One of these ideas called for developing a democracy that would represent the true will of the people. Until such a democracy had evolved, however, the KMT intended to promote a "limited" democracy without competing political parties until society had been educated and made prosperous and the citizenry had become morally virtuous.

The KMT's chairman, Chiang Kai-shek, assisted by his son Chiang Ching-kuo, defined the party's sacred mission as recovering mainland China from communist rule and transferring to it Sun Yat-sen's Three Principles of the People, as manifested in the modernization and democratization of Taiwan. To encourage the KMT in its grand mission, Chiang exhorted KMT members to overcome their communist defeat by using "that triumph [building a Sunist society on Taiwan] to comfort our leader, Sun Yat-sen, and those martyrs who died and are in heaven." Chiang Kai-shek thus reorganized the KMT and initiated the top-down democratic process by establishing local elections in 1950 and maintaining the fiction of a "constitutional" Republic of China on Taiwan.

An important "background condition" for Taiwan's democracy, to borrow a concept from Dankwart A. Rustow (who observed that in Sweden and Turkey a powerful sentiment for national unity had "precede[d] all the other phases of democratization"),[7] was that the majority of people must share a sense of national unity. In Taiwan two different sentiments of national unity competed, one shared by most mainlanders and another shared by many Taiwanese, yet they constituted a basis for both groups to embrace the dream of democracy.

Since its founding, the KMT's goal was a unified China. Having lost the civil war, the KMT and its supporters believed that transforming Taiwan into a model province based on Sunist doctrine could unify China. This sense of national mission made the KMT strongly dedicated to establishing a democratic China.

The political opposition, who had lived in a Taiwan separated from the mainland's governance since 1895 (except for those few years between late 1945 and 1949), believed that Taiwan's destiny should be a democratic Republic of Taiwan independent of the mainland. The February 28, 1947, uprising and its harsh suppression the by KMT reinforced those sentiments.

Although Taiwan's inhibited political center guided a top-down process of democratization, it often resorted to ruthless means to curb behavior it deemed illegitimate. This center's behavior was predicated on a mixture of policies that brutally suppressed dissident behavior and tightly regulated the populace while facilitating the opening up and reform of society. Such paradoxical actions flowed from a particular mind-set of the leadership. Extirpating behavior threatening to delegitimize the center's moral authority was perfectly justifiable, because such actions were necessary to guarantee the salvation of Chinese civilization. The center's top officials perceived themselves as sagelike, highly moral leaders trying to elicit that appropriate, voluntary behavior from society to save Chinese civilization and build a new society based on the doctrine of Sun Yat-sen. They never saw any contradiction in using martial law and promoting limited democracy to achieve a complete democracy later. Therefore we will never know the exact number of Taiwan's victims in those early years when limited democracy had just begun. The journalist Jiang Chunnan estimates that "more than ten thousand [political prisoners] went to jail."[8] The number might have been higher. Out of such paradoxical leadership behavior came the unexpected consequence of suppression and control while a civil society evolved that inhibited the political center and became the seedbed for political opposition.

By the early 1970s a group of disaffected KMT members, joined by college-educated youth and experienced local politicians, began criticizing the ruling party's style of guided, top-down democracy as insincere and phony. A real democracy, they claimed, would have competing political parties, a free press, and open national elections, but Taiwan had none of these. They argued that as long as the constitution was a dead letter, citizens had no civil rights. Equally important, this opposition grasped the importance of operating within the informal rules bounding opposition political behavior. Although the regime arrested and imprisoned many of these *dangwai* activists, their numbers grew.

By the late 1970s Taiwan's urbanization and manufacturing growth was generating a per capita income of more than US$3,000, meaning that the opposition now had the resources to hold discussion meetings and launch periodicals. As an enlarged, literate middle class began participating in local politics, the *dangwai* began entering candidates in the local and limited national elections. Thus in the late 1970s a free market process flourished, and a civil society emerged.

In the ideological market, Taiwanese heatedly discussed Western liberalism, modern Confucian humanism, Sunist doctrine, and even Taiwanese nationalism, a process that had commenced in a more limited way in the 1950s but in the late 1970s had meshed with four forms of advertising political beliefs and ideas. First, the ruling party's official ideology—the Three Principles of the

People—argued for a democracy without selfish interest groups and for adherence to the rule of law. Second, liberal intellectuals compared the political center's tolerance of a protodemocracy with the standards of Western democracy and found it lacking. Third, Taiwan's middle class extolled the virtues of the free market, striving for material improvement, and benefiting from Buddhist, Taoist, and Confucian religions. Finally, the press evaluated why different strata of voters supported their candidates and rejected those having extreme views. As these four advertising forms interacted, certain Chinese core values and beliefs were filtered out and valued as important for the practice of democracy.

Most elites and citizens had shared the utopian and Manichaean beliefs embodied in Confucianism and deeply distrusted their power holders. But engaging in elections, debating democracy, and evaluating the political center's performance were new experiences for everyone in Taiwan in the late 1970s and early 1980s. Gradually, more elites and citizens were willing to tolerate opposing opinions, agree to disagree, and play by the rules of democracy. When people realized that elections empowered them to make political choices, they wanted to expand the election process and elect national leaders directly. Meanwhile, the newly elected officials and representatives realized that the voters were judging their performance and could replace them if they were dissatisfied.

In the early 1980s people in Taiwan also began worrying about environmental pollution, and many farmers were unable to maintain their former standard of living. Declines in industries such as coal mining and textiles produced unemployment, and residents living near factories and nuclear reactors protested the incipient dangers.

Rising political expectations emboldened the *dangwai* to demand that the political center lift martial law and allow political parties to compete. In the political center, conservative KMT leaders worried about Taiwan's international isolation, PRC pressures to force a political settlement, Taiwan independence elements fomenting violence, and a leadership succession crisis. Believing that the populace was not ready for full democracy and that the current conditions did not justify lifting martial law, they demanded the opposition behave and accept the status quo. The opposition responded by trying to force the ruling party to allow an opposition party to form.

The top-down (KMT) and bottom-up *(dangwai)* approaches to democracy contained complex struggles over many political issues but centered on whether an authoritarian political system or a democracy could best solve the nation's problems. As local elections became routine and national elections evolved, disagreements between the *dangwai* and the political center's ruling party became more clearly delineated. The opposition, insistent that democracy was more suitable than authoritarianism for solving Taiwan's problems, argued as follows.

Conditions within Taiwan justified lifting martial law. More and more elites believed that political parties could compete and monitor one another, elect the best leaders, and satisfy the needs of the people. The constitution ought to be reactivated, elections should be held to reelect a new parliament and national assembly, and the people should elect their leaders directly. Civil rights must be restored to the people and all political prisoners released from prison. Social welfare policies should assist deprived farmers, laborers, pensioners, and so on. By challenging the political center to speed up political reform, the opposition put the ruling party on the defensive.[9] Many liberal KMT members sympathized with the *dangwai* and joined the struggle.

Taiwan's political life had now entered what Rustow has called a phase of "prolonged and inconclusive political struggle," which always is necessary before democracy can become a reality.[10] In Taiwan's case, democracy had become *the* primary aim for the opposition and even for many of the ruling party. For Chiang Ching-kuo, the KMT's aging and sick leader, democracy had also become integral to achieving his party's mission of unifying China.

## The Democratic Breakthrough

Taiwan could not have experienced a peaceful democratic breakthrough without great leadership, beginning with Chiang Kai-shek, who rebuilt the KMT and initiated limited democracy. Many KMT liberals and *dangwai* politicians also supplied leadership skills and, by insisting on tolerance and moderation in their struggle, pushed the bottom-up democratic process. But KMT leadership proved important, because powerful party conservatives resisted any political reform that would grant the *dangwai* party status. Only Chiang Ching-kuo, Chiang Kai-shek's son, had the power and charisma to restrain those hard-line conservatives from suppressing the *dangwai* and to lift martial law.

By 1980 Chiang's democratic vision began taking form, in which a "perfect" democracy developed in Taiwan could be transferred to the mainland. He had also conceived of a plan for democratization, but first he had to select a Taiwanese, Lee Teng-hui, as his vice president in February 1984, and then he had to wait two more years before he could launch his plan because of the intervention of various external and internal crises. Not until the spring of 1986 could he initiate political reform and announce in the fall of that same year that martial law would be lifted and replaced by a national security law.

Chiang took no action in late September 1986 when the DPP courageously but illegally established itself as a political party, thus affirming his commitment to democracy and the peaceful resolution of political disagreement.

So too did *dangwai* leaders restrain their extremist members from conducting violent demonstrations to demand the end of martial law. Taiwan now had entered the "decision phase" of its democratization.

But Chiang Ching-kuo died before the democratic breakthrough could be ensured, leaving the possibility that Taiwan's reform could lapse into what some have called pseudodemocracy, or the "existence of formally democratic political institutions, such as multiparty electoral competition, [that] masks (often in part to legitimate) the reality of authoritarian domination."[11] It remained for his successor, Lee Teng-hui, to consolidate the three essential conditions that Robert Dahl has argued are necessary for democracy.[12]

Lee's concept of democracy differed from Chiang's Confucianized democracy, which advocated a single party governing by virtue of its superior moral qualities and the indirect election of the nation's leaders by a national assembly. Pragmatic, sensitive to Taiwanese sentiments, and favoring the democracy of Japan and the West, with his unusual leadership skills Lee also defused crises and resolved political disagreements with his opponents. When he became KMT chairman, conservative politicians whose goals differed from his challenged him and had to be defeated before democracy became a reality.

## Partial Elite Convergence, Constitutional Reform, and Elections

Between the lifting of martial law on July 15, 1987, and mid-1992, Taiwan's political elites engaged in fierce struggle. The hard-core ruling party conservatives, long accustomed to holding power, did not want to share it with their opponents; the opposition extremists, although championing reform and democracy, believed in using violent means. Political leadership and mediating of disagreements were crucial if the ruling and opposition parties were to avoid violence and reversion to authoritarian rule.

Lee used the mediating skills of Chiang Yen-shih and others to patch up disagreements in the KMT, to achieve a political settlement with the opposition, and to sell his party on the idea that the direct election of the president and vice president was a good idea. He also mobilized party liberals and reform-minded opposition politicians to abolish the First National Assembly and carry out vital constitutional reform that expanded national elections.

In this period of rapid political change, many KMT seniors who had opposed their party's reforms retired. The younger Taiwanese politicians who replaced them typically supported Chairman Lee's leadership position and policies. This process, which Rustow has called "Darwinian selectivity in favor of convinced democrats," gave more party power to the chairman because those remaining hard-core conservatives, now a minority, either accepted their chairman's leadership or left the party.[13] Taiwan's democratic transition now entered the "habituation phase," in which a declining number of extremist politicians could not win support because everyone else was now playing by democratic rules.

## The Era of the Subordinated Political Center

Between December 1992 and spring 1996 Taiwan's elites increasingly complied with the democratic rules to resolve their disagreements, and there were few street demonstrations.[14] Although local and national elections involved ever greater sums of money and enormous amounts of time and energy, they had become a way of life, like the local elections of the past.

Broad voting trends revealed that the KMT had lost some popular support; its majority in the Legislative Yuan in 1996 was marginal, and it held far less than the two-thirds majority it had in the Second National Assembly. Even so, the KMT retained a working majority in local government and dominated the national government by its control of the Office of the President (President Lee won 54 percent of the vote in the March 23, 1996, presidential race). Voters believed that their charismatic, dynamic president, a Taiwanese, was one of them, and they supported the KMT.

But by late 1996 the executive branch seemed unable to initiate the reforms it wanted. The Office of the President was considering another National Affairs Conference to achieve some national consensus for further political reforms. The political center was now very much subordinated to the demands of civil society and the political parties. Yet the parties could not reach any consensus of what new policies to enact.

The KMT had co-opted many of the DPP's policy suggestions, making them appear to be its own to win voter support. (See table 15 for when the DPP made six programmatic criticisms of the KMT and when the KMT began adopting these as policies of its own to claim credit.) Thus the KMT could still win votes and manage the government, because the opposition party in 1996 was in disarray. Election results, as early as December 1991 through spring 1996, had revealed that voters rejected the DPP if they saw its message as exclusively devoted to establishing an independent Republic of Taiwan, for they feared war with the PRC. The majority of voters wanted the ROC's status in the international order improved, but not by antagonizing the PRC. They

TABLE 15
*KMT Policies Adopted after DPP Criticisms of Ruling Party*

| Issue | Date DPP advocates | Date put into effect |
|---|---|---|
| Lift martial law | May 19, 1986 | July 15, 1987 |
| Hold full parliamentary elections | December 25, 1987 | December 1991, 1992 |
| Elect governor, big-city mayors | March 12, 1988 | December 3, 1994 |
| Let exiled dissidents return | August 23, 1988 | July 7, 1992 |
| Abolish 1948 Temporary Provisions | December 12, 1988 | April 30, 1991 |
| Directly elect president | December 25, 1989 | March 23, 1996 |

SOURCE: Virginia Sheng, "DPP's Soul-Searching: To Oppose or Pitch In," *Free China Journal* 13, no. 17 (May 10, 1996), p. 7.

were capable, however, of voting a DPP politician into office to goad the KMT to perform better, as when they elected Chen Shui-bian in the Taipei city mayor's race of December 1994.

But in 1996 the DPP had only about seventy thousand members and limited financial resources, and party extremists still clung to their goal of establishing an independent Republic of Taiwan. The DPP leadership had also aged, virtually all of them having served prison time, and was at a loss for how to appeal to more than one-third of Taiwan voters.

Our approach to understanding the evolution of Taiwan's democracy did not postulate any necessary preconditions. In the former inhibited political center of martial law, strong sentiments of nationalism existed, just as they did among the opposition. Political elites both within and outside the inhibited political center had long struggled over which ideas and concepts could best resolve the problems facing the nation, and they finally agreed that democracy was best. The gradual convergence of the thinking of elites and citizens grew out of a Chinese political culture that, when readjusted, affirmed bargaining, compromise, public discourse, and consensus building. In that complex cultural readjustment process, some elites tried to oppose the tide of democracy, but they were restrained by other elites exercising their leadership skills. When official theory finally advertised that "political power resides with the people" *(zhuquan zaimin),* a concept gradually affirmed by intellectual, amateur, and mass media advertising, democracy seemed to have become a reality. Yet elite convergence was still not complete.

## The Future of Taiwan's Democracy

Alexis de Tocqueville pointed out that in America "parties, indeed, may be found which threaten the future of the Union; but there is none which seems to contest the present form of government or the present course of society."[15]

This is not the case in Taiwan, and for that reason Taiwan's political future is uncertain. There is a small group of Taiwanese politicians who are disenchanted with the present political institutions, ruling party, and government of Taiwan as well as with the regime's commitment to the unification of China. Will these Taiwanese nationalists continue to comply with the rules of democracy, or will they resort to other means to change the present polity?

As the past two centuries demonstrate, more and more nations have learned that democracy is a better way than violence to resolve conflicts over nationalistic, religious, racial, and other questions. As long as Taiwan's leaders, elites, and people can agree that democracy is the most suitable means to resolve disagreements, democracy can survive. Whether or not the ruling party shares more power with the opposition or is replaced by the opposition should not determine the fate of the first Chinese democracy.[16] Democracy will survive only if the people of Taiwan continue to love their democracy, fight to preserve it, and practice its moral and legal precepts.

*Chapter One: Posing the Problem: The Democratization of a Chinese Society*

1. Samuel P. Huntington, *The Third Wave: Democratization in the Late Twentieth Century* (Norman: University of Oklahoma Press, 1991), p. 16. Huntington's periodization allows for overlapping and change in the years that "wave" beginnings and reversals take place, because "it is often arbitrary to attempt to specify precisely when a regime transition occurs."

2. On January 1, 1912, Dr. Sun Yat-sen became the first provisional president of the Republic of China (ROC), which claimed sovereignty over mainland China. The Cairo conference of 1943 mandated that all Chinese territories occupied by imperial Japan would revert to the ROC at the end of World War II. On October 1, 1949, Mao Zedong officially proclaimed the establishment of the People's Republic of China (PRC). The ROC government relocated to Taiwan in 1949 but still claimed sovereignty over China until June 1994, when the Mainland Affairs Council, under the Executive Yuan, published an explanatory pamphlet titled *Relations across the Taiwan Strait.* The ROC's new position was that there was only "one China" comprising "two equal political entities," the ROC and the PRC. The ROC set aside the issue of which entity had sovereignty over "one China" and urged that both political entities try to build a special relationship based on trust and cooperation until negotiations could establish democratic elections to decide how to unite these "two equal political entities" into "one China."

3. *Zhongyang ribao* (Central daily news), May 19, 1949, p. 3. Under martial law, a person could receive the death penalty if charged and found guilty of any of the following: spreading rumors to arouse public passions against the government; organizing a public gathering that turned violent; stealing property or engaging in sabotage of economic activity; organizing strikes against business in the workplace; destroying public transportation property; damaging public utilities; carrying illegal weapons and ammunition; and encouraging school or university demonstrations.

4. For a chronology of Hsu Hsin-liang's activities, see *Lianhebao* (United daily news), November 28, 1986, p. 2. When the ROC government prohibited the publication of *Meilidao* (Formosa) in Taiwan, Taiwanese intellectuals in the United States began publishing this same journal there.

5. *Meilidao,* no. 105, September 18, 1982, p. 12.

6. *Zhongguo shibao* (China times), December 4, 1986, p. 2.

7. *Zili zaobao* (Independent morning post), January 29, 1990, p. 1.

8. *Lianhebao,* January 30, 1954, p. 1.

9. Lin Zi-yao, *One Author Is Rankling Two Chinas* (Taipei: Sing Kuang Book Co., 1989), p. 39.

10. "Taiwan Regime, in Drive on Dissidents, Jails Novelist and Other Intellectuals and Long-Haired Youths," *New York Times,* July 3, 1969, p. 3.

11. Interview with Bo Yang, July 1992.

12. Ibid.

13. Li Xiaofeng, *Taiwan minzhu yundong sishinian* (Forty years of trying to promote democracy in Taiwan) (Taipei: Zili wanbaoshe wenhua chubanbu, 1991), p. 129.

14. Intellectual elite mobilization of social strata has been described in Reinhard Bendix, *Kings or People: Power and the Mandate to Rule* (Berkeley: University of California Press, 1978).

15. For introducing this concept, see Ming K. Chan, "Decolonization without Democracy: The Birth of Pluralistic Politics in Hong Kong," in *The Politics of Democratization: Generalizing East Asian Experiences,* ed. Edward Friedman (Boulder, Colo.: Westview Press, 1994), pp. 161–81. This is the best brief description of the evolution of Hong Kong's limited democracy between 1989 and 1996.

16. See Ramon H. Myers, ed., *Two Societies in Opposition: The Republic of China and the People's Republic of China after Forty Years* (Stanford, Calif.: Hoover Institution Press, 1991), p. xvii. The analytic concepts regarding political centers described here were first developed by Thomas A. Metzger and further refined through discussions with Myers.

17. David Held, *Models of Democracy* (Stanford, Calif.: Stanford University Press, 1987). For reference to these three major models of democracy, see pp. 102, 184, and 204.

18. See Myers, *Two Societies in Opposition,* pp. xviii–xix, for these ten categories that describe and confirm the distinctive features of the "political center" typology.

19. Ibid., p. xviii.

20. We borrowed this concept, though we define it rather differently, from John Higley and Richard Gunther, eds., *Elites and Democratic Consolidation in Latin America and Southern Europe* (Cambridge: Cambridge University Press, 1993).

21. Our use of the term *democracy* is based on Robert A. Dahl, *Polyarchy: Participation and Opposition* (New Haven: Yale University Press, 1971), p. 2. Dahl argues there must be at least "eight guarantees" for these three necessary conditions to correspond to democracy. They are freedom to form and join organizations; freedom of expression; right to vote; eligibility for public office; right of political leaders to compete for support as well as their right to compete for votes; alternative sources of information; free and fair elections; and institutions for making government policies that depend on votes and other expressions. All these conditions existed in the ROC as of 1996. Most students of the worldwide democratic movement argue that three conditions denote the existence of democracy: meaningful and extensive competition among individuals and groups (especially political parties) for all effective positions of government power, at regular intervals and excluding the use of force; a high level of political participation to select leaders and policies through regular and fair elections; and a

level of civil and political liberties, such as freedom of expression, freedom of the press, freedom to form and join organizations, and freedom to ensure the integrity of political competition and participation. See also Robert A. Dahl, *Democracy and Its Critics* (New Haven: Yale University Press, 1989), and Larry Diamond, "The Globalization of Democracy," in *Global Transformation and the Third World*, ed. Robert O. Slater, Barry M. Schutz, and Steven R. Dorr (Boulder, Colo.: Lynne Rienner, 1993), p. 39.

22. We are again indebted to Thomas A. Metzger for this special use of the term *political life.*

## Chapter Two: Building a New Party

1. Lai Tse-han, Ramon H. Myers, and Wei Wou, *A Tragic Beginning: The Taiwan Uprising of February 28, 1947* (Stanford, Calif.: Stanford University Press, 1991), p. 66.

2. U.S. Department of State, *The China White Paper, August 1949* (Stanford, Calif.: Stanford University Press, 1967), p. xiv. Another publication that castigated the Kuomintang and left a memorable image of ineptness and corruption in readers' minds was Theodore H. White and Annalee Jacoby's *Thunder out of China* (New York: William Sloane, 1946). White and Jacoby blistered the KMT's right-wing leaders for their failures: "Under their stewardship Chinese political thought has lost all inner fruitfulness, has become dead and sterile. Their war record of leadership was one of progressive failure; they could supply no social dynamism to rally men forward, because they saw men not as men but as servile peasants. Their wisdom was reduced to the cunning of the marketplace; their strength became only an unbending stubbornness" (p. 311).

3. *Zongtong Jiang gong dashi changbian chugao* (The preliminary draft of collected materials describing the activities of Chiang Kai-shek, president), vol. 7, pt. 2 (Taipei: n.p., 1978), p. 241. Hereafter cited in text or notes as *CTCC* with appropriate volume, part, and page numbers.

4. Edwin Pak-wah Leung, ed., *Historical Dictionary of Revolutionary China, 1839–1976* (New York: Greenwood Press, 1992), pp. 76–77.

5. *CTCC*, vol. 7, pt. 2, p. 296.

6. Zhongyang gaizao weiyuanhui (Central Reform Committee), *Zongcai guanyu dang di gaizao zhi xunshi*(The president's instructions for reconstructing the party) (Taipei: Zhongyang gaizao weiyuanhui wenwu, gongyingshe, 1959), p. 23.

7. Ibid., p. 31.

8. Zhongyang gaizao weiyuanhui (Central Reform Committee), *Dangwu baogao*(Report on party affairs), vol. 1 (Taipei: n.p., 1952), p. 34.

9. Ibid., pp. 35, 36.

10. Xu Fuming, *Zhongguo guomindang di gaizao (1950–1952)* (Reform of the Chinese Kuomintang, 1950–1952) (Taipei: Zhengzhong shuju, 1986), p. 56.

11. Ibid., p. 59. See Ramon H. Myers and Tsai Ling, "Out of the Ashes of Defeat: Revitalizing the Kuomintang in Taiwan, 1950–1952," in Bianji weiyuanhui (Editorial committee), *Zhonghua minguo jianguo bashinian xueshu taolunji* (Proceedings of conference on eighty years history of the Republic of China, 1912–1991), vol. 1 (Taipei: Jindai Zhongguo chubanshe, 1991), p. 668.

12. Xu Fuming, *Zhongguo guomindang di gaizao (1950–1952)*, p. 62 (succeeding page references are given in the text).

13. See Song Huachun, "Gaizao hou di Nantou dangwu" (Party affairs in Nantou district after the reform), *Taiwan dangwu* (Taiwan political review), no. 13 (July 16, 1951): 20–25. This journal, launched January 16, 1951, by the CRC in Taipei, informed party members about rebuilding the KMT.

14. Gao Lin, "Jiashi woshi xiaozuzhang" (If I were the team leader), *Taiwan dangwu,* no. 47 (December 16, 1952): 28–29.

15. Zhong Yi, "Xiaozu jiatinghua" (The familylike character of the small team), *Taiwan dangwu,* no. 10 (June 1, 1951): 5–6.

16. These requests can be found in every issue of *Taiwan dangwu* for the period 1950–53.

17. "Zhengqiu xindangyuan gongzuo zhuanye" (A special article on the task of selecting new party members), *Taiwan dangwu,* no. 3 (February 16, 1951): 14–16.

18. Lo Tianzhun, "Jiceng zuzhi di zhongyaoxing" (The importance of having an organizational foundation), *Taiwan dangwu,* no. 43 (October 16, 1952): 54–55.

19. *Taiwan dangwu,* no. 3 (February 16, 1951), table 6.

20. *Gaizao* (Reform), nos. 47–48 (August 1, 1952): 33, 34.

21. Dickson and others (Hung-mao Tien, ed., *The Great Transition: Political and Social Change in the Republic of China* [Stanford, Calif.: Hoover Institution Press, 1989], p. 68) prefer the term *cell* to denote the Leninist character of the KMT. See Bruce J. Dickson, "The Lessons of Defeat: The Reorganization of the Kuomintang on Taiwan, 1950–52," *China Quarterly,* no. 133 (March 1993): 56–84. We prefer *team* because a small group continually interacted with society and performed services for society.

22. The KMT members we interviewed recalled 1949–52 as a period of defeat and a sense of certain death after the communist takeover of the island. They mentioned their great relief, as having escaped certain death, after the United States came to Taiwan's defense.

23. Sidney H. Chang and Ramon H. Myers, eds., *The Storm Clouds Clear over China: The Memoir of Ch'en Li-fu, 1900–1993* (Stanford, Calif.: Hoover Institution Press, 1993), pp. 235–36.

24. Ibid., p. 236.

25. Zhong Yi, "Ruhe guwu tongzhimen di geming qingxu" (How to encourage our comrades to have a revolutionary spirit), *Taiwan dangwu,* no. 40 (September 1, 1952): 6.

26. See *Taiwan dangwu,* no. 29 (March 16, 1952): 6–7; no. 50 (February 1, 1953): 28; no. 51 (February 16, 1953): 24.

27. Jiang Jieshi, "Bendang ying jianli zili ziqiang qunce qunli di xinjingshen" (This party should build a new spirit of self-reliance and self-strengthening along with a mass strategy and the people's power), *Gaizao,* no. 11 (February 1, 1951): 1.

28. "Zongcai xunce" (The words of the leader), *Taiwan dangwu,* no. 2 (February 1, 1951): 3.

29. In brief, Sun Yat-sen's Three Principles of the People is a doctrine for how China should become independent; how to build a new Chinese political order based on Western democratic theory and a Chinese-style, five-branch government with checks and balances; and how to establish a new economic order by state policies that equalize landownership rights, develop infrastructure and manufacturing, and guide

the market to minimize inequality and dampen swings in the business cycle. For a discussion and translation of Sun Yat-sen's essential writings, see Julie Wei, Ramon H. Myers, and Donald Gillin, eds., *Prescriptions for Saving China: Selected Translations of Sun Yat-sen* (Stanford, Calif.: Hoover Institution Press, 1994).

30. "Zhengshi dangbu chengliqian women di guannian yu taidu" (Our principles and attitudes before establishing the final party headquarters), *Taiwan dangwu,* no. 17 (September 16, 1951): 3.

31. Ni Wen-ya, "Fayang renai huzhu di meide" (Propagate the virtue of charitable self-help), *Taiwan dangwu,* no. 2 (February 1, 1951): 2–3.

32. Xiao Kang, "Fayang women shengming di guanghui" (Propagate the splendor in our lives), *Taiwan dangwu,* no. 52 (March 1, 1953): 48, 49.

33. Philip Selznick, *Leadership in Administration: A Sociological Interpretation* (Berkeley: University of California Press, 1984), pp. 91–100.

34. Kou Dehou, "Ganbu jueding yiqie" (The cadres decide everything), *Taiwan dangwu,* no. 2 (February 1, 1951): 22.

35. Ibid., p. 23.

36. See Myers and Tsai, "Out of the Ashes of Defeat," p. 112, for a fuller discussion of cadre training.

37. Wang Dexiu, "Dui fazhan jiceng dangwu di jidian yijian" (Some opinions regarding the base for our party's affairs), *Taiwan dangwu,* no. 15 (August 16, 1951): 6.

38. Selznick, *Leadership in Administration,* p. 90.

39. "Xiaozu zuzhi guiding" (The rules for the small committee organization), *Taiwan dangwu,* no. 1 ( January 16, 1950): 35–37.

40. Ling Jianan, "Xianji zuzhi baochi mimi di lilun guandian" (The theoretical principles for the secret organization at the district level), *Taiwan dangwu,* no. 48 ( January 1, 1953): 11, 20–23.

41. Ibid., p. 20.

42. Hung-mao Tien states that the KMT followed Leninist guidelines but was not Leninist because its ideology was Sun Yat-sen's doctrine. See Hung-mao Tien, *The Great Transition,* p. 1. See also Tun-jen Cheng and Stephan Haggard, eds., *Political Change in Taiwan* (Boulder, Colo.: Lynne Rienner, 1992), who regard the KMT as a quasi-Leninist party, and James A. Robinson, "The KMT as a Leninist Regime: Prolegomenon to Devolutionary Leadership through Institutions," *Political Chronicle: Journal of the Florida Political Science Association* 3, no. 1 (1991): 1–8. For another view of the KMT as a quasi-Leninist party, see Constance Squires Meaney, "Liberalization, Democratization, and the Role of the KMT," in Cheng and Haggard, *Political Change in Taiwan,* p. 95.

43. Robinson, "KMT as a Leninist Regime," p. 3, cites criteria that highlight the "enduring features of Leninist organization that marked the KMT into the eighties."

44. Zhang Qiyun, *Guomindang di xinsheng* (The rebirth of the Kuomintang) (Taipei: Zhongyang wenwu gongyingshe, 1953), p. 60. This statement of party intention was also the first article of the KMT's reform committee's charter. See *Gaizao* (Reform), nos. 47–48 (August 1, 1952): 1. See also Alfred de Grazia, trans., *Roberto Michels' First Lectures in Political Sociology* (New York: Harper Torchbooks, 1965), p. 139.

45. Lennard D. Gerson, comp., *Lenin and the Twentieth Century: A Bertram D. Wolfe Retrospective* (Stanford, Calif.: Hoover Institution Press, 1985), p. 125.

46. Quoted in V. I. Lenin, *State and Revolution* (New York: International, 1932), p. 79.

47. Ken Jowitt, *New World Disorder: The Leninist Extinction* (Berkeley: University of California Press, 1992), p. 1.

48. Selznick, *Leadership in Administration*, pp. 102–12.

49. The distinction between "hard" and "soft" authoritarian or dictatorial regimes is not easy to make. Political scientists concur that a "soft" regime can allow elections, limited free press, and some free speech, as in Mexico. See Richard R. Fagen and William S. Tuchy, *Political Privilige in a Mexican City* (Stanford, Calif.: Stanford University Press, 1972). We argue below that when the opposition and ruling elites agreed to adhere to formal and informal rules, as occurred in Taiwan after the 1960s, the inhibited political center had not become "soft" but still was a "hard" regime, as reflected by the authorities' increasing censorship controls in the late 1970s and early 1980s. See note 70 in chapter 3.

50. In the early 1940s, the CCP also possessed those sectlike characteristics of the KMT of the early 1950s. After 1950 the CCP lost its sectlike qualities as it increased membership and bureaucratized. For CCP policies that transformed China into a socialist collectivized society, see Roderick MacFarquhar and John K. Fairbank, eds., *The Cambridge History of China*, vol. 14, *The People's Republic*, part 1, *The Emergence of Revolutionary China, 1949–1965* (Cambridge: Cambridge University Press, 1987), pp. 51–258.

51. Hu Muchen and Wei Xiwen, *Zhongguo guomindang yu Taiwan* (The Chinese Kuomintang and Taiwan) (n.p.: Minjian zhishi banyuekan she, 1957), p. 57.

52. Dahrendorf defines life chances as "functions of [social] ligatures and options [choices]." See Ralph Dahrendorf, *Life Changes: Approaches to Social and Political Theory* (Chicago: University of Chicago Press, 1979).

53. See Hu and Wei, *Zhongguo guomindang yu Taiwan*, pp. 65–92.

54. Ibid., pp. 61–65.

55. Ibid., pp. 92–100.

56. "Kegui di pengbo qixiang" (A very precious, lively atmosphere), *Taiwan dangwu* 45 (November 16, 1952): 34.

57. Feng Naikuan, "Taoyuan tuixing shehui gaizao yundong di shikuang" (The truth about promoting the social reform movement in Taoyuan), *Taiwan dangwu* 47 (December 16, 1952): 34.

58. "Zhongshi juban sanmin zhuyi jiangxihui jingguo" (A report on how Taichung City conducted seminars on the Three Principles of the People), *Taiwan dangwu* 66 (April 16, 1953): 37. Also *Taiwan dangwu* 60 (July 1, 1953): 57 for similar activities in Pingdong district.

59. *Taiwan dangwu* 58 (June 1, 1953): 58 for team activities in I-lan, and ibid., 63 (August 16, 1953): 54.

60. "Jieshao yige youliang xiaozu" (To introduce an excellent work team), *Taiwan dangwu* 45 (November 16, 1952): 27.

61. "Gongzuo dongtai" (Work activities), *Taiwan dangwu* 44 (November 1, 1952): 42.

62. *Taiwan dangwu* 98 (February 1, 1955): 24. The party units in Taichung were elated about the success of work teams to help elect KMT-supported candidates in the

third-term elections of 1955. Roughly 80 percent of Taichung city's council had been KMT-supported candidates.

63. Lai, Myers, and Wou, *Tragic Beginning*, pp. 183–91.

## Chapter Three: The "Inhibited" Political Center

1. *Zhongyang ribao* (Central daily news), October 11, 1952, p. 1. At the 347th meeting on May 29, 1952, in Taipei, the KMT's CRC decided to convene the Seventh KMT Congress October 10–20. Several weeks later at its 359th meeting, the CRC approved that decision; that summer the party elected 175 party representatives to the congress. See Song Qun and Yu Wencao, eds., *Zhongguo guomindang Taiwan sishinian* (A forty-year history of the Chinese Nationalist Party in Taiwan) (Changchun: Jilin wenshi chubanshe, 1990), p. 25, and Zhong Gaizhi, ed., *Qiquan dahui zhongyao wenxian* (Imported documents of the seventh party congress) (n.p., April 1953), p. 2, for Chiang's speech.

2. Zhang Pinglun and Wu Wenchen, "Guomindang zhengzhi jiaose di yenbian" (The political role and evolution of the KMT), in *Zhonghua minguo minzhuhua guocheng, zhidu yu yingxiang* (The democratization of the Republic of China: Processes, organization, and influence), ed. Chang King-yuh (Taipei: Guoli zhengzhi daxue guoji guanxi yanjiusuo, 1992), p. 130. In 1983, KMT membership allegedly reached 2,121,000 members, or 11.37 percent of the population. Taiwanese made up 70 percent of the membership.

3. Ke Dehou, "Lun zhengdang zhengzhi" (An essay on political parties and politics), *Taiwan dangwu*, no. 25 (November 16, 1952): 7.

4. See Sidney H. Chang and Ramon H. Myers, eds., *The Storm Clouds Clear over China: The Memoir of Ch'en Li-fu, 1900–1993* (Stanford, Calif.: Hoover Institution Press, 1994), p. 102.

5. Ibid., pp. 105–6.

6. Lang Yuxian and Chen Wenjun, eds., *Minguo shibanian zhi sanshiwunian zhi xuanju shi* (A history of elections in the Republic of China, 1929–1946) (Taipei: Zhongyang xuanju weiyuanhui, 1987), p. 163.

7. Ch'ien Tuan-sheng, *The Government and Politics of China, 1912–1949* (Stanford: Stanford University Press, 1970), pp. 375–81.

8. For how the First National Assembly candidates were nominated and elected, see Dong Xiangfei, ed., *Zhonghua minguo xuanju gaikuang* (The circumstances regarding elections in the Republic of China), vol. 1 (Taipei: Zhongyang xuanju weiyuanhui, 1984) pp. 52–89.

9. Miao Chuanji, ed., *Zhongguo zhixian shi ziliao huibian* (A compendium of materials on the history of establishing a constitution in China) (Taipei: Guoshiguan, 1991), p. 641.

10. Ibid., p. 642.

11. Lang and Chen, *Minguo shibanian zhi sanshiwunian zhi xuanju shi*, p. 259.

12. *Lianhebao* (United daily news), January 30, 1954, p. 1.

13. Lang and Chen, *Minguo shibanian zhi sanshiwunian zhi xuanju shi*, p. 260.

14. Ibid.

15. Ibid., pp. 262–67.

16. Between February 19 and March 25, 1954, the First National Assembly elected Chiang Kai-shek as president and Chen Cheng as vice president (Chiang also served as KMT chairman). The National Assembly reelected the same team in March 1960; in March 1966 the Assembly reelected Chiang Kai-shek, with Yen Chia-kan as his running mate; in March 1972 the Assembly reelected the same team as president and vice president; when Chiang died in 1975, Yen Chia-kan assumed the presidency and Chiang Ching-kuo became KMT chairman; in March 1978 the Assembly elected Chiang Ching-kuo as president and Hsieh Tung-min, a Taiwanese, as vice president, while Chiang retained the KMT chairmanship; finally, in March 1984 the Assembly reelected Chiang as president and elected Lee Teng-hui, a Taiwanese, as vice president, with Chiang still presiding as KMT chairman. From 1949 until January 1987, when Chiang Ching-kuo died, Chiang Kai-shek and his son were the powerful leaders holding both the presidency and KMT chairmanship, in effect ruling Taiwan as a father and son team.

17. Hungdah Chiu, *Constitutional Development and Reform in the Republic of China on Taiwan (with Documents)*, Occasional Papers/Reprint Series in Contemporary Asian Studies, 2, no. 115 (Baltimore: Law School, University of Maryland, 1993), p. 16.

18. *Lianhebao*, December 21, 1969, p. 2.

19. Miao, *Zhongguo zhixian shi ziliao huibian*, pp. 645–46. After three previous revisions, the Temporary Provisions now contained eleven articles.

20. Lai Zuyi, "Zhongyang minyi daibiao jiti mai tudi" (The central government's people's representatives collectively purchased land), *Bashi niandai* (Eighties monthly), no. 1, no. 6 (November 1979): 66.

21. Ibid., pp. 66–67.

22. Weng Pingfang, "Dangwai guoda daibiao tan guomin dahui, kankan tamen zenmo shuo" (The *dangwai* National Assembly representatives discuss the National Assembly; Let us see what they have to say!), *Guanhuai* (Care) 7 (July 5, 1982): 13.

23. Ibid.

24. Peng Laike, "Lao guoda, liwei kuai qiao guangle" (The old National Assembly delegates and the Legislative Yuan members are rapidly passing away), *Zhonggulou* (Political monitors), no. 30 (December 28, 1984): 28.

25. Weng, "Dangwai guoda daibiao tan guomin dahui," p. 15.

26. For a review of these laws, see Ming-min Peng, "Political Offences in Taiwan: Laws and Problems," *China Quarterly*, no. 45 (July–September 1971): 471–93. All guarantees of civil liberties provided in the 1947 constitution were suspended by the imposition of martial law, which allowed the government to take legal action against any individuals it judged as threatening government legitimacy, disturbing the peace, or threatening national security.

27. Yan Zhirong, "Guangfu hou Taiji minxuan jingying zhengzhi fandui zhi yanjiu" (A study of Taiwan elite political opposition and elections after the restoration of Taiwan to the Republic of China's rule, 1945–1969) (Ph.D. diss., National Cheng-chih University's Institute of the Three Principles of the People, June 1993), p. 49. (Cheng-chih is romanized below as Zhengzhi.) Many more examples of arrests, trials, imprisonment, and executions can be found in *Taiwan no seiji kaikaku nempô: Oboegaku (1943–1987)* (see table 3).

28. Ibid.

29. Ibid.

30. From interviews with government officials in the Government Information Office and the Central China News Agency. Hung-mao Tien mentions that "Douglass Mendel estimated that between 1949 and 1955, over 90,000 political dissidents were arrested and over half of them executed." See his "Taiwan in Transition: Prospects for Socio-political Change," *China Quarterly*, no. 64 (December 1975): 629. Mendel's estimate is probably too high, but so far we simply do not know the true number of people who perished during the period of "white terror."

31. For a brief history of Lei Chen's life, see Chen Zaichun, "Lei Zhen xiansheng nianpu jianbian" (A brief annual record of Mr. Lei Chen), *Bashi niandai*, no. 9 (March 1981): 89–93.

32. Zhang Zhongdong, *Hu Shi, Lei Zhen, Yin Haiguang* (Hu Shih, Lei Chen, and Yin Hai-kuang) (Taipei: Zili wanbaoshe wenhua chubanbu, 1990), p. 76.

33. Ibid., p. 77.

34. Ibid., pp. 78–79.

35. Fu Zheng, ed., *Lei Zhen zhuanji* (Collected works of Lei Chen) (Taipei: Gueiguan tushu gufen youxian gongsi, 1989), 14:60 (succeeding references are given in the text).

36. Yan, "Guangfu hou Taiji minxuan jingying zhengzhi fandui zhi yanjiu," p. 50.

37. In *Meilidao* (Beautiful Formosa) 1, no. 2 (September 1979): 66, one article complained that the government closed magazines that were not communist-subversive. In *Meilidao* 1, no. 3 (October 1979): 7, an essay called for complete reform of the First National Assembly because that it did not represent China. On page 9, Fei Hsi-ping questioned Premier Sun Yun-suan as to why Taiwan's people could not organize political parties as guaranteed by the 1947 constitution and Sun's Three Principles of the People.

38. Minzhong ribao congshu (The daily masses compendium) *Meilidao shijian shimo* (The complete Meilidao incident) (Taipei: Minzhong ribao chubanshe, 1980), pp. 6–7.

39. See the detailed account by Taiwan renquan xiehui (Taiwan Human Rights Association), comp., *Gaoxiong shijian zhuanji* (A special report on the Kaohsiung incident) (Lencadia, Calif.: Taiwan renquan xiehui, 1980), pp. 16–29. Yao and Qiu were brutally beaten without reason.

40. Several journalists examined the Kaohsiung incident and discovered great discrepancies and conflicting stories. See Huang Defu, Huang Ji, and Chen Zhongjing, "Meilidao shijian; Zhenxiang zhuizong ji" (Undertaking an investigation to discover the truth about the Meilidao incident), *Zhonge zazhi* (Miscellany), nos. 134–37 (January–April 1980): 52–60. The authors relate that the police claimed to have pictures showing Yao and Ch'iu had not been beaten and that the prisoners had later injured themselves.

41. John Kaplan, *The Court-Martial of the Kaohsiung Defendants* (Berkeley: Institute of East Asian Studies, University of California, 1981), p. 17; *Zonghe yuekan* (Scooper monthly), no. 134 (January 1980), p. 54; see also Zhao Shaosheng, *Meilidao baodong shilu* (A true record of the Meilidao violence) (Taipei: Huanghe zazhi chubanshe, 1980), p. 60.

42. *Lianhebao*, December 12, 1980, p. 3.

43. Ibid.

44. See Taiwan renquan xiehui, *Gaoxiong shijian zhuanji*, p. 38.

45. Kaplan, *Court-Martial of the Kaohsiung Defendants*, p. 18.

46. Huang, Huang, and Cheng, "Meilidao shijian," p. 60.

47. The director-general, James C. Y. Soong of the ROC Government Information Office, made this statement. See Han Sheng, "Cechuan Meilidao baoxing zhenxiang" (A review of the true facts surrounding the Meilidao violence), *Youshi yuekan* (Youth monthly) 51–52, no. 1–6 (February 1980): 55.

48. Ibid.

49. *Zhonghua minguo xuanju shi*, pp. 523–24.

50. Ibid., pp. 528–29. The new election laws stipulated the criteria for qualified individuals to register as candidates and described the political behavior appropriate for competing in elections. These laws governed multimember district elections; anyone in the allowable quota of electable individuals could declare victory on receiving the highest number of votes.

51. Ibid., p. 521.

52. Ibid., p. 537.

53. Ibid., p. 540. For local election results from 1950 to 1980, see Dong Xiangfei, comp., *Zhonghua minguo xuanju gaikuang* (The election results of the Republic of China), vol. 2 (Taipei: Zhongyang xuanju weiyuanhui, 1984).

54. *Ziyou Zhongguo* (Free China) 16, no. 17 (April 1, 1957): 221.

55. Ibid. The Taiwanese candidate Xu Xinzhi, who easily could have defeated his KMT rival, was informed the day before voters cast their ballots that he must immediately begin serving his military draft. Xu had to withdraw. Were local elections rigged by the KMT? We have not discovered any such cases as yet.

56. See Tao Pai-chuan, ed., *Taiwan haineng genghao ma?* (Can Taiwan be even better?) (Taipei: Jingshi shuju, 1980), pp. 26–27.

57. Arthur J. Lerman, "National Elite and Local Politician in Taiwan," *American Political Science Review* 71, no. 4 (December 1977): 1406–22. Lerman correctly predicted that the national elite would not try "to rely on its own background and skills to determine what the will and needs of the people are" (p. 1421). Local politicians supported local elections and benefited from them, so that the national elite, as a nonelected group of outsiders, did not dare "repress the real elected leaders of the majority community." Ideologically committed to democracy, the KMT wanted to promote it while regulating its scope; when new conditions and pressures materialized, the KMT changed the rules to expand democracy.

58. Arthur J. Lerman, *Taiwan's Politics: The Provincial Assemblyman's World* (Washington, D.C.: University Press of America, 1978), pp. 53–57.

59. See Zhao Junwu, "Toushi xiajie difang xuanju; duoxiang biange duanqinei jueding" (Investigating the next term local elections; many reforms will soon be decided), *Liaowang zhoukan* (Outlook weekly), no. 1 (March 18, 1967): 24.

60. For improving the quality of political candidates, see *Liaowang zhoukan*, no. 3 (April 1, 1967): 24; for the importance of factions to elect political candidates, see Huang Te-fu, "Local Factions, Party Competition, and Political Democratization in Taiwan," *Guoli zhengzhi daxue xuebao* (Journal of National Zhengzhi University), no. 61 (June 1990): 723–45. Huang argues that local factions were a by-product of the multiple-candidate election system, or what he refers to as the "single non-transferable" election system. This same system helped the KMT to postpone opposition party

politics while fostering gradual, grassroots democratization. For factions in local elections, see Zhao Junwu, "Toushi xiajie difang xuanju; duoxiang bian> ge duanqinei jueding" (The next term local elections), *Liaowang zhoukan* (News weekly), no. 32 (October 21, 1967): 25–26. See also Zhao's article in the same magazine, no. 33 (October 28, 1967): 25–26 and no. 39 (December 9, 1967): 21–22.

61. "Taiwan xuanju zhidu di tese yu queshi" (Special features and deficiencies of Taiwan's local election system), *Shaodang zhoukan* (Challenge weekly), no. 93 (November 11, 1981): 23 and 30.

62. Li Xiaofeng, *Taiwan minzhu yundong sishinian* (The forty-year Taiwan democracy movement) (Taipei: Zili wanbaoshe wenhua chubanbu, 1991), p. 22.

63. Ibid., p. 124.

64. John F. Copper, with George P. Chen, *Taiwan's Elections: Political Development and Democratization in the Republic of China,* Occasional Papers/Reprint Series in Contemporary Asian Studies, no. 5 (Baltimore: University of Maryland Law School, 1984), p. 56. Between 1957 and 1989, the year 1977 marked the lowest percentage of seats won by the KMT: 72.73. For the period 1951 to 1985, the same was true for *xian* magistrates and city mayor elections, only 80 percent; this same pattern was reflected for the percentage of seats won by the KMT in the 1977 election for Taipei municipal council seats. See statistical tables in James A. Robinson, "The KMT as a Leninist Regime," *Political Chronicle* 3, no. 1 (1991): 1–8.

65. Based on interviews with top KMT officials in 1992–93.

66. *Lianhebao,* December 17, 1978, p. 3.

67. The discussion below is based on Copper and Chen, *Taiwan's Elections,* pp. 66–72; they state that "the 1980 precedent-setting election appeared to mark a transition from what theorists would call an authoritarian-technocrat system to a democratic-development one" (p. 72). We regard this election as a successful experiment in playing by the rules of democratic politics.

68. Our discussion is based on Thomas A. Metzger, "The Chinese Reconciliation of Moral-Sacred Values with Modern Pluralism: Political Discourse in the ROC, 1949–1989," in *Two Societies in Opposition: The Republic of China and the People's Republic of China after Forty Years,* ed. Ramon H. Myers (Stanford, Calif.: Hoover Institution Press, 1991), pp. 3–56.

69. We owe this point to Thomas A. Metzger from private conversations and his writings.

70. Tien Hung-mao, "Quanwei zhengdang guojia di zhuanxing: Taiwan fazhan jingyan," in Chang King-yuh, *Zhonghua minguo minzhuhua guocheng, zhidu yu yingxiang,* p. 70.

| Year | Number of Incidents | Confiscated Materials | Suspended Publication |
|------|---------------------|-----------------------|-----------------------|
| 1980 | 16 | 9 | 7 |
| 1981 | 1913 | 6 | |
| 1982 | 27 | 23 | 4 |
| 1983 | 33 | 26 | 7 |
| 1984 | 211 | 176 | 35 |
| 1985 | 275 | 260 | 15 |

71. Huang Hua, "Jianxingren tan guoshi" (A person whose sentence has been commuted discusses the nation's affairs), *Taiwan zhenglun* (Taiwan political review), no. 2 (September 1975): 43. Huang Hua's case is like that of the mainland dissident Wei Jingshen, who had served a long term of imprisonment in the 1980s, was released, and promptly resumed his criticisms of the PRC's lack of democracy. Wei was arrested in 1994 and sentenced in January 1995 to another long prison term.

72. Ibid.

73. Huang Hua, "Jianxingren di xinxin" (The beliefs of a prisoner whose sentence was commuted), *Taiwan zhenglun,* no. 3 (October 1975): 39.

74. Ibid.

75. Huang Hua, "Xiangren wei guo zhidao" (To be mutually tolerant is the way for the nation), *Taiwan zhenglun,* no. 4 (November 1975): 13.

76. The *Taiwan Political Review* also tried to delegitimize the First National Assembly by demanding that the government allow opposition parties to form, condemning the government for favoring offspring of mainlanders over native Taiwanese for university entrance, claiming the election system was unfair, arguing that the press was government controlled, and demanding the lifting of martial law. See Daniel K. Berman, *Words Like Colored Glass: The Role of the Press in Taiwan's Democratization Process* (Boulder, Colo.: Westview Press, 1992), p. 184.

77. "Women juexin wei yanlun ziyou fendou daodi" (We are determined to struggle to the end for free speech), *Meilidao* 1, no. 2 (September 1979): 66.

78. Fei Hsi-ping, "Xianzhi zudang shifou weixian, xiang xingzhengyuan tichu zhixun" (I asked the premier of the Executive Yuan if it is unconstitutional to limit and prevent parties from organizing), *Meilidao* 1, no. 3 (October 1979): 9.

79. Hong Sanxiong, *Fenghuo dujuancheng: Qishi niandai Taiwan daxuesheng yundong* (The city of the beacon: The student movement at National Taiwan University in the 1970s) (Taipei: Zili wanbaoshe wenhua chubanbu, 1993), pp. 94–95, for a description of the role of this office at National Taiwan University.

80. Deng Biyun, *Bashi niandai Taiwan xuesheng yundong shi* (A history of the Taiwan student movement in the 1980s) (Taipei: Qianwei chubanshe, 1993), pp. 3–5.

## Chapter Four: Legitimating a Political Opposition

1. In 1972 Kang Ning-hsiang introduced the term "no party, no faction" *(wudang wupai)* to distinguish himself from other election candidates. In 1975 Kuo Yu-hsin ran for the Legislative Yuan and called himself a nonparty person *(dangwai renshi),* and thereafter this term distinguised those political opponents who increasingly attacked the KMT as not being democratic and not promoting democracy fast enough. See Wang Xiaobo, "Taiwan di qiantu cong minzhu dao tongyi" (The future of Taiwan, from democracy to unification) (Taipei: Siji chuban shiye gongsi, 1981). See also Fan Yigong, "Xianjieduan di 'dangwai' " (The present stage of the *"dangwai"*), *Guanhuai zazhi* (CARE magazine), 28 (March 5, 1984): 38.

2. Wang To, *Dangwai di shengyin* (The voices of nonparty people) (Taipei: Changchao chubanshe, 1978). The Taiwanese Wang To was born in the poor fishing village of Badouzi. He graduated from National Zhengzhi University and became a famous

writer. This book is a series of interviews with leading *dangwai* politicians (p. 13). Succeeding page references are given in the text.

3. This question was raised in Xuanju ziliaoshi (Office for Election Materials), "Guomindang bixu huida yibaige wenti" (One hundred questions that the KMT ought to answer), *Bashi niandai* (Eighties monthly), no. 87 (October 25, 1985): 52.

4. Song Jitai, "Cong jingjiquan di fali tan Taiwan jieyan tizhi" (We can discuss Taiwan's martial law from the point of view of "emergency legal provisions"), *Nuanliu zazhi* (Current monthly), no. 114 (May 19, 1986): 9.

5. Ibid.

6. See editorial page by Lei Yuqi, "Qing Xingzhengyuan tongxia zhenben zhenshi wanjiu shehui weiji" (Please ask the Executive Yuan to act with determination to save our society from its current crisis), *Xinxingxiang* (New image), no. 13 (January 1983): 8.

7. Ibid.

8. Chen Yanghao, "Jin! Jin! Jin!" (Prohibit! prohibit! prohibit!), *Nuanliu zazhi* (Current monthly), no. 19 (January 20, 1984): 5. See also Chen Beidi, "Jinshu daguan" (A comprehensive overview of written censorship), *Bashi niandai*, no. 6 (November 1979): 28–37, for a listing of more than fifty examples of periodicals being closed down by the authorities.

9. Yu Yuehua, "Muwu xianfa di jinshu zhengce" (The policy of written censorship disregards the constitution), *Bashi niandai*, no. 6 (November 1979): 25.

10. Chen, "Jin! Jin! Jin!" p. 6.

11. Jiang Qunnan, editorial page, *Yazhouren* (Asian weekly), no. 17 (October 1982): 1. Jiang pointed out that the minister of interior, Lin Yang-kang, had told the Legislative Yuan that "the reason the government prohibits political parties is because the political behavior of an opposition party could divide society. That party also might not be vigilantly concerned about our national interests." Other officials stated that the "KMT has not yet completed the mission to recover the mainland," and "we already have three political parties." These were the stock answers the government used to rebut opposition demands to legalize multiple political parties.

12. Zheng Qianhe, "Yazi waijiao, kaizi waijiao" (The foreign policy of "doing nothing" and "spending foolishly"), *Bashi niandai*, no. 79 (August 17–23,1985): 36–37.

13. Jiang Liangren, "Zhengtan shang di wannianqing—Shen Chang-huan" (Shen Chang-huan is an evergreen tree on the political stage), *Bashi niandai*, no. 87 (October 19–25, 1985): 22.

14. Ibid., p. 24.

15. Editorial page titled "Guomindang di dalu zhengce" (The KMT's policy toward the mainland), *Yazhouren*, no. 22 (March 1983): 1.

16. See interview with an eighty-nine-year-old man who compared life under early Japanese colonial rule with that under KMT rule and stressed the unpredictable, chaotic life in Taiwan of the early 1980s, in Zhang Deming, "Congsu jianli shehui di fazhi chixu" (Speedily build a society based on legal harmony), *Yazhouren*, no. 23 (April 1, 1983): 26–29. The author claims that "the main reason we have not been able to build a society having legal harmony is because there basically is no freedom to criticize, no checks and balances, and no power of oversight" (p. 27).

17. Lü Nian, "Haoxi kailuo" (The opening of a good opera), *Yazhouren*, no. 23 (April 1, 1983): 18.

18. Ibid., p. 18. This critic went on to say that these legislators "do not know which year they were born or what world they belonged to" (p. 17).

19. Wu Feng-shan, *Wo neng wei quojia zuoxie shenmo?* (What can I do for my country?) (Taipei: Yuanjing chubanshe, 1978), p. 36.

20. Kang Ning-hsiang, "Baoxian, huxian, xingxian" (To preserve the constitution, protect the constitution, and enforce the constitution), *Yazhouren*, no. 23 (April 1, 1983): 33.

21. Ibid.

22. Huang Huangxiong, "Dangwai zai chufa" (The *dangwai* again take off), *Bashi niandai*, no. 16 (November 1981): 14. As one critic said, "In the 1970s the focus now shifted toward achieving an election equivalence with the ruling party" (p. 15).

23. Zheng Deming, "Junheng yu zhengdang zhengce" (The political policy of checks and balances and party politics), *Bashi niandai*, no. 16 (November 1981): 16.

24. Ibid.

25. Liu Zhijie, "Xuanju di guancha yu chensi" (Observations and reflections about the election), *Bashi niandai*, no. 8 (February 1981): 6. Even though KMT candidates spent lavishly for banquets and gifts to persuade voters, they were defeated.

26. Huang Yueqing, "Jianli zhengchang xuanju zhidu" (To establish an appropriate election system), *Bashi niandai*, no. 8 (February 1981): 11.

27. Sima Wenwu, "Dangwai suixianglu" (Random thoughts expressed by non-KMT politicians), *Nuanliu* (Current monthly), no. 10 (April 1983): 14.

28. Ling Ce, "Taiwan xuanmin toupiao xingwei chutan" (A preliminary study of the behavior of Taiwan voters), *Nuanliu*, no. 13 (July 1983): 36.

29. For these observations and those below, see ibid., pp. 38–39. After the victory of several *dangwai* candidates in 1980, a public survey carried out by the *Minzhong Daily* showed that the *dangwai* might win 35 percent of the popular votes. See Li Dichuan, "Quanli kaituo Gaoxiongshi di dangwai piaoyuan" (Let's go full blast to promote the election of *dangwai* candidates in Kaohsiung City), *Nuanliu*, no. 13 (July 1983): 30. As was so often the case, too many *dangwai* politicians shared an unwarranted optimism about voters' attitudes and beliefs. *Dangwai* success in scattered elections did not guarantee that an upward trend of popular support for *dangwai* candidates would continue.

30. Gao Wuxiong, "Wohu canglong di Gaoxiong" (Kaohsiung—the sleeping tiger and a dragon's lair), *Nuanliu*, no. 10 (April 1983): 46.

31. Ibid., p. 47.

32. Ibid.

33. Ibid., p. 48.

34. Gao Wuxiong, "Haojiu chen wongdi" (Good wine settles out in its container), *Nuanliu*, no. 11 (May 1983): 55.

35. Ibid., pp. 57–58.

36. Ibid.

37. Ibid., pp. 58–59.

38. *Lifayuan gongbao* (Proceedings of the Legislative Yuan), 17, no. 24 (March 24,

1981): 4–7. Six of the ten who signed were Fei Hsi-ping, Kang Ning-hsiang, Huan Huangxiong, Xu Runzshu, Huang Tienfu, and Zheng Deming.

39. Ibid., p. 4.

40. *Lifayuan gongba* 70, no. 23 (March 21, 1981): 5.

41. Ibid.

42. *Lifayuan gongbao* 71, no. 22 (March 17, 1982): 4.

43. Ibid., p. 6.

44. Ibid.

45. Ibid., p. 30.

46. "Bashi niandai minzhu zhengzhi fazhan" (Democratic political development in the 1980s), *Bashi niandai*, no. 9 (March 1981): 4–50.

47. Ibid., p. 13.

48. Ibid., p. 37.

49. Ibid., p. 39.

50. Ibid.

51. Ibid., p. 48.

52. See the appendix of Robert Bellah et al., *Habits of the Heart* (Berkeley: University of California Press, 1985).

53. John Dunn, *Rethinking Modern Political Theory: Essays, 1979–83* (Cambridge: Cambridge University Press, 1985), p. 8. We thank Thomas A. Metzger for his suggestion to refer to Dunn's concepts as forms of "advertising." We have added a fourth.

54. *Zhongyang ribao* (Central daily news), February 16, 1980, p. 1. We gratefully acknowledge the assistance of Thomas A. Metzger for the sources and quotes cited in this section.

55. Sun Yat-sen, *The Three Principles of the People: San Min Chu I, with Two Supplementary Chapters by President Chiang Kai-shek* (Taipei: Government Information Office, 1990), p. 326.

56. *Zhongyang ribao*, international ed., May 7, 1979, p. 3.

57. *Zhongyang ribao*, April 21, 1979, p. 1.

58. Nan Min, "Dangwai jinru qianchengdang shiqi" (The *dangwai* enters the pre-political party period), *Jiushi niandai* (Nineties) 197 (June 1986): 48.

59. Ibid.

60. Ibid.

61. Our comments about Chinese political culture in this section are drawn from Metzger's unpublished paper, "Political Repression and Political Culture in Contemporary Taiwan: The Kaohsiung Incident of December 10, 1979."

62. Thomas A. Metzger, *Escape from Predicament: Neo-Confucianism and China's Evolving Political Culture* (New York: Columbia University Press, 1977), chap. 3.

63. *Zhongyang ribao*, international ed,, December 30, 1979, p. 1.

64. *Shelun* (editorial), *Ziyou zhongguo* (Free China), 12, no. 2 (January 16, 1955): 1.

65. See *Zhongyang ribao*, February 11, 1980, p. 2; Bao siwen, "Zhonglun zazhi di xinxingshi" (The new characteristics of Chinese journals," *Shibao zhoukan* (China times weekly), January 27, 1980, p. 7; Zuo Gumo, "Ping Meilidao di baoli minzhu" (An evaluation of Meilidao's violent style of democracy), *Shibao zhoukan*, December 1979–January 1980, p. 7; Xuan Yuansui, "Dangwai renshi yu Gaoxiong shijian" (The *dangwai*

people and the Kaohsiung incident), *Mingbao yuekan* (Ming Pao monthly), February 1980, pp. 23–35; Peng Huaien, "Meilidao Gaoxiong shijian dui woguo minzhu fazhan di yingxiang" (The influence of the Meilidao incident in Kaohsiung district on the development of our nation's democracy), *Shibao zhoukan,* December 23, 1979, p. 7; Xia Zonghan, "Gaoxiong shijian pingyi" (An evaluation of the Kaohsiung incident), February 1980, pp. 37–45.

66. *Lianhebao* (United daily news), November 22, 1977, p. 7.

67. Ibid.

68. "Yefang Xu Xin-liang tan minzhu yu fazhi" (An evening talk with Hsu Hsin-liang on democracy and the legal system), *Zonghe yuekan* (Scooper monthly) 170 (January 1, 1978): 27. Hsu magnanimously praised the KMT, saying, "Although the KMT had a small setback in the election, their policies were pretty good, and their workers represent that party's success" (p. 15).

69. Ibid., p. 28. Hsu goes on to say: "The KMT has continuously promoted local elections. Therefore, the past twenty years the KMT has cultivated the voters' political awareness."

70. *Shelun* (editorial), *Lianhebao,* November 20, 1977, p. 3.

71. *Lianhebao,* November 22, 1977, p. 2.

72. *Shelun* (editorial), *Lianhebao,* November 22, 1977, p. 2.

73. Ibid.

74. John F. Copper, "Taiwan's Recent Election: Progress towards a Democratic System," *Asian Survey* 21, no. 10 (October 1981): 1034.

75. *Lianhebao,* December 7, 1980, p. 2.

76. Ibid. Yang went on to say: "The ruling party was self-disciplined and self-controlled, to show great progress. The election atmosphere was much better than in the past. One heard of bribery but not on any large scale."

77. Ibid.

78. Ibid. Foreign scholars also affirmed the significance of this election as demonstrating the regime's willingness to grant greater tolerance of a political opposition and revitalize ROC political institutions. See Richard L. Engstrom and Chu Chi-hung, "The Impact of the 1980 Supplementary Election on Nationalist China's Legislative Yuan," *Asian Survey* 24, no. 4 (April 1984): 447–458. See also Copper, "Taiwan's Recent Election, n. 48.

79. *Lianhebao,* December 8, 1980, p. 3.

80. Ibid.

81. *Lianhebao,* December 9, 1980, p. 2

82. Ibid.

*Chapter Five: Chiang Ching-kuo and the Decision to Democratize*

1. Some six hundred representatives and delegates attended the Tenth Party Congress (March 29 and April 9, 1969). By December 31, 1969, the party had 919,327 members, 86,772 teams, and 6,756 party unit areas *(qu).* See Zhongyang weiyuanhui (Central Committee), *Dangwu gongzuo baogao: Zhongguo guomindang di shici quanguo daibiaohui* (A report on our party's work: The Chinese Kuomintang Tenth Congress) (n.p.: n.d. [marked "top secret"]), p. 5.

2. See *Time* magazine, Asia edition, August 23, 1993, pp. 20–22. We thank Professor Tun-jen Cheng for the spring 1994 KMT announcement of party asset holding valuation. More recent estimates cite KMT assets valued at US$3 billion and as high as US$20 billion. According to Julian Baum's account, the KMT invests in more than one hundred companies and the party's top ten companies generated about US$100 million income in 1993. See Julian Baum, "The Money Machine," *Far Eastern Economic Review* 157, no. 32 (August 11, 1994): 62–64.

3. Hung-mao Tien, ed., *The Great Transition: Political and Social Change in the Republic of China* (Stanford, Calif.: Hoover Institution Press, 1989), p. 76, for a chart of the KMT's organization and roles in the late 1970s.

4. Some Western scholars have described KMT policies and rule as a *development-oriented authoritarian system*. See Jürgen Domes, "Political Differentiation in Taiwan: Group Formation within the Ruling Party and the Opposition Circles, 1979–1980," *Asian Survey* 21, no. 10 (October 1981): 1011. This term means that power is concentrated among a few elite groups; that power is used for development purposes and not to maintain entrenched interest groups; that various elite groups manage and represent different sectors of the polity; and that some political opposition is tolerated.

5. A survey of these developments can be found in Ramon H. Myers, "The Economic Transformation of the Republic of China on Taiwan," *China Quarterly*, no. 99 (September 1984): 500–528.

6. Our account of Chiang Ching-kuo's early life is based on the following: Howard L. Boorman and Richard C. Howard, eds., *Biographical Dictionary of Republican China*, vol. 1 (New York: Columbia University Press, 1967), pp. 306–12; Peng Weiwen, ed., "Jiang zongtong Jiang gong xiansheng dashi jianbian" (A brief account of the major happenings in the life of the president, Mr. Chiang Ching-kuo), *Chuanjian* (Global view monthly), December 1, 1987, pp. 26–27; Jiang Nan, *Jiang Jingguo zhuan* (A biography of Chiang Ching-kuo) (Los Angeles: Luntanbao, 1984), p. 15.

7. See mimeographed English copy of *Chen Jieru Jiang Zhuan* (The biography of Chen Jieru and Chiang Kai-shek) (n.p.: n.d. [archives of the Hoover Institution]), p. 127. When Jieru met Chiang Kai-shek's first wife, Chiang Fuk-mei, several months earlier in Fenghua county, Fuk-mei (Madame Mao) had described Ching-kuo as a "good boy and very sensible, but terribly afraid of his father" (p. 107).

8. Ibid., p. 129.

9. Ibid., pp. 131–32.

10. Wang Sheng, *Wo so liaojie di Jiang zongtong, Jingguo xiansheng* (The president, Mr. Chiang Ching-kuo, whom I know) (Taipei: Liming wenhua gongsi, 1981), p. 4.

11. Former officials like Chen Li-fu, Yü Kuo-Hwa, and Sun Yun-Suan assert that Chiang Ching-kuo firmly believed in Sunist doctrine (interviews with Sun and Yu in 1990 and with Chen in 1992). In our interview with Chang Tsu-yi, he claimed that Chiang's Sunist ideas were responsible for his promoting democracy in the ROC. Chiang's strategy was to use martial law to prevent communist subversion while improving Taiwan's socioeconomic conditions. In the distant future martial law could be lifted and democracy developed. For Chiang Ching-kuo, *sanmin zhuyi* meant freedom, democracy, and a fairly equitable distribution of wealth and income.

12. Chiang Ching-kuo, "Women shi renmin di gongpu" (We are the servants of the people), in *Jiang Jingguo xiansheng quanji* (Collected works of Mr. Chiang Ching-kuo),

comp. Jiang Jingguo xiansheng zhuanji bianji weiyuanhui (Editorial Committee for the Collected Works of Mr. Chiang Ching-kuo), vol. 1 (Taipei: Government Information Office, 1991), p. 95. For other examples of Chiang's emphasis on *sanmin zhuyi*, see vol. 12, pp. 186, 335–37, 372, 416–20, 521, 538–42, 545–46, and 581–83. Cited hereafter as *CCKCC*, with appropriate volume and page numbers.

13. See Chang Lin, "Jiangxi Gannan shiqi di Chiang zhuanyuan" (Chiang's special duties while serving in the southern districts of Jiangxi Province), in *Jiang Jingguo di shuibian* (The different careers of Chiang Ching-kuo) (Taipei: Dangan congkan bianji weiyuanhui, 1985), pp. 12–24.

14. For Chiang Ching-kuo's role in the Nationalist recovery of Manchuria after 1945, see Donald Gillin and Ramon H. Myers, eds., *Last Chance in Manchuria: The Diary of Chang Kia-ngau* (Stanford, Calif.: Hoover Institution Press, 1989).

15. Wu Guozhen (author of handwritten manuscript), Huang Zhuozhun (recorder), and Liu Yungcheng (editor), *Wu Guozhen zhuan* (The biography of Wu Kuo-chen) (Taipei: Zuyou shibao, 1995), pp. 447–48.

16. Ibid., p. 453.

17. Ibid., p. 458. Wu also charged Chiang Kai-shek and his son with being responsible for launching the "white terror" campaign of the early 1950s. "They lost mainland China, and they now only have Taiwan, so they have established a self-defense system which is extreme in its form. Their attitude is that one cannot be soft in dealing with enemies. If there is a choice, it is better to kill three thousand people than to miss one important enemy" (p. 448).

18. Edwin A. Winckler, "Elite Political Struggle, 1945–1985," in *Contending Approaches to the Political Economy of Taiwan,* ed. Edwin A. Winckler and Susan Greenhalgh (Armonk, N.Y.: M. E. Sharpe, 1988), p. 158.

19. Interview with Chang Tsu-yi.

20. Ihara Kichinosuke, *Taiwan no seiji kaikaku nempō oboegaku (1943–1987)* (Taiwan political reform yearbook memoir [1943–1987]) (Nara, Japan: Tezukayama University, Department of Liberal Arts, 1992), pp. 221–22.

21. *CCKCC*, 14:243 (succeeding page references are given in the text).

22. On December 28, 1975, Chiang stated: "Our national plan in the short term is to defend the offshore islands and Taiwan. Our national plan in the long term is to recover the China mainland and build a Republic of China based on the Three Principles of the People" (ibid., 10:540).

23. Our emphasis of this first-time statement by Chiang.

24. Our emphasis to show Chiang equated democracy with Confucian ethics.

25. Song Zuli, *Guoce, guoshi, guoyun* (Our nation's policies, state of affairs, and destiny) (Taipei: Guanghua chuban gongsi, 1979), p. 13.

26. The biographical account by Wang Sheng often lapses into the legendary (note 10).

27. Jiang Nan, *Jiang Jingguo zhuan* (A biography of Chiang Ching-kuo) (Monte Bello, Calif.: Meiguo luntanbao, 1985); and Liu Yungxi, *Jiang Jingguo zai Tai sanshinian* (Chiang Ching-kuo's thirty years in Taiwan) (Hong Kong: Dalian yinshua gongsi, 1985).

28. Our comments below about Chiang are based on interviews with government officials such as Chang Tsu-yi, who prepared his speeches and served as deputy secre-

tary-general of the Office of the President from 1976 until the late 1980s, and Jiao Renhe, director of the Confidential Information Section of the Office of the President in August 1992.

29. Liu, *Jiang Jingguo zai Tai sanshinian*, p. 238. Chiang noted these same qualities in Lee Teng-hui, and the two men became very close in Chiang's final years.

30. Ibid.

31. Ibid., pp. 238, 246, 247, 253.

32. Interview with Chang Tsu-yi.

33. Ibid.

34. Based on interview with Wei Xiaomeng, the daughter of James Wei.

35. Based on an interview with former premier Lee Huan in summer 1992.

36. See Parris Chang, "Taiwan in 1983: Setting the Stage for Power Transition," *Asian Survey* 24, no. 1 (January 1984): 122–23, who states that the government took no action against politicians in the 1983 elections but severely banned their magazines.

37. Interview with Sun Yun-suan in 1992.

38. For a discussion of these ten projects see Song, *Guoce, guoshi, guoyun*, p. 41. They were the following: the north-south superhighway; a nuclear power plant; Taoyuan International Airport; China Steel Corporation; China Shipbuilding Corporation; Petroleum-Chemical Corporation; Taichung harbor development; electrification of railways; Pei-hua Railroad; and Suao harbor development.

39. Xu Li, "Jiangjia zhi xia jueqi di zhishu guanliao" (The technocrat-bureaucrats who have been promoted during the rule of the Chiang family), *Minzhu zhengzhi* (*Democratic politics*, no. 40 (November 21, 1984): 27.

40. Ibid., p. 28.

41. Zhang Bojia, "Cong zongtong daxuan dao Guomindang quanli zhuanhuan" (From the presidential election to the change in KMT power), *Guanhuai zazhi* (*CARE magazine*) 26 (January 5, 1984): 34. See also Maria Hsia-Chang, "Political Succession in the Republic of China on Taiwan," *Asian Survey* 24, no. 4 (April 1984): 423–46. The author examines a number of possible vice presidential choices for Ching-kuo and argues that Sun would be the ideal running mate and successor.

42. Zhang, "Cong zongtong daxuan dao Guomintang quanli zhuanhuan," p. 35.

43. Li Ru-shui, "Li Denghui you zheige jihuima?" (Does Lee Teng-hui have a chance?), *Zhengchijia*, no. 9 (April 10, 1984): 9.

44. Yan Yinmo, "Li Denghui yu Taiwan weilai" (Lee Teng-hui and Taiwan's future), *Zhengchijia*, no. 2 (February 21, 1984): 21. The Taiwanese vice president at the time, Sheh Tung-min, was reported to have been eager to continue as Ching-kuo's running mate.

45. Yang Aili, *Sun Yunxuan zhuan* (A biography of Sun Yun-suan) (Taipei: Tianxia zazhi, 1989), p. 260, 261.

46. He Su, "Taiwanren zidi toujiao zhengrong" (Taiwan's children now compete), *Zhengchijia*, no. 3 (February 28, 1984): 6.

47. Sima Wenwu, "Shui gan jie Jiang Jingguo di ban?" (Who dares to succeed Chiang Ching-kuo?), *Bashi niandai* (Eighties monthly), special issue (February 22, 1984), p. 7.

48. Interviews with various party elders.

49. Liu, *Jiang Jingguo zai Tai sanshinian*, p. 250. In Hao Pei-tsun's diary of his

recollections of Chiang Ching-kuo, Hao remarks that "after Vice President Hsieh decided to retire, if there was any necessity to nominate a Taiwanese vice president, Lee Teng-hui would be the number one candidate." Hao went on to praise Lee's educational qualifications, character, and religious beliefs. He also related that Chiang had told him he selected Lee Teng-hui because political circumstances necessitated appointing a Taiwanese vice president and that the nation needed to have able Taiwanesem assume high leadership positions. See Hao Pei-tsun, *Jingguo Xianshen Wannian* (The late years of Mr. Chiang Ching-kuo), ed. Wan Lixing) (Taipei: Tianxia wenhua chuban gufen youxian gongsi, 1995), p. 130.

50. See Xiang Lin, "Shui gai cheng 'dangjin' zhi jiu?" (Who can shoulder the blame for suppressing the formation of a political party?"), *Qiuhaitang* (Begonia magazine) 43 (June 1, 1986): 35.

51. Lin Antai, "Jiang Jingguo neng tupo minzhu pingjing ma?" (Can Chiang Ching-kuo break the democratic bottleneck?), *Zongheng zhoukan* (Comprehensive weekly) 110, no. 63 (October 1986): 14.

52. Ibid., p. 15.

53. Ibid., p. 13.

54. Based on interviews with Vice President Lee Teng-hui in 1986.

55. To our knowledge, no KMT top leaders ever privately proposed or publicly advocated immediate political reform. There seems to have been general agreement in their ranks that the status quo was satisfactory. Our interviews with party leaders like Mah Soo-lay and others also lead us to believe that not one top KMT official was even aware that Chiang planned political reform at the party's March 1986 Third Plenum. Yet Lee Huan reminded us that Chiang Ching-kuo, as early as the mid-1970s, had talked to him about the necessity of the KMT's undertaking another reform like that launched between 1950 and 1952.

56. Such events are mentioned in *Taiwan no seiji kaikaku nempō*, p. 284.

57. Yun-han Chu, *Crafting Democracy in Taiwan* (Taipei: Institute for National Policy Research, 1992), p. 55, for percentage share of votes in regional districts and occupational districts in elections of 1980 and 1983, and p. 57 for distribution of seats in the Legislative Yuan. In 1980 and 1983 the KMT won fifty-six and sixty-one seats, respectively, to the *dangwai*'s six seats in both elections. To prepare for the December 1983 elections, two hundred *dangwai* candidates convened on October 23, 1983, and agreed that "All of the people in Taiwan should determine the future of Taiwan" would be their basic campaign message to the voters. See *Taiwan no seiji kaikaku nempô*, p. 274.

58. For a discussion of this *dangwai* setback, see Zhao Jing, "Yijiu basan xuanzhan huigu" (Looking back at the 1983 election war), *Jianjing guanchang* (Progress), no. 18 (December 10, 1983): 7–11. See also editorial in same issue, "Zhankai xuanhou chongjian gongzuo" (New tasks for the postelection period), pp. 4–5, which claims that quarrels between *dangwai* leaders and successful KMT methods to win votes for their candidates were the main reasons for the 1983 *dangwai* setback.

59. See *Taiwan no seiji kaikaku nempô*, p. 285. The *dangwai* activities described in the next few paragraphs are taken from this same yearbook of Taiwan political developments.

60. Li Xiaofeng, *Taiwan minzhu yundong sishinian* (The forty-year Taiwan democracy movement) (Taipei: Zili wanbaoshe wenhua chubanbu, 1991), p. 140.

61. Ibid., p. 201.

62. Quoted from Wuyue yiri zudang" (Forming a party on May first), *Minzhu shidai zhoukan* (Democratic age weekly), no. 118 (May 5, 1986): 5.

63. *Taiwan no seiji kaikaku nempô*, p. 295.

64. Zeng Xinyi, "Dangwai yao canxuan yeyao zudang" (The *dangwai* want to participate in elections and also to form a party), *Minzhu tiandi zhoukan* (Democratic road weekly), no. 18 (July 1, 1985): 32.

65. Xu Yiwen, "Liji chengli minzhudang" (Immediately form a democratic party), *Minzhu tiandi zhoukan*, no. 18 (July 1, 1985): 31. See the editorial in the same issue by Zheng Nanrong, "You rexue you danqi jiu zudang" (With hot blood and courage we can form a party), p. 1, which refers to Shih Ming-teh's dramatic appeal to his political comrades to form a democratic party as soon as possible.

66. See Tao Pai-chuan, *Chuangyi zaoshi; tupo nijing* (To create and set the stage for a breakthrough amidst adversity) (Taipei: Yujing chuban shiye gongsi, 1982), p. 77, where Tao argues for free political parties to compete as a necessary basis for having real political democracy.

67. Ibid., p. 287.

68. Ibid., p. 288.

69. Tao Pai-chuan, *Zhengzhi yu lianhuan* (Political jade rings) (Taipei: Beishui chexin jijinhui, 1986), p. 18.

70. We are indebted to Thomas A. Metzger for this insight.

71. Based on interviews with leading KMT officials.

72. Between 1978 and 1989, Dr. Wei Yung, as head of the Research, Development, and Evaluation Commission of the Executive Yuan, initiated various government surveys of public opinion. If we exclude measures of public attitudes toward pollution and social services, all other indicators reflect high popular approval of government, averaging between 65 and 80 percent public approval for ROC government's policies. See Wei Yung, "Xian jieduan Taiwan xuanju wenhua di tedian yu fazhan" (Special features and development of Taiwan's election culture in the current period), paper presented at a conference sponsored by *Zhongguo shibao* (China times), July 7–9, 1992, in Taipei.

73. Based on interviews with leading KMT officials.

74. Tao Pai-chuan, *Weiyan weixing bang youdao* (In this period of crisis, our nation has found a solution) (Taipei: Beishui chexin jijinhui, 1989), p. 14.

75. For Yüan's comments, see *Lianhebao* (United daily news), March 28, 1986, p. 2.

76. Ibid.

77. Ibid. for Hu Fu's comments.

78. *Taiwan no seiji kaikaku nempô*, pp. 294–95.

79. Our story is based mainly on Karl Fields, "The Anatomy of a Financial Scandal: The Rise and Fall of the Cathay Business Group," paper delivered at the Center for Chinese Studies Spring Regional Seminar, Berkeley, April 27, 1991.

80. Ibid., p. 22.

81. See James C. Hsiung, "Taiwan in 1985: Searching for Solutions," *Asian Survey*

26, no. 1 (January 1986): 93–101, which describes the trial of government officials charged with authorizing the murder of Henry Liu, coal mine cave-ins, and a serious fire at the No. 3 Nuclear Power Plant.

82. At the twelfth session of the Third Plenum, March 29–April 1, 1986, 950 KMT members met to discuss party affairs and reelect central committee and standing committee members. The main theme of the meeting, according to the Taipei press, was to review the past and plan a strategy for the future. See *Lianhebao*, March 29, 1986, p. 1. This meeting marked the beginning of Taiwan's great political transition. Scholars reviewing Taiwan in 1986 never conveyed the enormous significance of the decisions made by Chiang Ching-kuo: first, to initiate political reform and then, in October, to take no action to arrest the DPP leaders. See John F. Copper, "Taiwan in 1986: Back on Top Again," *Asian Survey* 27, no. 1 (January 1987): 81–91.

83. *Lianhebao*, March 30, 1986, p. 3.

84. *Taiwan no seiji kaikaku nempô*, p. 313.

85. See interview with Mah Soo-lay in *Zhongyang ribao* (Central daily news), international ed., November 9, 1986, p. 1.

86. Along with Ma, Yen Chia-kan convened a twelve-person committee whose members included Shieh Tung-min, Lee Teng-hui, Ku Cheng-kang (who died shortly thereafter), Yu Kuo-hwa, Ni Wen-ya, Yuan Shou-chien, Shen Chang-huan, Lee Huan, Ch'iu Chuang-huan, and Wu Po-hsiung. On May 12 they began their work.

87. We attribute Taiwan's democratic breakthrough mainly to Chiang Ching-kuo's decision to liberalize the "inhibited" political center. Hao Pei-tsun's diary about Chiang Ching-kuo confirms our view. Hao relates the following: "I feel that he [Chiang Ching-kuo] was reacting to the demands of the opposition and to pressures from the international order, but basically Chiang alone conceived the idea for Taiwan's democratization." See *Jing-kuo xianshen wannian*, p. 1. Our evidence and argument have been organized according to the following schema: (1) as early as the mid-1970s Chiang cherished the goal of democracy and wanted to realize his father's dream and his party's mission of unifying China under Sun Yat-sen's Three Principles of the People; (2) Chiang perceived between 1980 and 1984 that he had to take decisive political action to expand democracy; (3) with the ROC already internationally isolated between 1980 and 1986, a small opposition movement threatening to compete with the KMT for political power, PRC pressures upon Taiwan mounting, United States pressures for political change increasing, the liberal wing of the KMT pressing for political reform, Chiang ill and aging, and other societies democratizing, there was no action other than democratization that Chiang preferred or ever regarded as about equal; and finally, (4) Chiang knew how to initiate democratization, he was still physically able to do so in the worsening circumstances between 1984 and 1986, and at the timely moment he used his power to act by selecting a successor to complete his mission should he suddenly die. For a discussion of this logical schema, which is based on G. H. Von Wright's intentionalist explanation of historical events, see Rex Martin, "G. H. Von Wright on Explanation and Understanding: An Appraisal," *History and Theory* 19, no. 2 (1990): 207–8.

*Chapter Six: Political Conflict and Lifting Martial Law*

1. On September 28, 1986, Fei Hsi-ping and others founded the DPP, but in 1989 Fei left that party because of differences of opinion with the DPP leadership.

2. *Lianhebao* (United daily news), March 15, 1986, p. 1.

3. The data presented here can be found in Council for Economic Planning and Development, *Taiwan Statistical Data Book, 1995* (Taipei: Council for Economic Planning and Development, 1995).

4. "Wuyue yiri zudang" (Forming a party on May 1), *Minzhu shidai zhoukan* (Democratic age weekly), no. 118 (May 5, 1986): 4–5.

5. In the same journal issue, see "Zudang zhihou jiuhui Taiwan" (After organizing a party, we will immediately return to Taiwan), p. 7.

6. Editorial page, "Jianli xindang–dajia yiqi lai" (Create a new party—everybody come and join), *Bashi niandai zhoukan* (Eighties monthly), no. 119 (May 12, 1986): 2–3.

7. Jiang Feng, "Jiang Jingguo shuo: Congqian wo dui dangwai zhiyou yuan" (Chiang Ching-kuo says: In the past I only had contempt for the *dangwai*), *Bashi niandai zhoukan*, no. 122 (June 2, 1986): 4.

8. Ibid., p. 5.

9. Li, *Taiwan minzhu yundong sishinian*, p. 255.

10. Ibid., p. 227.

11. Ibid., p. 228.

12. Ibid., p. 230.

13. *Zili wanbao* (Independent evening post), August 10, 1986, p. 2.

14. Li, *Taiwan minzhu yundong sishinian*, p. 233.

15. *Zhongguo shibao* (China times), September 29, 1986, p. 2.

16. Li, *Taiwan minzhu yundong sishinian*, p. 238.

17. Ibid., p. 240.

18. *Zhongguo shibao*, September 29. 1986, p. 2.

19. *Lianhebao*, October 7, 1986, p. 2. We are not certain this single poll represented public opinion, but previous polls had suggested public apathy.

20. *Taiwan ribao* (Taiwan daily), October 12, 1986, p. 2.

21. *Zhongyang ribao* (Central daily news), October 1, 1986, p. 3.

22. *Zhongyang ribao*, December 2, 1993, p. 1.

23. Ibid.

24. Ibid.

25. *Zili wanbao*, November 16, 1986, p. 2.

26. *Zhongguo shibao*, April 16–20, 1988, p. 2.

27. *Zili zaobao* (Independent morning post), April 16, 1988, p. 1.

28. *Zhongguo shibao*, April 17, 1988, p. 2.

29. See pamphlet titled "DPP," published in Taipei, spring 1988, p. 27.

30. Ibid., pp. 13–14.

31. Ibid., pp. 15–27.

32. These six subcommittees, comprising twelve KMT standing committee members, were divided into two groups: group one had the task of drafting a new national security law and an organization law for political parties; the second group was in charge of planning how to reform local governance, replace the old national representatives elected on the mainland, improve social stability, and reform the KMT.

33. Interviews with former KMT top leaders.
34. *Lianhebao,* October 3, 1986, p. 1.
35. Li, *Taiwan minzhu yundong sishinian,* p. 242.
36. *Lianhebao,* October 19, 1986, p. 1.
37. *Lianhebao,* December 11, 1986, p. 1.
38. For some discussion of the history and impact of martial law on Taiwan, see *Zhongguo shibao,* October 21, 1986, p. 2. See also the editorial in *Xinxinwen* (Journalist), no. 9 (May 11–17, 1987): 4–5.
39. *Lianhebao,* October 24, 1986, p. 1. In late February 1987 Premier Yu told the Legislative Yuan that it must pass the new national security law and then draft and approve a new law for political parties to compete. See also *Lianhebao,* February 25, 1987, p. 1.
40. *Lianhebao,* November 29, 1986, p. 1.
41. *Lianhebao,* December 24, 1986, p. 1.
42. *Lianhebao,* March 12, 1987, p. 2.
43. This was the assessment offered by Li Xiaofeng in his history of Taiwan's forty years of political opposition to KMT rule. See Li, *Taiwan minzhu yundong sishinian,* p. 247.
44. Ibid., p. 248.
45. Ibid., p. 249.
46. Ibid., p. 250.
47. *Lianhebao,* November 7, 1986, p. 2.
48. See *Lianhebao,* November 15, 1986, p. 1, and November 21, 1986, p. 1.
49. *Lianhebao,* November 21, 1986, p. 3.
50. *Lianhebao,* November 23, 1986, p. 3.
51. Ibid.
52. Ibid.
53. *Lianhebao,* December 4, 1986, p. 3.
54. *Lianhebao,* December 5, 1986, p. 3.
55. *Lianhebao,* December 7, 1986, p. 1.
56. Ibid.
57. For information on the 1983 election see chapter 3, table 5.
58. Yun-han Chu, *Crafting Democracy in Taiwan* (Taipei: Institute for National Policy Research, 1992), p. 61.
59. Wu Mutian, "Zhangwo minyi dongxiang," *Lianhebao,* December 7, 1986,p.1.
60. Ibid.
61. Ibid.
62. *Lianhebao,* March 13, 1987, p. 2.
63. *Lianhebao,* March 17, 1987, p. 2.
64. For a review of these social movements, see Hsin-huang Michael Hsiao, "The Changing State-Society Relation in the ROC, Economic Change, the Transformation of the Class Structure, and the Rise of Social Movements," in *Two Societies in Opposition: The Republic of China and the People's Republic of China after Forty Years,* ed. Ramon H. Myers (Stanford, Calif.: Hoover Institution Press, 1991), pp. 127–40.
65. Chu, *Crafting Democracy in Taiwan,* p. 104. It is worth noting that the participants in these 1987 protests became more numerous: for example, in 1986 there were

five social protests numbering more than 5,001 persons; in 1987, seven; and in 1988, twelve (p. 105). These large protests were aimed at the central government.

66. Editorial, *Lianhebao*, March 31, 1987, p. 2.

67. Jiang Liangren, "Jinji zhanting si-yi-jiu" (Urging a halt for the moment: The April 19 demonstration), *Xinxinwen*, no. 6 (April 20–26, 1987): 10.

68. Lin Pingming, "Wu ersi women zai xiang jian" (On May 24 will we meet again?) *Xinxinwen*, no. 6 (April 20–26, 1987): 18.

69. Ibid., p. 20.

70. Hu Yuanhui, *Lianhebao*, May 16, 1987, p. 2.

71. Ibid.

72. Chen Qingxi, *Lianhebao*, May 16, 1987, p. 2.

73. The following description of the May 19 demonstration is based on *Zili wanbao*, May 20, 1987, p. 2; and "Shizilushang shier xiaoshi" (Twelve hours on the streets and intersections), *Xinxinwen*, no. 11 (May 25–31, 1987): 18–58.

74. *Lianhebao*, May 21, 1987, p. 2.

75. Ibid.

76. Ibid.

77. Ibid.

78. Chu, *Crafting Democracy in Taiwan*, pp. 104–5.

79. *Zhongyang ribao*, June 6, 1987, p. 2.

80. *Lianhebao*, June 7, 1987, p. 2.

81. *Zhongyang ribao*, June 9, 1987, p. 2.

82. *Lianhebao*, June 11, 1987, p. 2.

83. Jing Zhiren, *Lianhebao*, June 14, 1987, p. 2.

84. *Lianhebao*, June 13, 1987, p. 2.

85. *Zili wanbao*, June 13, 1987, p. 2.

86. Ibid.

87. "Kan wan jietou lianxuju yihou" (After seeing the television series), *Xinxinwen*, no. 3 (June 15–21, 1987): 4–5.

88. *Lianhebao*, June 14, 1981, p. 1.

89. *Zhongguo shibao*, June 16, 1987, p. 1.

90. *Lianhebao*, June 23, 1987, p. 1.

91. *Zhongyang ribao*, June 24, 1987, p. 1.

92. *Zhongyang ribao*, June 25, 1987, p. 1.

93. *Zili wanbao*, July 8, 1987, p. 2.

94. *Zhongyang ribao*, July 15, 1987, p. 1.

## Chapter Seven: The First Election after the Lifting of Martial Law

1. Editorial, "Fanxing shi wei zou geng changyuan di lu: Yijiu baqi di huigu" (To reevaluate ourselves in order to travel a longer road: A review of 1987), *Xinxinwen zhoukan* (Journalist weekly), no. 42 (December 28, 1987–January 3, 1988): 7.

2. Ibid.

3. Jiang Liangren, "Chiang zongtong liuxia di yichan" (The legacy of President Chiang Ching-kuo), *Xinxinwen zhoukan*, no. 45 (January 18–24, 1988): 20.

4. Ibid.

5. Ibid.

6. Ibid.

7. *Lianhebao* (United daily news), October 28, 1986, p. 1.

8. *Lianhebao*, October 29, 1986, p. 1. Cheng Shui-chih stated that the new law would require "parties to register according to their type of activity as well as the conditions of each group, in which there must be at least fifteen candidates competing for city and provincial elected seats or thirty candidates competing for district government seats."

9. *Lianhebao*, November 6, 1987, p. 1.

10. Wang Lixing, *Wukuei* (With a clear conscience) (Taipei: Tienxia wenhua chubanshe, 1994), p. 40.

11. Ibid.

12. Interview with Ma Ying-chiu.

13. Wang, *Wukuei*, p. 42.

14. "Zhu Gaujeng di yanlei" (The tears of Ju Gau-jeng), *Xinxinwen zhoukan*, no. 45 (January 18–24, 1988): 52.

15. Hua Yiwen and Guo Hongzhi, "Dang wo tingdao zheige xiaoxi shi" (When I heard the news), *Xinxinwen zhoukan*, no. 45 (January 18–24, 1988): 18.

16. These were the questions raised by Huan Guochang, "Taipei di xiayibu" (The next step for Taipei), *Xinxinwen zhoukan*, no. 45 (January 18–24, 1988): 70.

17. Xu Han, *Li Denghui di qishinian* (The seventy years of Lee Denghui) (Taipei: Kaijin wenhua shiye youxian gongsi, 1993), pp. 25–26. Lee Jinlung's first son joined the imperial Japanese army in World War II and disappeared while serving in the Philippines. His third son, Lee Bingnan, is a general manager in a business enterprise.

18. Ibid., p. 37.

19. Li Da, *Li Denghui zhuan* (Biography of Lee Teng-hui) (Hong Kong: Guangjiaojing chubanshe, 1988), p. 44.

20. Ibid., p. 45.

21. Xu, *Li Denghui di qishinian*, p. 76.

22. Li, *Li Denghui zhuan*, pp. 49–50.

23. Observers like Xu Han (see his *Li Denghui di qishinian*, p. 83) argue that Chiang Ching-kuo selected Lee as vice president because he had no political supporters, was morally upright, was not obligated to anyone, and had no son to promote. As a Christian, Lee had close ties with the Presbyterian Church in northern Taiwan that could serve to check the radical Presbyterian Church in the south. Chiang also wanted an able Taiwanese to deal with the Taiwan nationalist movement, both overseas and at home. Finally, Lee's selection would demonstrate to United States authorities that mainlanders and Taiwanese could get along and that equality and justice existed for everyone in Taiwan, irrespective of ethnicity.

24. Our account is based on Zhou Yukou, *Li Denghui di yiqian tian* (Lee Teng-hui's first one hundred days) (Taipei: Maitian chubanshe, 1993), pp. 29–40.

25. Sima Wenwu, "Li Denghui di 100 tian" (The first hundred days of Lee Teng-hui), *Xinxinwen* (Journalist), no. 58 (April 18–24, 1988): 21.

26. Ibid., pp. 21–22.

27. Nan Fangshuo, "Li Denghui diyinian di chengjidan" (A one-year report card on Lee Teng-hui), *Xinxinwen*, no. 96 (January 9–15, 1989): 22–23.

28. Guo Hongzhi, "Zongtong nianzhong kaoji, minzhong gei ta jifen?" (How did the people score the president in terms of their year-end evaluation?), *Xinxinwen,* no. 96 (January 9–15, 1989): 26–32.

29. Chen Minfeng, Wei Hongwu, and Liao Fuxun, "Ni zenyang kan zhei yiwen Taiwanren yuanshou?"(What do you think about the Taiwanese leader?), *Xinxinwen,* no. 96, (January 9–15, 1989): 35.

30. For a good description of this congress see *Zili zaobao* (Independent morning post), January 2, 1988, p. 2.

31. Minzhudang dangan (A file on the DPP), "Zheichang ji yu tuzi di youxi wanle haojiu haojiu" (The game of chicken and rabbit has been going on for a long time), *Xinxinwen zhoukan,* no. 120 (June 26–July 4, 1989): 58.

32. Hua Yiwen, "Xian shi xindi, dang shi jiudi" (The line is new, but the party is old), *Xinxinwen zhoukan,* no. 129 (August 28–September 3, 1989): 42.

33. The Public Officials Election and Recall Law of the Republic of China was first promulgated on May 14, 1980, and amended three more times, the last time on August 2, 1991. Its 113 articles (the law of August 2, 1991) outline the functions played by the Central Election Commission and the rules and sanctions governing voters and candidates.

34. "Activists Steal Limelight from Taiwan Politicians," *Straits Times,* November 20, 1989, p. 6.

35. Taiwan's new freedoms and this election encouraged exiled dissidents like Guo Beihong to return to Taiwan and appear at political rallies like that for Zhou Huiying, who ran for the Taiwan Provincial Assembly, and Lu Xiuyi, running for the Legislative Yuan. See "Police Confident of Nabbing Kuo," *China Post,* November 24, 1989, p. 15. On the evening of November 29, police captured an exiled dissident named Columbus Leo, secretary-general of the overseas World Formosan Association (WFA), near a church on Changan East Road in Taipei. Two other dissidents recently deported were also alleged to be in Taiwan: Robert C. Tsai of the Central Committee of the Formosan Independence League, and Shane Lee, president of the WFA. They had allegedly sneaked into Taiwan by using passports belonging to other citizens. See "Dissident Leo Arrested on Way to Campaign Rally," *China Post,* November 30, 1989, p. 12.

36. One newspaper even published a 123-article draft constitution for a hypothetical Republic of Taiwan. See *Zili zaobao,* November 16, 1989, pp. 9–10. Foreign newspapers also reported breaking this taboo. See Andrew Quinn, "Call for Independence Breaks Taiwan Taboo," *Korean Herald,* November 10, 1989, p. 8.

37. *Lianhebao,* November 22, 1989, pp. 3–4.

38. Ibid., p. 4.

39. Ibid. Arguing against Taiwan independence, James C. Y. Soong stated that support for Taiwan independence was a "queer sound coming from an ivory tower" that would "turn Taiwan into another Beirut." See James C. Y. Soong, *Lianhebao,* November 22, 1989, p. 3. Even the DPP's top leaders split on the Taiwan independence issue. Xie Changting endorsed the idea of a new constitution and a new country, but Chen Shui-bian declared that a new country does not necessarily mean an independent Taiwan. Lin Wenlang believed that an independent Taiwan would greatly damage the economy and cause a catastrophe; Lin Zhengjie opposed changing the name of the country. See *Lianhebao,* November 22, 1989, p. 3.

40. Julian Baum and James A. Robinson, "Party Primaries in Taiwan: Footnote or Text in Democratization?" *Asian Affairs* 20, no. 2 (summer 1993): 88–98. We measure KMT history from the year 1894, when the Xingzhonghui was founded and later called the KMT.

41. In every county and city, powerful lineages or clans operate patron-client networks to grant favors and allocate political power. These clans also advanced their candidates. Local politicians ignored these clans at their peril. These powerful factions or cliques are described in a special report titled "Dangyi kewei zongjin zhiyi bukewei" (You can go against the party but not the clans), *Shibao zhoukan* (China times weekly), no. 601 (September 3–9, 1989): 194–95.

42. For the KMT primary, more than 900,000 KMT members cast their ballots at 1,250 polling stations. Voter turnout was 46 percent, compared with the 30 percent average voter turnout in United States primaries. Later figures show that the KMT had registered 670 candidates, but only 212 could be nominated by the party according to law. See Wu Wen-cheng and Chen I-hsin, "Constructive Controversies," *Free China Review* 39, no. 12 (December 1989): 41.

43. "Xuanju 'reshenzhan' wenti chongchong" (Problems pile up in the election warmup for war), *Yazhou zhoukan* (International Chinese newsweekly), July 2, 1989, p. 12.

44. Yang Taixun, *Zhongguo shibao* (China times), July 26, 1989, p. 2.

45. "Minjindang quanli 'duoquan' " (The DPP goes all out to seize power), *Yazhou zhoukan,* November 12, 1989, pp. 8–9. This same faction was also called the "New Country" faction.

46. Ibid.

47. See *Yazhou zhoukan,* July 2, 1989, p. 13.

48. See *Yazhou zhoukan,* November 12, 1989, p. 9.

49. Ibid., p. 8. See also Cao Youfen, "Fengyun qi, Shanhe dong" (The winds and clouds swirl, the mountain streams roar), *Yuanjian zazhi* (Global view monthly), October 15, 1989, p. 22.

50. Ibid., pp. 8–9.

51. Ibid., p. 8.

52. Ho Ying, "KMT Divides Regional Races into Three 'Combat Zones,' " *China News,* November 22, 1989, p. 12.

53. Cao, "Fengyun qi, Shanhe dong," p. 22.

54. Ibid., p. 23.

55. Fu's remarks had a double meaning. *Fangshi* can mean lovemaking between married couples as well as "matters concerning housing" to refer to Assemblyman Fan, who served on a committee investigating public housing. See *Zhongguo shibao,* November 23, 1989, p. 2.

56. Ibid.

57. *Zili zaobao,* November 3, 1989, p. 3.

58. *Zhongguo shibao,* November 19, 1989, p. 4.

59. *Zili zaobao,* November 5, 1989, p. 3.

60. *Zili zaobao,* November 18, 1989, p. 2. Another group of intellectuals, critical of the ruling party, declared they were politically "neutral," endorsed Yu Ching, and ranked all the DPP candidates in the races for city mayor and county magistrates as

better than their KMT rivals. None of these KMT candidates received a single endorsement among these academics, who called themselves the Society for Uprightness and Clarity (Zhengshe). Even the popular KMT candidate Chao Shao-kang, who won the highest number of votes in a previous election, was ranked twenty-eighth in this evaluation report, a niche below Xu Xiaodan, the notorious stripper. See "Self-Styled 'Neutral' Professors Give Edge to Opposition Candidates," *China News*, November 28, 1989, p. 12. Lei Yuchi, chairman of the minor Dagong Party, running for legislator in Taipei county, filed a lawsuit at the Taipei district prosecutor's office against Professor Yang Guoshu, president of the Zhengshe. See "Opposition Candidate Sues Group over Inaccurate Survey," *China Post*, November 30, 1989, p. 11.

61. Gabriel Fok, "Electioneering Begins," *Free China Journal* 6, no. 89 (November 20, 1989): 1. The popular KMT politician Chao Shao-kang listed all his achievements and activities in a seven-page newsletter. See "Zhao Shaokang di qushi" (The story of Chao Shao-kang), *Chao Shao-kang tongxin zazhi* (Chao Shao-kang newsletter), no. 11. At least 105 election candidates placed advertisements, costing a total of NT$50 million, or roughly US$1.9 million, by November 30, 1989. Wang Linglin, an independent, topped the list, spending NT$5.8 million, or about US$230,000. See "105 Candidates Spend NT$50 million on Advertising," *China Post*, November 30, 1989, p. 11.

62. *Zili zaobao*, November 20, 1989, p. 3.

63. *Lianhebao*, November 1, 1989, p. 2.

64. Ibid.

65. Ibid. Their names were listed as Zang Pingzhao, Huang Chiquang, Hsu Mingde, Wu Yili, and Wan Linglin.

66. *Lianhebao*, November 23, 1989, p. 5. The DPP also circulated photocopies of a KMT advertisement announcing a public rally for KMT candidates running for the Legislative Yuan after which each voter would receive a gift. The authors received this evidence from the DPP Taipei City headquarters.

67. *Lianhebao*, November 6, 1989, p. 3.

68. *Lianhebao*, November 7, 1989, p. 1.

69. *Lianhebao*, November 6, 1989, p. 3.

70. See advertisement in *Minshengbao* (People's daily), December 1, 1989, p. 32.

71. Ibid.

72. See the special report "Wu Dunyi: Ban yici ganjing pingan di xuanju; Zhu Gaozheng: Diyi dadang shi 'jinniudang' " (Wu Den-yih: To manage a clean, peaceful election; Ju Gau-jeng: The number one big party is a party of "golden oxen"), *Yuanjian zazhi*, October 15, 1989, p. 40. We summarize the opinions of these two party members.

73. For this debate, see "Wu Dunyi: Guomindang guochu gongxian; Zhu Gao-Zheng: Guomindang zhishi meiba Taiwan tuokua" (Wu Den-yih: The KMT's past merits; Ju Gau-jeng: The KMT has only blocked Taiwan's progress), *Yuanjian zashi*, October 15, 1989, p. 45.

74. Ibid., p. 46.

75. Ibid., p. 50. See the special report "Wu Dunyi: Dui Guomindang shenchu wennuan di shou; Zhu Gaozheng: Bizhe yanjing tou Minjindang" (Wu Den-yih: Stretch out your warm hands to the KMT; Ju Gau-jeng: Close your eyes and cast your vote for the DPP), *Yuanjian zazhi*, October 15, 1989, p. 50.

76. Ibid., p. 44.

77. Ibid., p. 45.

78. Ibid., p. 50.

79. "Shou buwan nüren shi, kan buwan xuanju xiu" (Endless talk about women; continuous shows of election), *Xinxinwen* (Journalist), no. 142 (November 27, 1989): 20.

80. Cao, "Fengyun qi, Shanhe dong," pp. 23 and 27. This poll interviewed 2,544 persons over twenty years of age and eligible to vote in Taipei, Taipei, Yilan, Zhanghua, Nantou, Gaoxiong, and Pingdong counties and in Taichung, Taipei, and Chiai cities. See p. 34 for a brief account of this survey.

81. Ibid., p. 27. This same poll revealed that 61 percent had not decided how they would vote; 15 percent had decided how they would vote, and 13 percent admitted they did not know how they would vote. See p. 33.

82. Guo Hongzhi, "Minjindang yao kan di shuzi" (The data the DPP wants to see), *Xinxinwen zhoukan*, no. 117 (June 5–11, 1989): 14.

83. *Lianhe wanbao* (United evening news), November 22, 1989, p. 5. In counties like Changhua, where thirteen candidates were running for the Legislative Yuan, voter apathy had become so noticeable that only six of the competing candidates had decided to attend the political rallies. See *Lianhe wanbao*, November 22, 1989, p. 5.

84. *Zhongshi wanbao* (China times express), December 2, 1989, p. 4.

85. *Zhongguo shibao*, December 1, 1989, p. 3.

86. *Lianhebao*, December 2, 1989, p. 2.

87. Ho Ying, "Over 12 Million Eligible in Tomorrow's Big Vote," *China News*, December 1, 1989, p. 12.

88. Ho Ying and Lin Hua, "Heavy Security in Place for Election Today," *China News*, December 2, 1989, p. 12.

89. *Zhongguo shibao*, December 3, 1989, p. 1.

90. "Demonstrations Surround Tainan Government Building," *China Post*, December 4, 1989, p. 11. Some minor violence also occurred in Taoyuan and Nantou counties and in Hsinchu and Taichung cities.

91. *Lianhe wanbao*, December 7, 1989, p. 3. Of the 841 votes cast at polling station 71, Li Yaqiao received 776, Li Zongfan only 35, and Cai Sijie 14, with 16 votes not clearly marked. These votes exactly matched the election committee's recount report, so no error had been made at polling station 71, as Li Zongfan had charged.

92. "Sanxiang gongzhi xuanju jiexiao" (Announcing three elections for public officials), *Zhongguo shibao*, December 3, 1989, p. 1.

93. *Shijie ribao* (World journal daily news), December 4, 1989, p. 1.

94. *Zhongyang ribao* (Central daily news), December 4, 1989, p. 6.

95. This same evaluation was repeated by a one scholar in Beijing: "In the elections, the Democratic Progressive Party (DPP) achieved great developments, whereas the Kuomintang (KMT) suffered unprecedented setbacks." See Foreign Broadcast Information Service, *Daily Report: China*, December 26, 1989, p. 52.

96. *Zhongguo shibao*, December 6, 1989, p. 2.

97. *Lianhebao*, December 8, 1989, p. 2.

98. "Li Denghui zhuxi jiang fabiao tanhua" (KMT chairman Lee Teng-hui will deliver a speech and hold discussions), *Zhongguo shibao*, December 6, 1989, p. 2.

99. See editorial, *Lianhebao*, December 7, 1989, p. 2.

100. "Hanxiang" (Winter fragrance), *Lianhebao,* December 9, 1989, p. 25.

101. *Zili zaobao,* December 5, 1989, p. 2.

102. *Zhongguo shibao,* December 6, 1989, p. 4.

103. Shelley Rigger, "The Risk of Reform: Factional Conflict in Taiwan's 1989 Local Elections," *American Journal of Chinese Studies,* no. 2 (October 1994): 144–47, for the case of Li Yikun.

104. Countless voters told us they were voting for the first time for the DPP to check and balance the KMT.

105. *Lianhebao,* December 7, 1989, p. 4. In the January 1990 election for councils and small-town mayors the KMT won 77 percent of the former and 91 percent of mayorships, mainly because the DPP failed to run candidates.

## Chapter Eight: Democracy's First Crisis

1. Hung-mao Tien, ed., *The Great Transition: Political and Social Change in the Republic of China* (Stanford, Calif.: Hoover Institution Press, 1989), p. 113.

2. *Lianhebao* (United daily news), February 18, 1990, p. 1.

3. Lin Yinting, "Neidou zhong di yimei huoqi: Lee Huan" (A live chip in the inner struggle for power: Lee Huan), *Yuanjian zazhi* (Global view monthly), no. 44 (January 15, 1990): 26–28.

4. Wang Xingqing, "Li Denghui timing Li Yuanzi, Guomindang neidou dengchang" (Lee Teng-hui nominates Li Yuan-zu, and the power struggle within the KMT begins), *Xinxinwen* (Journalist), no. 153 (February 12–18, 1990): 11.

5. *Zili zaobao* (Independent morning post), February 15, 1990, p. 1.

6. *Lianhebao,* February 11, 1990, p. 3.

7. *Lianhebao,* February 12, 1990, p. 3.

8. Ibid.

9. Ibid.

10. Ibid. Among the key leaders who voted for secret balloting were Hau Pei-tsun, Lee Huan, Lin Yang-kang, and Sun Yun-suan. Among those who favored the stand-up method were James C. Y. Soong, Kao Yu-jen, Ch'iu Chuang-huan, and Wu Po-hsiung.

11. Interviews with President Lee Teng-hui.

12. *Zili zaobao,* February 12, 1990, p. 1.

13. *Zili wanbao* (Independent evening post), February 11, 1990, p. 1.

14. Ibid.

15. *Lianhebao,* February 13, 1990, p. 2.

16. *Lianhe wanbao* (United evening news), March 1, 1990, p. 1.

17. Ibid.

18. *Zili zaobao,* March 1, 1990, p. 2.

19. *Zili zaobao,* March 3, 1990, p. 1.

20. Our account of this meeting is based on the following accounts: *Lianhebao,* February 20, 1990, pp. 1, 3; *Lianhe wanbao,* February 19, 1990, p. 3; *Zili zaobao,* February 20, 1990, p. 1.

21. *Lianhebao,* February 20, 1990, p. 3.

22. *Lianhe wanbao,* March 3, 1990, p. 1.

23. Ibid. Those who maneuvered to promote the Lin-Chiang ticket in the National Assembly supported Lee Huan, Hau Pei-tsun, etc. The rival coalitions supported either Lee Teng-hui or Lee Huan. Bitter about being bypassed as vice president and increasingly worried about President Lee's ideas for constitutional reform and a PRC policy, Lee Huan and others now considered the National Assembly's new presidential and vice presidential ticket.

24. *Lianhebao,* March 4, 1990, p. 1.

25. *Zhongguo shibao* (China times), March 4, 1990, p. 1.

26. *Lianhe wanbao,* March 4, 1990, p. 1.

27. *Lianhe wanbao,* March 5, 1990, p. 1.

28. *Zili zaobao,* March 6, 1990, p. 1.

29. Ibid.

30. *Lianhe wanbao,* March 7, 1990, p. 1.

31. *Zili zaobao,* March 8, 1990, p. 3, for various comments by major political figures.

32. Ibid.

33. *Zhongguo shibao,* March 8, 1990, p. 1.

34. *Zhongguo shibao,* March 9, 1990, p. 1.

35. One report states that people warned Lin not to "betray" Taiwanese interests by being a pawn in the mainlander power structure and to "give the first Taiwanese a chance." See Chang Mau-kuei, "Toward an Understanding of the Sheng-chi wen-t'i in Taiwan: Focusing on Changes after Political Liberalization," in *Ethnicity in Taiwan: Social, Historical, and Cultural Perspectives,* ed. Chen Chung-min, Chuang Ying-chang, and Huang Shu-min (Taipei: Institute of Ethnology, Academia Sinica, 1994), p. 101.

36. *Lianhebao,* March 9, 1990, p. 1.

37. Ibid. Premier Lee Huan refused to accept Wang's request, and Wang again tendered his resignation on March 27, declaring, "I simply want to take a rest and prepare myself for the long road ahead." *China Post,* March 28, 1990, p. 6.

38. For a discussion of this Chinese sense of "predicament," see Thomas A. Metzger, *Escape from Predicament: Neo-Confucianism and China's Evolving Political Culture* (New York: Columbia University Press, 1977), chap. 3.

39. *Zhongguo shibao,* March 10, 1990, p. 1. Information would surface much later that Zai Hongwen, a business tycoon and politician, personally visited Lin to convey to him the fears of Taiwanese businesspeople who believed it best that Lin step down. We thank Tun-jen Cheng for this insight.

40. *Zili wanbao,* March 10, 1990, p. 1. On that same day, the Taipei stock market shot up 440 points as investors, who now believed that political stability had been restored, confidently purchased stock and set off a bull market.

41. *Lianhe wanbao,* March 10, 1990, p. 1. See also *Lianhebao,* March 11, 1990, p. 1, for how both men announced their withdrawal from the race. Pressures on Chiang Wei-kuo to resign had come from critical remarks by Chiang Hsiao-wu, the ROC representative to Japan and nephew of Chiang Wei-kuo, who had flown to Taipei to hold a press conference and denounce Chiang Wei-kuo's intention to run on the ticket. See *Zhongguo shibao,* March 10, 1990, p. 3. See also Chang Hsiao-yen's remarks about Chiang's candidacy (p. 3).

42. *Lianhe wanbao,* March 16, 1990, p. 1.

43. *Lianhe wanbao*, March 11, 1990, p. 1.

44. *Zhongguo shibao*, March 13, 1990, p. 1.

45. Ibid.

46. *Zhongguo shibao*, March 15, 1990, p. 1. Other newspapers, however, reported a period of two hours and longer times for the Committee to deliberate and decide.

47. Government Information Office, Republic of China, *Constitution, Republic of China* (Taipei, n.d.), pp. 55–57. These eleven articles had been passed in accordance with paragraph 1 of Article 174 of the constitution.

48. *Zhongyang ribao* (Central daily news), international ed., March 16, 1990, p. 1.

49. Even the party's newspaper, *Zhongyang ribao*, interpreted the committee's action as expanding the National Assembly's power and condemned its action. See *Zhongyang ribao*, international ed., March 15, 1990, p. 1. Some committee members, elected from Taiwan, were also criticized for trying to extend their term of office beyond the allowed two years.

50. *Zili zaobao*, March 14, 1990, p. 1.

51. "President Lee Called to End Political 'Farce,' " *China Post*, March 16, 1990, p. 16.

52. "Military Police Drag away Fourteen DPP Deputies," *China Post*, March 17, 1990, p. 12.

53. *Zhongguo shibao*, March 17, 1990, p. 1.

54. *Lianhe wanbao*, March 17, 1990, p. 1.

55. *Zhongguo shibao*, March 18, 1990, p. 1.

56. *Zhongguo shibao*, March 16, 1990, p. 1.

57. "Retirement of Aging Reps Second Most Urgent Issue," *China Post*, March 29, 1990, p. 12. The *China Times* had surveyed 834 adults, and 80 percent stated that the National Assembly had no function to perform and that they were furious about the committee's four recommendations. Only 13 percent stated that the assembly represented the will of the people. "Yuban minzhong buman guodai suowei" (Over half the people are dissatisfied with the behavior of the National Assembly), *Zhongyang ribao*, international ed., March 18, 1990, p. 1.

58. *Lianhebao*, March 18, 1990, p. 1.

59. *Zili zaobao*, March 19, 1990, p. 1.

60. *Lianhebao*, March 19, 1990, p. 1. The idea for such a conference must be attributed to President Lee. As will be seen in the next chapter, all political parties and most of the elite were deeply suspicious of the conference and believed the president was trying to use the meeting for the benefit of the KMT and himself.

61. *Lianhebao*, March 19, 1990, p. 1; *Zhongyang ribao*, international ed., March 18, 1990, p. 1.

62. *Zili wanbao*, March 19, 1990, p. 1.

63. *Zili zaobao*, March 21, 1990, p. 1.

64. *Lianhebao*, March 22, 1990, p. 1.

65. *Lianhe wanbao*, March 22, 1990, p. 1.

66. Ibid.

*Chapter Nine: Achieving a Partial Political Settlement*

1. "Guoshi huiyi choubeihui minyi diaocha zhiyi" (A survey of public opinion by the National Conference's preparatory committee) (June 26, 1990), p. 2. This survey was cited by Hungdah Chiu, "The National Affairs Conference and Constitutional Reform in the Republic of China on Taiwan," paper prepared for a hearing on Taiwan before the House Subcommittee on Asian and Pacific Affairs, October 11, 1990.

2. According to *Lianhebao* (United daily news), March 24, 1990, p. 2, the term *guoshi huiyi* means "a meeting to decide the ROC's destiny," not a "national affairs conference," as translated in the foreign press and in Taiwan's English-language newspapers. However, we use the term National Affairs Conference as a shorthand reference for the definition above.

3. *Lianhebao*, April 2, 1990, p. 3.

4. *Lianhe wanbao* (United evening news), March 28, 1990, p. 1. A definitive list of the twenty-four invited members is in *Lianhe wanbao*, April 4, 1990, p. 3.

5. *Lianhe wanbao*, April 2, 1990, p. 1.

6. *Lianhe wanbao*, March 29, 1990, p. 3.

7. *Lianhebao*, April 14, 1990, p. 1.

8. *Lianhebao*, May 9, 1990, p. 1.

9. Ibid.

10. *Lianhe wanbao*, May 10, 1990, p. 3.

11. *Zhongguo shibao* (China times), May 15, 1990, p. 1.

12. *Zili zaobao* (Independent morning post), June 23, 1990, p. 2.

13. *Lianhe wanbao*, April 29, 1990, p. 3.

14. *Lianhebao*, June 24, 1990, p. 2.

15. *Zhongguo shibao*, June 25, 1990, p. 1.

16. These goals are expressed in *Lianhebao*, April 6, 1990, p. 2. See also Tien Hungmao's op-ed piece in *Zhongguo shibao*, May 21, 1990, p. 3. Tien also wanted the conference to abolish the "temporary provisions" and end the "period of communist suppression."

17. Chen Fangming, "Guojia gaizao yingyou Taiwanshi di shiye" (There should be a vision of Taiwan history for restructuring the state), *Xinwenhua* (New culture) 16 (May 1990): 64.

18. Chang Minggui, *Lianhe wanbao*, March 30, 1990, p. 2. See also the author's op-ed piece in *Zili zaobao*, March 31, 1990, p. 3.

19. Yang Taixun, "Ruhe kai yige chenggong di guoshi huiyi" (How to hold a successful National Affairs Conference), *Zhongguo luntan* (China tribune) 350 (April 5, 1990): 29.

20. "Guoshi huiyi yu xianzheng gaige" (The National Affairs Conference and the reform of the constitution and the polity), *Zhongguo luntan*, 350 (April 5, 1990): 7.

21. Chen Wenyan, *Zili wanbao* (Independent evening post), May 27, 1990, p. 5.

22. Chen Zheming, "Diyi jieduan gulian rengong, dier jieduan weiwo duzun" (The first stage is bitterly practicing the act of patience: The second stage is for me alone to have respect), *Xinxinwen* (Journalist), no. 173 (July 2–8, 1990): 12.

23. Ibid., p. 13.

24. Tong Qingfeng and Chen Donghao, "Duibuqi, wo tuichu! guoshihui zen shou-

chang?" (I am sorry, but I am going to withdraw! How will the National Affairs Conference party end?), *Xinxinwen*, no. 173 (July 2–8, 1990): 16–17.

25. Ibid., p. 18.

26. Liao Fushun, "Hu tui li sui weile nazhuang?" (When the fox retreats, another follows; For what purpose?), *Xinxinwen*, no. 173 (July 2–8, 1990): 20–24.

27. Tong Qingfeng, "Zhishi fenzi qieneng beiren shoubian?" (How can the intellectuals be utilized by people?), *Xinxinwen*, no. 173 (July 2–8, 1990): 26.

28. Ibid., p. 27.

29. *Zili wanbao*, March 24, 1990, p. 1. On March 26, DPP chairman Huang Hsin-chieh said that Chiang Yen-shih had not yet discussed the National Affairs Conference with him and that the party's central committee was setting up a six-person group to organize a research team to study how to prepare the conference. See *Lianhe wanbao*, March 26, 1990, p. 3.

30. Ibid.

31. *Zhongguo shibao*, March 30, 1990, p. 2.

32. *Lianhebao*, April 2, 1990, p. 3.

33. Ibid.

34. Ibid.

35. *Lianhe wanbao*, April 3, 1990, p. 3.

36. *Zhongguo shibao*, April 4, 1990, p. 3.

37. *Zhongguo shibao*, April 3, 1990, p. 3.

38. *Lianhebao*, April 5, 1990, p. 3.

39. *Zili wanbao*, April 9, 1990, p. 2.

40. *Zhongguo shibao*, April 10, 1990, p. 1.

41. *Zhongguo shibao*, May 14, 1990, p. 2.

42. *Zili wanbao*, May 14, 1990, p. 5.

43. *Lianhebao*, May 15, 1990, p. 3.

44. *Zili zaobao*, June 21, 1990, p. 2.

45. *Zhongguo shibao*, April 1, 1990, p. 2.

46. *Zhongguo shibao*, June 16, 1990, p. 2.

47. *Zili wanbao*, June 18, 1990, p. 2.

48. *Lianhebao*, June 25, 1990, p. 4. This survey was conducted by nonmainstream KMT members eager to show that support for the National Affairs Conference was minimal. We thank Tun-jen Cheng for this information.

49. *Zhongguo shibao*, June 19. 1990. p. 1.

50. *Lianhe wanbao*, June 7, 1990, p. 1.

51. Cheng Wenlong, "Women dui 'guoshi huiyi' di kanfa yu qiwang" (Our opinions and expectations of the National Affairs Conference), *Tongling* (Leader magazine), no. 58 (May 1990): 8. Mr. Cheng is the chief editor of *this* monthly.

52. *Lianhebao*, June 14, 1990, p. 3.

53. *Lianhebao*, May 14, 1990, p. 2.

54. *Lianhebao*, April 23, 1990, p. 3.

55. *Lianhebao*, March 27, 1990, p. 3.

56. *Lianhebao*, June 18, 1990, p. 2.

57. *Zili zaobao*, June 18, 1990, p. 2.

58. Ibid.

59. *Zhongguo shibao,* June 15, 1990, p. 2.

60. *Zhongguo shibao,* June 25, 1990, p. 3.

61. *Lianhebao,* June 26, 1990, p. 2.

62. *Zhongguo shibao,* June 15, 1990, p. 1.

63. *Lianhebao,* June 16, 1990, p. 2. See also Weng Wenjing, "Taiwan di zhengzhi renwu xuyao jiangdi yinjie" (Taiwan's politicians ought to change their tune), *Xinxinwen,* no. 172 (June 25–July 1, 1990): 54–55, for an interview with Peng Ming-min. Ding Mou-shih, head of the Washington, D.C., North American Coordination Council, had even telephoned Peng urging him to participate in the National Affairs Conference.

64. *Zili wanbao,* June 28, 1990, p. 2.

65. *Lianhe wanbao,* June 28, 1990, p. 1. Also *Zhongguo shibao,* June 28, 1990, p. 1.

66. *Zhongguo shibao,* June 28, 1990, p. 1.

67. *Lianhebao,* June 28, 1990, p. 1. The eight individuals who refused to participate were Hu Fu, Li Hongxi, Yang Guoshu, Peng Ming-min, Chen Tangshan, Chu Yun-han, Wang Shixian, and Xuan Yiwen.

68. *Zili wanbao,* June 28, 1990, p. 1. For the first time in their history, the KMT and DPP met and discussed their different visions of democracy and how to achieve them.

69. *Lianhe wanbao,* June 28, 1990, p. 1.

70. *Zili zaobao,* June 29, 1990, p. 3. *Zili zaobao,* June 29, 1990, p. 3. Huang Hsin-chieh tried to talk her into participating, but on June 30 she withdrew.

71. *Zili zaobao,* June 29, 1990, p. 3.

72. Ibid., p. 1.

73. *Zhongguo shibao,* June 29, 1990, p. 4.

74. *Lianhebao,* June 30, 1990, p. 2.

75. Chang Chun-hung, *Lianhebao,* June 30, 1990, p. 2.

76. Ibid.

77. *Zili wanbao,* June 29, 1990, p. 2.

78. *Zili wanbao,* June 30, 1990, p. 2.

79. Ibid. James C. Y. Soong, however, replied, "I believe Taiwan politics have reached a new stage of political party politics. In order for the parties to have a normal competitive relationship, they still have a long way to go. But President Lee respects the DPP and wants a consensus with it; but it takes both sides to make that effort."

80. *Zili zaobao,* June 30, 1990, p. 2. Because the liberal wing of the KMT participated in this conference, the resolution favoring direct presidential elections had carried.

81. *Zhongguo shibao,* June 29, 1990, p. 4. See also Weng Wenjing, "Guomindang Qizui bashe, gaigepai hezong lianheng" (The Kuomintang is at odds with itself, and the Reform Coalition pulls together), *Xinxinwen,* no. 173 (July 2–8, 1990): 35–37. Wu Yijing examines the Reform Coalition's organization in "Gaozhu lianmeng dachi, jinji Yuanshan zhanchang" (Raising high the banner of alliance, the Reform Coalition presses its attack on the battlefield at the Grand Hotel), ibid., pp. 38–39.

82. *Zili zaobao,* June 30, 1990, p. 2; see also *Zhongguo shibao,* July 1, 1990, p. 4. See also the detailed tables in *Zili zaobao,* July 2, 1990, p. 3.

83. *Zhongguo shibao,* June 30, 1990, p. 2.

84. *Zili zaobao,* June 30, 1990, p. 3.

85. Ibid.

86. *Lianhebao,* July 1, 1990, p. 1.
87. Ibid., p. 2.
88. Ibid.
89. *Zili wanbao,* June 30, 1990, p. 5.
90. *Zhongguo shibao,* July 2, 1990, p. 4.
91. Ibid.
92. Ibid.
93. *Lianhebao,* July 3, 1990, p. 1.
94. Ibid.
95. *Zhongguo shibao,* July 3, 1990, p. 2.
96. Ibid.
97. Ibid., p. 3.
98. *Zili wanbao,* July 3, 1990, p. 5.
99. *Lianhebao,* July 3, 1990, p. 2.
100. *Lianhebao,* July 4, 1990, p. 1.
101. *Zhongguo shibao,* July 3, 1990, p. 3.
102. Huang Hsin-chieh, *Lianhebao,* July 3, 1990, p. 3.
103. Ibid.
104. Ibid.
105. Ibid.
106. *Zhongguo shibao,* July 4, 1990, p. 2.
107. *Lianhebao,* July 4, 1990, p. 2.
108. *Zhongguo shibao,* July 4, 1990, p. 5.
109. Ibid.
110. Ibid.
111. Ibid.
112. Ibid., p. 3.
113. *Zhongguo shibao,* July 5, 1990, p. 1.
114. Ibid.
115. Ibid.
116. Ibid.
117. *Zili wanbao,* July 4, 1990, p. 6.
118. *Lianhebao,* July 6, 1990, p. 2. The DPP leadership continued to demand that the committee be created. Chang Chun-hong declared that his party would urge the KMT to create that committee to reform the constitution and reorganize the National Assembly. See *Lianhe wanbao,* July 5, 1990, p. 3.
119. *Zili wanbao,* July 9, 1990, p. 1.
120. *Lianhebao,* July 10, 1990, p. 2.
121. Ibid. On November 2, 1990, DPP adviser Hsu Hsin-liang, still disappointed with the outcome of the national conference, declared that the DPP would hold a national conference sometime in the first half of 1991. According to Hsu, "One hundred and fifty will be invited to participate. The conference will be a true people's representation." See Grace Tsai, "DPP to Set up Its Own National Affairs Conference," *China News,* November 2, 1990, p. 3. This conference never materialized.
122. *Zhongguo shibao,* July 5, 1990, p. 5.
123. Ibid., p. 3. Our discussion below is based on this detailed discussion meeting.

124. Nan Fangshuo, "Zhege yinying yulai yuda: Shengji qingxu bei guoshi huiyi chongxin tiaoqi" (The shadow becomes larger and larger; The birthplace issue is stirred up again at the National Affairs Conference"), *Xinxinwen*, no. 173 (July 2–8, 1990): 40–45.

125. Hou Lichai, "Guoshi huiyi haoxiang meiyou kaiguo yiyang" (The National Affairs Conference has created a new crisis for Taiwan politics), *Zhonghua zazhi* (China journal) 28, no. 325 (August 1990): 10–14.

126. Sima Wenwu, "Guoshi huiyi haoxiang meiyou kaiguo yiyang" (It seems as if the National Affairs Conference never really happened), *Xinxinwen*, no. 183 (September 10–16. 1990): 2.

127. Hu Chiu-yuan, "Guoshi huiyi shi shenmo? Yao zuo shenmo? (What is the National Affairs Conference? What does it want to do?), *Zhonghua zazhi*, 28, no. 325 (August 1990): 15.

128. *Zhongguo shibao*, July 7, 1990, p. 3.

129. *Zili zaobao*, (Independent morning post), July 5, 1990, p. 5.

130. *Zhongguo shibao*, July 6, 1990, p. 1.

131. Ibid.

132. Ibid.

133. *Zili zaobao*, July 6, 1990, p. 1.

134. Ibid.

135. *Lianhe wanbao*, July 6, 1990, p. 3.

136. *Zili zaobao*, July 7, 1990, p. 3.

137. Ibid.

138. Ibid.

139. Remarks by a former leading government official and a KMT leader we interviewed in Taipei.

## Chapter Ten: Preparing for Constitutional Reform

1. *Zhongyang ribao* (Central daily news), February 18, 1992, p. 3.

2. *Zhongguo shibao* (China times), February 27, 1988, p. 2.

3. Ibid.

4. *Lianhebao* (United daily news), February 4, 1989, p. 2.

5. *Lianhebao*, March 2, 1989, p. 2.

6. *Zili zaobao* (Independent morning post), July 3, 1989, p. 2.

7. *Lianhebao*, July 6, 1989, p. 4.

8. Our account is taken from *Lianhebao*, July 21, 1989, p. 4.

9. Editorial, *Lianhebao*, August 10, 1989, p. 2.

10. *Lianhebao*, August 29, 1989, p. 4. See also the table in *Zili zaobao*, April 3, 1990, p. 2, for when different parties and groups wanted the senior representatives to retire.

11. *Shoudu zaobao* (Capital times), April 3, 1990, p. 2.

12. *Ziyou shibao* (Freedom times), April 4, 1990, p. 2.

13. *Zili wanbao* (Independent evening post), April 5, 1990, p. 2; see also *Lianhebao*, April 5, 1990, p. 2.

14. *Lianhebao*, May 31, 1990, p. 4.

15. *Zhongyang ribao*, June 23, 1990, p. 3; *Zhongguo shibao*, June 22, 1990, p. 2.

16. *Lianhebao,* July 17, 1990, p. 4.

17. Based on an interview conducted with Irwine W. Ho in Taipei, December 24, 1991.

18. See *Gongshang shibao* (Commercial times), January 9, 1991, p. 2, and editorial in *Lianhebao,* March 30, 1991, p. 2.

19. *Gongshang shibao,* April 4, 1991, p. 2.

20. *Lianhebao,* February 27, 1991, p. 1.

21. *Lianhebao,* January 19, 1991, p. 7. Estimates were that holding the April 1991 meeting would require the government to spend NT$250 million, or US$10 million. The government spent NT$130 million, or nearly US$4.3 million, to hold the eighth meeting of the First National Assembly in February–March 1990. By repeatedly mentioning the vast sums of money spent to support the First National Assembly, the press tried to mobilize public opinion to reform the institution.

22. *Lianhebao,* March 29, 1991, p. 2.

23. Our description of the last (April 1991) meeting of the First National Assembly is based on "Zhengzhi diantang lunwei jingwuchang" (The political temple has been downgraded to become a boxing arena), *Shibao zhoukan* (China times weekly), no. 321 (April 20–26, 1991): 8–11.

24. *Republic of China Yearbook, 1993* (Taipei: Republic of China, Government Information Office, 1993), pp. 728–29.

25. "Guotong you zhangai; chongtu nan zhixi" (There are obstacles preventing communication, and it has been difficult to prevent conflict), *Shibao zhoukan,* no. 321 (April 20–26, 1991): 12, 13.

26. The discussion forum *(zuotanhui)* always allowed intellectuals and scholars to evaluate political events and elite political behavior as well as to suggest a course of policy. Since the 1970s the media used this political institution for elite mobilization of public opinion and to exchange information. See *Zhongguo shibao,* February 3, 1991, p. 9.

27. *Zhongguo shibao,* December 5, 1990, p. 4.

28. *Zhongguo shibao,* May 17, 1991, p. 2. Chao Shao-kang argued that "Articles 100 and 101 are no longer appropriate for the ROC's rapidly changing society and democratization."

29. Ibid. Huang, a legal authority in the Legislative Yuan, insisted on revising only Articles 100 and 101 and making no further revision of the criminal code.

30. *Lianhebao,* May 21, 1991, p. 2.

31. *Lianhebao,* May 22, 1991, p. 2.

32. Ibid.

33. *Zhongguo shibao,* September 3, 1991, p. 4.

34. Ibid. See also *Zhonghua ribao* (Greater China times), September 24, 1991, p. 2.

35. By mid-September 1991, the KMT had reluctantly agreed that it must concede to DPP pressure and at least revise Article 100. See *Zhongyang ribao,* September 17, 1991, p. 2.

36. For example, see *Ziyou shibao,* September 23, 1991, p. 4.

37. *Zhongguo shibao,* September 28, 1991, p. 4.

38. *Lianhebao,* October 2, 1991, p. 3.

39. *Zhongyang ribao,* March 1, 1992, p. 1.

40. *Zhongyang ribao,* May 16, 1992, p. 1.

41. *Zhongguo shibao*, May 19, 1992, p. 3.

42. Zang Zhunxiong, *Taiwan shibao* (Taiwan times), May 25, 1992, p. 3.

43. Article 174 of the 1947 constitution states that three-fourths of the National Assembly delegates must ratify any amendment to the constitution and at least two-thirds of the Assembly must be present. This KMT majority of delegates could divide, and many might join with the political opposition. Controlling 75 percent of the delegates gave the KMT enough power to revise the 1947 constitution.

44. *Free China Journal* 8, no. 77 (November 4, 1991): 2.

45. "Ge jiu ge wei, yubei . . . " (On your mark, get set . . . ), *Shibao zhoukan*, U.S. edition, no. 346 (October 12–18, 1991): 6.

46. "Chongfeng di haojiao xiangle" (The bugle's sound has launched the battle), *Xinxinwen* (Journalist), no. 248 (December 9–15, 1991): 20–21. See also "Guodai xuanju: Guomindang yipian guangming" (As for the Second National Assembly election, the KMT has a bright side), *Jiushi niandai* (Nineties), no. 259 (August 1991): 31–33.

47. "Guomindang dangwu jiangzuo zhongda gexin" (The KMT Party affairs will undertake a major reform), *Shibao zhoukan*, no. 322 (May 4–6, 1991): 29. Many tasks performed by the Mainland Affairs Committee were assigned to the Department of Defense Intelligence Bureau, and tasks performed by the Overseas Affairs Section went to the Overseas Chinese Committee.

48. *Lianhebao*, October 3, 1991, p. 3. The team was composed of Li Yuan-zu, vice president; James C. Y. Soong, KMT secretary-general; Chen Zhungzhang, head of the Party Work Committee; Wang Xuqing, head of Taiwan Provincial Party headquarters; Chien Han-sung, Taipei party chief; Hwang Ching-fong, another Taipei party chief; and Hong Mengchi, chief of the party's general management section.

49. *Zhongguo shibao*, September 19, 1991, p. 3. James C. Y. Soong and others conferred with party elders Lee Huan, Shieh Tung-min, and Ch'iu Chuang-huan; with Sung Shixuan, Pan Chen-chew, Kuan Chung, and Chen Li-an, who represented middle-aged party veterans; and with Chien Han-sung, Hwang Ching-fong, and Wang Xuqing, who were younger, lower-rank party officials.

50. "Ge jiu ge wei, yubei . . . " *Shibao zhoukan*, October 12–18, 1991, p. 7. This screening committee was also led by Vice President Li along with Premier Hau Pei-tsun, Chiang Yen-shih, Lin Yang-kang, James C. Y. Soong, Wu Po-hsiung, and Lien Chan. This committee had several meetings to conclude its screening work.

51. *Zhongguo shibao*, October 3, 1991, p. 2.

52. *Zhongguo shibao*, September 19, 1991, p. 2.

53. Xu Yangming, ed., *Renmin zhixian huiyi shilu* (A record of the meeting of the People's Draft Constitution) (Taipei: Minzhu jinbudang zhongyang dangbu, 1991), p. 12.

54. *Zhongyang ribao*, August 23, 1991, p. 2. This prompted Vice Minister of Public Affairs Chen Mengling of the Ministry of Internal Affairs to say: "If the Department of Justice decides this behavior violates the law, the only principle we can adopt is to warn the DPP party to desist or dissolve the party."

55. "Ge jiu ge wei, yubei . . . ," *Shibao zhoukan*, no. 346 (October 12–18, 1991): 7.

56. See "Taidu zhixian you jinbeng er songchi" (The taut bowstring of Taiwan independence has slackened), *Shibao zhoukan*, no. 347 (October 19–25, 1991): 18–24.

57. *Shijie ribao* (World journal daily news), November 18, 1991, p. 1.

58. "Dangxuan luoxuan jie xiaolian" (To be elected or not to be elected, they are all happy), *Shibao zhoukan*, no. 347 (October 19–25, 1991): 3.

59. *Zhongshi wanbao* (China times express), December 18, 1991, p. 2. See also *Zhongguo shibao*, September 23, 1991, p. 2, which reported that Chairman Hsu Hsin-liang believed his party could win 30 percent of the votes, while Wu Nairen, head of the New World faction, contended that a figure between 20 and 30 percent was more realistic.

60. *Shibao zhoukan*, no. 346 (October 12–18, 1991): 9.

61. *Lianhebao*, October 3, 1991, p. 3. A fourth party, called the Workers' Party (Gongdang), also nominated candidates. See *Lianhebao*, October 3, 1991, p. 3.

62. *Zhongyang ribao*, November 23, 1991, p. 1. For the 225 district seats the KMT nominated 192, and the DPP 105; for the 80 nondistrict seats the KMT nominated 75, and the DPP 45; and for the 20 overseas seats the KMT nominated 20, and the DPP 121. See *Zhongguo shibao*, November 15, 1991, p. 4.

63. *Xinxinwen* called the election "simple but the most complex election in recent years." The future of both parties greatly depended on this election's outcome. See "Chongfeng di haojiao xiangle," *Xinxinwen*, no. 248 (December 9–15, 1991): 20–21.

64. Our comments about party platforms are drawn from *Zhongguo shibao*, November 18, 1991, p. 4.

65. *Zhongguo shibao*, September 20, 1991, p. 4.

66. *Zhongguo shibao*, November 29, 1991, p. 2.

67. *Zhongguo shibao*, December 3, 1991, p. 4.

68. *Zhongguo shibao*, November 14, 1991, p. 4.

69. Ibid.

70. "Bei timing xuezhe dushi xiuxian xiaozu chengyuan" (The nominated scholars are all members of the Constitutional Revision Committee), *Xinxinwen*, no. 244 (November 11–17, 1991): 25.

71. "Yiguandao liangbaiwan daoqing ye huanbudao yige mingo" (Two million members of the Yiguandao could not even have someone nominated), *Xinxinwen*, no. 244 (November 11–17, 1991): 24–28.

72. *Zhongguo shibao*, November 14, 1991, p. 4.

73. *Lianhebao*, September 22, 1991, p. 4.

74. "Shusheng canxuan weihe erzhan?" (For what purpose do the scholars participate in elections, and for what reason?), *Yuanjian zazhi* (Global view monthly), no. 63 (August 15, 1991): 55.

75. *Lianhebao*, November 25, 1991, p. 4.

76. *Zhonghua shehui minzhudang jiben gangling* (The basic charter of the China Social Democratic Party) (Taipei: China Social-Democratic Party, 1991), p. 5.

77. *Zhongguo shibao*, December 4, 1991, p. 2.

78. Ibid.

79. *Lianhebao*, December 13, 1991, p. 2.

80. *Lianhebao*, December 12, 1991, p. 3.

81. *Zhongguo shibao*, November 11, 1991, p. 4.

82. *Zhongguo shibao*, December 18, 1991, p. 2.

83. *Zhongshi wanbao*, December 20, 1991, p. 2.

84. *Zhongshi wanbao*, December 19, 1991, p. 2.

85. *Zhongshi wanbao*, December 20, 1991, p. 2.

86. *Zhongguo shibao*, December 20, 1991, p. 6.

87. *Zhongshi wanbao*, December 20, 1991, p. 9. One DPP candidate hired 100 tables of food to be continuously served to voters, but his rival KMT candidate hired 360 tables for continuous food service *(liushuixi)*.

88. *Lianhebao*, December 15, 1991, p. 4.

89. *Zhongguo shibao*, December 19, 1991, p. 5.

90. *Lianhebao*, December 13, 1991, p. 4.

91. *Zhongguo shibao*, November 20, 1991, p. 4.

92. *Lianhebao*, December 15, 1991, p. 4.

93. *Zhongguo shibao*, December 11, 1991, p. 4.

94. "134 Election Cases Reported," *China News*, December 18, 1991, p. 3.

95. "Candidates Violate Rules," *China News*, December 18, 1991, p. 3.

96. *Zhongguo shibao*, December 21, 1991, p. 4.

97. Ibid.

98. Ibid., p. 1.

99. *Lianhebao*, December 22, 1991, p. 1. All data discussed below are from this source.

100. Chen Shouguo, "Taiwan xuanmin foujue le Taidu suqiu" (Taiwan voters reject the idea of an independent Taiwan), *Zhongguo shibao zhoukan*, no. 1 (January 5–11, 1992): 46.

101. Our comments are based on *Lianhebao*, December 22, 1991, p. 3. Lin Zhuoshui was beaten by 20,487 votes.

102. *Zhongshi wanbao*, December 22, 1991, p. 6.

103. *Zili zaobao*, December 23, 1991, p. 3.

104. Interview with Mrs. Maysing Yang, director of the DPP foreign affairs department, who blamed the DPP's defeat on the KMT's having "bought" the election.

105. *Minzhong ribao* (Commons daily), December 23, 1991, p. 4.

106. "Jinhou dadi shi zhengti dabing tuan zhanfang Kang Ning-hsiang" (Henceforth, we fight for a total united war: An interview with Kang Ning-hsiang), *Jiushi niandai*, no. 264 (January 1992): 54.

107. *Zili zaobao*, December 24, 1991, p. 2.

108. Ibid.

109. *Zhongguo shibao*, December 23, 1991, p. 3.

110. Nicholas D. Kristof, "A Dictatorship That Grew Up," *New York Times Magazine*, February 16, 1992, sec. 6, p. 20. See also "Ruling Party Wins Big Victory in Taiwan Vote," *San Francisco Sunday Examiner and Chronicle*, December 22, 1991, p. 3.

111. *Zhongguo shibao*, January 3, 1992, p. 2.

112. Chen Shouguo, *Zhongguo shibao*, January 3, 1992, p. 2.

113. *Lianhebao*, January 6, 1992, p. 3.

114. *Lianhebao*, March 5, 1992, p. 2.

115. Tien Hung-mao, *Zhongguo shibao*, January 21, 1992, p. 2.

116. *Zhongguo shibao*, January 2, 1992, p. 2.

117. *Zhongguo shibao*, January 22, 1992, p. 2.

118. *Zhongguo shibao*, January 12, 1992, p. 2.

119. *Zhongguo shibao*, February 23, 1992, p. 2.

120. *Zhongguo shibao*, March 4, 1992, p. 2.

## Chapter Eleven: Reforming the Constitution

1. *Zhongguo shibao* (China times), March 6, 1992, p. 1.
2. *Zhongguo shibao*, March 7, 1992, p. 2.
3. Ibid. Chiang defended President Lee's action by saying that "President Lee has no personal selfishness. He wants all ideas to be presented and to listen to them." He also tried to calm fears that President Lee and Premier Hau had been feuding by revealing that the two leaders frequently met, discussed all matters, and cooperated to achieve compromise on issues that divided them. Chiang described them as "giving in on small matters to gain on the big issues."
4. Ibid.
5. *Lianhe wanbao* (United evening news), March 7, 1992, p. 3.
6. *Zhongguo shibao*, March 7, 1992, p. 2.
7. *Zhongguo shibao*, March 8, 1992, p. 2.
8. *Zhongguo shibao*, March 9, 1992, p. 4.
9. *Zhongguo shibao*, March 8, 1992, p. 2.
10. Ibid.
11. Ibid.
12. *Zhongguo shibao*, March 17, 1992, p. 6.
13. *Lianhebao* (United daily news), March 26, 1992, p. 1.
14. Interviews with leading KMT officials in summer 1992.
15. *Zhongguo shibao*, March 9, 1992, p. 1.
16. *Zhongguo shibao*, March 10, 1992, p. 2.
17. Ibid.
18. Ibid. The KMT had not based its campaign on indirect election of the president and vice president, in fact always downplaying that issue.
19. Ibid.
20. *Zhongguo shibao*, March 11, 1992, p. 3.
21. Editorial, *Lianhebao*, March 14, 1992, p. 2.
22. *Zhongguo shibao*, March 13, 1992, p. 2.
23. Ibid. See also *Zhongguo shibao*, March 16, 1992, p. 3.
24. *Zili zaobao* (Independent morning post), March 14, 1992, p. 2.
25. *Lianhe wanbao*, March 14, 1992, pp. 1 and 3.
26. *Zili zaobao*, March 15, 1992, p. 2.
27. *Lianhebao*, March 15, 1992, p. 3. See also *Zili zaobao,* March 15, 1992, p. 3.
28. Party members like Yü Mu-ming had long insisted that central committee debates be decided by members casting secret ballots. For this reason Yü demanded the Third Plenum abide by procedural rules so that the election issue could be resolved once and for all in the KMT (interview, July 1992). Those opposed to this approach feared that casting ballots might strengthen party factions and divide the party. They wanted to build consensus, postpone serious issues, and compromise. *Zili zaobao,* March 16, 1992, p. 3. On March 15 Lee Huan said, "China should comprise only the Republic of China, and the five-power constitution should be preserved and taken to the mainland to be adopted there." Lee argued that overseas Chinese could not participate in direct elections, and direct elections would reduce the powers of the National Assembly. Ch'iu Chuang-huan, formerly supportive of President Lee, now sided with

Lee Huan and other critics of direct election. See *Zhongshi wanbao* (China times express), March 16, 1992, p. 2.

29. *Zhongguo shibao*, March 17, 1992, p. 4. Chiang Yen-shih argued that neither President Lee nor those supporting the direct election procedure had lost any battle; the real issue was that democratic free speech had prevailed within the KMT.

30. *Zhongguo shibao*, March 21, 1992, p. 2.

31. *Lianhebao*, March 26, 1992, p. 1.

32. In his travels about the island in late 1991, President Lee learned that the majority of people wanted direct election of a president. Government surveys also showed that north of Taichung city only 40 percent of voters supported indirect election, whereas south of Taichung only 20 supported indirect election. The president wanted this issue debated in the party in order to educate the conservatives demanding indirect elections. The president believed that roughly twenty of the thirty-one standing committee members wanted direct elections. A majority in society wanted direct elections, but a vocal conservative minority in the KMT opposed it. The president refused to take sides in the Third Plenum debate, accepted the compromise of a three-year waiting period, and opted for patience, realizing that direct elections would be held. (Interview with President Lee, July 16, 1992.) Wang Ying-chieh, a wealthy mainland businessman elected to the National Assembly, agreed with President Lee's judgment that many KMT central committee members believed direct election would be interpreted as a step toward Taiwan independence. Postponing direct elections for three years would allow people to understand the concept. (Interview with Wang Ying-chieh, July 16, 1992.)

33. *Zhongguo shibao*, March 26, 1992, p. 2.

34. *Lianhebao*, March 23, 1992, p. 2. Of 1,879 persons polled, almost 60 percent were undecided about whom they would vote for, but 31.3 percent supported Lee, 4.5 percent Lin Yang-kang, 1.5 percent Ch'iu Chuang-huan, 0.4 percent Hsu Hsin-liang, and 0.3 percent Huang Hsin-chieh. If Lee did not run, support increased to 30 percent for Lin Yang-kang and 20 percent for Hau Pei-tsun. About 42 percent stated they would vote for the KMT and 30.4 percent for other parties.

35. *Lianhebao*, January 2, 1992, p. 2.

36. *Lianhebao*, January 13, 1992, p. 2.

37. *Zhongguo shibao*, February 16, 1992, p. 2.

38. *Zhongguo shibao*, March 3, 1992, p. 3.

39. A DPP National Assembly representative from the United States, Dr. Chang Fu-mei, expressed amazement that the KMT leadership reversed its position and opted for direct elections. (Based on interview with Dr. Chang Fu-mei, June 1992.)

40. *Lianhebao*, March 13, 1992, p. 3.

41. Ibid.

42. The head of the KMT delegation in the National Assembly, Shieh Lung-sheng, was instructed to carry out the KMT's Third Plenum resolution to decide the issue of electing a president before May 20, 1996, and mobilize KMT delegates to approve articles to the constitution. *Zhongguo shibao*, March 23, 1992, p. 2.

43. *Zili zaobao*, March 18, 1992, p. 2.

44. The leader of the DPP National Assembly delegation, Cai Shiyuan, declared,

"The DPP will prepare its own statement for the oath." See *Lianhebao,* March 18, 1992, p. 4. Interviews with Wang Ying-chieh and Ma Ying-chiu.

45. Interview with Wang Ying, July 1992. Wang said the DPP did not recognize the ROC, so why should the Ying-chieh grant them any authority in the National Assembly? Shieh Lung-feng also stated that the KMT originally wanted to give the DPP a deputy secretary-general position, but their actions outraged the KMT delegates because the DPP did not recognize the existence of the ROC, only Taiwan independence. See also *Zhongguo shibao,* March 24, 1992, p. 2. At the last National Assembly meeting (spring 1991) on March 13, DPP delegate Chang Chun-hong expressed a desire to be deputy secretary-general, but after the first two days the KMT delegates strongly resolved not to give the position to the DPP.

46. The DPP delegates were at first hurt and then outraged by the KMT's refusing to give them some power of the chair committee to manage assembly activities. (Interview with DPP delegate Chang Fu-mei, June 1992.)

47. *Zhongguo shibao,* March 21, 1992, p. 2, describes the day's opening ceremony and President Lee's speech. For a day-to-day chronology of the National Assembly convention, see Liao Fuxun and Lin Yingqiu, "Ayi xianfa tan zhengzhu" (Sadness for the constitution; regret about our politics), *Xinxinwen* (Journalist), no. 273 (May 31– June 6, 1992): 20–27. See chronology of events for March 20.

48. Interview with Shieh Lung-sheng, July 1992.

49. *Zhongguo shibao,* March 25, 1992, p. 2.

50. *Zili zaobao,* March 27, 1992, p. 2.

51. Ibid. See Liao and Lin, "Ayi xianfa, tan zhengzhu," for events of March 26–30; *Lianhebao,* March 27, 1992, p. 2.

52. *Zhongguo shibao,* March 29, 1992, p. 2.

53. *Zhongguo shibao,* March 30, 1992, p. 4.

54. Ibid.

55. Ibid.

56. *Zili zaobao,* April 14, 1992, p. 2. Wang Ying-chieh was an elected KMT delegate to the National Assembly.

57. *Lianhebao,* April 15, 1992, p. 2.

58. Ibid.

59. Ibid.

60. *Lianhebao,* April 28, 1992, p. 2.

61. Ibid.

62. *Lianhebao,* April 29, 1992, p. 2.

63. *Zili zaobao,* April 29. 1992, p. 3. We translate the expressive *guoda shuang* as "feel so good"; it connotes erotic sensation.

64. Ibid. Assembly delegate Shieh Lung-sheng even said, "The Legislators should save the AIDS for themselves." Other assembly delegates called the parliamentarians "national thieves" *(guoze)* and "the cause of national disorder" *(Guojia di luanyuan).*

65. Interview with Shieh Lung-sheng, July 1992.

66. *Zhongguo shibao,* March 19, 1992, p. 2.

67. *Zhongguo shibao,* May 16, 1992, p. 2.

68. Ibid.

69. Ibid.

70. *Zili zaobao*, May 19, 1992, p. 3.

71. *Zhongguo shibao*, May 20, 1992, p. 2. One KMT delegate personally told President Lee that "if the National Assembly allows the Legislative Yuan to extend their term, it is like having your wife raped and then apologizing to the person, and that is ridiculous." The same delegate then said to the president: "If legislators must have a term of four years, I will chop off my head and hand it to you."

72. *Zili zaobao*, May 22, 1992, p. 3.

73. *Zili zaobao*, May 19, 1992, p. 3.

74. *Zhongguo shibao*, March 19, 1992, p. 2.

75. *Lianhebao*, March 27, 1992, p. 3.

76. *Lianhebao*, April 5, 1992, p. 2.

77. "Minjindang siyijiu zoushang qiongtu molu" (The DPP's April 19 demonstration cannot go any further), *Dujia baodao* (Scoop weekly), no. 195 (April 22–28, 1992): 18–28, for a detailed account of the events preceding and marking the April 19 demonstration.

78. *Zili zaobao*, April 20, 1992, p. 2.

79. *Zili zaobao*, April 21, 1992, p. 2.

80. Ibid.

81. *Zili zaobao*, April 23, 1992, p. 2.

82. Ibid.

83. "Zhongxiao xilu shizi lukoushang namian pojiu di luqizhi" (At the crossroads of Zhongxiao West Road, there is a tattered green flag), *Xinxinwen*, no. 262 (April 26–May 2, 1992): 16.

84. *Zili zaobao*, April 30, 1992, p. 2.

85. Ibid. Some DPP delegates referred to Shieh as "one of those delegates who wants to expand his power; he has no self-respect, and he is a disgrace."

86. See editorial, *Lianhebao*, April 28, 1992, p. 2. This same columnist also blamed the KMT for not carrying out political reform and for tilting too sharply toward the mainland so as to discourage consensus within the KMT. But he urged the two parties to negotiate and undertake reform and concluded there was no place for a third political party in the ROC.

87. *Lianhebao*, April 19, 1992, p. 2.

88. See editorial by Yang Xiancun, *Zhongguo shibao*, April 22, 1992, p. 4. Yang asserted that the DPP always had ignored the fact that most people had more confidence in the KMT than the DPP to manage Taiwan. Moreover, the DPP's inability to understand what the people really wanted was the root cause of the DPP's failure to win voters' support for its members.

89. Ibid., p. 19.

90. Zhang Zuojin, "Fenxi minzhu jinbudang di jinbu yu minzhu" (An analysis of the democracy and progress of the Democratic Progressive Party), *Yuanjian zazhi* (Global view monthly), no. 71 (May 1992): 56.

91. *Zhongguo shibao*, April 1, 1992, p. 2. The assembly's daily expenditures amounted to about US$200,000 (according to the late 1992 exchange rate of NT$25 per US$1). If the assembly convened for seventy days, the total expenditure was about

US$14.0 million, or NT$350 million. See *Zhongguo shibao,* May 30, 1992, p. 2. Salaries came to NT$180 million (US$7.2 million), and transport, per diem expenses, honoraria, and such amounted to another NT$130 million (US$5.2 million).

92. These proposals and recommendations can be found in Guomin dahui mixuzhu (Secretariat of the National Assembly), comp., *Dierci guomin dahui lingshihui xiuxian tian* (Proposals submitted at the Second Provisional National Assembly to Revise the Constitution) (Taipei: Secretariat of the National Assembly, April 1992), pp. 1–366; and by the same author: *Dierci guomin dahui lingshihui yiban tiao—fu yuan xiuxian tiao gaiwei yiban tiao ershiliu jian* (General proposals submitted at the Second Provisional National Assembly—appendix of the original constitutional articles for revision, which became twenty-six general proposals) (Taipei: Secretariat of the National Assembly, April 1992), pp. 1–366. All proposals were read to the Assembly and then reviewed by the first review committee, which voted whether to permit the proposal to be screened at a second reading. At the second reading, a proposal was reviewed and, if approved, went to the third reading. At this final stage only the wording could be altered; in substance, the proposal remained unchanged. (Interview with Shieh Lungsheng.)

93. For the eight articles, cited as Articles 11–18, see *Zhongyang ribao* (Central daily news), international ed., May 29, 1992, p. 1.

94. On April 20, only 186 people attended the Assembly, but 268 were required for a quorum. The chairman dismissed the Assembly that day. See *Zili zaobao,* April 21, 1992, p. 4. The DPP delegates as well as all other non-KMT delegates did not attend that day, leaving only a small number of KMT delegates.

95. *Lianhebao,* May 15, 1992, p. 1.

96. *Lianhebao,* May 3, 1992, p. 2.

97. *Lianhebao,* May 5, 1992, p. 2.

98. *Zhongguo shibao,* May 26, 1992, p. 2; *Zhongguo shibao,* May 27, 1992, p. 1; also *Lianhe wanbao,* May 27, 1992, p. 1. The ruling party planned to study whether the assembly should have a permanent secretariat *(yizhang),* etc.

99. *Zhongguo shibao,* May 29, 1992, p. 2.

100. Ibid.

101. Ibid.

102. *Lianhebao,* May 3, 1992, p. 2.

103. Tien Hung-mao, *Zhongguo shibao,* May 29, 1992, p. 2.

104. Ibid.

105. Yang Taixun, *Lianhebao,* March 16, 1992, p. 2.

106. Zhou Yangshan, *Lianhebao,* March 14, 1992, p. 4.

107. *Zhongguo shibao,* March 5, 1992, p. 4.

108. Sima Wenwu, "Batiao shengsuo ba Li Denghui di shengwang tuodao gudi" (The eight articles, like strands of a rope, have ensnared Lee Teng-hui and dragged him down), *Xinxinwen,* no. 273 (May 23–June 6, 1992): 28–29.

109. Xuezhe guoshi zuotan (Scholars discuss national affairs), "Xiuxian hu? Huixian hu?" (Revising the constitution or destroying it?) *Guoshi pinglun* (China forum), no. 1 (July 7, 1992): 7, 10, 12, 13.

110. *Zili zaobao,* May 28, 1992, p. 3.

111. *Zili zaobao,* May 29, 1992, p. 2.

112. Ibid. One group tried to obtain one million signatures to condemn the National Assembly, but this movement quickly collapsed.

## Chapter Twelve: Resolving Political Disagreements

1. Bernard Bailyn, comp., *The Debate on the Constitution* (New York: Library of America, 1993), parts 1–2.

2. Xing Zhiren, *Xianfa lunheng* (Essays on constitutional law) (Taipei: Dongda tushu gongsi, 1991), pp. 574–75.

3. Xu Yangming, ed., *Minzhu daxianzhang shilu* (The authentic record of the democratic constitutional draft) (Taipei: Minzhu jinbudang zhongyang dangbu, 1991), pp. 286–306 for the preliminary constitutional draft and pp. 310–25 for the final version.

4. Xing Zhiren, *Xianfa lunheng,* p. 575.

5. Susan Yu, "Opposition Party Tactics Slow First Day of National Assembly," *Free China Review* 11, no. 17 (May 6, 1994), p. 1.

6. Susan Yu, "Assemblymen Weigh Changes in Constitution," *Free China Journal* 11, no. 18 (May 13, 1994): 7.

7. Susan Yu, "Constitutional Session Stalled," *Free China Journal* 11, no. 26 (July 8, 1994): 2.

8. Ibid.

9. Susan Yu, "Constitutional Reforms Pass, Including Direct Presidential Vote," *Free China Journal* 11, no. 30 (August 5, 1994): 1.

10. Wang Lixing, *Wukuei* (With a clear conscience) (Taipei: Tienxia wenhua chubanshe, 1994), p. 64.

11. "Most Taiwan People Are Satisfied with the Performance of Premier Hau Pei-tsun's Cabinet, but They Are Worried about Taiwan's Economic Climate," Taipei CNA, November 23, 1992, in *JPRS Report: China,* December 22, 1992, pp. 66–67.

12. Wang, *Wukuei,* p. 287.

13. Liao Fushun, "Li Yuan-ts'u Plays Infield Strategist; Sung Hsin-lien Performs as Outfield Fighter—Preliminary Agreement Reached on National Security Bureau Subordination Issue," *Xinxinwen* (Journalist), no. 203 (February 3, 1991): 14–15, in *JPRS Report: China,* May 8, 1991, pp. 100–102.

14. Wang, *Wukuei,* p. 288. See also *Li Denghui yijiu jiusan* (Lee Teng-hui, 1993) (Taipei: Zhou Yukou, 1994), p. 24.

15. Wang, *Wukuei,* p. 214.

16. Ch'en Yu-hsin, "Has Wang Chien-hsuan Caused the Tight Lee-Hao Relationship to Break?" *Xinxinwen,* no. 292 (October 16, 1992): 26–28, in *JPRS Report: China,* November 24, 1992, pp. 37–38.

17. Wang, *Wukuei,* p. 287; see also Liu Chien-sheng, "Do Lee and Hao Rule the Taiwan Military Jointly?" *Jiushi niandi,* no. 1 (January 1, 1991): 52–53, in *JPRS Report: China,* April 30, 1991, pp. 95–97.

18. *JPRS Report: China,* December 22, 1992, p. 66. See also Li Chiung-yueh, "Refute China Dream—Voices from Mainlanders and Taiwanese," *Zili wanbao* (Independent evening post), October 14, 1992, p. 1, in *JPRS Report: China,* November 30, 1992, p. 35; and Wang, *Wukuei,* p. 288.

19. Chen Shan-jung, "Yeh Chu-lan Says Hao Po-tsun Held Secret Military Meeting," *Zili wanbao*, January 29, 1993, p. 1, in FBIS, *Daily Report: China*, February 9, 1993, p. 67. DPP legislator Yeh Chu-lan said: "On 23 January, Hau Pei-tsun convened the 'Eighth Meeting on Military Affairs' with a dozen or so of active-duty and retired generals—including Huang Hsing-chiang, Chen Ting-chung, and Hsu Li-nung—at his official residence in Shihlin to discuss their involvement in political strife." The Defense Ministry on February 8 denied any acts of disloyalty to the country and the constitution.

20. Ju Gau-jeng's open letter titled "The World Is So Vast, No One Man Can Rule It Alone" was a paid advertisement in numerous newspapers on January 13, 1993.

21. Zhou, *Li Denghui di yiqian tian*, p. 41.

22. Ibid., p. 61. The government praised Hau's services. See *Daily Report: China*, February 8, 1993, pp. 70–71.

23. Zhou, *Li Denghui di yiqian tian*, p. 135.

24. Ibid.

25. Ibid., p. 136.

26. See *Xinxinwen*, no. 380 (June 19–25, 1994): 25 (caption under photo of the former premier).

27. See Lien Chan, "The ROC's Rule in a Multilateral World Order," *Free China Journal* 11, no. 27 (July 15, 1994): 7.

28. *Lianhebao* (United daily news), November 14, 1986, p. 1.

29. Jiang Xueqin, "Zhuxi jiaozhuo, danggong miwang" (The chairman is eager, but the party workers are puzzled), *Xinxinwen*, no. 9 (May 11–17, 1987): 26.

30. Ibid.

31. Zhen Yuxin, "Ruguo Guomindang bu xihuan beiren zuocheng 'biaoben' " (If the KMT does not want to be regarded as a false model), *Xinxinwen*, no. 216 (April 29 May 5, 1991): 43.

32. *Zhongyang ribao* (Central daily news), December 7, 1989, p. 1.

33. "[Guan pai] zhuzhong zuzhi dongyuan; [Song pai] pianxiang xingzheng guanli" (Kuan's group emphasizes organization and mobilization; Soong's group stresses administration and management), *Xinxinwen*, no. 216 (April 29–May 5, 1991): 44–45.

34. *Lianhebao*, April 2, 1991, p. 4. Another report announced that the ninety-two special areas *(qu)* would be cut to sixty-five, and that personnel at the elite level would be reduced 50 percent. See *Chingnian ribao* (Youth daily), April 25, 1991, p. 2.

35. Zhen Yuxin, "Laoxiong, ni gei wo shiwan, wo ye buhui gei ni liyi" (Old brother, you gave $100,000, but I cannot give you any of the profits), *Xinxinwen*, no. 216 (April 29–May 5, 1991): 47. Hsu Li-te headed a party committee to manage the party's endowment.

36. *Zili wanbao*, June 8, 1990, p. 2.

37. See the excellent discussion of DPP and KMT factionalism by Tun-jen Cheng and Yung-ming Hsu, "Issue Structure, the DPP's Factionalism, and Party Realignment," in *Taiwan's Electoral Politics and Democratic Transition*, ed. Hung-mao Tien (Armonk, N.Y.: M. E. Sharpe, 1996), pp. 151–52.

38. Li Ta-kuo, "Political Roots of Money Politics," *Zili wanbao*, September 24, 1992, p. 14, as published in Foreign Broadcast Information Service, *JPRS Report: China*, December 4, 1992, p. 34.

39. Wu Nai-te, "Ludicrous Lee Teng-hui and Hau Pei-tsun," *Zili wanbao*, October 27, 1992, in *JPRS Report: China*, November 30, 1992, p. 38.

40. Chi Yen-ling, "The Kuomintang Still Cannot Kick the Habit—Its Addiction to Martial Law," *Xinxinwen*, no. 283 (August 12, 1992): 36–37, in *JPRS Report: China*, December 4, 1992, p. 35.

41. Ibid., p. 36.

42. Sima Wenwu, "KMT Works for Its Own Destruction; DPP Waits to Take Over," *Xinxinwen*, no. 325 (June 5, 1993): 11, in *JPRS Report: China*, August 17, 1993, p. 37.

43. Ti Ying and Yang Ai-li, "Taiwan's Self-Examination," *Tianxia*, no. 145 (June 1, 1993): 20–25, in *JPRS Report: China*, August 2, 1993, pp. 41–43.

44. *Zhongguo shibao* (China times), July 30, 1993, p. 2.

45. Ch'iu Ming-hui, "Jaw Shau-kong Interviewed on Motives, Process in Forming New Party," *Xinxinwen*, no. 333 (August 21, 1993): 57–59, in *JPRS Report: China*, December 3, 1993, p. 41.

46. Ibid.

47. *Zhongguo shibao*, July 30, 1993, p. 2, for a KMT defense of President Lee.

48. *Zhongguo shibao*, August 11, 1993, p. 3.

49. *Lianhebao*, August 11, 1993, p. 1.

50. *Lianhebao*, July 23, 1993, p. 2.

51. Ibid. Another example of that Chinese optimism that all problems can be solved if leaders behave in a proper, moral way.

52. *Lianhebao*, May 18, 1993, p. 2. By July 21 the Central Committee membership had been increased from 180 to 210 and the supplementary list of members to 105. See *Zhongguo shibao*, July 21, 1993, p. 2. By so increasing party delegates, the congress had 1,773 voting representatives.

53. Ibid.

54. *Zhongguo shibao*, August 18, 1993, p. 2. The votes favoring this proposal reveal that many party delegates wanted to have an arrangement to check the chairman's power as well as to mollify the nonmainstream faction and discourage their leaving the party.

55. Ibid.

56. *Lianhebao*, August 19, 1993, p. 2. Hau and Lin, considered to be the nonmainstream faction opposing the chairman, were checked by Li and Lien, who strongly supported the chairman.

57. *Zili wanbao*, August 18, 1993, p. 1.

58. See *Xinxinwen*, no. 455 (November 19–25, 1995): 26–27, 38, 41–42, and 45.

59. Ibid.

60. Interview with a leading journalist on March 25, 1996.

61. Lee Teng-hui, *Zhongyang ribao*, April 23, 1994, p. 1.

62. In recent years many opposition politicians' memoirs have appeared, describing their treatment by police and security personnel and their prison life. For an account of Shih Ming-Teh's twenty-five years in prison, see Li Ang, *Shi Mingde qian zhuan* (The biography of Shih Ming-teh) (Taipei: Qianwei chubanshe, 1993); Li Ao, *Li Ao zu zhuan you huiyi* (The autobiography and memoir of Li Ao) (Taipei: Chuanneng chubanshe, 1987); Liu Zhoulian, *Chongshen Meilidao* (The retrial of the Meilidao) (Taipei: Zili wanbao, 1991).

63. Our assessment of the DPP's violent behavior is based on unpublished research and a paper written by Dr. Liao Ta-chi, "An Authoritarian Regime: A Legislator's Role in Promoting Democracy—an Examination of the Extra-institutional Strategies of Taiwanese Legislators," paper prepared for a conference on the role of legislatures in emerging democratic societies, May 26–28, 1993, in Paris. See also Tsao I-hui and Lin Chia-chun, "Is There Any Other Way, Aside from Fighting?" *Xinxinwen*, no. 201 (January 20, 1991): 32, 35–40, in *JPRS Report: China*, April 30, 1991, pp. 97–103.

64. Chiu Ming-hui, "Independence Faction Flag—Taiwan Professors' Association Supplies Theoretical Basis for Taiwan Independence," *Xinxinwen*, no. 197 (December 23, 1990): 62–63, in *JPRS Report: China*, April 16, 1991, pp. 104–6.

65. *Shijie ribao* (World journal daily news), May 2, 1994, p. 1.

66. Chen Donghao, "Wei le zhuxi baozuo, tamen du qiangzhu zuo 'heilian' " (Because of the chairman's position, they all competed to become the "black face"), *Xinxinwen*, no. 241 (October 20–27, 1991): 40.

67. Ibid.

68. *Taiwan no seiji kaikaku nempyô*, p. 293.

69. Ibid.

70. Cheng and Hsu, "Issue Structure, the DPP's Factionalism, and Party Realignment," p. 149.

71. Ch'en Chien-hsun, "The DPP's Battle Plan and Defection-Inciting Tactics relating to the County Magistrate and Mayoral Elections," *Xinxinwen*, no. 333 (July 31, 1993): 48–50, in *JPRS Report: China*, October 12, 1993, pp. 40–41.

72. Ibid.

73. Joseph Bosco, "Faction versus Ideology: Mobilization Strategies in Taiwan's Elections," *China Quarterly*, no. 137 (March 1994): 50–62.

74. Susan Yu, "Separatists to Form New Party," *Free China Journal* 3, no. 32 (August 23, 1996): 2.

75. This section is based on Jiang Yiping and Li Zuxun, *Lishui er xing: Xindang gushi* (Swimming against the tide: the story of the new party) (Taipei: Shangzhou wenhua shiyeh gufen yuxiang gongsi, 1994), pp. 28–29, 47, 58–59, 61–63, 81, 86–76, and 125.

76. Chao Shao-kang proposed to run for the Keelung city mayor's office, Yü Muming for Taoyuan district head, Li Ching-hua for Taichung city mayor, Zuo Chuan for Tainan city mayor, and Kuan Chung for Kaohsiung district head.

77. For long-term voting trends of the Legislative Yuan and county magistrates and city mayor elections, see Huang-mao Tien, "Elections and Taiwan's Democratic Development," in Tien, *Taiwan's Electoral Politics and Democratic Transition*, pp. 16–17. For the 1995–96 elections see table 14.

78. *Lianhebao*, March 18, 1996, p. 7.

79. Ibid.

80. Susan Yu, "KMT Goes to the Polls Confident of Victory but Ready for a Fight," *Free China Journal* 11, no. 92 (December 11, 1992): 7.

81. Lu Huan-jung, "Both Parties Have Gained in Popularity, but Fewer Votes Can Be Considered Shoo-ins—Our Magazine Polls the People on Their Satisfaction with and Support for the KMT and the DPP," *Xinxinwen*, no. 289 (September 26, 1992): 48–50, in *JPRS Report: China*, November 30, 1992, pp. 36–37.

82. Ch'iu Ming-hui and Yang Sheng-ju, "Billionaire Politicians; Midas Touch Financial Management Skill," *Xinxinwen,* no. 345 (October 23, 1993): 41–42, in *JPRS Report: China,* January 10, 1994, pp. 38–41.

83. Ting Wei-kuo, "If Half of the Country in Taiwan Turns 'Green' from 'Blue,' " *Caixin* (Wealth magazine), no. 135 (June 1, 1993): 160–63, in *JPRS Report: China,* August 23, 1993, pp. 42–44.

84. Susan Yu, "Revisions to ROC Election Law Studied," *Free China Journal* 10, no. 47 (July 2, 1993): 1.

85. Susan Yu, "KMT Share of Positions Drops Slowly over Years," *Free China Journal* 10, no. 67 (November 19, 1993): 8.

86. Susan Yu, "KMT Captures 15 of 23 Posts in Three-Way Election," *Free China Journal* 10, no. 69 (December 3, 1993): 1.

87. James A. Robinson, "KMT Retains Majority of Local Offices," *Free China Journal* 11, no. 5 (February 4, 1994): 7.

88. Julian Baum, "Spring Cleaning: Old-Style Politicians Hit by Corruption Indictments," *Far Eastern Economic Review,* April 28, 1994, p. 18. For a detailed account of how the KMT, Office of the President, Executive Yuan, and Judicial Yuan began cooperating in February and March to carry out an islandwide investigation of political corruption in the January 1994 election, see *Zili wanbao,* March 16, 1994, p. 2.

89. *Zili wanbao,* March 19, 1994, p. 2.

90. *Zili wanbao,* June 27, 1994, p. 3.

91. *Zili wanbao,* June 22, 1994, p. 3.

92. *Zili wanbao,* June 23, 1994, p. 1.

93. "Neiwai baofa hezi dazhan" (A great nuclear war explodes inside and outside the Legislative Yuan), *Xinxinwen,* no. 381 (June 26–July 2, 1994): 24–25.

94. *Zili wanbao,* July 1, 1994, p. 3.

95. Virginia Sheng, "Legislature Approves Budget for Fourth Nuclear Power Plant," *Free China Journal* 11, no. 27 (July 15, 1994): 1.

96. Chen Yisheng, ed., *Maixiang minzhu duli zhi lu* (To march on the road to democratic independence) (Taipei: Qianwei chubanshe, 1993), p. 114.

97. Jiang Dianming, ed., Xiao Jing, deputy editor, and Zhou Zhihuai, *Jiushi niandai zhi Taiwan* (Taiwan in the nineties) (Beijing: Zhongguo youyi chuban gongsi, 1993), pp. 126–34.

98. Sun Qingyu, ed., *Minjindang xianxiang* (The reality of the DPP) (Taipei: Rizhitang wenhua shiye youxian gongsi, 1992), p. 127.

99. Shima Ryôtarô, "Basho no kurishimi: Taiwanjin ni umareta hiai" (A place of agony: The tragedy of having been born a Taiwanese), *Shûkan asahi,* May 6–13, 1994, p. 44.

100. Ibid., p. 49.

101. *Renmin ribao,* June 17, 1994, p. 5.

102. *Zhongguo shibao,* July 6, 1995, pp. 2 and 10.

103. David W. Chen, "Taiwan's President Tiptoes around Politics at Cornell," *New York Times,* June 10, 1995, p. 4.

*Chapter Thirteen: Conclusion: The Evolution of the First Chinese Democracy*

1. For an approach crediting the socioeconomic changes in Taiwan with the Taiwanization of KMT rule, and its political reforms with facilitating democratization, see Hung-mao Tien, "The Transformation of an Authoritarian Party-State: Taiwan's Developmental Experience," *Issues and Studies* 25, no. 7 (July 1989): 105–33, and Hung-mao Tien, *The Great Transition: Political and Social Change in the Republic of China* (Stanford, Calif.: Hoover Institution Press, 1989). Another approach has stressed that democratization is a process of learning by doing through electoral competition to engineer "a transitional process of an authoritarian party-state." See Teh-fu Huang, "Electoral Competition and Democratic Transition in the Republic of China," *Issues and Studies* 27, no. 10 (October 1991): 97–123; Fu Hu, "The Electoral Mechanism and Political Change in Taiwan," in *In the Shadow of China: Political Developments in Taiwan since 1949*, ed. Steve Tsang (London: Hurst, 1993), pp. 134–68. For another approach arguing that the top-down democratic process represented the relaxing of authoritarian rule over society, see Edwin A. Winckler, "Institutionalization and Participation on Taiwan: From Hard to Soft Authoritarianism?" *China Quarterly* 99 (September 1984): 481–99. This methodology was also applied earlier by Hung-chao Tai, "The Kuomintang and Modernization in Taiwan," in *Authoritarian Politics in Modern Society: The Dynamics of Established One-Party Systems*, ed. Samuel P. Huntington and Clement H. Moore (New York: Basic Books, 1970), pp. 406–35. As for analyzing the opposition-driven, bottom-up democratic process, which the works listed above neglect to mention, see Tun-jen Cheng, "Democratizing the Quasi-Leninist Regime in Taiwan," *World Affairs* 41 (July 1989): 471–99; C. L. Chiou, *Democratizing Oriental Despotism: China from 4 May 1919 to 4 June 1989 and Taiwan from 28 February 1947 to 28 June 1990* (London: St. Martin's Press, 1995); Ching-chan Hwang, *An Entrepreneurial Analysis of Oppposition Movements*, Occasional Papers/Reprints Series in Contemporary Asian Studies, 6, no. 131 (Baltimore: School of Law, University of Maryland, 1995), chap. 5.

2. Our narrative emphasizes that the political opposition tried to form an opposition party that might have induced the KMT to order massive arrests and even resort to violent suppression. That never took place because Chiang Ching-kuo restrained his party's hard-core conservatives and agreed to the party's existence. Chiang acted this way because he had conceived of a new vision for Taiwan's democracy and a plan to realize that vision. For very different views of why Chiang Ching-kuo decided to launch political reform, see Andrew J. Nathan and Helena V. S. Ho, "Chiang Ching-kuo's Decision for Political Reform," in *Chiang Ching-kuo's Leadership in the Development of the Republic of China on Taiwan*, ed. Shao-chuan Leng (New York: University Press of America, 1993). Another democratic-breakthrough explanation argues that a strong political opposition challenged the KMT while the KMT was afflicted with leadership difficulties. Wakabayashi Masahiro states, "The decision to declare liberalization was unavoidable because of the following: the multiple effects of greater degrees of freedom and the emerging movement to demand greater power to participate in decision making by the nonincorporated social sector of the party-nation system; the challenge of the nonparty forces as well as the prospect of a political power succession crisis owing to the worsening health of Chiang Ching-kuo; and the fumbling responses

of the KMT ruling elite, who opposed any movement of political opposition." See Wakabayashi Masahiro, *Taiwan: Bunretsu kokka to minshuka* (Taiwan: State disintegration and democratization) (Tokyo: Tôkyô daigaku shuppankai, 1992), pp. 212–13.

3. The match-up between ideological-political cultural change and practicing democracy also resembles *elective affinity*, the term Max Weber borrowed from Goethe to connect ideas and interests rather than saying "correspondence," "reflection," or "expression." Only in a process that is routine or institutionalized do individuals "elect" the features of an idea with "which they have an 'affinity' or a point of 'coincidence,' or 'convergence.'" See H. H. Gerth and C. Wright Mill, *From Max Weber: Essays in Sociology* (New York: Oxford University Press, 1958), p. 63. We thank Thomas A. Metzger for this term and source.

4. Lucian W. Pye has argued that Chinese elite attitudes and beliefs toward political authority changed after remnants of the KMT regime moved to Taiwan in 1949. See Lucian W. Pye, with Mary W. Pye, *Asian Power and Politics: The Cultural Dimension of Authority* (Cambridge: Harvard University Press, 1985), pp. 228–36. See also Pye's assessment of local elections, which he described as real democracy, in "Taiwan's Development and Its Implications for Beijing and Washington," *Asian Survey* 26, no. 6 (June 1986): 611–29. Our findings not only confirm Pye's insight but build on his work by showing that different ways of expressing beliefs and visions by political advertising had converged, so that elites slowly adjusted their political cultural values and beliefs to practice democracy.

5. Hung-mao Tien, Teh-fu Huang, Fu Hu, Yun-han Chu, and other social scientists in Taiwan have analyzed elections in great depth and by new methods. See also John F. Copper, *Taiwan's 1991 and 1992 Non-supplemental Elections: Reaching a Higher State of Democracy* (New York: University Press of America, 1994); John F. Copper, *A Quiet Revolution: Political Development in the Republic of China* (Washington, D.C.: Ethics and Public Policy Center, 1988); Hung-mao Tien, ed., *Taiwan's Electoral Politics and Democratic Transition: Riding the Third Wave* (Armonk, N.Y.: M. E. Sharpe, 1996). Recent research in Taiwan explores how age, education, and ethnicity have influenced voting patterns. See Liu I-chou, "Generational Divergence in Party Image among Taiwan Electorate," *Issues and Studies* 31, no. 2 (February 1995): 87–114; Chen-shen Yen, "Sandong Bu Guoban and Political Stability in Taiwan: The Relevancy of Electoral System and Subethnic Cleavage," *Issues and Studies* 31, no. 11 (November 1995): 1–15.

6. Aside from Harvey J. Feldman, ed., *Constitutional Reform and the Future of the Republic of China* (Armonk, N.Y.: M. E. Sharpe, 1991), very little of substance has been written in English about how the 1947 constitution influenced Taiwan's democratic evolution, but there is an extensive literature on this topic in Chinese.

7. Dankwart A. Rustow, "Transition to Democracy: Toward a Dynamic Model," *Comparative Politics* 2, no. 3 (April 1970): 351. We thank Larry Diamond for bringing this important essay to our attention.

8. Quoted from Feldman, *Constitutional Reform and the Future of the Republic of China*, p. 156.

9. Cheng, "Democratizing the Quasi-Leninist Regime in Taiwan," pp. 471–79.

10. Rustow, "Transition to Democracy," p. 352.

11. Larry Diamond, Juan J. Linz, and Seymour Martin Lipset, *Politics in Developing*

*Countries: Comparing Experiences with Democracy* (Boulder, Colo.: Lynne Rienner, 1995), p. 8.

12. These three conditions include meaningful competition for positions of government power through routine, free, and fair elections; wide political participation to select leaders and their policies so that no social group is excluded from citizenship rights; a high level of civil equality under a rule of law so that the citizens can express their views and interests and vigorously contest policies and offices. See Diamond, Linz, and Lipset, *Politics in Developing Countries*, pp. 6–7; Robert A. Dahl, *A Preface to Democratic Theory* (Chicago: University of Chicago Press, 1956), chap. 3; Robert A. Dahl, *Polyarchy: Participation and Opposition* (New Haven: Yale University Press, 1971), p. 2; Robert A. Dahl, *Democracy and Its Critics* (New Haven: Yale University Press, 1989); and Larry Diamond, "The Globalization of Democracy," in *Global Transformation and the Third Wave*, ed. Robert O. Slater, Barry M. Schutz, and Steven R. Dorr (Boulder, Colo.: Lynne Rienner, 1993), p. 39.

13. Rustow, "Transistion to Democracy," p. 358.

14. Recently, several political scientists have argued that the December 1992 election for a new Legislative Yuan was a critical turning point for Taiwan's democratization because it epitomized "conflict displacement in democratic transition." See Tse-min Lin, Yun-han Chu, and Melvin J. Hinich, "Conflict Dispslacement and Regime Transition in Taiwan: A Spatial Analysis," *World Politics* 48, no. 4 (July 1996): 453–81. We submit that conflict displacement in Taiwan's democratic transition terminated after the December 1991 election to replace the First National Assembly and the DPP's willingness to participate in the National Assembly's reform of the 1948 constitution. Changing these political rules let Taiwan's national elections become a reality, and conflict displacement was ensured. The December 1992 election for a new Legislative Yuan made it possible for political parties to begin to practice coalition politics.

15. Alexis de Tocqueville, *Democracy in America* (New York: Vintage Books, 1956), 1:184.

16. Even without any political turnover or complete elite convergence in the near future, if Taiwan's new generation of politicians and their parties can still abide by the principles of democracy to resolve disagreements, maintain freedom, and preserve civil liberties, Taiwan's democracy should gradually become consolidated, as theorized by political theorists such as Samuel P. Huntington, "Democracy for the Long Haul," Juan J. Linz and Alfred Stepan, "Toward Consolidated Democracies," and Guillermo O'Donnell, "Illusions about Consolidation," all in *Journal of Democracy* 7, no. 2 (April 1996): 3–51. Crucial for democracy's consolidation, according to Larry Diamond, are freedom of expression and protection of civil liberties to ensure individual freedoms. See Larry Diamond, "Is the Third Wave Over?" *Journal of Democracy* 7, no. 3 (July 1996): 20–37. A good example of Taiwan's political parties amicably building political consensus occurred in late December 1996 at the National Development Conference organized by the Office of the President, where politicians and elites were urged to freely express their opinions on diverse political issues.

Owing to limitations of space we list only the main primary materials used in this study and exclude Chinese, Japanese, and Western monographs (already cited in notes), Western journals and newspapers, and Chinese government and subcentral government publications (both Chinese and English are cited in notes), scholarly dissertations, pamphlets, and miscellanea (already cited in notes).

## CHINESE NEWSPAPERS

*Gongshang shibao* (Commercial times)
*Lianhe wanbao* (United evening news)
*Lianhebao* (United daily news)
*Minshengbao* (Popular life times)
*Minzhong ribao* (Commons daily)
*Shijie ribao* (World journal daily news)
*Shoudu zaobao* (Capital times)
*Taiwan ribao* (Taiwan daily)
*Taiwan shibao* (Taiwan times)
*Zhongguo shibao* (China times)
*Zhonghua ribao* (Greater China times)
*Zhongshi wanbao* (China times express)
*Zhongyang ribao* (Central daily news)
*Zili wanbao* (Independent evening post)
*Zili zaobao* (Independent morning post)
*Ziyou shibao* (Freedom press)

## CHINESE JOURNALS AND NEWSLETTERS

*Bashi niandai* (Eighties monthly)
*Gaizao* (Reform)
*Guanhuai zazhi* (Care magazine)
*Guoli Zhengzhi daxue xuebao* (Journal of National Zhengzhi University)
*Guoshi pinglun* (China forum)

*Jiushi niandai* (Nineties)
*Liaowang zhoukan* (Outlook weekly)
*Meilidao* (Beautiful Formosa)
*Mingbao yuekan* (Ming pao monthly)
*Minzhu tiandi zhoukan* (Democratic world weekly)
*Nuanliu zazhi* (Current monthly)
*Qiuhaitang* (Begonia magazine)
*Shaodang zhoukan* (Challenge weekly)
*Shibao zhoukan* (China times weekly)
*Taiwan dangwu* (Taiwan party affairs)
*Taiwan zhenglun* (Taiwan political review)
*Tongling* (Leader magazine)
*Xinwenhua* (New culture)
*Xinxinwen zhoukan* (Journalist weekly)
*Xinxinxiang* (New phenomena)
*Yazhou zhoukan* (International Chinese newsweekly)
*Yazhouren* (Asian weekly)
*Youshi yuekan* (Youth monthly)
*Yuanjian zazhi* (Global view monthly)
*Zhengzhijia* (Statesman weekly)
*Zhongguo luntan* (China tribune)
*Zhuoyue* (Excellence)
*Zonghe yuekan* (Scooper monthly)
*Zongheng zhoukan* (Comprehensive weekly)

## INTERVIEWS (TAPES AND NOTES)

| Date | Name and Status | Topics |
|------|-----------------|--------|
| 1990 | Lee Teng-hui. President, ROC | National affairs; election of 1990 president and vice president Constitutional reform |
| | Li Yuan-tzu (Li Yuan-zu). Vice president, ROC | |
| | Chen Li-fu. Senior adviser to the president | KMT retreat from mainland to Taiwan; 1951 KMT party reform Chiang Ching-kuo; Taiwan democratization, 1988–90 |
| | Sun Yun-suan (Sun Yun-hsuan). Senior adviser to the premier, 1978–84 | |
| | Yu Kuo-hwa (Yü Kuo-hua). Senior adviser to the president, premier, 1984–89 | Chiang Ching-kuo; democracy; *dangwai*; DPP |
| | Chiang Lien-ju. National policy adviser | National affairs and KMT |

1990–91
1992

Kang Ning-hsiang. DPP legislator

Lee Huan. Senior adviser to the president, premier, 1989–90


Chang Tsu-yi. National policy adviser; deputy secretary-general to the president, 1978–88
James C. Y. Chu (Chu Chi-ying). Director-general, Department of Cultural Affairs, KMT
Ma Ying-chiu (Ma Ying-jeou). Vice chairman, MAE
Chiang Wego (Chiang Wei-kuo). Secretary-general, NSC; president, Society for Strategic Studies
Ch'iu Chuang-huan. Senior adviser to the president
Ma Shu-li (Ma Soo-lay) (KMT). Senior adviser to the president; secretary-general, KMT, 1985–87
Bo Yang (Yidong). Writer
Zhang Zoujin. Publisher, *Lianhe wanbao* (United evening news)
Ding Tingyu. Director, Gallup poll
Yu Mu-ming. KMT legislator


Hsu Hsin-liang. Chairman, DPP
Chang Chun-hong. Secretary-general, DPP
Chen Fu-mei (Chang Fu-mei). DPP member; National Assembly representative
Chien Han-sung (Chien Han-sheng). Director, Taipei City Committee, KMT
Ju Gau-jeng (Chu Kao-cheng). Chairman, Chinese Social Democratic Party
Chang King-yuh (Chang Ching-yü). President, NCU
Chiao Jen-ho. Director, Confidential Information Section, Office of the President

Kang's role in *dangwai;* his magazine, *Bashi niandai* (Eighties monthly); DPP
1951 KMT party reform; lifting of martial law; Chiang Ching-kuo's political life; democratization in Taiwan
Chiang Ching-kuo as a person and as a politician


1986, 1991 KMT party reform


Unification consultation; non-mainstream KMT; Taiwan independence
Chiang Ching-kuo; Lee Teng-hui; Hau Pei-tsun
Ways of electing the president and vice president
Martial law; 1986 KMT party reform

His views regarding KMT and social change
Freedom of press; lifting of press law; Lee Teng-hui and his politics
KMT; DPP; Lee Teng-hui's policy toward mainland
New KMT alliance; constitutional reform
DPP party

Election of 1991 KMT and DPP
DPP


KMT


Legislative Yuan; KMT and DPP


Early KMT press control

Chiang Ching-kuo; 1986 party reform; democracy

Shaw Yü-ming (Shao Yü-ming).
Director, GIO
Irwine W. Ho (Ho I-wu). Senior
adviser to the president
Wang Ying-chieh. National As-
sembly representative, KMT
Shieh Lung-sheng (Hsieh Lung-
sheng). Chairman, National As-
sembly, KMT
Wang Xingqing (Nan Fang-
shuo). Chief editor, *Xinxinwen*
(Journalist)
Shirley W. Y. Kuo (Kuo Wan-
Jung). Chairman, Council for
Economic Planning and Devel-
opment
Yanghuang Meixing
Liang Su-jung (Liang Su-yung).
Senior adviser to the president
Huang Hsin-chieh. Member,
NA; adviser, DPP
Jason C. Hu (Hu Chih-chiang).
Director-general, GIO
Liao Cheng-hao. Adviser, Execu-
tive Yuan
Lien Chan. Premier, ROC
Nan Fangshuo (Wang Xing-
qing)

1993

GIO and the press; KMT

National Assembly; retreat of the
elders; NA members
Direct presidential elections

National Assembly; constitutional revision

Lee Teng-hui; Hau Pei-tsun; general social development
KMT and government policies

1993 election
KMT; Lee Teng-hui

Kao-hsiung incident; DPP; his
views of KMT

Hau Pei-tsun and Lien Chan

Mainland China policy
Political and constitutional reform
Editor-in-chief, *Xinxinwen zhoukan* (Journalist weekly)

Numbers in *italic* denote charts; those in **boldface** denote tables.

strations, 141–46, 147–48, 251–52, 258–60,
277; political goals of, 174; and presidential elections, 244, 245, 258–60; proposes
constitutional reforms, 240, 241, 266–67,
269; reformed, 238–39; on reunification,
134–35, 201, 279–80, 291; seeks political reforms, 208–9, 210, 212, 213–14, 341n. 118;
structure of, 135, 278; violence by members of, 222, 223, 278
Deng Jie, 184, 185, 191

economic reform, 25, 42–44
*Eighties Monthly*, 88, 109, 131
elections: competition in, 61, 63, 82, 164, 238;
*dangwai* compete in, 63, 82–86, 93, 99–
100, 137–40; DPP vote-buying in, 167, 288,
346n. 87; held, 4–5, 16, 163–64, 166–72; institutionalized, 97–99; KMT vote-buying
in, 61, 73, 88, 167, 235–36, 237–38, 274, 288,
318n. 25, 333n. 66, 346nn. 87 & 104; laws regarding, 162, 314n. 50, 331n. 33; quotas in,
59; successful candidates in, 60–61, 96,
120; urged, 108; violence in, 168, 171–72;
voters turnout: —before 1984, 60, 61–62,
64–65, 96–97; —in 1989, 164, 171, 332n. 42,
334n. 83; —in 1991–96, 236, 282, **284–85**,
287–88; —demographics of, 83
elections, legislative: pre-1989, 98, 136–40; in
1989, 166–72; in 1992–96, 282, **284**
elections, local: authorized, 43; in 1951–81,
59–65, 96–97; in 1992–94, 287–88; results
of, 282–83, 335n. 105
elections, national, 282, 283–87
elections, National Assembly, 229–39, 269,
**284–85**, 343n. 21
elections, presidential: methods of, 177, 178,
240, 340n. 80; National Affairs Conference
discusses, 208–9, 210–11, 214–15; in 1996,
283, **284–85**
elections, primary, 163–66, 332n. 42
elections, supplementary, 49–50, 63–64, **65**,
112, 136–40

Fan Zhengzong, 166
Farmers' Rights and Interests Association,
177
Fei Hsi-ping: challenges martial law, 68, 86–
87, 128, 313n. 37; founds DPP, 327n. 1;
founds Public Policy Association, 121;

leads demonstration, 143, 145; praises Sun
Yun-suan, 116
*Free China Fortnightly*, 53, 55, 60
freedom of assembly, 146–47, 162
Fu Zhongxiung, 166

General Agreement on Tariffs and Trade
(GATT), 291–92
governmental structure, 10–12, 263, 267,
268–69; reforming of, 240–41, 243–44,
246, 248, 261–62
Gu Ying, 96
Guo Guoji, 84
Guo Peihong, 226
Guo Yidong, 5

Hau Pei-tsun, 269–71; on KMT voting
method, 335n. 10; leaves KMT, 269; New
KMT Alliance supports, 274; opposes Lee,
183, 189–90, 275–76, 353n. 19; political
views of, 203, 245, 248
Ho, Irwine W., 185–86, 221, 227
Hong Qichang, 186, 258
Hong Shaonan, 223
Hou Lichai, 213
Hou Xikai, 220
Hsieh, Tung-min, 246, 312n. 16, 323n. 44
Hsu Hsin-liang, 76; attends National Affairs
Conference, 202, 205, 207; complains
about National Affairs Conference, 206,
212, 341n. 121; as DPP leader, 2–3, 231–32,
277, 278; on election of president, 252; ex-
ile of, 2–3, 137, 305n. 4; founds Taiwan
Democratic Party, 130; and magistracy, 63,
82; on National Assembly election, 237;
and political demonstrations, 109, 259;
praises KMT, 320n. 68–69; urges democra-
tization, 2–3, 96
Hu Fu, 124–25, 200, 210, 211, 263
Hu Hanmin, 47
Huang Chaohui, 186–87, 188
Huang Erxuan, 165
Huang Hsin-chieh: attends National Affairs
Conference, 201, 202, 207; criticizes KMT,
50, 74; on DPP defeat, 237; on election of
president, 252; forms Nonparty Organization to Promote Elections throughout the
Province, 6; heads DPP, 277; on National
Affairs Conference goals, 204, 212, 339n.
29; in political demonstrations, 57, 58,

**Library of Congress Cataloging-in-Publication Data**

Chao, Linda.

  The first Chinese democracy : political life in the Republic of
China on Taiwan / Linda Chao and Ramon H. Myers.

      p.   cm.

  Includes bibliographical references and index.

  ISBN 0-8018-5650-7 (alk. paper)

  1. Democracy—China.   2. China—Politics and government—
1976–   3. China—Relations—Taiwan.   4. Taiwan—Relations—
China.   I. Myers, Ramon H., 1929– .   II. Title.

JQ1516.C426 1998

320.95124'9'09049—dc21                                    97-18847
                                                          CIP